Southern Living®

2023 Annual Recipes

SKILLET
STUFFED PEPPERS
(PAGE 144)

DEEP-DISH
SKILLET BROWNIES
(PAGE 41)

MILLET SALAD WITH BUTTER
BEANS, OKRA, AND GARLICKY
MARINATED TOMATOES
(PAGE 102)

PORK CHOPS WITH
CAROLINA BARBECUE
SAUCE, SMOKED BUTTER,
AND BRAISED ONIONS
(PAGE 101)

BLACKBERRY-
LIME PORCH PUNCH
(PAGE 174)

CHOCOLATE-PEANUT
BUTTER ICEBOX CAKE
(PAGE 162)

STRUDEL WITH
FRIED APPLES
(PAGE 230)

The Four Legs of Our Table

Dear Friends,

Our approach to food in the pages of *Southern Living* rests on four legs, a bit like the tables we gather around with family and friends.

First, there's **tradition**. These are the beloved dishes of the South that celebrate the uniqueness of our region, like crispy Fried Oysters (page 57), Heavenly Key Lime Pie (page 132), a simple-but-perfect Creole Tomato Sandwich (page 149), or Micah's Buttermilk Biscuits (page 192).

Trends are the flip side of tradition. We feature what's fresh in the food world, showcasing recipes from great chefs like fried chicken from Sara Bradley of freight house in Paducah, Kentucky (page 317), and celebrated Savannah baker Cheryl Day's small-batch jams (page 134). We also aim to expand palates and pantries with dishes like Barbecue Jackfruit Sandwiches (page 146) and Chocolate Cake with Tahini Buttercream (page 226).

And then there is **technique**. With more than 55 years of testing and developing recipes in our Test Kitchen, we have plenty of tips and strategies to help you improve your cooking skills so you'll be guaranteed great results every time. Craving a restaurant-quality meal? See "4 Steps to a Great Skillet Steak" (page 44). Learn how to "Love Your Leftovers" with a batch of Potato-Peel Chips (page 66). Or upgrade your grilling game with a fresh new marinade (page 120).

Last but not least, there is **seasonality**. We highlight what's bountiful and beautiful at a particular time of year, whether that's a Crawfish Roll (page 47) in March, a Strawberry Shrub (page 96) made with perfectly ripe berries in May, or a slice of Apple-and-Clove Spice Cake (page 208) in September.

The book you're holding contains every recipe that graced the pages of *Southern Living* in 2023, a collection of dishes that represents all four of the sturdy legs of Southern cooking.

Lisa Cericola
Deputy Food Editor
Southern Living magazine

Contents

Top-Rated Recipes

We cook, we taste, we refine, we rate—and at the end of each year, our Test Kitchen shares the highest-rated recipes from each issue exclusively with *Southern Living Annual Recipes* readers

January–February

- Skillet Beer-Cheese Dip with Pretzel Bites (page 15) This crowd-pleaser really needs no introduction—the name says it all. It's one of our tailgating go-tos, and we're pretty sure it'll become one of yours too.
- Grapefruit-Cream Cheese Hand Pies (page 24) This recipe calls for grapefruit marmalade, which may be tricky to find in your regular supermarket. Look for it online or in specialty shops. The combination of the fresh flavor of grapefruit with a sweetened cream cheese filling—all encased in flaky pastry you can just pick up and eat with your hands—is outstanding and definitely worth the effort of it takes to make this recipe.
- Green Chile Mac and Cheese with Chicken (page 33) Take comfort food to an whole new level. You'll never want "ordinary" mac and cheese again after you give this one a try. A hint of heat and great chile flavor is a great complement to the creamy richness of the macaroni and cheese.

GRAPEFRUIT-CREAM CHEESE HAND PIES

- Deep-Dish Skillet Brownies (page 41) A high-sided cast-iron skillet is the secret to success when making this decadent dessert. If your family fights over the corners of regular brownies, these will keep the peace. They're served in wedges, so there are no corners—everyone gets a delectable, crusty edge!

March

- Crawfish Fried Rice (page 47) We try to make the most of crawfish season by finding fresh new ways to use this star ingredient. This dish comes together in only 20 minutes, so it can elevate a weeknight dinner to something special.
- Skillet-Roasted Cabbage Wedges with Hot Bacon Dressing (page 51) The iconic "wedge salad" was our inspiration for this delicious dish. Cook the cabbage until it turns a deep golden brown for the best results, and bake up a quick batch of cornbread to sop up the juices.
- Barbecue-Pork Pizza (page 61) This popular pie calls for cooking your own pork shoulder, but if you're pressed for time, pick up some shredded pork from your favorite BBQ spot and follow the simple steps to pizza perfection.
- Skillet Beef Enchiladas (page 59) There's no rolling involved with this hearty recipe, so it's perfect for a weeknight meal. And the ground beef filling makes enough for a pot of chili later in the week.
- Lemon Lush (page 65) Luscious layers of lemon and cream combine with a sweet and flaky crust in this fresh twist on a nostalgic favorite. It's a must-serve dessert at your next get-together.

April

- Easter Egg Lemon Cake with Whipped Cream Topping (page 74) As beautiful as it is delicious, this adorable cake will be the star of your Easter buffet. If you don't have time to make the cake from scratch, a boxed lemon cake mix makes a perfectly fine substitute.
- Prosciutto-Wrapped Chicken Cutlets with Haricots Verts (page 85) We love how the prosciutto gets delightfully crisp as it cooks—and the tanginess of the mustard combines beautifully with it. We like this chicken paired with haricots verts, but roasted or steamed asparagus or a side salad makes a lovely accompaniment too.
- Spring-Vegetable Sheet Pan Quiche (page 87) Sheet-pan recipes are still wildly popular because they're simple and incredibly versatile—but who would have thought the trend could be applied to classic quiche? Baking this brunch favorite in a sheet pan instead of a standard pie dish yields more servings—a perfect solution when you're feeding a crowd.
- Roasted Lamb with Fresh-Herb Sauce (page 93) This gorgeous lamb roast makes a spectacular centerpiece for an Easter feast. In a twist on tradition, it swaps Day-Glo mint jelly for a fresh herb sauce.

May

- Strawberry Ranch Water (page 97) Move over, margarita! This refreshing (and super simple) cocktail will soon become your new favorite. Cheers!
- No-Bake Honey Cheesecake (page 109) We created this recipe with the busy cook in mind. With only 20 minutes hands-on time, you can whip it up in no time and it looks

NO-BAKE HONEY CHEESECAKE

(and tastes) like you spent hours in the kitchen.

- Spiced-Up Shoestring Fries (page 111) No need to cut your own potatoes for homemade fries. Toss a bag of frozen fries with our secret spice mix, and nobody will know you didn't make them from scratch.
- Quick and Easy Cream Cheese Danish (page 116) Squares of puff pastry provide the foundation for these breakfast treats you can fill with your favorite fruits and toppings. The possibilities are endless.

June–July
- Blackened Fish Tacos (page 131) We love to top these tacos with our Spicy Slaw (page 131), but if hot and spicy food isn't for you, top with your favorite basic slaw recipe.
- Mango Salsa (page 132) We have tested and tasted hundreds of salsa recipes over the years and this one has received rave reviews from our test kitchen staff. It pairs well with crab cakes, tacos, or even grilled chicken.
- Skillet Stuffed Peppers (page 144) We bumped up the flavor of traditional stuffed peppers—which usually call for a ground beef filling—with Italian sausage. They're baked in the same skillet the meat is cooked in, so they make a one-pan, one-dish meal.

- Cracker-Crust Tomato Pie (page 150) We took a classic Southern staple and lightened it up just a bit. It's still juicy and cheesy with a crisp crust, but swapping saltines for traditional pastry and lightening up a few ingredients makes it more waistline-friendly. It's every bit as good as the original.
- Any-Berry No-Bake Cheesecake (page 136) One simple recipe, three tasty variations, and the best part: there's no baking required.

August
- Shagadelic (page 159) With a perfect balance of tart grapefruit and sweet honey, this is a real summer refresher—and a real conversation-starter to boot!
- Key Lime-Coconut Icebox Cake (page 161) This no-bake cake adds the flavor of coconut to a classic Southern pie. Pipe the whipped cream topping with a star tip for a beautiful presentation.
- Pepper Sauce Watermelon Wedges (page 170) This cool party snack hits on all cylinders—sweet, spicy, and salty. Wedges of juicy watermelon are sprinkled with hot pepper vinegar, sliced peppers, black pepper, and flaky salt.
- BLT Pasta Salad (page 180) We love celebrating summer tomatoes with a classic BLT, but switching it up is fun too. This picnic-perfect pasta salad has all of the elements of a BLT on bread—and then some.
- Pimiento Cheese Flatbread (page 185) Our love of pimiento cheese is so powerful, we're always looking for newfangled ways to use it. This Italy-meets-the-South flatbread gets a double dose of the stuff—it's sprinkled on before baking and served alongside the warm wedges as a spread.

September
- Peanut Butter-Banana Blondies (page 197) There's a secret ingredient that makes these brownies incredibly moist with a delicate crumb. It may surprise you!
- Creamy Corn Jalapeño Poppers (page 215) Sweet corn and a blend of mozzarella and Cheddar cheeses—and a hit of umami-rich miso—make these poppers irresistible. If you're a fan of firey food, leave a few of the jalapeño seeds in the chile shells before filling and baking.
- Smothered Steaks with Mushroom Sauce (page 224) This recipe comes together in under 30 minutes, but it's fancy enough for entertaining. Beef tenderloin is seared and then smothered with a rich and creamy wild mushroom sauce. Serve it with Roasted Cheddar Broccoli (page 224), steamed and buttered haricots verts, or roasted broccoli or Brussels sprouts, depending on your mood and the season.
- Strudel with Fried Apples (page 230) Serve slices of this strudel warm from the oven with big dollops of vanilla ice cream. We used Honeycrisp apples, but you can substitute with your favorite variety and get the same delicious results.

SMOTHERED STEAKS WITH MUSHROOM SAUCE

SAUSAGE-KALE STRATA

October

- Banana Layer Cake with Caramel Icing (page 237) This elegant cake comes together quickly and calls for a few simple ingredients you probably have on hand. The recipe can also be used for cupcakes or a sheet cake, if that suits you better.
- Bacon-Wrapped Pork Tenderloin "Filets" (page 250) If you love a bacon-wrapped beef filet but are looking for a less expensive option, you must give this recipe a try. It received rave reviews in our Test Kitchen and is sure to become one of your new favorites.
- Sausage-Kale Strata (page 251) Leftover sourdough bread is the star of this hearty and delicious breakfast casserole. Italian sausage and kale combine for an unbelievably tasty dish—with a hint of healthy.
- Chipotle-Maple Almonds (page 255) This interesting twist on classic spiced nuts is sweet, salty, smoky, and crunchy—it will be a welcome addition to your preholiday dinner cocktail munching. Make a double batch to keep on hand for last-minute holiday gift-giving.

November

- Ginger Loaf Cake (page 259) The smell of this lovely loaf cake baking in the oven will get you in a festive fall (or holiday) spirit. Ginger lovers, rejoice—it calls for a ½ cup of minced fresh ginger! Perfect with a cup of coffee or hot mulled cider.
- Whipped Goat Cheese with Smoky Bacon Jam (page 260) Whipped feta is all the rage these days—this indulgent dip applies the same concept to goat cheese. It's truly a special treat served with Easy Fried Crackers (page 260).
- French Onion Deviled Eggs (page 264) Who doesn't love deviled eggs? Topped with Crispy Gruyère Onions, this recipe takes the all-time party favorite up a big notch.
- Cheesy Scallion Stuffing with Sesame Seeds (page 268) Looking for a side that's familiar but inspired? Food writer and chef Eric Kim puts a Korean spin on traditional Southern "dressing."
- Possum Pie (page 276) You may need a nap after eating a slice of this very special pie with a pecan shortbread crust, vanilla cream cheese filling, and chocolate pudding topping, but you'll have sweet dreams.

GINGER LOAF CAKE

December

- Satsuma Upside-Down Cake (page 296) This gorgeous cake looks like a jewel-encrusted box—and it absolutely radiates with the flavor of sweet, in-season satsuma mandarins. Lightly spiced with cloves and made tender with buttermilk, it's an enchanting holiday dessert.
- Cranberry Old-Fashioneds (page 295) Get into the spirit of the season with this classic cocktail given a holiday twist. Made with Cranberry Simple Syrup and garnished with orange peel and Boozy Cranberries, it's sure to make merriment at your next holiday gathering.
- Spicy Cheese Straws (page 334) Rich, buttery, tangy, and pleasantly spicy and salty, these fan-favorite cocktail nibbles never get old. This recipe turns up the heat just a smidge with cayenne and Aleppo pepper—and smoked paprika.
- Sausage-and-Black-Eyed Pea Soup with Greens (page 313) Got hungry holiday houseguests rolling in? Greet them with a big pot of this hearty and warming soup. Bake up a batch of your favorite cornbread to go along with it.
- Freight House Fried Chicken (page 317) We Southerners love fried chicken all year long—for summer picnics, Sunday suppers, or any other time friends and family gather. Make this super-crispy, joyously juicy fried chicken from chef Sarah Bradley for feasting whatever holiday you celebrate this time of year.

January–February

Who's Ready to Party?

Warm up winter gatherings with these crowd-pleasing dips

SKILLET BEER-
CHEESE DIP WITH
PRETZEL BITES

Skillet Beer-Cheese Dip with Pretzel Bites

ACTIVE 25 MIN. - TOTAL 45 MIN.

SERVES 8

- 8 hickory-smoked bacon slices, coarsely chopped (1 cup)
- 1 (12-oz.) pkg. frozen pretzel bites, salt packet reserved
- 1 (8-oz.) pkg. cream cheese, softened
- 1 (8-oz.) block sharp Cheddar cheese, shredded (about 2 cups)
- 1 (7-oz.) block Havarti cheese, shredded (about 1¾ cups)
- ½ cup (4 oz.) IPA-style beer
- 2 Tbsp. whole-grain mustard
- ½ tsp. garlic powder
- ⅛ tsp. cayenne pepper
- 2 Tbsp. finely chopped fresh chives

1. Preheat oven to 400°F. Heat a 9-inch cast-iron skillet over medium-high. Add chopped bacon, and cook, stirring often, until fat is rendered and bacon is almost crisp, about 8 minutes. Remove from heat. Using a slotted spoon, transfer bacon to a paper towel-lined plate, and set aside. Reserve 1 tablespoon drippings in skillet.
2. Toss together pretzel bites and 2 tablespoons water on a rimmed baking sheet. Sprinkle half of reserved salt packet evenly over pretzel bites, tossing until coated, and set aside. Discard remaining half of reserved salt packet.
3. Stir together cream cheese, Cheddar, Havarti, beer, mustard, garlic powder, and cayenne pepper in a medium bowl until thoroughly combined. Spoon cheese mixture into skillet, and spread in an even layer. Bake in preheated oven until hot and bubbly around edges, about 15 minutes. Remove from oven, and let cool 5 minutes. (Do not turn off oven.)
4. While dip cools, bake pretzel bites at 400°F until heated through, about 5 minutes. Arrange pretzel bites around edges of dip in skillet; sprinkle center evenly with chives and reserved bacon. Serve dip immediately with any remaining pretzel bites.

Skillet Taco Dip

(Photo, page 17)

ACTIVE 30 MIN. - TOTAL 1 HOUR

SERVES 8

- 2 lb. lean ground beef
- 1 medium-size red onion, finely chopped (1½ cups), divided
- 1 (15-oz.) can seasoned black beans (such as Bush's), drained and rinsed
- 2 (1-oz.) envelopes taco seasoning mix
- 10 oz. Cheddar cheese, shredded (about 2½ cups)
- 2 plum tomatoes, chopped (1 cup)
- ¼ cup sliced scallion (from 1 medium scallion)
- ¼ cup chopped fresh cilantro
  Tortilla chips and sour cream, for serving

1. Preheat oven to 375°F. Heat a 12-inch cast-iron skillet over medium-high. Add ground beef, and cook, stirring often, until crumbly and cooked through, about 10 minutes. Add 1¼ cups of the red onion; cook, stirring often, until onion is tender, about 3 minutes. Add black beans, taco seasoning, and 1 cup water; stir until beef is well coated, about 1 minute. Remove from heat. Stir in 1 cup of the cheese. Sprinkle with remaining 1½ cups cheese.
2. Bake in preheated oven until cheese is melted and lightly browned, about 25 minutes. Let cool 5 minutes. Sprinkle evenly with tomatoes, scallion, fresh cilantro, and remaining ¼ cup red onion. Serve hot with tortilla chips and sour cream.

Skillet Spinach-Artichoke Dip

(Photo, page 16)

ACTIVE 30 MIN. - TOTAL 1 HOUR

SERVES 8

- 2 Tbsp. unsalted butter
- 1 medium-size yellow onion, chopped (2 cups)
- 3 (5-oz.) pkg. fresh spinach, coarsely chopped (14 cups)
- 2 (12-oz.) jars marinated quartered artichoke hearts, drained and coarsely chopped (3 cups)
- 1 (8-oz.) pkg. cream cheese, softened
- 1 (6-oz.) pkg. finely shredded Parmesan cheese
- 1 cup mayonnaise
- 2 tsp. grated lemon zest plus 3 Tbsp. fresh juice (from 2 lemons)
- 1-2 Tbsp. hot sauce (such as Tabasco), to taste
- 2 (8-oz.) blocks Monterey Jack cheese, shredded (about 4 cups)
  Crackers, pita chips, or crudités, for serving

1. Preheat oven to 375°F. Melt butter in a 12-inch cast-iron skillet over medium. Add onion; cook, stirring often, until onion softens and begins to turn light golden brown, about 10 minutes. Add spinach in 2 batches, stirring until spinach is wilted before adding next batch; cook over medium, stirring often, until liquid evaporates, 4 to 6 minutes. Remove from heat.
2. Stir marinated artichokes, cream cheese, Parmesan, mayonnaise, lemon zest and juice, hot sauce, and 3½ cups of the Monterey Jack cheese into the spinach mixture in the skillet until well combined. Spread in an even layer, and sprinkle with remaining ½ cup Monterey Jack.
3. Bake in preheated oven until cheese on top is lightly golden brown, about 25 minutes. Let stand 5 minutes. Serve hot with crackers, pita chips, or crudités.

SKILLET SPINACH-
ARTICHOKE DIP
(PAGE 15)

SKILLET TACO DIP
(PAGE 15)

The Beauty of Beets

Sweet, colorful, and healthy to boot, these root vegetables brighten up dinnertime

JUMP-START SUPPER
Roast the beets up to three days in advance to get some of the prep work done ahead.

Rainbow Beet Galette
ACTIVE 15 MIN. · TOTAL 2 HOURS
SERVES 6

Preheat oven to 400°F. Toss together 1½ lb. **small beets** (a combination of trimmed red, golden, and/or candy cane beets), ¼ cup **extra-virgin olive oil**, and 1 tsp. **kosher salt** in a large bowl. Separate beets by color onto different large pieces of aluminum foil, piling them in the center. Fold foil over each pile; seal to create packets. Place foil packets on a baking sheet. Bake in preheated oven until beets can be easily pierced with a knife, about 1 hour. Remove from oven, and keep oven on. Carefully open packets, and let beets cool until easy to handle, about 10 minutes. Using a paper towel, remove skins from cooled beets. Slice beets into ¼-inch rounds. Set aside. Roll ½ (14.1-oz.) pkg. **refrigerated piecrusts** (1 piecrust) into a 14-inch round on a piece of parchment paper lightly dusted with **all-purpose flour.** Spread dough with 1 (5.2-oz.) pkg. **garlic-and-herb spreadable cheese** (such as Boursin), leaving a 2-inch border. Arrange sliced beets in a circular pattern on top of cheese, overlapping slices slightly. Fold dough edges over beets and in toward the center, pleating as needed. Beat 1 **large egg,** and brush on dough. Sprinkle evenly with **flaky sea salt.** Transfer parchment paper with galette to a baking sheet. Bake at 400°F until crust is deeply browned, about 30 minutes. Drizzle with additional **olive oil;** garnish with **fresh tender herbs** (such as dill and chives). If desired, drizzle with **honey.** Serve immediately.

Speedy Steak Salad

A fresh way to enjoy a comforting meat-and-potatoes supper

Cast-Iron Steak Salad

ACTIVE 30 MIN. - TOTAL 30 MIN.
SERVES 4

- 12 oz. baby gold potatoes (about 12 potatoes)
- 1 (about 1¼-lb.) strip steak, at room temperature
- 1¼ tsp. kosher salt, divided
- ¾ tsp. black pepper, divided
- 1 Tbsp. canola oil
- 2 Tbsp. sherry vinegar
- 1½ tsp. Dijon mustard
- 1 tsp. pure maple syrup
- ¼ cup extra-virgin olive oil
- 3 anchovy fillets, finely chopped (1½ Tbsp.), optional
- 2 garlic cloves, finely chopped (2 tsp.)
- 1 (5-oz.) pkg. mixed greens (about 5 cups)
- 1 medium shallot, thinly sliced (about ¼ cup)
- ¾ oz. Parmigiano-Reggiano cheese, shredded (about ¼ cup)

1. Place potatoes in a medium-size microwavable dish. Add 3 tablespoons water, and cover with a lid or plate. Microwave on HIGH until potatoes are tender when pierced with a fork, 4 to 5 minutes. Uncover and let cool slightly, 6 to 8 minutes.

2. While potatoes cool, pat steak dry with paper towels; sprinkle evenly with ¾ teaspoon of the salt and ½ teaspoon of the pepper. Heat a large cast-iron skillet over medium-high until it starts to smoke. Add canola oil, and place fatty edge of steak in skillet; cook, holding steak upright using tongs, until fat is browned and begins to render, about 2 minutes. Turn steak onto 1 flat side; cook, undisturbed, until it starts to brown, about 2 minutes. Flip and cook, undisturbed, 2 more minutes. Cook, turning occasionally, until an instant-read thermometer inserted in thickest portion of steak registers 125°F for medium-rare, about 6 to 8 minutes, or to desired degree of doneness. Turn steak to the opposite edge of the fatty long edge, holding it upright using tongs, and cook until browned, about 1 minute. Transfer steak to a cutting board, and let rest 8 to 10 minutes; reserve 1 tablespoon drippings in skillet. Reduce heat to medium.

3. While steak rests, gently crush potatoes using bottom of a flat glass until potatoes crack but are still intact. Add to drippings in skillet, and sprinkle with ¼ teaspoon of the salt. Cook, turning every 1 to 2 minutes, until potatoes are golden brown and crispy, about 4 minutes. Remove from heat.

4. Whisk together vinegar, Dijon mustard, maple syrup, and remaining ¼ teaspoon each salt and pepper in a small bowl. Gradually whisk in olive oil until smooth and combined. Whisk in chopped anchovies (if desired) and garlic. Pour 2 tablespoons dressing into a large bowl; add mixed greens, sliced shallot, and shredded Parmigiano-Reggiano cheese, tossing until lightly coated. Transfer salad to a large platter. Slice steak against the grain, and place it and potatoes evenly on top of salad. Drizzle with 2 tablespoons dressing, and serve with remaining dressing on the side, if desired.

CALORIES: **441** – CARBS: **19 G** – FAT: **24 G**

The Big Squeeze

Texas prides itself on many things, including its stellar grapefruit varieties, which are as bold as the state itself

FLORIDA MAY HAVE ITS ORANGES, and California may have its grapes. But Texas sets the standard when it comes to plump, vibrant, intensely sweet grapefruit. The outstanding varieties that hail from the Lone Star State have a lush concentration of juice and colorful flesh ranging from fiery orange and pink to deep red. It's one of their most prized exports.

Scientists believe that a hybrid of the pomelo, one of the oldest and largest citrus fruits, was found in Barbados during the mid-18th century. This mix of a pomelo (*Citrus grandis*) and a sweet orange (*C. sinensis*) is what we now consider to be a grapefruit (*C. paradisi*). Later, seeds were brought to Florida and Texas for cultivation. Some historians claim that the fruit got its name because it grows in grapelike clusters, but others say it's due to the tart flavor, like that of an unripe grape.

Texas' contribution to the country's grapefruit production started in 1893 with initial plantings of white and pink varieties. The success of these crops led to extensive groves throughout the Lower Rio Grande Valley. Known locally as "the Valley," this unique area offers well-drained soil, excellent sunshine, and subtropical coastal humidity, which results in sweet, fleshy produce. You'll also find other types of citrus here, but grapefruit leads the pack.

A.E. Henninger, a McAllen, Texas, farmer, is credited with discovering a red mutation in his orchard in 1929. This ruby-color outlier (now called Redblush) was the first grapefruit to receive a U.S. patent. Throughout the mid-1900s, farmers in the Valley kept discovering new kinds of red grapefruit, which they cultivated and patented. These robust mutations soon became the heart of grapefruit production, making Texas famous for its red varieties. In 1993, the state legislature declared it the official fruit of Texas, citing its economic success as well as its many nutritional benefits and palate-pleasing qualities.

The original varieties featured yellow-orange exteriors and were described as "golden oranges." Over the past century, the state has become known for the more pigmented versions. Rio Star combines the two reddest kinds, Star Ruby and Rio Red. Ruby Sweet includes the popular Ruby Red and others such as Ray Ruby and Henderson. The Flame type, known for having few seeds, has more subtle tones of red.

Texas grapefruit season typically runs from mid-fall to spring (October through April), with local farm stands and grocery stores selling luscious fruit by the bushel. If you can't find the right variety near you, G and S Groves and Bell's Farm to Market ship throughout the U.S. Enjoy them for breakfast with a sprinkle of sugar, or try something new with one of these wonderfully sweet-tart desserts.

Mini Grapefruit Upside-Down Cakes

ACTIVE 20 MIN. · TOTAL 1 HOUR
SERVES 6

- 3 grapefruit (any combination of white, pink, and red)
- 1 cup granulated sugar, divided
- 1 cup all-purpose flour
- ½ cup almond flour
- 1 tsp. baking powder
- ½ tsp. kosher salt
- ½ cup unsalted butter, softened, plus more for greasing ramekins
- 2 large eggs
- 2 tsp. grated grapefruit zest
- ½ cup sour cream
- ⅓ cup whole milk
- Sweetened whipped cream, for serving (optional)

1. Preheat oven to 350°F. Remove and discard peel and pith from grapefruit. Cut 2 (¼-inch-thick) rounds from each grapefruit. Reserve remaining grapefruit for another use. Grease 6 (8-ounce) ramekins with butter. Sprinkle 2 teaspoons sugar onto bottom and sides of each ramekin. Press 1 grapefruit round in bottom of each ramekin, trimming to fit. Set aside.

2. Whisk together all-purpose flour, almond flour, baking powder, and salt in a medium bowl. Set aside.

3. Beat butter and remaining ¾ cup sugar in a large bowl with an electric mixer on high speed until light and fluffy, about 4 minutes. Add eggs 1 at a time, beating well after each addition. Beat in zest. Reduce mixer speed to low; add flour mixture to butter mixture, alternating with sour cream and milk in 2 additions and beating until incorporated after each addition. Spoon batter over grapefruit rounds.

4. Arrange ramekins evenly on a rimmed baking sheet. Bake in preheated oven until a wooden pick inserted in center of cakes comes out clean, 24 to 26 minutes. Remove from oven. Let cool in ramekins 10 minutes. Run a knife around edge of each ramekin, and invert cakes onto plates. Serve warm. Top with whipped cream, if desired.

GRAPEFRUIT
PAVLOVA
(PAGE 24)

GRAPEFRUIT-
CREAM CHEESE
HAND PIES
(PAGE 24)

Grapefruit Meringue Pie

ACTIVE 40 MIN. - ACTIVE 1 HOUR, 10 MIN.,
PLUS 3 HOURS CHILLING

SERVES 8

CRUST

- 1½ cups crushed graham crackers (from about 11 cracker sheets)
- 2 Tbsp. granulated sugar
- ½ tsp. ground ginger
- ¼ tsp. kosher salt
- 5 Tbsp. unsalted butter, melted

FILLING

- 1¼ cups granulated sugar
- ⅓ cup cornstarch
- 2 Tbsp. grated grapefruit zest plus 1¼ cups fresh juice (from 2 Ruby Red grapefruit)
- 4 large egg yolks
- 4 Tbsp. unsalted butter, cubed

MERINGUE

- 4 large egg whites
- ¼ tsp. cream of tartar
- ½ cup granulated sugar

1. Prepare the Crust: Preheat oven to 350°F. Stir together crushed graham crackers, sugar, ginger, and salt in a large bowl until combined. Stir in melted butter. Transfer to a 9-inch pie plate, pressing firmly into bottom and up sides. Bake until Crust is set and light golden brown, 12 to 14 minutes. Transfer to a wire rack; let cool completely, about 20 minutes.

2. Prepare the Filling: Whisk together sugar and cornstarch in a medium saucepan. Whisk in grapefruit juice, ½ cup water, and egg yolks; cook over medium heat, whisking constantly, until thickened, 6 to 8 minutes. Remove from heat; whisk in butter until melted and combined. Pour mixture through a fine mesh strainer into a heatproof bowl. Stir in grapefruit zest until combined.

3. Pour Filling into cooled Crust. Place a piece of plastic wrap directly on surface of Filling. Refrigerate until set, about 3 hours.

4. Prepare the Meringue: Beat egg whites and cream of tartar with an electric mixer on high speed until frothy, about 1 minute. Gradually beat in sugar. Continue beating until sugar is dissolved and stiff peaks form, about 4 minutes.

5. Remove plastic wrap from surface of pie. Spoon Meringue over chilled pie. Using a kitchen torch, toast Meringue until lightly browned. (Alternatively, broil pie on center rack of the oven 6 inches from heat source until just browned, 2 to 3 minutes, watching carefully to prevent Meringue from burning.)

Grapefruit-Cream Cheese Hand Pies

(Photo, page 23)

ACTIVE 15 MIN. - TOTAL 1 HOUR, 10 MIN.

SERVES 6

- 1 (14.1-oz.) pkg. refrigerated piecrusts (2 piecrusts)
  All-purpose flour, for work surface
- ½ cup cream cheese, softened
- ⅓ cup granulated sugar
- 6 Tbsp. grapefruit marmalade
- 1 large egg, beaten
- 2 Tbsp. turbinado sugar
- 1 cup powdered sugar
- 2 Tbsp. fresh grapefruit juice (from 1 grapefruit)

1. Preheat oven to 400°F. Line a large baking sheet with parchment paper; set aside. Unroll piecrusts on a lightly floured work surface. Using a 5-inch round cutter, cut out 3 rounds from each crust. Discard any remaining scraps.

2. Beat cream cheese and granulated sugar with an electric mixer on high speed until smooth, about 2 minutes. Dollop 1 rounded tablespoon cream cheese mixture onto the center of each dough round. Top each with 1 tablespoon marmalade. Brush some of the beaten egg around edge of each filled pastry; reserve remaining beaten egg. Fold each pastry in half to enclose the filling; using a fork, press edges to seal. Place sealed pastries on prepared baking sheet. Refrigerate until chilled, about 15 minutes.

3. Brush pies with remaining beaten egg, and sprinkle evenly with turbinado sugar. Bake in preheated oven until golden brown, 18 to 22 minutes. Remove from oven. Let cool on baking sheet about 20 minutes.

4. Whisk together powdered sugar and grapefruit juice in a small bowl until smooth. Drizzle over cooled hand pies, and serve.

Grapefruit Pavlova

(Photo, page 22)

ACTIVE 15 MIN. - TOTAL 1 HOUR,
PLUS 1 HOUR, 15 MIN. COOLING

SERVES 8

- 4 large egg whites (about ⅔ cup)
- ¼ tsp. cream of tartar
- ¼ tsp. kosher salt
- ¾ cup granulated sugar
- 2-3 drops red food coloring gel (optional)
- 3 large pink grapefruit
- 2 Tbsp. seedless raspberry jam
- 1½ cups heavy whipping cream
- ½ cup sour cream
- ¼ cup powdered sugar
  Fresh mint leaves, for garnish

1. Preheat oven to 250°F. Line a baking sheet with parchment paper; set aside. Beat egg whites with a stand mixer fitted with a whisk attachment on high speed until foamy, about 1 minute. Beat in cream of tartar and salt until soft peaks form, about 1 minute. Gradually add granulated sugar in a slow, steady stream. Continue beating until egg whites are very stiff and sugar is almost dissolved, about 4 minutes. If using food coloring, beat in 1 drop at a time until meringue reaches desired shade.

2. Using an offset spatula or the back of a spoon, spread meringue onto prepared baking sheet, forming a 9-inch round with a 6-inch-wide indention in the center. Bake in preheated oven for 45 minutes. Turn oven off, and let meringue cool in oven for 45 minutes. Remove from oven, and let cool to room temperature about 30 minutes.

3. Remove and discard peel and pith from grapefruit. Working over a bowl, cut grapefruit into segments; reserve juice in bowl, and discard membranes. Stir together jam and 1 tablespoon reserved grapefruit juice in a medium bowl. Add segments; stir gently to combine. Set aside.

4. Beat whipping cream, sour cream, and powdered sugar with an electric mixer on high speed until stiff peaks form, about 2 minutes. Spoon whipped cream mixture onto center of cooled meringue. Top evenly with grapefruit mixture. Garnish with fresh mint leaves. Serve immediately.

GRAPEFRUIT
MERINGUE PIE

POMELO
OLIVE OIL
CAKE

Pomelo Olive Oil Cake

ACTIVE 15 MIN. - TOTAL 1 HOUR,
PLUS 1 HOUR, 15 MIN. COOLING

SERVES 8

- 2 cups bleached cake flour
- ½ cup fine yellow cornmeal
- 1½ tsp. baking powder
- ½ tsp. baking soda
- ½ tsp. kosher salt
- 3 large eggs
- 1 cup granulated sugar
- 2 Tbsp. grated pomelo zest plus ½ cup fresh juice (from 1 pomelo)
- 1¼ cups extra-virgin olive oil, plus more for greasing pan
  Powdered sugar, for dusting cake
  Pomelo wedges, for serving

1. Preheat oven to 350°F. Grease a 9-inch springform pan with oil. Line bottom of pan with parchment paper. Place pan on a baking sheet lined with foil; set aside.
2. Whisk together flour, cornmeal, baking powder, baking soda, and salt in a medium bowl until combined. Set aside.
3. Beat eggs, granulated sugar, and pomelo zest in a large bowl with an electric mixer on high speed until mixture is thickened, doubled in size, and pale yellow, about 5 minutes. With mixer running on high speed, gradually stream in olive oil, and beat until combined. Reduce mixer speed to low; add flour mixture to egg mixture alternating with the pomelo juice in 3 additions, beginning and ending with the flour mixture. Scrape down sides of bowl. Pour batter into prepared pan. Tap pan gently on work surface to remove any bubbles.
4. Bake in preheated oven until a wooden pick inserted in center of cake comes out clean, 45 to 55 minutes. Let cool in pan for 15 minutes. Remove from pan, and let cool on a wire rack for 1 hour. Gently dust the top of cake with powdered sugar. Cut cake into 8 slices; top each slice with a pomelo wedge, and serve.

Go for the Gold (or Red, White, Pink, or Green)

1. White
This mouth-puckering fruit was originally found in Barbados, and it was the first kind of grapefruit planted in the U.S. Its pale yellow flesh packs an intense tart flavor and subtle floral aroma. Use it in simple syrups and cocktails or in recipes with warm spices.

2. Red
Smaller and sweeter than the pink types, these grapefruit are great for baking or just enjoying alone as a snack. The best-known red variety is the orange-skinned Ruby Red, which has been integral in Texas' commercial grapefruit industry.

3. Pomelo
Pomelos have lime green skin; flesh that ranges from pale yellow to red; and a bitter, thick pith. While their flavor is similar to grapefruit, pomelos tend to be larger, about the size of a small melon. They're easy to peel and yield beautiful large segments ideal for salads.

4. Pink
Supermarket bestsellers, these grapefruit are popular for good reason. With a mild tang and a balanced sweetness, they're top picks for juicing. Although they are golden on the outside, their flesh can range in color from pale pink to vibrant coral.

A FEW THINGS TO KNOW ABOUT GRAPEFRUIT
To choose the best of the bunch, seek out one that feels a bit heavy for its size, which indicates a juicy interior. Avoid those with lumpy skin or soft spots, which are signs that the citrus is past its prime. Serve chilled segments with granola and yogurt at breakfast, or add some to a salad of butter lettuce, toasted pine nuts, avocado slices, and your favorite vinaigrette. You can use the zest in rubs or marinades for seafood, chicken, or pork. And you'll never go wrong mixing freshly squeezed Texas grapefruit juice with tequila, soda water, and lime to make a refreshing paloma.

A Tale of Two Dumplings

There's more than one way to make the South's most comforting dish

PICK ANY FIVE SOUTHERNERS at random, and it's a safe bet that the chicken and dumplings on their dinner tables will be as unique as they are. The farther north you tread, the more likely you'll encounter dumplings scooped from a loose batter and then dropped into the bubbling broth. In the Deep South, they might be rolled as thick as slim biscuits (this is sometimes referred to as "chicken and pastry") or as thin as fat noodles (often called "chicken and slicks"). Some folks like theirs brothy with a confetti of diced carrot and sliced celery; others prefer it plain and simple with a splash of cream and a dash of pepper.

The roots of this popular dish are layered deep in our history, running under regions, through social classes, and across time. While one of the first printed recipes for it appears in a community cookbook from Virginia published in 1878, the DNA of chicken and dumplings can be traced back to meals simmered by Africans and Europeans centuries earlier.

The list of Southern icons who've stirred up a pot of chicken and dumplings is long and laudable. Country-cooking great Edna Lewis rolled her dumplings thin, cutting them into neat diamond shapes. Community activist and cookbook author Toni Tipton-Martin opts for easier drop dumplings, but she dresses up her chicken by browning it in butter or bacon fat for extra flavor and adds a generous glug of white wine to enrich the bubbling broth.

I grew up with my grandmother May's recipe. She was a first-grade teacher who moonlighted selling furs at McRae's department store; my grandfather worked at a car dealership. They didn't have much, but they usually had enough. While she prepared most things from scratch, she did rely on modern conveniences: Her dumplings were made using a boxed baking mix,

and her chicken came from a can. While she held nothing against fresh vegetables and herbs, there weren't any in sight.

I cooked this dish with her just once, during a family reunion in Sardis, Mississippi. My grandmother had prepared chicken and dumplings hundreds of times without a hiccup, but on this evening, something happened. Whether it was distraction, dementia, or simply a thin pot on an unfamiliar stove, the dumplings scorched. I remember her frustration; my mother trying to convince her that they tasted fine. "They do NOT taste fine, Judy," she said, her normally sweet voice turning steely and stern, reminding us that her faculties and dignity were still very much intact. There was only one thing to do—start over.

With so many of my food memories shaped by my grandmother, I'm shocked that this is the only time I can remember cooking with her. The recollections are mere flashes—pulled chicken, a flour-dusted counter, a simmering pot. A tight biscuit dough, rolled flatter than seemed right. Floured fingers slipping soft dominoes of dough into the bubbling broth. Dutiful, dedicated stirring, with an occasional nervous scrape of the wooden spoon across the bottom of the pan for extra reassurance. Then, at long last, a final taste. They were better than fine, she proclaimed. Just right.

When I set out to re-create her recipe (she never wrote it down), I whispered a plea to the heavens for her forgiveness as I made small changes to suit my palate. With a choice of dumplings, herbs, and vegetables, my version (at right) meets you where you are. Start from scratch, if you have time, picking the dumpling style that speaks to you. If you're in a hurry, by all means, take a store-bought shortcut. The right way to prepare chicken and dumplings is just how you like them. The only wrong way is to not make them at all. —Josh Miller

Chicken and Your Favorite Dumplings

ACTIVE 35 MIN. - TOTAL 55 MIN.

SERVES 4

- 2 (1-lb.) bone-in chicken breasts
- 6 cups lower-sodium chicken broth
- 1 small yellow onion, halved
- 2 medium celery stalks, divided (1 stalk is optional)
- 2 large carrots, peeled, divided (1 carrot is optional)
- 2 (5-inch) fresh thyme or flat-leaf parsley sprigs, plus chopped leaves for garnish
- ½ tsp. kosher salt
- ½ tsp. black pepper, plus more for garnish
  Rolled or Drop Dumplings (recipes, opposite)
- ½ cup heavy whipping cream (optional)
- 1 Tbsp. all-purpose flour (optional)

1. Place chicken, broth, and onion in a large Dutch oven. Cut 1 celery stalk and 1 carrot in half crosswise; add to Dutch oven with thyme or parsley sprigs, salt, and pepper. Bring to a boil over high; reduce heat to low. Cover and simmer, undisturbed, until chicken is cooked through and easily pulls away from bone, about 20 minutes. Remove chicken; let cool slightly. Using 2 forks, pull chicken apart into bite-size pieces; discard skin and bones, herb sprigs, and cooked vegetables, reserving broth in Dutch oven.
2. Prepare Rolled or Drop Dumplings as directed opposite. Return broth to a simmer over medium-low. Thinly slice remaining carrot and celery stalk, if desired; add to broth with pulled chicken. If desired, whisk together cream and flour in a small bowl until smooth; stir into broth. Gradually add dumplings to broth. Cover and simmer gently over low, until dumplings are cooked through, about 8 minutes for Rolled Dumplings or 10 minutes for Drop Dumplings. Remove from heat. Garnish with pepper and chopped thyme or parsley.

DROP
DUMPLING
DOUGH

ROLLED
DUMPLING
DOUGH

Drop Dumplings

Stir together 1 cup **all-purpose flour**, ½ cup **fine yellow cornmeal**, 1 tsp. **baking powder**, and ¾ tsp. **kosher salt** in a medium bowl. Stir in ¾ cup **whole buttermilk** and 2 Tbsp. melted **unsalted butter** until dough comes together. Let stand 5 minutes. Drop tablespoons of dough into broth; cook as directed.

Rolled Dumplings

Stir together 1½ cups **all-purpose flour**, 1½ tsp. **baking powder**, and ¾ tsp. **kosher salt** in a medium bowl. Using a fork, cut in 3 Tbsp. cubed cold **unsalted butter** until flour mixture is crumbly. Stir in ½ cup plus 2 Tbsp. **whole buttermilk** until dough comes together. Roll out dough to ¼-inch thickness on a well-floured work surface; cut into 2- x 1-inch rectangles. Add dumplings to broth; cook as directed.

CHICKEN AND
ROLLED DUMPLINGS

ROTISSERIE CHICKEN SHORTCUT
Preroasted birds are a busy person's lifesaver.
Discard the skin and bones, and then pull the
meat into bite-size chunks. Prepare the broth
as directed on page 28, omitting raw chicken.
Add the pulled chicken with the dumplings in
Step 2, and proceed as directed.

FROZEN DUMPLINGS SHORTCUT
Frozen dumplings will satisfy your cravings with minimal effort. Prepare the recipe as directed on page 28 through Step 1, adding the frozen dumplings when the broth is simmering in Step 2. Cook according to package directions.

CHICKEN AND
DROP DUMPLINGS

Flash in the Pan

Whip up a speedy skillet pasta in 40 minutes or less

Fettuccine with Collards and Bacon

ACTIVE 40 MIN. - TOTAL 40 MIN.
SERVES 4

- 1 lb. uncooked fettuccine
- 4 garlic cloves, divided
- ¼ cup extra-virgin olive oil
- 1 cup panko breadcrumbs
- ¼ tsp. kosher salt, plus more for salting water
- 8 thick-cut bacon slices, chopped
- 1 medium-size yellow onion, finely chopped (1½ cups)
- ¼ tsp. crushed red pepper, plus more for garnish
- 1 lb. fresh collard greens, stemmed and thinly sliced (about 6 cups)
- 4 oz. Pecorino Romano cheese, grated (about 1 cup), plus more for garnish

1. Bring a large pot of salted water to a boil over high. Add fettuccine; cook until al dente, about 8 minutes. Reserve 1½ cups cooking water; drain pasta, and transfer to a large heatproof bowl.
2. Grate 1 garlic clove. Heat olive oil in a large skillet over medium-high. Add panko, salt, and grated garlic; cook, stirring often, until panko is golden brown, 3 to 4 minutes. Transfer to a bowl, and set aside. Wipe skillet clean.
3. Add bacon to same skillet; cook over medium, stirring often, until crisp, about 12 minutes. Transfer cooked bacon to a plate, reserving drippings in skillet. Mince remaining 3 garlic cloves. Add onion, red pepper, and minced garlic to drippings in skillet. Cook, stirring often, until onion is tender, about 5 minutes. Add collards; cook, stirring often, until just tender, about 5 minutes. Add cooked fettuccine and bacon, cheese, and reserved 1½ cups cooking water. Continue cooking over medium, tossing occasionally until sauce coats noodles, about 2 minutes.
4. Remove from heat, and sprinkle with panko mixture. Garnish with additional cheese and crushed red pepper. Serve immediately.

A TRICK FOR TENDER GREENS
To avoid tough collard greens, fold each leaf in half and then tear or slice off the stem.

Green Chile Mac and Cheese with Chicken

ACTIVE 15 MIN · TOTAL 15 MIN
SERVES 4

- 4 Tbsp. unsalted butter
- 1 large poblano chile, chopped (about 1 cup)
- 3 Tbsp. all-purpose flour
- 3 cups whole milk
- ½ tsp. kosher salt
- ¼ tsp. ground cumin
- 8 oz. white processed cheese (such as Velveeta), cubed (about 1¼ cups)
- 8 oz. sharp Cheddar cheese, shredded (about 2 cups), divided
- 3 cups shredded rotisserie chicken
- 12 oz. medium-size shell pasta (about 3 cups), cooked and drained
  Fresh cilantro, for garnish

1. Preheat oven to broil with rack about 10 inches from heat source. Melt butter in a large broiler-safe skillet over medium-high. Add poblano, and cook, stirring often, until tender, about 3 minutes.

2. Add flour, and cook, stirring constantly, until bubbly, about 1 minute. Whisk in milk; cook, whisking often, until mixture thickens, about 5 minutes. Stir in salt and cumin. Add processed cheese and 1½ cups of the Cheddar, stirring until melted, 1 minute. Stir in chicken and cooked pasta; remove from heat.

3. Sprinkle with remaining ½ cup Cheddar. Broil in preheated oven until cheese is lightly browned, about 4 minutes. Garnish with cilantro.

SOME (DON'T) LIKE IT HOT

Poblano peppers are typically about half as spicy as jalapeños; for an even milder mac, remove the ribs or use Anaheim chiles.

FOR GOOD MEASURE
Put a measuring cup in the colander to help you remember to reserve some pasta water for the sauce.

Lemon-Pepper Shrimp Scampi

ACTIVE 35 MIN. - TOTAL 35 MIN.
SERVES 4

- 1 lb. uncooked spaghetti
- 1½ lb. jumbo peeled, deveined raw shrimp, tails removed
- 2 tsp. kosher salt, divided, plus more for salting water
- 1 tsp. black pepper, divided, plus more for serving
- 4 Tbsp. extra-virgin olive oil, divided
- 6 Tbsp. unsalted butter, divided
- 1 large shallot, finely chopped (about ⅓ cup)
- 6 garlic cloves, thinly sliced (about 3 Tbsp.)
- 1 cup dry white wine (such as Pinot Grigio)
- ½ cup chopped fresh flat-leaf parsley (from 1 bunch), plus more for garnish
- 2 tsp. grated lemon zest plus 4 Tbsp. fresh juice (from 2 lemons)

  Grated Parmesan cheese, for serving

  Lemon wedges, for serving

1. Bring a large pot of salted water to a boil over high. Add spaghetti; cook until al dente, 7 to 8 minutes. Reserve 1 cup cooking water; drain pasta, and transfer to a large bowl.
2. Pat shrimp dry with a paper towel; sprinkle with 1 teaspoon of the salt and ½ teaspoon of the pepper.
3. Heat 2 tablespoons of the olive oil in a 12-inch skillet over medium-high. Add half of the shrimp; cook, undisturbed, until browned on 1 side, 2 to 3 minutes. Stir shrimp, and transfer to a plate. Repeat with remaining oil and shrimp.
4. Add 4 tablespoons of the butter to drippings in skillet; add shallot, garlic, and remaining 1 teaspoon salt and ½ teaspoon pepper. Cook over medium-high, stirring often, until shallot is just tender, about 3 minutes. Stir in wine, scraping up any browned bits from bottom of pan; cook, undisturbed, until reduced by half, 2 to 3 minutes. Reduce heat to medium, and add cooked shrimp (and any accumulated juices), parsley, lemon zest and juice, cooked spaghetti, reserved 1 cup cooking water, and remaining 2 tablespoons butter. Cook over medium, tossing together until sauce becomes glossy and coats noodles evenly, 2 to 3 minutes.
5. Remove from heat; top with grated cheese and more black pepper. Garnish with parsley, and serve with lemon wedges.

Beefy Skillet Lasagna

ACTIVE 30 MIN. - TOTAL 40 MIN.

SERVES 4

- 1 Tbsp. extra-virgin olive oil
- 1 lb. lean ground beef
- 3 medium garlic cloves, minced (about 1 Tbsp.)
- 1 tsp. kosher salt
- ½ tsp. fennel seeds
- ¼ tsp. crushed red pepper
- 1 (24-oz.) jar marinara sauce
- 10 uncooked lasagna noodles, broken into 2-inch pieces (4 to 5 cups)
- 1 cup whole-milk ricotta cheese
- 4 oz. shredded low-moisture mozzarella cheese (about 1 cup)
- 2 oz. Parmesan cheese, grated (about ½ cup)
- ¼ cup chopped fresh basil, plus whole leaves for garnish

1. Heat oil in a 12-inch cast-iron skillet over medium-high. Add beef, and cook, stirring occasionally, until crumbled and browned, about 5 minutes. Add garlic, salt, fennel seeds, and crushed red pepper; cook, stirring constantly, until fragrant, about 1 minute. Stir in 1½ cups water, scraping up any browned bits on bottom of skillet.

2. Using tongs, stir in marinara and lasagna noodle pieces, ensuring pieces are submerged in sauce. Bring to a boil over medium-high; cover, reduce heat to low, and simmer until noodles are just tender, 15 to 20 minutes, uncovering during last 5 minutes of cooking. While mixture cooks, preheat oven to broil with oven rack about 10 inches from heat source.

3. Stir together ricotta, shredded mozzarella, grated Parmesan, and chopped basil in a medium bowl until combined; dollop over cooked noodle mixture in skillet.

4. Broil in preheated oven until cheese is melted and lightly browned, about 5 minutes. Garnish with basil leaves.

LIGHTEN IT UP
Reduce fat by replacing all or half of the beef with ground turkey or hot Italian chicken sausage.

Creamy Andouille Pasta

ACTIVE 35 MIN. · TOTAL 35 MIN.

SERVES 4

- 1 lb. uncooked penne pasta
- 1 lb. andouille sausage, cut into ½-inch-thick slices
- 4 Tbsp. unsalted butter
- 1 medium-size red bell pepper, chopped (about 1 cup)
- 1 small Vidalia onion, finely chopped (about 1 cup)
- 4 Tbsp. all-purpose flour
- 3 cups whole milk
- 2 tsp. Cajun seasoning
- ¾ tsp. kosher salt, plus more for salting water
- 4 oz. pepper Jack cheese, shredded (about 1 cup)

  Thinly sliced scallions, for garnish

  Hot sauce, for garnish

1. Bring a large pot of salted water to a boil over high. Add pasta; cook until al dente, about 11 minutes. Drain and set aside.

2. Place sausage in a cold 12-inch skillet. Cook over medium-high, stirring often, until browned, 5 to 8 minutes. Transfer sausage to a plate.

3. Reduce heat to medium; add butter to drippings in skillet, stirring until melted, about 1 minute. Add chopped red bell pepper and Vidalia onion. Cook, stirring often, until onion is tender, about 3 minutes. Add flour; cook, stirring constantly, until lightly toasted, about 1 minute. Increase heat to medium-high; whisk in milk, and cook, whisking constantly, until mixture thickens, about 5 minutes. Stir in Cajun seasoning, salt, and reserved sausage. Add cheese, stirring until just melted, about 1 minute.

4. Remove from heat, and stir in cooked pasta. Garnish with sliced scallions and hot sauce.

GO SLOW

Start cooking the sausage in a cold skillet; the gradual increase in heat will render more of the flavorful drippings.

Let's Go Dutch, Baby

For a fun Valentine's Day breakfast, try this puffy oversize pancake

Chocolate Dutch Baby with Berries

ACTIVE 25 MIN. - TOTAL 45 MIN.
SERVES 4

- ½ cup all-purpose flour
- ¼ cup granulated sugar
- 3 Tbsp. unsweetened cocoa
- ¼ tsp. plus a pinch kosher salt, divided
- 3 large eggs, at room temperature
- 1 cup whole milk, at room temperature
- 1½ tsp. vanilla extract, divided
- 2 Tbsp. unsalted butter
- ½ cup heavy whipping cream
- 2 Tbsp. powdered sugar
- ¼ tsp. ground cinnamon
- ½ cup sliced fresh strawberries
- ½ cup fresh raspberries
- Flaky salt, to taste (optional)

1. Place a 10-inch cast-iron skillet in oven with rack in lower-third position. Preheat oven to 425°F. (Do not remove skillet while oven preheats.)
2. Whisk together all-purpose flour, granulated sugar, cocoa, and ¼ teaspoon of the salt in a medium bowl. Whisk together eggs, milk, and 1 teaspoon of the vanilla in a medium bowl until well combined. Gradually whisk about half of the milk mixture into flour mixture until smooth. Gradually whisk in remaining milk mixture until thoroughly combined.

3. Carefully remove hot skillet from preheated oven; add butter, and swirl to melt and coat skillet. Working quickly, pour batter into skillet. Bake in preheated oven until puffed and brown around edges, 18 to 22 minutes.
4. Meanwhile, whisk together heavy cream, powdered sugar, cinnamon, and remaining ½ teaspoon vanilla and pinch of kosher salt in a bowl until soft peaks form, 45 seconds. Chill, covered, until ready to serve.
5. Remove Dutch baby from oven. Top with whipped cream and berries; sprinkle with flaky salt, if using. Serve immediately.

Chocolate-Orange Dutch Baby

Prepare recipe as directed through Step 2, adding 2 tsp. grated **orange zest** to egg-milk mixture. Proceed with recipe as directed through Step 3; omit Step 4. In Step 5, spoon 1 cup **mixed orange slices** (such as blood oranges and navel oranges) on top of Dutch baby instead of whipped cream and berries; drizzle with **maple syrup.**

Chocolate-Cherry-Almond Dutch Baby

Prepare recipe as directed through Step 2, substituting **almond extract** for vanilla extract. Proceed with recipe as directed through Step 3; omit Step 4. In Step 5, spoon 1 (5.3-oz.) container **vanilla whole-milk yogurt** on top of Dutch baby instead of whipped cream and berries; swirl in ½ cup well-stirred **cherry preserves.** Sprinkle evenly with **toasted sliced almonds.**

The Sweet Side of Rice

This globally loved grain makes a delicious dessert

POPULAR FROM SOUTHEAST ASIA to South America, rice can turn up on the table at any meal of the day. In South Carolina, as well as parts of West Africa, some say that the Lord's Prayer could be edited to read "Give us this day our daily rice" instead of bread.

In the early 1990s, Karen Hess, a legendary American culinary historian, published a book called *The Carolina Rice Kitchen*. Following an insightful introductory essay on the importance of the African hand in the cooking of the Carolinas, there are myriad recipes for rice, including breads and even restorative gruels for the sick. Many vividly demonstrate the culinary connections between the Lowcountry and the rice-growing areas of West Africa. Recipes such as purloo (a hearty one-pot dish that's prepared with seafood or meat), red rice, and rice pudding (one of my favorite uses for this grain) transformed the food in this region.

As anyone with a collection of cookbooks about cuisines around the world can attest, there are many ways to create rice pudding. The possibilities range from Indian kheer (flavored with rose water and cardamom seeds) to different types of arroz con leche and arroz con dulce in the Hispanic world, as well as the South African version that's made tangy with lemon zest. Some are soupy, and others stiff. The dish can bake in the oven, be cooked in a double boiler, or rely strictly on the stovetop.

When it comes to this dessert, I am a purist and believe the fewer ingredients the better. Rice that's cooked simply and enhanced with minimal additions is my idea of perfection. It's all about the mouthfeel of the creamy texture and the toothsomeness of the grain. This version, which is prepared in a skillet, suits me best. Buttered Rum Raisin Sauce dresses it up, but it's just as tasty enjoyed on its own. –Jessica B. Harris

Creamy Skillet Rice Pudding

ACTIVE 50 MIN. - TOTAL 1 HOUR
SERVES 4

- 1½ Tbsp. unsalted butter
- ½ cup uncooked Arborio rice
- 3½ cups whole milk
- ½ cup heavy whipping cream
- ¼ cup packed light brown sugar
- 1 vanilla bean pod, halved lengthwise
- ¼ tsp. kosher salt
- 2 large egg yolks
  Buttered Rum Raisin Sauce, for serving (recipe at right)
- 3 Tbsp. toasted sliced almonds

1. Melt butter in a large (12-inch) cast-iron skillet over medium. Add rice, and cook, stirring constantly, until toasted and fragrant, 1 to 2 minutes. Add whole milk, heavy cream, brown sugar, vanilla bean pod halves, and kosher salt; bring to a simmer over medium, stirring often. Reduce heat to medium-low to maintain a steady simmer. Simmer, stirring often, until rice is tender and mixture has thickened, 30 to 35 minutes. Remove from heat; discard vanilla bean pod halves.
2. Beat egg yolks with a whisk in a medium bowl. Ladle in about ½ cup of the hot pudding mixture, whisking constantly to temper the eggs. Pour warmed egg mixture back into skillet. Stir mixture constantly until well combined, about 1 minute. Let cool slightly, about 10 minutes. (Pudding will continue to thicken as it cools.)
3. To serve warm, divide pudding evenly among 4 bowls. Spoon Buttered Rum Raisin Sauce evenly over the bowls; sprinkle with almonds. To serve chilled, transfer pudding to an airtight container and place plastic wrap directly on the surface. Chill until cold, about 3 hours. Top with warm Buttered Rum Raisin Sauce and almonds.

Buttered Rum Raisin Sauce

ACTIVE 10 MIN. - TOTAL 40 MIN.
SERVES 4

- ½ cup golden raisins
- ⅓ cup (2⅔ oz.) dark rum
- ½ cup packed light brown sugar
- ½ tsp. kosher salt
- ⅛ tsp. ground cinnamon
- 2 Tbsp. unsalted butter, cut into 2 pieces

1. Stir together golden raisins and rum in a small saucepan with a tight-fitting lid. Bring mixture to a simmer over medium; cover, and remove from heat. Let stand until raisins are plumped, about 30 minutes.
2. Uncover saucepan, and stir in sugar, 1 tablespoon water, salt, and cinnamon. Bring mixture to a simmer over low, stirring often to dissolve sugar. Let simmer, undisturbed, for 1 minute. Remove from heat; stir in butter, 1 tablespoon at a time, until sauce is thick and glossy. Transfer sauce to an airtight container, and chill until ready to use, up to 4 days. To reheat, place sauce in a microwavable bowl and microwave on HIGH until hot, about 2 minutes.

The Historical Weight of Rice

This grain is a potent connector between the culinary and agricultural cultures of coastal South Carolina and Georgia and those of West Africa—from southern Senegal through Sierra Leone. It is the rice-growing knowledge and the brutal labor by both enslaved Africans in the South and their ancestors on the other side of the Atlantic that created the wealth of the Lowcountry planters. In fact, it is said that the rice fields that enslaved people formed along the coast are large enough to be seen from space.

Go Deep

The trick to outrageously rich, superthick brownies? A high-sided cast-iron skillet

DEEP-DISH
SKILLET
BROWNIES

How Do You Take Your Brownies?

Sweet, salty, or crunchy—there are plenty of ways to dress up the classic

Deep-Dish Skillet Brownies

ACTIVE 15 MIN. - TOTAL 50 MIN.,
PLUS 1 HOUR COOLING

SERVES 8

5	Tbsp. unsalted butter, plus more for skillet
¼	cup canola oil
1¼	cups 60% to 70% cacao bittersweet chocolate chips, divided
¾	cup granulated sugar
¾	cup packed light brown sugar
2	tsp. vanilla extract
2	large eggs, at room temperature
½	cup all-purpose flour
¼	cup Dutch-process cocoa
½	tsp. kosher salt
¼	tsp. baking soda
	Ice cream (optional)

1. Preheat oven to 350°F. Lightly grease a 9- or 10-inch cast-iron skillet with butter.

2. Place butter and oil in a large microwavable bowl; microwave on MEDIUM (50% power) until butter melts and mixture is warm, about 2 minutes. Stir in ½ cup of the chocolate chips until melted and smooth, about 1 minute. Whisk in granulated sugar, brown sugar, vanilla, and eggs until combined and smooth. Fold in flour, cocoa, kosher salt, and baking soda until just combined.

3. Stir in remaining ¾ cup chocolate chips. Pour batter into prepared skillet.

4. Bake in preheated oven until edges are puffed and a wooden pick inserted in center comes out mostly clean, about 32 minutes for fudgy brownies and up to 40 minutes for chewier brownies. Cool in skillet on a wire rack 1 hour before serving. Top with ice cream, if desired.

White Chocolate-Strawberry Brownies

Prepare recipe as directed through Step 2. In Step 3, stir ¼ cup each chopped white chocolate and crushed freeze-dried strawberries into batter with remaining chocolate chips. Pour batter into skillet; bake as directed. Remove from oven; top with ¼ cup each chopped white chocolate and crushed freeze-dried strawberries.

Coconut-Almond-Fudge Brownies

Prepare recipe as directed through Step 2. In Step 3, stir ¼ cup each shredded coconut and toasted sliced almonds into batter with remaining chocolate chips. Pour batter into skillet; bake as directed. Remove from oven; top with ¼ cup each shredded coconut and toasted sliced almonds. Cool 30 minutes; drizzle with ¼ cup hot fudge.

Peanut-and-Pretzel Brownies

Prepare recipe as directed through Step 2. In Step 3, stir 3 Tbsp. chopped honey-roasted peanuts and ¼ cup crushed pretzel twists into batter with remaining chocolate chips. Pour batter into skillet, and top mixture with an additional 3 Tbsp. chopped honey-roasted peanuts and ¾ cup crushed pretzel twists. Bake as directed.

Salted Caramel-S'mores Brownies

Prepare recipe as directed through Step 2. In Step 3, stir ½ cup each mini marshmallows and crushed graham crackers into batter with remaining chocolate chips. Pour batter into skillet; bake as directed. Remove from oven; top with ½ cup each mini marshmallows and crushed graham crackers, pressing to adhere. Cool 30 minutes; drizzle with ¼ cup salted caramel sauce.

Next-Level Nachos

Whether you watch the Super Bowl for the football or the commercials,
Test Kitchen Professional Ivy Odom has party-ready recipes that will steal the show

WHEN THE SUPER BOWL rolls around, I don't really pay attention to which teams are playing or who's performing during halftime. As with any good party in the South, the main priority is the food. Watching the game at home provides certain perks that you can't enjoy at tented tailgates. There's nothing like sneaking away to the kitchen to whip up a last minute dish while hungry fans are grazing away on premade snacks.

Best served hot off the stove, these Corn-and-Smoked Sausage Nachos will be devoured before the end of the first quarter. Inspired by my mother's jalapeño popper dip, this creamy corn-studded cheese sauce blankets the crunchy tortilla chips in the best way (though Mama swears by a potato chip for any dip that includes a base of cream cheese and sweet onions). To make things even better, I add Alabama-made Conecuh sausage—beloved throughout the South for its rich flavor. If you can't find it in your local supermarket, your favorite smoked sausage will work.

Another Mama-approved tip? Set up a beverage station where folks can make their own drinks, so you don't have to play bartender all night. Ranch water is a simple mix of tequila, sparkling water, and lime juice and is always a crowd-pleaser. My pretty pomegranate version (recipe at right) is a fruity, tangy twist on the classic. Add these recipes to your game-day lineup, and you'll have happy fans regardless of the final score.

Corn-and-Smoked Sausage Nachos

ACTIVE 30 MIN. · TOTAL 30 MIN.
SERVES 6

- 1 lb. hickory-smoked sausage (such as Conecuh), chopped (about 4 cups)
- 1½ cups fresh yellow corn kernels (from 3 ears)
- 1 cup chopped sweet onion (from 1 small onion)
- ¼ tsp. kosher salt
- 2 tsp. Creole seasoning, divided
- 1 (8-oz.) pkg. cream cheese, softened
- ½ cup half-and-half
- 8 oz. thick tortilla chips (such as Tortiyahs!)
- 1 small jalapeño chile, finely chopped (about ¼ cup)
- 1 scallion, thinly sliced (about 1 Tbsp.)

1. Heat a 12-inch cast-iron skillet over medium-high. Add sausage; cook, stirring occasionally, until browned, about 8 minutes. Transfer sausage to a paper towel-lined plate using a slotted spoon; set aside. Reserve 2 tablespoons drippings in skillet; discard remaining drippings.

2. Add corn, chopped onion, salt, and 1½ teaspoons of the Creole seasoning to drippings in skillet; cook, stirring occasionally, until vegetables are tender, 5 to 8 minutes. Add softened cream cheese and half-and-half, stirring until cream cheese melts, about 1 minute. Remove from heat.

3. Place tortilla chips in a large skillet or on a platter. Spoon corn mixture evenly over chips; top with reserved sausage, jalapeño, and scallion. Sprinkle with remaining ½ teaspoon Creole seasoning. Serve immediately.

Pomegranate Ranch Water

ACTIVE 5 MIN. · TOTAL 5 MIN.
SERVES 1

Fill a double old-fashioned glass with ice. Add ¼ cup **blanco tequila**, 6 Tbsp. **sparkling water** (such as Topo Chico), 2 Tbsp. fresh **lime juice**, and 2 tsp. bottled **pomegranate juice**; stir to combine. Garnish with a **lime wheel**.

HEAT THINGS UP
Use spicy Italian or andouille sausage (instead of the smoked kind) to give these nachos an extra kick.

COOKING SCHOOL
TIPS AND TRICKS FROM THE SOUTH'S MOST TRUSTED KITCHEN

4 Steps to a Great Skillet Steak
Hint: A little butter goes a long way

1.
LET IT REST
Allow the steak to stand at room temperature for 30 minutes. This is important because it helps the meat cook more evenly. Pat both sides dry with a paper towel. Season the steak generously with kosher salt (about 1 teaspoon per pound) and plenty of freshly cracked black pepper.

2.
USE A HOT SKILLET
Heat a cast-iron skillet over high until very hot, about 5 minutes. Coat the bottom of the pan with 1 to 2 tablespoons of vegetable oil. Add the steak, pressing down with a spatula for an even sear. Cook until the steak easily releases from the pan, 1 to 2 minutes. Flip; cook 1 to 2 minutes more.

3.
ADD FAT (AND FLAVOR)
Reduce heat to medium-low; add 2 tablespoons butter, a few sprigs of woody herbs (like thyme or rosemary), and 1 to 2 smashed garlic cloves to the skillet. Carefully tilt the pan to one side; use a spoon to baste the steak with the melted butter. Continue to cook until it reaches desired doneness.

4.
LET IT REST (AGAIN)
Remove the steak from the skillet. Transfer it to a plate. Cover loosely with foil (if desired), and allow it to sit for about 10 minutes to give the juices time to reabsorb into the steak. Using a sharp knife, slice the meat against the grain, cutting perpendicular to the muscle fibers, for the most tender results.

(NOT) TOO HOT TO HANDLE

SILICONE
Lodge's Silicone Hot Handle Holder is colorful and dishwasher-safe; it shields your hands from temperatures up to 500°F. $8; lodgecastiron.com

LEATHER
Smithey's handcrafted, double-layered Leather Skillet Sleeve comes in two sizes, including an extended length for more protection. This design is timeless, just like a good skillet. $25; smithey.com

SKILLET SMARTS

■ When not in use, skillets should be clean, bone-dry, and lightly coated with oil.

■ If stacking, add a paper towel between pans to protect the surfaces.

■ Store them in the oven to avoid splashes and steam from the sink or stovetop. (Just remember to remove them before preheating.)

March

Tail Spins

Crawfish hit their peak this month. Go beyond the usual boil with these speedy recipes

CRAWFISH
ROLLS

Crawfish Rolls

ACTIVE 10 MIN. - TOTAL 10 MIN., PLUS 30 MIN. CHILLING

SERVES 8

Stir together ½ lb. peeled cooked **crawfish tails** (or ½ lb. frozen peeled cooked crawfish tails, thawed and drained), ¼ cup finely chopped **celery**, 1½ Tbsp. **mayonnaise**, 1 Tbsp. **fresh lemon juice** (from 1 lemon), 1 tsp. **Dijon mustard**, 1 tsp. finely chopped **fresh dill**, 1 tsp. grated **garlic**, ¾ tsp. **kosher salt**, and ¼ tsp. **smoked paprika** in a medium bowl until well combined. Cover with plastic wrap, and chill until cold and flavors combine, at least 30 minutes or up to 2 days. Divide crawfish mixture evenly among 8 **brown-and-serve dinner rolls**, toasted and split from top. Sprinkle evenly with 1½ Tbsp. thinly sliced **fresh chives**. Serve with **lemon wedges,** if desired.

Creamy Crawfish Soup

ACTIVE 35 MIN. - TOTAL 35 MIN.

SERVES 6

Melt 6 Tbsp. **unsalted butter** in a large saucepan over medium. Whisk in 6 Tbsp. **all-purpose flour**; cook, whisking constantly, until bubbling and golden brown, 3 to 4 minutes. Add 2 cups chopped **fennel** (from 1 large bulb, reserving fronds for garnish), 1½ cups chopped **plum tomatoes** (from 2 medium tomatoes), 1½ cups chopped **yellow onion** (from 1 medium onion), 2 tsp. **kosher salt**, 1 tsp. **black pepper**, and ¼ tsp. **cayenne pepper.** Cook, stirring often, until vegetables are tender, 4 to 5 minutes. Whisk in 4 cups **seafood or vegetable stock**; bring to a boil over medium. Reduce heat to low, and stir in ½ lb. peeled cooked **crawfish tails** (or ½ lb. frozen peeled cooked crawfish tails, thawed and drained). Simmer, stirring occasionally, until thickened,

CRAWFISH FRIED RICE

10 to 15 minutes. Remove pan from heat. Using an immersion blender, process mixture until completely smooth, about 1 minute. Return pan to low heat, and stir in 1 cup **heavy whipping cream** and ½ lb. **crawfish tails.** Cook, stirring occasionally, until heated through, about 5 minutes; stir in 1 Tbsp. **fresh lemon juice** (from 1 lemon). Drizzle with **olive oil,** and sprinkle with fennel fronds and more **black pepper.**

Crawfish Fried Rice

ACTIVE 20 MIN. - TOTAL 20 MIN.

SERVES 6

Heat 1 tablespoon **vegetable oil** in a large skillet or wok over medium. Add 3 lightly beaten **large eggs,** and cook, stirring often, until eggs are just set, about 1 minute. Transfer to a bowl, and wipe pan clean. Heat 1 tablespoon **vegetable oil** in pan over high. Add 1 cup finely chopped **carrot** (from 2 medium carrots), and cook, stirring often, until mostly tender, 2 to 3 minutes. Add 1 Tbsp. finely chopped **garlic** (from 3 medium garlic cloves) and 1 tsp. minced **fresh ginger** (from 1 [1-inch] piece fresh ginger); cook, stirring constantly, until fragrant, about 1 minute. Stir in 2 tsp. **toasted sesame oil** and 1 tablespoon **vegetable oil.** Add 4 cups cooked and cooled **jasmine white rice,** spreading in an even layer; cook, stirring occasionally, until rice is lightly toasted, 3 to 4 minutes. Add 1 lb. peeled cooked **crawfish tails** (or 1 lb. frozen peeled cooked crawfish tails, thawed and drained), ½ cup thinly sliced **scallions** (from 4 scallions), ½ cup **frozen sweet peas,** 2 Tbsp. **soy sauce,** 1 tsp. **kosher salt,** and cooked eggs; cook, stirring constantly, until liquid is absorbed, 3 to 4 minutes. Drizzle with more **soy sauce,** and serve.

Turning Heads

Don't judge it by its humble looks. Cabbage is the unsung darling of the vegetable aisle

WHEN I THINK OF CABBAGE, one of my earliest memories comes to mind. I am a tiny, barefoot girl standing in dense, damp, dark earth that looks like crumbled chocolate cake, the kind of topsoil found in the rich bottomland along the South Fork of the New River in North Carolina. Parallel rows of plump green cabbage heads stretch out as far as I can see. I now think of them as giant thumbtacks, with their long taproots sunk deep, holding the very ground in place so it wouldn't slide off the slope or slip over the bank into the river. I moved down off those mountains four decades ago, but those images from childhood still serve as my placeholder, ensuring that part of my past won't be swept away and lost either. To this day, I keep a timeworn vintage cabbage sack, large enough to hold 50 pounds of the veggies going to market, pinned next to my front door as a memento of my Appalachian roots.

You see, my family has raised cabbage on their farms and in their kitchen gardens in the Blue Ridge Mountains for generations, endowing me with a lifelong devotion to this delightful, and perhaps underappreciated, heirloom vegetable. My cabbage-centric upbringing might make me biased, but it doesn't make me wrong.

People use the phrase "as common as a cabbage" as though that were a bad thing. Being able to easily find and enjoy it fresh year-round is only one of the reasons that I adore this charming veggie. We can cook it all sorts of ways (or not, because it's equally delicious and useful raw).

A whole head keeps for weeks in the fridge—far longer than other leafy greens and, for that matter, longer than its culinary cousins like broccoli, Brussels sprouts, and cauliflower. That enduring quality means it's ready to step up when we need it, a brilliant solution on busy weeks when we never get around to a fresh-vegetable run. It's also one of the best bargains, especially during colder months when local harvests are harder to come by.

These recipes hang on to the best parts of what's familiar and comforting about cabbage, but they also add excitement with updated techniques and flavors. If you're not already a fan, you will be soon. –Sheri Castle

Stuffed-Cabbage Soup

Stuffed cabbage rolls are beloved on many family supper tables, but wrapping those leaves takes time. This hearty soup delivers all of the same delicious ingredients—like beef, rice, tomato sauce—a lot quicker. Serving the dish warm but not piping hot allows the subtle flavors to come through and improves the consistency. A sprinkle of fresh dill and a squeeze of bright lemon make the perfect finishing touches.
ACTIVE 20 MIN. · TOTAL 1 HOUR, 10 MIN.
SERVES 6

- 1 lb. ground round
- 1 medium-size yellow onion, chopped (2 cups)
- 1 tsp. kosher salt
- ½ tsp. black pepper
- 2 Tbsp. chopped garlic (4 garlic cloves)
- ½ tsp. ground cinnamon
- 3¾ cups beef consommé (from 3 [10½-oz.] cans)
- 3½ cups tomato sauce (from 2 [15-oz.] cans)
- 6 cups chopped green cabbage (from 1 small head)
- 2 medium carrots, thinly sliced (1 cup)
- ½ cup uncooked long-grain white rice
- 2 Tbsp. dark brown sugar
- 1 Tbsp. Worcestershire sauce
- 1 dried bay leaf
- 2 Tbsp. fresh lemon juice (from 1 lemon), plus lemon wedges for serving
- 2 Tbsp. chopped fresh dill, plus dill sprigs for garnish

1. Cook ground round, onion, salt, and pepper in a small Dutch oven or large saucepan over medium-high, stirring often, until meat is no longer pink, about 5 minutes. Stir in garlic and cinnamon, and cook, stirring constantly, 1 minute.
2. Stir in consommé and tomato sauce. Bring to a low boil over medium. Stir in cabbage, carrots, rice, brown sugar, Worcestershire, and bay leaf. Return to a boil over medium. Reduce heat to low; cover and simmer until rice is tender, about 25 minutes.
3. Remove from heat, and let stand, uncovered, 15 minutes. Remove and discard bay leaf; stir in lemon juice and chopped fresh dill. Ladle evenly into 6 bowls. Garnish with dill sprigs; serve with lemon wedges.

CABBAGE AND NOODLES
WITH SMOKED SAUSAGE

Cabbage and Noodles with Smoked Sausage

Because cabbage keeps nicely for weeks, as do the noodles and fully cooked sausage, it's easy to have ingredients you need for this dish on hand. Pay attention to the order of the steps: Preheating the water for the pasta prevents the lightly cooked vegetable mixture from getting too soft while the noodles boil.

ACTIVE 30 MIN. - TOTAL 55 MIN.

SERVES 8

- 2 Tbsp. olive oil, divided
- 12 oz. cooked smoked sausage (kielbasa or andouille), cut into ½-inch rounds
- 2 medium-size red, yellow, and/or orange bell peppers, cut into thin strips (about 3 cups)
- 1 medium-size yellow onion, cut into thin strips (about 2 cups)
- 1 head savoy cabbage, very thinly sliced (about 8 cups)
- 4 large garlic cloves, thinly sliced (about 2 Tbsp.)
- 1 tsp. kosher salt, plus more to taste
- ½ tsp. black pepper, plus more to taste
- ½ cup heavy whipping cream
- ½ tsp. crushed red pepper
- 1 (8-oz.) pkg. wide egg noodles
- ¼ cup loosely packed fresh basil leaves, thinly sliced

1. Heat 1 tablespoon of the oil in a Dutch oven over medium-high. Add sausage, and cook, stirring occasionally, until browned, about 3 minutes. Transfer sausage to a plate, reserving drippings in Dutch oven. Set sausage aside.
2. Heat remaining 1 tablespoon oil with reserved sausage drippings in Dutch oven over medium-high. Add bell peppers and onion; stir with a wooden spoon, scraping bottom of Dutch oven to loosen any browned bits, adding a splash of water, if needed.
3. Stir in cabbage, garlic, salt, and black pepper. Cover and cook until vegetables are just tender, 5 to 7 minutes. Stir in cream and crushed red pepper. Add reserved sausage and any accumulated juices on plate, and stir to combine. Cover and keep warm over very low heat.
4. Bring a large pot of salted water to a boil over high. Add the noodles; cook according to package directions until al dente. Drain noodles, and stir into sausage mixture. Stir in basil, and add more salt and black pepper to taste. Serve hot.

Red Cabbage with Cider and Pecans

(Photo, page 52)

The secret to great cabbage texture is cooking it only until tender, well before it gives up and becomes mushy. In this recipe, it is sautéed with apple slices in cider. The fruity sweetness is balanced by a splash of tangy apple cider vinegar, which helps preserve the vegetable's pretty red hue.

ACTIVE 30 MIN. - TOTAL 45 MIN.

SERVES 8

- 4 Tbsp. unsalted butter
- 2 Tbsp. granulated sugar
- 1½ tsp. kosher salt, plus more to taste
- 1 tsp. black pepper, plus more to taste
- 1 large onion, thinly sliced (about 3 cups)
- 8 cups shredded red cabbage (from 1 large cabbage)
- 1 large sweet, crisp apple (such as Honeycrisp), cored and thinly sliced (about 2 cups)
- ½ cup unfiltered apple cider
- 3 Tbsp. unfiltered apple cider vinegar
- ⅓ cup candied or toasted pecan halves
- 2 oz. crumbled goat cheese (about ⅓ cup)

1. Melt butter in a large saucepan over medium-high. Stir in sugar, salt, and pepper. Add onion, and stir to coat. Reduce heat to medium, and cook, stirring occasionally, until onion softens and begins to turn golden, 4 to 5 minutes.
2. Stir in cabbage and apple. Add cider; stir to coat mixture in saucepan. Cover and cook, tossing occasionally with tongs, until cabbage is just tender, 10 to 12 minutes. Remove from heat, and stir in vinegar. Season with more salt and pepper to taste.
3. Transfer mixture to a serving bowl. Sprinkle cabbage mixture with pecans and goat cheese. Serve slightly warm or at room temperature.

Skillet-Roasted Cabbage Wedges with Hot Bacon Dressing

(Photo, page 53)

Many of us were raised on "fried" cabbage made in a big black skillet. Here, wedges are cooked until they turn deep golden with caramelized edges. Slathered with a warm dressing made from bacon, mustard, and cider vinegar, this side becomes a complete dinner if you serve it with some hot cornbread to sop up the juices.

ACTIVE 20 MIN. - TOTAL 1 HOUR

SERVES 4

- 8 thick-cut bacon slices, cut crosswise into thin strips
- 1 small head green cabbage, cut into 8 (2½-inch-thick) wedges
- 1 tsp. kosher salt
- ¼ cup honey
- ¼ cup whole-grain Dijon mustard
- 2 Tbsp. apple cider vinegar
- 1 tsp. cracked pepper

1. Preheat oven to 450°F. Cook bacon in a 12-inch cast-iron skillet over medium, stirring occasionally, until bacon is crisp and browned, about 15 minutes. Remove from heat. Using a slotted spoon, transfer bacon to a bowl, reserving 7 tablespoons of the drippings in skillet. Transfer reserved drippings from skillet to a small saucepan, and set aside. Do not wipe skillet clean.
2. Arrange cabbage wedges, cut side down, in skillet, nestling them close together. Brush tops with 1 tablespoon of the reserved drippings. Sprinkle with salt. Roast in preheated oven until cabbage is tender when pierced with a knife and deeply browned in spots, 20 to 25 minutes.
3. Heat remaining 6 tablespoons bacon drippings over low until warm, about 45 seconds. Remove from heat, and whisk in honey, mustard, vinegar, and pepper. Drizzle honey-mustard mixture over cabbage. Sprinkle with reserved bacon.

RED CABBAGE WITH
CIDER AND PECANS
(PAGE 51)

SKILLET-ROASTED
CABBAGE WEDGES WITH
HOT BACON DRESSING
(PAGE 51)

CREAMED CABBAGE-AND-LEEK GRATIN

A Cabbage Cheat Sheet

KNOW THE VARIETIES: Cabbage can be divided into two main categories: European and Asian. The former includes green (also known as white), red or purple, and savoy—the ones we use most often in Southern recipes. The latter includes napa and bok choy. The differences have more to do with texture than flavor, though the Asian cabbages are less sweet.

FOCUS ON FRESHNESS: To select a great head of cabbage, start by picking it up. It should feel heavy and dense with no wilted or yellowed leaves. A generous covering of loose, floppy outer leaves is good because they are Mother Nature's way of protecting the head. (Many recipes tell us to discard all of the outer layer, but unless it is wilted or ripped, there's no reason to.) The cut end of the stalk should be smooth with no cracks or fissures.

STORE IT THE RIGHT WAY: One of the best things about whole cabbages is that they stay fresh for several weeks when kept cool and dry. If one has lots of outer leaves, just place it in the crisper drawer of the fridge. If it's already peeled down to the firm inner head, store it loosely wrapped in a vegetable bag. Once it's been cut, cover the exposed side to avoid moisture loss, and trim away any slightly darkened areas before the next use.

Creamed Cabbage-and-Leek Gratin

This comforting, surprisingly easy gratin is a new take on classic scalloped or creamed cabbage. The well-seasoned sauce and buttery, cheesy topping make this dish special enough for a dinner party. Grate the cabbage yourself, which is easy to do with a food processor's shredding disk. Please resist the tempting shortcut of preshredded cabbage; it won't have the moisture and freshness this recipe deserves.

ACTIVE 25 MIN. · TOTAL 1 HOUR, 5 MIN.

SERVES 8

- 7 Tbsp. unsalted butter, divided
- 1 small head green cabbage, cored and grated (about 8 cups)
- 2 medium leeks, thinly sliced (about 2 cups)
- 1½ tsp. kosher salt, divided
- 5 Tbsp. instant flour (such as Wondra) or all-purpose flour
- 2 cups whole milk
- 1 tsp. black pepper
- ½ tsp. dry mustard
- ½ tsp. freshly grated nutmeg
- ¼ tsp. cayenne pepper
- 4 oz. Gruyère cheese, shredded (2 cups)
- 2 Tbsp. fresh thyme leaves
- 1½ cups fresh breadcrumbs
- 3 oz. Parmesan cheese, shredded (¾ cup)

1. Preheat oven to 350°F. Lightly coat a 2½-quart gratin dish or shallow baking dish with cooking spray.

2. Melt 1 tablespoon of the butter in a Dutch oven over medium. Stir in cabbage, leeks, and 1 teaspoon of the salt. Cover and cook, stirring often, until barely tender, 5 to 7 minutes. Remove from heat, and cover to keep warm.

3. Melt 5 tablespoons of the butter in a small saucepan over medium. Whisk in flour; cook, whisking constantly, 2 minutes. (Do not let flour brown.) Whisk in milk; cook, stirring constantly with a heatproof spatula until mixture has thickened, about 2 minutes. Stir in black pepper, dry mustard, nutmeg, cayenne pepper, and remaining ½ teaspoon salt. Add Gruyère cheese, and stir until melted. Stir in thyme. Fold cheese mixture into warm cabbage mixture, and pour into prepared baking dish.

4. Stir together breadcrumbs and Parmesan in a small bowl. Microwave remaining 1 tablespoon butter in a small microwavable bowl on HIGH until melted, 30 to 40 seconds. Drizzle melted butter over breadcrumb mixture, and toss well. Sprinkle evenly over top of gratin.

5. Bake in preheated oven until golden brown on top, about 30 minutes. Let stand at least 10 minutes before serving.

The World Is His Oyster

For North Carolina chef and writer Bill Smith,
shucking this coastal delicacy is like opening a memory box

I HAVE NO MEMORY of not eating oysters.

My father, Bill Smith Sr., delivered the U.S. mail for his entire working life. (During World War II, he was assigned to an army post office in Calcutta, India.) For a few years, while I was still living at home, his route included parts of Pamlico County on the North Carolina coast. Back in those days, people would often leave presents for postal workers, especially around the holidays. We sometimes kept a gifted basket of oysters under a wet burlap bag in our basement. (I should note here that the health department says you should never ever keep raw bivalves unrefrigerated–even in the basement.)

Along the East Coast, everyone actually obeyed the rule about eating oysters in the "R" months: They were considered out of season in warm weather. People thought they got too large and became sort of milky. It turns out, they aren't unsafe at other times of the year, just less appetizing.

We mainly prepared them three ways: in a stew, roasted over a fire, or raw. I still prefer these uncomplicated recipes. I've often said that one of the hardest things for a chef to learn is when to leave well enough alone. Unfussy oysters reinforce this point of view.

The arrival of a bushel of oysters was occasion enough for a party. It was fairly common for people to have permanent roasting pits at home. They usually had some kind of metal frame to hold the corrugated iron sheets on which the bivalves were roasted. Then that wet burlap bag was thrown over them.

My Uncle Alex hosted many of these roasts. Although he lived downtown, his backyard was fenced in, so it could contain all the carrying on. Everyone helped themselves, so we learned at a young age how to dodge the smoke and avoid burning our fingers. He terrified us kids by eating the pea crabs alive as they scurried out of newly opened oysters. It took me years to try one of those, and even then it was roasted, not alive.

Oyster stew, on the other hand, was always soothing. How can something so simple be so delicious? If you don't have to do the shucking, it can be ready in a snap. It's almost not even a recipe at all. It seems strange to me now, but it was often brought to us when we were sick. My father's mother would ask for it when she became frail, and sometimes bedridden, in old age.

Fried oysters would most likely be part of a fish fry. My mother's side of the family was Roman Catholic and didn't eat meat on Fridays, so we had a lot of those. It was supposed to serve as a kind of penance, but I had no complaints.

Here in coastal North Carolina, oyster fishing was done in the wild until recently. The people who gathered them for a living could lease out beds during the busy season. Then development, pollution, and climate change began to affect our wild seafood populations. This has happened all along the Southern coast. Happily, people in the industry–often the younger members of old fishing families–have realized that oysters can be successfully and safely farmed, which allows for them to be somewhat protected from these threats.

Then there are the more personal struggles: A few of my relatives suddenly became allergic to oysters after eating them their whole lives. Their doctors told them that this isn't uncommon, just bad luck. I hate to think what I would do if this happened to me. I'm in favor of oysters any way they show up–even in drinks. I'm especially fond of the beer-tomato juice cocktail known as the michelada. One time, when I ordered one in Mexico City, the waiter asked if I would prefer it regular or extraordinario. "Why, extraordinary, of course!" I replied. It came with a spoon because half a dozen raw oysters had been stirred into the drink. It was a showstopper.

Buying the Best Bivalves

Follow these tips to source and store fresh oysters

WHEN TO GET THEM: You can call off the dogs now—it's okay to eat oysters in months without an "R" in their names. However, they do taste best when the weather is colder.

WHAT TO LOOK FOR: Unshucked oysters should be displayed on ice; avoid any sold from tanks. Select those with closed shells. They should have a fresh, briny scent and feel heavy for their size.

HOW TO STORE: Place unshucked oysters in a bowl, cover with a damp kitchen towel, and refrigerate for up to three days. Use shucked oysters the day you buy them.

SIMPLE OYSTER STEW

Simple Oyster Stew

ACTIVE 30 MIN. · TOTAL 30 MIN.

SERVES 2

- 12 oysters in the shell, scrubbed, or 12 fresh shucked oysters in liquid
- 2 cups whole milk
- ¾ tsp. kosher salt
- ½ tsp. black pepper
- 2 Tbsp. butter, softened
- 2 Tbsp. thinly sliced scallion (from 1 scallion)
- Oyster crackers, for serving

1. Working with 1 oyster at a time, hold it in the palm of your hand with an oven mitt to prevent cutting yourself; position oyster so that curved side of shell faces down and flat side faces up. Insert an oyster or paring knife between shell halves near the hinge. Pry open oyster, and drain liquor into a small bowl. Run knife under oyster to release it from shell; discard shell. Place oyster on a plate. Repeat procedure with remaining oysters. (Alternatively, if using preshucked oysters, place a fine mesh strainer over a small bowl, and drain shucked oysters.) Set oysters and liquor aside.

2. Heat milk in a small saucepan over medium, stirring occasionally, until milk begins to bubble around edges of pan and a little bit of steam rises off the surface, about 6 minutes. Stir in oysters and oyster liquor. (If using preshucked oysters, add about ¾ cup reserved liquor.) Cook over medium, stirring constantly, until oysters just begin to curl and firm up, about 2 minutes. Stir in salt and pepper. Remove pan from heat.

3. Divide butter evenly between 2 soup bowls. Transfer oysters from pan to bowls using a spoon; carefully pour hot milk mixture over oysters. Sprinkle evenly with sliced scallion. Serve with oyster crackers.

FRIED OYSTERS

Fried Oysters

ACTIVE 25 MIN. · TOTAL 50 MIN.

SERVES 2

- Peanut oil, for frying
- 1 cup self-rising flour
- 1 cup corn flour (such as Maseca)
- ½ tsp. kosher salt, plus more to taste
- ½ tsp. black pepper
- 2 dozen fresh shucked Select oysters in liquid, drained, divided
- Lemon wedges, for serving
- Cocktail sauce or mayonnaise mixed with Sriracha, for serving

1. Pour oil to a depth of ¾ inch in a 12-inch cast-iron skillet; heat oil over medium-high to 370°F.

2. Whisk together self-rising flour, corn flour, salt, and pepper in a wide, shallow baking dish. Shake off excess liquor from oysters. Working with 1 oyster at a time, dredge 12 oysters in flour mixture. Place on a large plate. Dredge oysters in flour mixture again, gently shaking off excess.

3. Add dredged oysters to hot oil, and cook, turning occasionally using a slotted spoon or spider skimmer, until golden brown, 3 to 4 minutes. (Immediately begin cooking them once they are breaded; the crust won't be as crisp if breading sits and becomes soggy.) Drain oysters on a paper towel-lined plate. Sprinkle with additional salt to taste, and serve immediately with lemon wedges and cocktail sauce. Return oil to 370°F. Repeat dredging, cooking, and serving process with remaining oysters.

Cook Once; Eat Twice

Leverage your leftovers into tasty, time-saving dinners

Chicken Schnitzel with Cabbage-Carrot Slaw

ACTIVE 30 MIN. - TOTAL 1 HOUR

SERVES 4

- 4 tsp. spicy brown mustard
- 1 cup vegetable oil, divided
- 6 Tbsp. bread-and-butter pickle brine, divided
- 3¼ tsp. kosher salt, divided
- 1 tsp. black pepper, divided
- 8 cups shredded red cabbage (from 1 large head cabbage)
- 1½ cups matchstick carrots
- 3 Tbsp. finely chopped shallot (from 1 small shallot)
- 3 Tbsp. chopped fresh flat-leaf parsley, plus more for garnish
- 1 cup all-purpose flour
- 3 large eggs, beaten
- 3 cups panko breadcrumbs
- 8 (4½-oz.) chicken breast cutlets (⅓ inch thick)
  Lemon wedges, for serving

CHICKEN SCHNITZEL WITH CABBAGE-CARROT SLAW

1. Whisk together mustard, ¼ cup of the oil, 4 tablespoons of the pickle brine, ¾ teaspoon of the salt, and ¼ teaspoon of the pepper in a large bowl. Add red cabbage, carrots, shallot, and parsley; toss to coat. For leftovers, remove 2 cups of the cabbage-carrot slaw and store in an airtight container in the refrigerator up to 2 days. Set aside remaining slaw mixture.

2. Place flour, eggs, and panko in 3 separate shallow bowls. Season chicken cutlets evenly with 2 teaspoons of the salt and the remaining ¾ teaspoon pepper. Dredge each cutlet in flour (shaking off any excess), dip in egg, and dredge in panko to coat, pressing lightly to adhere. Place coated chicken cutlets on a parchment paper-lined baking sheet. Discard any remaining flour, egg, and panko.

3. Preheat oven to 200°F. Heat ½ cup of the oil in a 12-inch nonstick skillet over medium. Working in batches, place cutlets in hot oil. Cook until golden brown, crispy, and a thermometer

inserted into thickest portion registers 165°F, about 3 minutes per side. Remove cutlets from skillet; place on a wire rack set inside a rimmed baking sheet. Place baking sheet in preheated oven to keep warm while repeating process with remaining cutlets, adding remaining ¼ cup oil to skillet as needed.

4. Wipe skillet clean, and heat over medium. Add reserved cabbage-carrot slaw to skillet with remaining 2 tablespoons pickle brine and ½ teaspoon salt; cook, tossing constantly, until cabbage is wilted, 3 to 4 minutes. Place 4 cutlets on a platter with slaw. Garnish with additional parsley, and serve with lemon wedges.

5. For leftovers, cool remaining chicken schnitzel cutlets to room temperature, about 30 minutes. Refrigerate cutlets in an airtight container up to 2 days.

Crispy Chicken Sandwiches

ACTIVE 10 MIN. - TOTAL 15 MIN.

SERVES 4

Place 4 **leftover chicken schnitzel cutlets** on a wire rack set inside a rimmed baking sheet. Preheat oven to 400°F. Bake cutlets until heated through, 10 to 12 minutes. Melt 2 Tbsp. **butter** in a large skillet over medium. Toast 4 **brioche hamburger buns** in batches, cut sides down, until golden brown, about 1 minute, adding butter as needed. Remove buns from pan; spread 1 Tbsp. **mayonnaise** over cut sides. Cut each cutlet in half. Place 5 **pickle chips** on bottom half of each bun; top each with 2 cutlet halves and ½ cup **leftover cabbage-carrot slaw.** Cover with top halves of buns.

Skillet Beef Enchiladas

ACTIVE 30 MIN. · TOTAL 1 HOUR, 5 MIN.
SERVES 4

- 2 Tbsp. olive oil
- 3 cups chopped yellow onion (from 2 medium onions)
- 2 Tbsp. minced garlic (from 6 cloves)
- 2 lb. 90/10 lean ground beef
- 1 cup unsalted beef stock
- 2 (1-oz.) envelopes low-sodium taco seasoning mix
- 2 cups red chile enchilada sauce (such as Frontera)
- 1 (15-oz.) can black beans, drained and rinsed
- 10 (6-inch) corn tortillas, each cut into 8 wedges
- 8 oz. shredded Mexican 4-cheese blend (2 cups)

Chopped fresh cilantro, for garnish

Thinly sliced jalapeño chiles, for garnish

1. Heat oil in a large cast-iron skillet over medium-high. Add chopped onion; cook, stirring occasionally, until softened and translucent, about 8 minutes. Add minced garlic; cook, stirring constantly, until fragrant, about 1 minute. Add beef; cook, stirring with a wooden spoon until crumbly and no longer pink, about 6 minutes.

2. Stir in beef stock and taco seasoning; bring to a boil. Cook, stirring often, until sauce has thickened slightly, about 90 seconds. Remove from heat.

3. For leftovers, transfer 2 cups of the beef mixture to a bowl and cool completely, about 30 minutes. Cover and refrigerate up to 2 days.

4. Preheat oven to broil with rack about 6 inches from heat source. Stir enchilada sauce and beans into remaining seasoned beef in skillet. Place cut tortillas in an even layer on surface of beef mixture, and gently fold into the mixture until fully coated and well distributed. Top evenly with cheese. Broil until cheese is melted and browned in spots, about 4 minutes.

5. Remove from oven; top with cilantro and jalapeño slices. Serve immediately.

Easy Chili Con Carne

ACTIVE 20 MIN. · TOTAL 20 MIN.
SERVES 4

Add 2 cups **leftover seasoned beef**, 2 cups **unsalted beef stock**, 2 Tbsp. **tomato paste**, 1 (15-oz.) can **diced tomatoes** (undrained), and 1 (15-oz.) can **pinto beans** (drained and rinsed) to a large Dutch oven; bring to a boil over medium-high. Reduce heat to medium, and gently boil, stirring occasionally, until thickened and saucy, 12 to 15 minutes. Season with 1 tsp. **kosher salt**. Divide chili among 4 bowls. Top evenly with 1 sliced **avocado** and ¼ cup **sour cream**. Garnish with crushed baked **tortilla chips** and chopped **fresh cilantro**.

HONEY-SOY GLAZED PORK CHOPS

browned and a thermometer inserted into thickest portion registers 130°F, 2 to 3 minutes per side. For leftovers, transfer 2 pork chops to a plate and cool completely. Meanwhile, repeat with 2 tablespoons of the vegetable oil and remaining 4 pork chops, adding 1 tablespoon oil to skillet for each batch. Place 4 cooked pork chops on a plate; tent with foil to keep warm. Do not wipe skillet clean.
4. Add remaining 2 tablespoons vegetable oil to drippings in skillet. Heat oil over medium-high; add Broccolini, tossing to coat with drippings. Add sliced mushrooms, remaining 1 teaspoon garlic, and ¼ cup water; cover and cook, tossing occasionally, until mushrooms are tender and Broccolini is tender-crisp, about 8 minutes. Season with remaining ½ teaspoon salt and ¼ teaspoon pepper. For leftovers, transfer about a third of the Broccolini and ¾ cup mushrooms to a plate. Let vegetables cool to room temperature.
5. Divide warm pork chops and remaining vegetables among 4 plates. Spoon 2 tablespoons of the honey-soy mixture over each pork chop. Garnish with sliced scallions, and serve. Refrigerate 2 cooled pork chops and cooled vegetable mixture in separate airtight containers up to 2 days.

Stir-Fried Pork and Noodles
ACTIVE 15 MIN. - TOTAL 20 MIN.
SERVES 4

Heat 2 tsp. **vegetable oil** in a large nonstick skillet over medium-high. Add 2 lightly beaten **large eggs;** cook, stirring often, until scrambled, about 1 minute. Transfer eggs to a bowl. Slice 2 **leftover glazed pork chops;** add to skillet with **leftover honey-soy sauce mixture.** Bring to a boil over medium; cook, stirring occasionally, until pork is heated through, about 3 minutes. Add 1 cup chopped **leftover Broccolini;** ¾ cup **leftover mushrooms;** ½ tsp. **kosher salt;** ½ tsp. **crushed red pepper;** and 1 (8-oz.) pkg. **rice stick noodles,** cooked according to package directions. Stir in scrambled eggs. Cook over medium, tossing constantly, until well combined and noodles absorb sauce, about 1 minute. Remove from heat, and garnish with thinly sliced **scallions.**

Honey-Soy Glazed Pork Chops
ACTIVE 25 MIN. - TOTAL 40 MIN.
SERVES 4

- ½ cup honey
- ½ cup lower-sodium soy sauce
- 2 Tbsp. oyster sauce
- 2 Tbsp. rice vinegar
- 1 tsp. sesame oil
- 3 tsp. minced garlic (from 2 cloves), divided
- 1 tsp. cornstarch
- 6 Tbsp. vegetable oil, divided
- 6 (6 oz. each) boneless pork chops (¾ inch thick)
- 2 tsp. kosher salt, divided
- ¾ tsp. black pepper, divided
- 12 oz. Broccolini
- 12 oz. sliced cremini mushrooms
  Thinly sliced scallions, for garnish

1. Stir together honey, soy sauce, oyster sauce, rice vinegar, sesame oil, and 2 teaspoons of the garlic in a medium bowl. Transfer ¾ cup of the honey-soy mixture to an airtight container; refrigerate until ready to use, up to 3 days.
2. Transfer the remaining honey-soy mixture (about ½ cup) to a small saucepan. Stir in cornstarch, and bring to a simmer over medium; cook, stirring occasionally, until sauce is thickened and coats the back of a spoon, about 2 minutes. Remove from heat; cover to keep warm.
3. Heat 2 tablespoons of the vegetable oil in a large cast-iron skillet over medium. Season pork chops with 1½ teaspoons of the salt and ½ teaspoon of the pepper. Add 2 pork chops to skillet, and cook over medium, turning once, until

Barbecue-Pork Pizza

ACTIVE 30 MIN. - TOTAL 2 HOURS, 55 MIN.
SERVES 4

- 3½ lb. boneless pork shoulder (Boston butt), trimmed and cut into 6 cubes
- 1 medium-size yellow onion, trimmed, peeled, and quartered
- 6 large garlic cloves
- 1 Tbsp. kosher salt
- 1 cup barbecue sauce, divided
- 1 Tbsp. olive oil
- 16 oz. fresh pizza dough, at room temperature
- 8 oz. shredded low-moisture, part-skim mozzarella cheese (about 2 cups), divided
- ½ cup thinly sliced red onion (from 1 small onion)
- ⅓ cup drained, sliced pepperoncini peppers
- Fresh cilantro leaves, for garnish

1. Combine pork shoulder, yellow onion, garlic, and salt in a large Dutch oven with water to cover. Bring to a boil over medium-high; reduce to a simmer. Cover and cook over medium-low, turning occasionally, until meat pulls apart easily with a fork, about 2 hours.
2. Remove pork from Dutch oven. Place on a cutting board; shred using 2 forks. Discard fat. For leftovers, transfer 3 cups shredded pork to a medium bowl and cool completely, about 30 minutes. Store, covered, in refrigerator up to 2 days.
3. Transfer remaining 2 cups shredded pork to a separate medium bowl. Add ¼ cup of the barbecue sauce, and toss to coat.
4. Preheat oven to 450°F. Coat a (15- x 10-inch) rimmed baking sheet with oil. Gently stretch or roll pizza dough to cover bottom of pan. Spread remaining ¾ cup barbecue sauce over dough, leaving a ½-inch border. Sprinkle evenly with 1½ cups of the mozzarella. Top evenly with shredded pork, red onion, and pepperoncini peppers. Sprinkle evenly with remaining ½ cup shredded mozzarella.
5. Bake in preheated oven until crust is golden brown and mozzarella is bubbly, 18 to 20 minutes. Let stand 5 minutes; cut into slices, and garnish with cilantro leaves.

Quick Pork Ragù

ACTIVE 30 MIN. - TOTAL 30 MIN.
SERVES 4

Heat 2 Tbsp. **olive oil** in a Dutch oven over medium. Add 2 cups chopped **yellow onion** and 1 cup chopped **carrots**; cook, stirring often, until softened, about 8 minutes. Add 1 Tbsp. minced **garlic** and 1 Tbsp. **tomato paste**; cook, stirring, about 1 minute. Add ⅓ cup **dry red wine** to pan, stirring to release any browned bits. Cook until liquid is almost evaporated, about 2 minutes. Stir in 1 tsp. kosher salt, ½ tsp. black pepper, ¼ tsp. **crushed red pepper**, and 1 (28-oz.) can **crushed San Marzano plum tomatoes.** Bring to a boil; reduce to a simmer. Cover and cook 10 minutes. Stir in 3 cups **leftover shredded pork**; cook until heated through, about 2 minutes. Divide 1 lb. cooked **pappardelle pasta** among 4 bowls; top with pork mixture. Top with grated **Parmesan cheese** and chopped **fresh flat-leaf parsley.**

Baked Lemon-Thyme Salmon

ACTIVE 15 MIN. - TOTAL 1 HOUR, 10 MIN.
SERVES 4

- ½ cup fresh lemon juice (from 3 lemons)
- 1 Tbsp. minced garlic (from 2 medium cloves)
- 1 Tbsp. Dijon mustard
- 1 Tbsp. honey
- ⅓ cup plus 4 tsp. olive oil, divided
- 1 Tbsp. fresh thyme leaves, plus 6 (3-inch) sprigs, divided
- 6 (6-oz.) skin-on salmon fillets (1 to 1½ inches thick), patted dry
- 1½ lb. baby Yukon Gold potatoes, quartered lengthwise
- 3¾ tsp. kosher salt, divided
- 1 lb. fresh green beans, trimmed
- ¾ tsp. black pepper, divided
- 1 medium lemon, thinly sliced crosswise
- 2 Tbsp. butter, cubed

1. Preheat oven to 425°F with racks in top third and middle positions. Whisk together lemon juice, garlic, mustard, honey, ⅓ cup of the oil, and thyme leaves in a medium bowl until combined. For leftovers, transfer ½ cup of the lemon mixture to an airtight container and store in refrigerator up to 5 days.
2. Place salmon fillets in a 13- x 9-inch baking dish. Pour remaining lemon juice mixture over salmon, turning to coat. Set aside to marinate for 10 minutes at room temperature.
3. Meanwhile, toss together baby Yukon Gold potatoes, 2 teaspoons of the oil, and 1½ teaspoons of the salt on a rimmed baking sheet lined with parchment paper. Bake in preheated oven 10 minutes. Remove from oven, and push potatoes to one half of the baking sheet. On the other half of the baking sheet, toss green beans, ¾ teaspoon of the salt, ¼ teaspoon of the pepper, and remaining 2 teaspoons oil until green beans are fully coated.
4. Season marinated salmon with remaining 1½ teaspoons salt and ½ teaspoon pepper. Top salmon with thyme sprigs, lemon slices, and butter cubes.

5. Place baking dish with salmon on top rack and baking sheet with vegetables on middle rack. Bake at 425°F until potatoes and green beans are tender and salmon is flaky and a thermometer inserted into the thickest portion registers 135°F, about 25 minutes, stirring vegetables halfway through cook time. Remove salmon and vegetables from oven. Transfer 4 salmon fillets, 2½ cups potatoes, and 3 cups green beans to a platter. Serve.
6. For leftovers, let remaining salmon fillets, potatoes, and green beans cool completely, about 30 minutes. Refrigerate the salmon and vegetables in separate airtight containers up to 2 days.

Salmon Niçoise Salad

ACTIVE 10 MIN. - TOTAL 10 MIN.
SERVES 4

Let **leftover lemon juice mixture** come to room temperature; shake to recombine. Toss 7 oz. **mixed baby greens** with ¼ cup of the lemon juice mixture, ½ tsp. **kosher salt**, and ¼ tsp. **black pepper** in a large serving bowl. Using a fork, flake 2 **leftover salmon fillets** into chunks; arrange over dressed greens with 1 cup **leftover potatoes**, 1 cup **leftover green beans**, 1 cup halved **cherry tomatoes**, ½ cup halved pitted **Kalamata olives**, and 2 peeled and quartered **hard-cooked eggs**. Drizzle with remaining ¼ cup lemon mixture.

Hole in One

Turn basic biscuits and eggs into a fun, company-worthy breakfast

DON'T CRISP THOSE STRIPS
Pliable parcooked bacon is the secret to keeping these eggs inside their biscuit shells.

Egg in a Biscuit

ACTIVE 15 MIN. · TOTAL 35 MIN.
SERVES 8

- 8 bacon slices
- 1 (16.3-oz.) can refrigerated buttermilk biscuits (8 biscuits)
- 2 oz. sharp Cheddar cheese, shredded (about ½ cup)
- 8 large eggs
- ¼ tsp. kosher salt
- ¼ tsp. black pepper
  Chopped fresh chives

1. Preheat oven to 400°F. Line a large rimmed baking sheet with parchment paper.

2. Working in 2 batches, cook bacon in a large skillet over medium-low until partially cooked but not crisp, 10 to 15 minutes. Set bacon aside.

3. Pat each biscuit into a 3½-inch-wide round. Using a 2-inch round cutter, cut a circle from center of each biscuit. Place biscuit rings and centers on prepared baking sheet. Bake in preheated oven until puffed but still pale, about 8 minutes. Do not turn oven off.

4. Cut bacon slices in half crosswise. Drape 2 bacon pieces over holes in biscuit rings; sprinkle each with 1 tablespoon cheese. Press bacon and cheese into biscuit holes to create wells. Separate eggs, placing egg whites in a medium bowl and 1 egg yolk in each biscuit well. Whisk egg whites until just frothy. Spoon about 1 tablespoon egg white over each yolk. Sprinkle filled biscuit rings evenly with salt and pepper.

5. Bake biscuit rings and centers until biscuits are golden brown and eggs are just set, 10 to 12 minutes. Garnish with chives.

The Right Stuff

Top sweet potatoes with savory fillings for fast and wholesome meals

Quick "Baked" Sweet Potatoes

ACTIVE 5 MIN. · TOTAL 20 MIN.
SERVES 4

Prick 4 medium **sweet potatoes** all over with a fork; place in a microwavable dish. Cover with plastic wrap, and microwave on HIGH for 5 minutes.

Uncover and turn potatoes over; cover and microwave on HIGH until tender, about 5 minutes. Let stand 5 minutes. Cut a lengthwise slit down center of each potato, and fluff flesh with a fork. Place potatoes on a baking sheet, and add desired filling (recipes at right).

Barbecue Pork- and Slaw-Stuffed Sweet Potatoes

ACTIVE 20 MIN. · TOTAL 25 MIN.
Toss 12 oz. **pulled pork** with ½ cup **barbecue sauce**; divide among potatoes. Broil until crispy, 3 minutes. Combine 1 Tbsp. each **olive oil** and **apple cider vinegar**, 1½ tsp. each **Dijon mustard** and **honey**, and ½ tsp. **salt** in a bowl. Add ¾ cup shredded **cabbage**, ¼ cup thinly sliced **red onion**, and chopped **chives**; toss to coat. Top potatoes with slaw.

CALORIES: **415** – CARBS: **35 G** – FAT: **19 G**

Cheesy Chipotle Chicken-Stuffed Sweet Potatoes

ACTIVE 20 MIN. · TOTAL 30 MIN.
Combine 2 cups shredded **cooked chicken**, 1 chopped canned **chipotle chile**, 1 tsp. **kosher salt**, ½ tsp. **black pepper**, ¾ cup shredded **Cheddar cheese**, and ¼ cup **whole-milk yogurt**; divide among potatoes. Top with ¼ cup more cheese. Broil 3 minutes. Top with ¼ cup more yogurt, ¼ cup **salsa**, and chopped fresh **cilantro**.

CALORIES: **375** – CARBS: **29 G** – FAT: **14 G**

Beans- and Greens-Stuffed Sweet Potatoes

ACTIVE 30 MIN. · TOTAL 30 MIN.
Cook ¾ cup chopped **yellow onion** in 1 Tbsp. **olive oil** in a pan over medium heat 5 minutes. Add 6 cups chopped **collard greens**, 1 cup no-salt-added **canned white beans**, ½ cup **chicken stock**, 1 tsp. **salt**, and ¼ tsp. **crushed red pepper**. Cook 12 minutes. Add 1 Tbsp. **red wine vinegar**. Divide among potatoes; garnish with ¼ cup **bacon**.

CALORIES: **226** – CARBS: **42 G** – FAT: **3 G**

The Slice Is Bright

Delight citrus fans with this nostalgic layered dessert

CRUSH IT
Use a food processor to blitz the sandwich cookies into fine crumbs for the crust.

Lemon Lush

ACTIVE 30 MIN. - TOTAL 45 MIN.,
PLUS 4 HOURS CHILLING
SERVES 12

1   (19.1-oz.) pkg. cream-filled vanilla sandwich cookies, crushed (about 4½ cups)
½   cup butter, melted
2   (8-oz.) pkg. cream cheese, softened
2   tsp. lemon zest plus 3 Tbsp. fresh juice
1½ cups powdered sugar, divided
3   cups heavy whipping cream
3   cups whole milk
2   (3.4-oz.) pkg. lemon instant pudding mix and pie filling
    Lemon slices, for garnish

1. Coat a 13- x 9-inch freezer-safe baking dish with cooking spray, and line the dish with parchment paper.
2. Stir crushed cookies and melted butter in a large bowl until combined. Press firmly into bottom of prepared baking dish in an even layer. Freeze until firm, about 10 minutes.
3. Meanwhile, beat cream cheese, lemon zest and juice, and 1¼ cups of the powdered sugar in a large bowl with an electric mixer on high speed until fluffy, about 3 minutes. Place heavy whipping cream and remaining ¼ cup powdered sugar in a large bowl; beat with a mixer on high until stiff peaks form, about 2 minutes. Fold 1 cup of the whipped cream into cream cheese mixture. Spread mixture over crust; freeze until set, about 10 minutes.
4. Whisk milk and pudding mix in a large bowl until smooth and thickened, 2 to 4 minutes. Spread pudding over cream cheese mixture in crust. Chill until pudding sets slightly, about 15 minutes.
5. Gently spread remaining whipped cream over pudding. Chill, covered, until firm, at least 4 hours or up to 24 hours. Garnish with lemon slices. Store, covered, in refrigerator up to 4 days.

COOKING SCHOOL

LOVE YOUR LEFTOVERS

The best ways to reheat food so it tastes like it was just served. (Yes, even fish)

FISH
Wrap cooked fillets in foil with 1 tablespoon water; place on a baking sheet. Warm in a 250°F oven until center is heated through, about 20 minutes.

CHICKEN
Warm ¼ cup chicken broth over medium-low heat in a skillet. Add cooked chicken; cover and cook until warmed through, turning often, about 10 minutes.

PIZZA
Heat pizza slices in a nonstick skillet over medium heat until crust is crisp, 2 to 3 minutes. Add 1 teaspoon water; cover and cook until cheese is melted, about 1 minute more.

Smarter Storage
Swap single-use plastics for reusable items

SQUARED UP
Freeze easy-to-thaw portions of soups, stews, and sauces with Souper Cubes' silicone molds. 1-Cup Tray (holds four portions); *soupercubes.com*

HUG IT OUT
Save onion and avocado halves with these dishwasher-safe and airtight produce covers from Food Huggers. Eco Starter Bundle; *foodhuggers.com*

THAT'S A WRAP
Abeego's reusable beeswax paper grips onto bowls or containers to seal and protect what's inside, no plastic needed. Variety Square (three pack); *abeego.com*

PUT A LID ON IT
These silicone covers from GIR create tight suction on any sturdy bowl or pan and can be used in the microwave or oven up to 550°F. Round Suction Lid; *gir.co*

WASTE NOT

Transform your kitchen scraps with these easy recipes

CITRUS SIMPLE SYRUP
Cut 1 cup **citrus peels** into ¾-inch strips. Bring 1 cup each **granulated sugar** and **water** to a boil in a medium saucepan over high. Add peels; simmer until syrup thickens slightly, 15 to 20 minutes. Let cool.

POTATO-PEEL CHIPS
Preheat oven to 400°F. Toss together 1 cup **potato peels,** 2 Tbsp. **olive oil,** ½ tsp. **smoked paprika,** and ¼ tsp. **kosher salt.** Spread evenly on a parchment-lined baking sheet. Bake until crispy, 10 to 11 minutes. Season to taste.

SPINACH PESTO
Pulse 2 cups packed **fresh spinach,** ½ cup grated **Parmesan,** ¼ cup **toasted walnuts,** and 1 **garlic clove** in a food processor until chopped. With processor running, slowly add ½ cup **olive oil** until smooth.

April

CHEESY ARTICHOKE
DIP WITH SPRING
CRUDITÉS

Eat Your Heart Out

Tender and slightly tart, fresh artichokes are easier to cook than
you think—and now's the best time to enjoy them

Cheesy Artichoke Dip with Spring Crudités

ACTIVE 15 MIN. · TOTAL 35 MIN.

SERVES 12

1. Preheat oven to 450°F. Coat an 8-inch
square baking dish with cooking spray.
2. Place 8 oz. softened **cream cheese,**
½ cup **mayonnaise,** ½ cup **sour cream,**
½ cup grated **Parmesan,** 3 Tbsp. minced
shallot, 1 tsp. chopped **garlic,** 1 Tbsp.
fresh thyme leaves, ½ tsp. **kosher salt,**
¼ tsp. **black pepper,** and ½ cup grated
low-moisture part-skim mozzarella
in a food processor. Process until
combined, about 20 seconds. Drain
2 (14-oz.) cans **artichoke hearts packed
in water;** pat dry, and chop. Add to
food processor; pulse to combine,
about 2 pulses. Transfer to prepared
baking dish. Top with additional ½ cup
mozzarella.
3. Bake in preheated oven until
browned, about 15 minutes. Let stand
5 minutes before serving. Serve with
radishes, snap peas, endive leaves, and
baby carrots and **cucumbers.**

Roasted Artichokes with Creamy Garlic Dipping Sauce

ACTIVE 25 MIN. · TOTAL 1 HOUR, 10 MIN.

SERVES 6

1. Preheat oven to 400°F. Cut 1 **lemon** in
half; set 1 half aside. Trim ½ inch off tops
and stems of 6 small (8 to 10 oz. each)
fresh artichokes. Remove small outer
leaves around stems. Using a peeler, peel
green skin from stems. Cut 1 artichoke
in half lengthwise; using a spoon,
scoop out fuzzy center. Rub cut side of
artichoke with lemon half. Repeat with
remaining artichokes; place cut side up
on a large rimmed baking sheet.
2. Squeeze reserved lemon half over
artichokes. Thinly slice another **lemon,**
and place slices on baking sheet
with artichokes. Drizzle with 6 Tbsp.
olive oil. Add 2 **garlic heads,** halved

ROASTED ARTICHOKES
WITH CREAMY GARLIC
DIPPING SAUCE

crosswise, and 2 fresh **rosemary sprigs;**
sprinkle with 1 tsp. **kosher salt** and
¼ tsp. **pepper.** Flip artichokes cut side
down. Cover tightly with foil.
3. Roast in preheated oven until
artichokes are tender, 45 to 55 minutes.
Squeeze garlic from skins into a small
bowl; mash with a fork, and stir in 1 cup
mayonnaise, 1 tsp. **Dijon mustard,** and
½ tsp. each **salt** and **pepper.** Transfer
artichokes and lemons to a platter;
garnish with chopped fresh **parsley.**
Serve with sauce.

FLAVOR UPGRADE

To make the Cheesy Artichoke Dip even
better, make the Roasted Artichokes
(at left) and swap in 2 cups chopped
roasted hearts for the canned.

Island Treasure

For Florida native Shanika Graham-White, a beloved Jamaican recipe
is an Easter tradition that connects her past with the present

EASTER HAS ALWAYS been a big deal to Shanika Graham-White. When she was a child growing up in Orlando, the holiday was a lively affair peppered with the tastes, sounds, and scents from the island of Jamaica, her family's native home. Graham-White, author of the cookbook *Orchids & Sweet Tea: Plant-Forward Recipes with Jamaican Flavor & Southern Charm* and creator of the popular wellness blog of the same name, still anticipates it each year with childlike fervor. For her, Easter is a day when her two cultures and places can shine.

"Our extended family celebrates Easter the way most people do Thanksgiving," she says. "It's a big, fun gathering with lots of music and really great food that fuses my island and Southern roots." At the heart of their spread, which includes Jamaican classics like jerk chicken and curried goat as well as Southern favorites like macaroni and cheese, is the Jamaican spice bun.

This deeply aromatic, sweet yet zingy quick bread is filled with assertive warm spices (allspice, cinnamon, and nutmeg) that are punctuated with dried fruit (like raisins and cherries). Its signature dark color typically comes from a combination of ingredients like Guinness stout and browning sauce, a thick and viscous reduction of burnt-sugar essence that's an indispensable staple in the Caribbean pantry. (You can order many different brands of the product from Amazon.) A Jamaican spice bun is a cousin to the British hot cross bun—from which it is believed to have descended. Although it's enjoyed year-round, it's most popular during the Lenten season, when many Christians abstain from eating meat. In Jamaica, the spice bun is usually served with a hefty slice of marigold-yellow processed cheese, which is considered an essential pairing.

The spice bun that Graham-White makes for her family's Easter celebration—an event that usually draws about a dozen people and stretches throughout much of the day—varies slightly from the typical Jamaican version that she grew up eating. Her adaptation shows her own touch. "My mother is a nurse, and I spent a significant amount of time understanding how to heal some of my own postpartum health ailments with food," she explains. "So it's really important for me to have most of my recipes include healthier components." To achieve greater nutritional balance without sacrificing the spice bun's complex taste, Graham-White nixes the Guinness stout, instead opting for a combination of molasses and browning sauce to achieve the rich, earthen shade. She also goes with almond milk to reduce some of the dairy.

Even with those slight changes, this recipe is a cherished tradition that Graham-White says she is honored to bequeath to the next generation. "My 6-year-old son, Kameron, helps me bake the spice bun now, and it's a really special moment," she says. "Through this recipe, I get to share with him about Jamaica, our family, and our heritage."

Jamaican Easter Spice Bun

ACTIVE 15 MIN. - TOTAL 1 HOUR, 25 MIN.,
PLUS 1 HOUR, 30 MIN. COOLING
SERVES 8

- ¼ cup unsalted butter, melted, plus more for greasing loaf pan
- ¾ cup dried cherries
- ¾ cup raisins
- Boiling water
- 3 cups all-purpose flour
- 1 Tbsp. baking powder
- 2 tsp. ground cinnamon
- 1 tsp. ground nutmeg
- 1 tsp. ground allspice
- ½ tsp. fine sea salt
- 1½ cups milk (whole milk or dairy-free milk alternative)
- ½ cup packed light brown sugar
- ¼ cup cane syrup or pure maple syrup
- 1 Tbsp. unsulphured molasses
- 2 tsp. browning sauce (such as Grace Browning, optional)
- 1 tsp. vanilla extract
- 1 egg, at room temperature
- Cheese slices (such as American, optional)

1. Preheat oven to 350°F. Lightly grease a 9- x 5-inch loaf pan with butter; line with parchment paper. Set aside.
2. Place dried cherries and raisins in a medium bowl. Cover with boiling water, and let soak until softened, about 5 minutes. Drain and rinse fruit; set aside.

SPICY AND SWEET
Whole star anise makes a pretty (but optional) topper for this deeply flavored quick bread.

FAMILY TIME: SHANIKA WITH HER HUSBAND, DARNELL; SON, KAMERON; AND DOG, KOFFEE

3. Whisk together flour, baking powder, cinnamon, nutmeg, allspice, and salt in a large bowl until combined. Whisk together melted butter, milk, brown sugar, cane syrup, molasses, browning sauce (if desired), and vanilla in a separate large bowl until combined, brown in color, and smooth. Whisk in egg. Add milk mixture to flour mixture, stirring gently until batter is combined. (It should be thick but stirrable with a wooden spoon or spatula.) Fold in reserved cherries and raisins.

4. Transfer batter to prepared loaf pan, spreading evenly with a spatula. Bake in preheated oven until a wooden pick or knife inserted in middle of bread comes out clean, about 1 hour to 1 hour, 15 minutes.

5. Remove from oven, and let cool in loaf pan for 10 minutes. Gently remove bread from pan, and let cool completely on a wire rack, about 1 hour, 30 minutes. Slice bread, and serve with cheese, if desired.

Spring by the Slice

Easy to bake and take, these sheet cakes will be the talk of every get-together this season, from Easter to birthdays and baby showers

Strawberry Patch Cake

ACTIVE 45 MIN. - TOTAL 1 HOUR, 15 MIN.,
PLUS 1 HOUR, 30 MIN. COOLING

SERVES 16

STRAWBERRY CAKE

- Baking spray
- 2¾ cups unbleached cake flour
- 2 tsp. baking powder
- ¾ tsp. kosher salt
- ½ tsp. baking soda
- 1 lb. very ripe fresh strawberries, hulled, divided
- 1½ cups granulated sugar
- ¾ cup unsalted butter, softened
- 1 large egg, at room temperature
- 2 large egg whites, at room temperature
- ⅓ cup whole buttermilk
- 1¾ tsp. vanilla extract
- Red food coloring gel (optional)

BERRY-MARSHMALLOW FROSTING

- 2 Tbsp. freeze-dried strawberries (from 1 [0.8-oz.] pkg.)
- ¾ cup butter
- 1 (7-oz.) container marshmallow creme
- 2 cups powdered sugar
- 1-2 Tbsp. whole milk

ADDITIONAL INGREDIENTS

- Miniature marshmallows
- Yellow candy-coated milk chocolate pieces
- Fresh strawberries, halved if large

1. Prepare the Strawberry Cake: Preheat oven to 350°F. Coat a 13- x 9-inch baking pan with baking spray; line bottom of pan with parchment paper. Whisk together flour, baking powder, salt, and baking soda in a medium bowl.
2. Place 1 cup of the strawberries in a food processor; pulse until chopped, 3 to 5 times. Set chopped berries aside. Place remaining strawberries in food processor; process until pureed, about 30 seconds. (You should have ¾ cup puree.) Set aside.
3. Beat granulated sugar and butter in a stand mixer fitted with a paddle attachment on medium-high speed until pale and fluffy, about 3 minutes. Add egg followed by egg whites, 1 at a time, beating on medium speed just until blended after each addition. Beat in buttermilk, vanilla, reserved chopped strawberries, and puree, and, if using, a few drops food coloring until blended and desired color is reached, about 30 seconds. Gradually add flour mixture in thirds, beating on low speed just until incorporated after each addition, stopping to scrape down sides as needed.
4. Spoon batter into prepared pan, spreading evenly. Bake in preheated oven until golden around edges and a wooden pick inserted in center of cake comes out clean, 30 to 35 minutes.

Transfer pan to a wire rack; cool completely, about 1 hour, 30 minutes.
5. Meanwhile, prepare the Berry-Marshmallow Frosting. Process freeze-dried strawberries in a food processor until finely ground, 1 minute. Set aside. Beat butter in a stand mixer fitted with a paddle attachment on medium-high speed until creamy and smooth, 2 minutes. Add marshmallow creme; beat until combined, 2 minutes. Add 1 cup of the powdered sugar; beat on low speed until well blended. Add 1 tablespoon milk, ground strawberries, and remaining 1 cup powdered sugar, beating until smooth. If frosting is stiff, beat in remaining 1 tablespoon milk. Chill until ready to use.
6. Use kitchen shears to cut marshmallows in half diagonally. Spread frosting over cake. Arrange marshmallow halves in groups of 5 to form flowers around edges of cake; press a candy-coated chocolate in center of each flower. Garnish cake with strawberries.

Very Carrot Cake with Maple-Cream Cheese Frosting

ACTIVE 25 MIN. - TOTAL 55 MIN., PLUS 1 HOUR COOLING

SERVES 15

CARROT CAKE

Baking spray

- 2½ cups all-purpose flour
- 1 cup granulated sugar
- ⅔ cup dark brown sugar
- 2 tsp. baking powder
- 2 tsp. ground cinnamon
- 1 tsp. ground ginger
- ¾ tsp. kosher salt
- ½ tsp. baking soda
- ¼ tsp. ground nutmeg
- 1 cup whole milk
- ¾ cup vegetable oil
- 3 large eggs, at room temperature
- 1¾ tsp. vanilla extract
- 4 large carrots, peeled and shredded (2 cups)
- 1 cup toasted walnuts, roughly chopped
- ½ cup golden raisins, roughly chopped

MAPLE-CREAM CHEESE FROSTING

- ½ cup unsalted butter, softened
- 1 (8-oz.) pkg. cream cheese, softened
- 2 Tbsp. pure maple syrup
- 1 tsp. vanilla extract
- 2 cups powdered sugar, sifted

Green food coloring gel

ADDITIONAL INGREDIENTS

Orange candy-coated almonds (such as Jordan almonds)

Green candy sprinkles in assorted sizes

1. Prepare the Carrot Cake: Preheat oven to 350°F. Coat a 13- x 9-inch baking pan with baking spray, and line bottom of pan with parchment paper. Whisk together flour, granulated sugar, brown sugar, baking powder, cinnamon, ginger, salt, baking soda, and nutmeg in a medium bowl. Whisk together milk, oil, eggs, and vanilla in a large liquid measuring cup.

2. Pour egg mixture into flour mixture; stir to combine. Fold in carrots, walnuts, and raisins. Pour batter into prepared pan, spreading evenly. Bake in preheated oven until a wooden pick inserted in center of cake comes out clean, 30 to 35 minutes. Transfer pan to a wire rack; cool completely, about 1 hour to 1 hour, 30 minutes.

3. Meanwhile, prepare the Maple-Cream Cheese Frosting: Beat butter in a stand mixer fitted with a paddle attachment on medium-high speed until smooth and creamy, about 2 minutes. Add cream cheese; beat until light and fluffy, 2 to 3 minutes. Add maple syrup and vanilla; beat on medium speed until well blended, about 30 seconds, scraping down sides of bowl as needed. Reduce speed to low; add 1 cup of the powdered sugar, beating until well blended. Add remaining 1 cup powdered sugar, and beat until smooth and combined. Chill until ready to use.

4. Reserve ⅛ cup of the frosting in a small bowl. Stir in green food coloring, and transfer to a piping bag fitted with a small writing tip; set aside. Spread remaining Maple-Cream Cheese Frosting over cake.

5. Arrange candy-coated almonds on top of cake in rows. Pipe leaves onto 1 end of each almond with reserved green frosting. Garnish with sprinkles.

Easter Egg Lemon Cake with Whipped Cream Topping

(Photo, page 76)

ACTIVE 35 MIN. - TOTAL 1 HOUR, 5 MIN., PLUS 1 HOUR COOLING

SERVES 16

LEMON CAKE

Baking spray

- 3 cups unbleached cake flour
- 2 tsp. baking powder
- ¾ tsp. baking soda
- ¾ tsp. kosher salt
- 1¼ cups buttermilk
- 1 Tbsp. grated lemon zest plus ¼ cup fresh juice (from 3 small lemons)
- 1¼ tsp. vanilla extract
- 1½ cups granulated sugar
- ¾ cup unsalted butter, softened
- 2 large eggs, at room temperature

WHIPPED CREAM TOPPING

- ½ tsp. unflavored gelatin (from 1 [¼-oz.] envelope)
- 1¼ cups heavy whipping cream
- ¼ cup powdered sugar
- 1 tsp. vanilla extract

ADDITIONAL INGREDIENTS

Blue, yellow, and pink candy sprinkles of various shapes

Green candy sprinkles

1. Prepare the Lemon Cake: Preheat oven to 350°F. Coat a 13- x 9-inch baking pan with baking spray, and line bottom of pan with parchment paper. Whisk together flour, baking powder, baking soda, and salt in a medium bowl. Whisk together buttermilk, lemon zest and juice, and vanilla in separate medium bowl.

2. Beat granulated sugar and butter in a stand mixer fitted with a paddle attachment on medium-high speed until mixture is pale and fluffy, about 3 minutes. Add eggs, 1 at a time, beating on medium speed just until blended after each addition. Gradually add flour mixture in thirds, alternating with buttermilk mixture, beating on low speed just until blended after each addition, stopping to scrape down sides of bowl as needed.

3. Spoon batter into prepared pan, spreading evenly. Bake in preheated oven until golden around edges and a wooden pick inserted in center of cake comes out clean, about 30 minutes. Transfer pan to a wire rack; cool completely, 1 hour to 1 hour, 30 minutes.

4. Meanwhile, prepare the Whipped Cream Topping: Sprinkle gelatin over 4 teaspoons water in a small microwavable bowl. Let stand 5 minutes to hydrate. Microwave gelatin on HIGH in 5-second intervals until melted, about 15 seconds total. Beat cream, sugar, and vanilla in a stand mixer fitted with a whisk attachment on medium-high speed until thickened. With mixer running, slowly stream in gelatin mixture; beat until stiff peaks form, about 30 seconds. Chill until ready to use.

5. Spread Whipped Cream Topping over Lemon Cake. Cut an 8- x 10-inch egg shape from center of a 12- x 16-inch sheet of parchment paper; discard egg shape to create a stencil. Gently lay stencil over cake; top as desired with blue, yellow, and pink sprinkles. Remove stencil; add green sprinkles around edges of cake. Store, covered, in refrigerator until ready to serve, up to 1 day.

VERY CARROT CAKE
WITH MAPLE-CREAM
CHEESE FROSTING

EASTER EGG LEMON
CAKE WITH WHIPPED
CREAM TOPPING
(PAGE 74)

CHOCOLATE CHICK
CAKE (PAGE 79)

BLOOMING
HUMMINGBIRD
CAKE

Blooming Hummingbird Cake

ACTIVE 45 MIN. - TOTAL 1 HOUR,
15 MIN., PLUS 1 HOUR, 30 MIN. COOLING

SERVES 16

HUMMINGBIRD CAKE

- Baking spray
- 2¾ cups unbleached cake flour
- 2 tsp. baking powder
- 2 tsp. ground cinnamon
- ½ tsp. kosher salt
- ½ tsp. baking soda
- 1⅓ cups granulated sugar
- ¾ cup unsalted butter, softened
- 3 large eggs, at room temperature
- 1¼ tsp. vanilla extract
- 2 small bananas, mashed (about ⅔ cup)
- 1 (8-oz.) can crushed pineapple in juice, undrained
- 1 cup roughly chopped toasted pecans

CREAM CHEESE FROSTING

- ½ cup butter, softened
- 1 (8-oz.) pkg. cream cheese, softened
- 1¼ tsp. vanilla extract
- 2 cups plus 2 Tbsp. powdered sugar, sifted
- ⅛ tsp. kosher salt

ADDITIONAL INGREDIENTS

- Dried pineapple rings
- White pearl candy sprinkles
- Fresh mint leaves

1. Prepare the Hummingbird Cake: Preheat oven to 350°F. Coat a 13- x 9-inch baking pan with baking spray; line bottom of pan with parchment paper. Whisk together flour, baking powder, cinnamon, salt, and baking soda in a medium bowl.
2. Beat granulated sugar and butter in a stand mixer fitted with a paddle attachment on medium-high speed until mixture is pale and fluffy, about 3 minutes. Add eggs, 1 at a time, beating just until blended after each addition, about 1 minute. Reduce mixer speed to medium; beat in vanilla and mashed bananas until combined, about 30 seconds. Gradually add flour mixture in thirds, beating on low speed just until combined after each addition, stopping to scrape down sides as needed. Use a spatula to fold in pineapple and pecans.

3. Spoon batter into prepared pan, spreading evenly. Bake in preheated oven until golden around edges and a wooden pick inserted in center of cake comes out clean, 30 to 35 minutes. Transfer pan to a wire rack, and cool completely, about 1 hour, 30 minutes.
4. Meanwhile, prepare the Cream Cheese Frosting: Beat butter in a stand mixer fitted with a paddle attachment on medium-high speed until smooth and creamy, about 2 minutes. Add cream cheese; beat until light and fluffy, about 3 minutes. Add vanilla; beat until well blended, about 30 seconds. Reduce speed to low; beat in 1 cup of the powdered sugar until well blended, about 30 seconds. Add kosher salt and remaining 1 cup plus 2 tablespoons powdered sugar, and beat until smooth and combined, about 1 minute. Chill until ready to use.
5. Spread frosting over cake. Form flowers on top of cake with dried pineapple rings. Fill center of each flower with white pearl sprinkles; garnish with mint leaves.

Chocolate Chick Cake

(Photo, page 77)

ACTIVE 25 MIN. - TOTAL 55 MIN., PLUS 1 HOUR COOLING

SERVES 16

CHOCOLATE CAKE

- Baking spray
- 2 cups all-purpose flour
- 1½ cups granulated sugar
- 1 cup unsweetened cocoa
- 1½ tsp. baking powder
- 1 tsp. instant espresso powder
- ¾ tsp. kosher salt
- ½ tsp. baking soda
- 2 large eggs, at room temperature
- 1½ cups whole buttermilk
- ⅔ cup vegetable oil
- 1¼ tsp. vanilla extract

CHOCOLATE FROSTING

- 2½ cups powdered sugar
- ¾ cup unsweetened cocoa
- ½ cup unsalted butter, softened
- ¼ cup whole milk
- 1¼ tsp. vanilla extract
- ⅛ tsp. kosher salt

ADDITIONAL INGREDIENTS

- 1 cup candy-coated milk chocolate eggs (such as Cadbury Mini Eggs)
- 7-8 miniature chocolate chicks

1. Prepare the Chocolate Cake: Preheat oven to 350°F. Coat a 13- x 9-inch baking pan with baking spray; line bottom of pan with parchment paper. Whisk together flour, granulated sugar, cocoa, baking powder, espresso powder, salt, and baking soda in a medium bowl. Whisk together eggs, buttermilk, oil, and vanilla in a large liquid measuring cup.
2. Pour egg mixture into flour mixture; stir to combine. Pour into prepared pan, spreading evenly. Bake in preheated oven until a wooden pick inserted in center of cake comes out clean, 30 minutes. Transfer pan to a wire rack; cool completely, 1 hour to 1 hour, 30 minutes.
3. Meanwhile, prepare the Chocolate Frosting: Beat powdered sugar, cocoa, butter, milk, vanilla, and salt in a stand mixer fitted with a whisk attachment on low speed, 1 minute. Increase speed to medium; beat until light and fluffy, stopping to scrape down sides as needed, 3 minutes. Chill until ready to use.
4. Spread frosting over cake. Lightly crush ¼ cup of the candy-coated eggs; set aside. Sprinkle remaining ¾ cup whole candy-coated eggs over cake, pressing slightly into frosting. Sprinkle with reserved crushed eggs, pressing slightly into frosting as needed. Arrange chocolate chicks on cake as desired.

Pass the Potatoes, Please!

Rutabaga revs up this healthier take on a popular side

Potato-and-Rutabaga Gratin

Trading the traditional cream for milk cuts more than 100 calories per serving and slashes the saturated fat while delivering a dish that's still rich and satisfying.

ACTIVE 25 MIN. · TOTAL 55 MIN.

SERVES 8

- 1½ lb. Yukon Gold potatoes, scrubbed and cut into ⅛-inch-thick slices (from 5 potatoes)
- 1 (1-lb.) rutabaga, peeled, trimmed, and cut into ⅛-inch-thick slices
- 4 (5-inch) fresh thyme sprigs, plus leaves for garnish
- 1½ tsp. kosher salt
- 1 tsp. grated garlic
- ¾ tsp. Dijon mustard
- ½ tsp. black pepper
- 2½ cups whole milk, divided
- 3 Tbsp. all-purpose flour
- 4 oz. Gruyère cheese, shredded (about 1 cup), divided

1. Preheat oven to 400°F with rack about 10 inches from heat source. Add potatoes, rutabaga, thyme sprigs, salt, garlic, Dijon mustard, pepper, and 2 cups of the milk to a large saucepan. Bring to a simmer over medium, gently turning vegetables occasionally. (Vegetables will not be submerged.) Cover and reduce heat to low. Simmer, turning vegetables occasionally and stirring to prevent sticking, until vegetables are almost tender, about 12 minutes.

2. Whisk together flour and remaining ½ cup milk in a small bowl until smooth. Stir flour mixture into simmering vegetable mixture. Cook, stirring occasionally, until thickened, about 1 minute. Remove from heat; discard thyme sprigs. Spoon half of the vegetable mixture into a 10-inch broiler-safe cast-iron skillet or 2-quart baking dish. Sprinkle with ½ cup of the cheese. Top with remaining vegetable mixture, arranging potato and rutabaga slices as desired. Sprinkle evenly with remaining ½ cup cheese.

3. Bake, uncovered, in preheated oven until mixture is bubbling around edges, 15 to 20 minutes. Increase oven temperature to broil (keep gratin in oven). Broil until golden brown, 1 to 2 minutes. Remove gratin from oven, and let cool 10 minutes. Sprinkle with thyme leaves, and serve warm.

Before Recipe Makeover:

CALORIES: **405** – FIBER: **3 G** – FAT: **34 G**

After Recipe Makeover:

CALORIES: **192** – FIBER: **5 G** – FAT: **7 G**

GOOD FOR YOU!
Rutabagas are high in fiber, potassium, and several antioxidants. Be sure to peel and discard the thick skin before cooking.

Devilishly Good

Bet you can't eat just one bite of this spiced–up, ultracreamy party dip

Deviled Crab Dip

ACTIVE 20 MIN. - TOTAL 50 MIN.
SERVES 6

- ⅓ cup finely chopped red bell pepper (from 1 small pepper)
- 2 Tbsp. finely chopped seeded jalapeño chile (from 1 chile)
- ½ (8-oz.) pkg. cream cheese, softened
- ½ cup mayonnaise
- ¼ cup chopped fresh parsley
- ½ tsp. grated lemon zest plus 1 tsp. fresh juice
- 1½ tsp. seasoned salt (such as Lawry's)
- ½ tsp. Worcestershire sauce
- ¾ tsp. Old Bay seasoning, divided
- 8 oz. fresh jumbo lump crabmeat, drained and picked over, or canned lump crabmeat
- 18 saltine crackers, finely crushed
- 2 oz. sharp Cheddar cheese, shredded (about ½ cup)
- 2 Tbsp. unsalted butter, melted

  Baguette slices, endive leaves, sweet mini peppers, carrots, radishes, sugar snap peas, and celery stalks, for serving

1. Preheat oven to 400°F. Stir together bell pepper, jalapeño, cream cheese, mayonnaise, parsley, lemon zest and juice, seasoned salt, Worcestershire sauce, and ½ teaspoon of the Old Bay seasoning in a medium bowl until blended. Gently fold in crabmeat, and transfer to a 1-quart baking dish.
2. Stir together crushed saltines, Cheddar, butter, and remaining ¼ teaspoon Old Bay seasoning in a medium bowl until crackers are moistened. Sprinkle evenly over crabmeat mixture in baking dish.
3. Bake in preheated oven until dip is bubbling and cracker topping is golden brown, 25 to 30 minutes. Serve hot with baguette slices and desired vegetables.

CRAB CHECK
Pick through the crabmeat carefully to remove any stray bits of shell.

Spring Mix

Change up your chicken routine with the season's freshest vegetables

Lemony Roast Chicken with Rainbow Carrots

ACTIVE 20 MIN. · TOTAL 1 HOUR, 35 MIN.
SERVES 4

- 1 (4- to 5-lb.) whole chicken, patted dry
- ½ tsp. black pepper
- 2 tsp. kosher salt, divided
- 2 large lemons, divided
- 1 garlic head, halved crosswise
- 8 (6-inch) fresh herb sprigs (such as thyme, oregano, parsley, or dill), plus more for garnish
- 1½ lb. small rainbow carrots, peeled
- 1½ cups chicken stock
- 2 Tbsp. olive oil

1. Preheat oven to 425°F. Sprinkle chicken with pepper and 1½ teaspoons of the salt. Cut 1 of the lemons in half, setting aside 1 half. Cut other lemon into ¼-inch–thick slices. Place 1 lemon half, garlic head halves, and herb sprigs in cavity of chicken. Tie legs together with kitchen twine; tuck wing tips under chicken. Place it, breast side up, in a roasting pan. Arrange carrots and lemon slices around chicken; sprinkle with remaining ½ teaspoon salt. Pour stock over carrots; drizzle chicken with olive oil.
2. Bake in preheated oven until a thermometer inserted into thickest portion of thigh registers 165°F, about 1 hour, 15 minutes, stirring vegetables halfway through bake time.
3. Transfer chicken, carrots, and lemon slices to a platter. Squeeze reserved lemon half into drippings; stir. Remove and discard twine. Pour drippings over chicken and carrots. Garnish with herb sprigs.

SUPER SPUDS
Omit the carrots, and use 1½ pounds halved new potatoes; they soak up the pan drippings even better.

TURNIP THE VOLUME
Not a radish fan? Prepare the recipe as directed, substituting 1 pound peeled baby turnips with greens. Halve or quarter any larger turnips, if needed.

Crispy Chicken Thighs with Roasted Radishes

ACTIVE 20 MIN. · TOTAL 45 MIN.

SERVES 4

- 4 (8-oz.) bone-in, skin-on chicken thighs
- 1½ tsp. kosher salt, divided
- ¾ cup all-purpose flour
- ½ tsp. black pepper, plus more for garnish
- 1 cup whole buttermilk
- 1 lb. radishes with greens
- 2 Tbsp. unsalted butter
- 1 Tbsp. olive oil
- 3 garlic cloves, smashed
- 2 tsp. apple cider vinegar
- 1 tsp. honey
- 1 tsp. chopped fresh oregano, plus more leaves for garnish
- Flaky sea salt

1. Preheat oven to 425°F. Sprinkle chicken thighs with ¾ teaspoon of the salt. Whisk together flour, pepper, and ¼ teaspoon of the salt in a shallow dish. Place buttermilk in a separate shallow dish. Working with 1 piece at a time, dip chicken in buttermilk, turning to fully coat; place chicken in flour mixture, turning to coat. Transfer to a wire rack set inside a rimmed baking sheet, and set aside.

2. Cut greens from radishes; roughly chop greens, and cut radishes in half. Keep radishes and greens separate; set aside.

3. Melt butter in a 12-inch cast-iron skillet over medium-high; add oil. Add chicken thighs to skillet, skin side down; cook, undisturbed, until golden brown, about 5 minutes. Flip chicken thighs, and arrange radishes and garlic around chicken thighs; sprinkle with remaining ½ teaspoon salt. Bake, uncovered, in preheated oven, stirring radishes and garlic halfway through bake time, until a thermometer inserted into thickest portion of chicken registers 165°F, 20 to 25 minutes.

4. Transfer chicken to a plate using a slotted spatula. Heat radish mixture in skillet over medium-high. Stir in chopped radish greens, vinegar, honey, and oregano; cook, stirring constantly, until greens are wilted, about 1 minute.

5. Return chicken to skillet, skin side up. Sprinkle with flaky sea salt, pepper, and oregano.

Chicken Leg Quarters with Asparagus and Buttermilk Ranch

ACTIVE 20 MIN. - TOTAL 45 MIN.

SERVES 4

- 4 (12-oz.) chicken leg quarters
- 1 tsp. smoked paprika
- ½ tsp. onion powder
- 1½ tsp. kosher salt, divided
- ¾ tsp. black pepper, divided
- ½ cup whole buttermilk
- ½ cup sour cream
- ¼ cup mayonnaise
- 1 Tbsp. chopped fresh dill, plus more for garnish
- 2 garlic cloves, finely grated
- 2 tsp. fresh lemon juice (from 1 lemon)
- 2 lb. fresh asparagus, trimmed
- 1 Tbsp. olive oil

1. Preheat oven to 425°F. Pat chicken dry with paper towels. Stir together smoked paprika, onion powder, 1 teaspoon of the salt, and ¼ teaspoon of the pepper in a small bowl. Sprinkle seasoning mixture evenly over chicken, gently patting into skin. Arrange chicken on a large aluminum foil-lined rimmed baking sheet. Bake until a thermometer inserted into thickest portion of chicken registers 150°F, 20 to 25 minutes.

2. Meanwhile, whisk together buttermilk, sour cream, mayonnaise, dill, garlic, lemon juice, ¼ teaspoon of the salt, and remaining ½ teaspoon pepper in a small bowl until smooth. Cover with plastic wrap, and store in refrigerator until ready to serve.

3. Move chicken to 1 side of baking sheet. Add asparagus to opposite side; drizzle with oil, and sprinkle with remaining ¼ teaspoon salt. Bake at 425°F until a thermometer inserted into thickest portion of chicken registers 165°F, 10 to 15 minutes. Drizzle chicken and asparagus with about ¼ cup buttermilk dressing; garnish with dill. Serve with remaining buttermilk dressing.

CARROT GOLD
Prefer carrots? Omit the asparagus, and add 2 pounds peeled carrots around chicken in Step 1. Sprinkle carrots with ¼ teaspoon salt; drizzle with 1 tablespoon olive oil. Bake until chicken is done, 35 to 45 minutes. Drizzle with dressing, and garnish as directed in Step 3.

Prosciutto-Wrapped Chicken Cutlets with Haricots Verts

ACTIVE 25 MIN. - TOTAL 35 MIN.
SERVES 4

- 4 (5- to 6-oz.) chicken breast cutlets
- 2 Tbsp. Creole mustard
- ½ tsp. black pepper, plus more for garnish
- ¾ tsp. kosher salt, divided
- 12 prosciutto slices, divided
- 4 tsp. fresh tarragon leaves, divided, plus more for garnish
- 1 Tbsp. unsalted butter
- 1 Tbsp. olive oil
- 1 lb. trimmed haricots verts (French green beans)
- ⅛ tsp. crushed red pepper
- Lemon wedges, for serving

1. Preheat oven to 375°F. Rub chicken cutlets with mustard; sprinkle with black pepper and ½ teaspoon of the salt. Place 3 prosciutto slices on a piece of parchment paper, slightly overlapping each slice by about 1 inch to create a square shape. Sprinkle 1 teaspoon of the tarragon leaves over prosciutto. Place 1 chicken cutlet crosswise in center of prosciutto; lift edges of parchment to help wrap prosciutto around chicken. Place wrapped cutlet, seam side down, on a large plate. Repeat with remaining prosciutto, tarragon, and chicken.

2. Add butter and oil to a large ovenproof skillet; heat over medium-high until butter melts. Add chicken cutlets, seam sides up, and cook, undisturbed, 3 to 4 minutes. Flip, and bake in preheated oven until a thermometer inserted into thickest portion of chicken registers 165°F, 8 to 10 minutes.

3. Transfer chicken from skillet to a large plate using a slotted spatula. Heat drippings in skillet over medium-high. Add haricots verts, remaining ¼ teaspoon salt, and crushed red pepper; cook, stirring often, until tender, 2 to 4 minutes. Return chicken and any juices to skillet; garnish with more tarragon and black pepper. Serve with lemon wedges.

SNAP TO IT

For a pop of sweetness, prepare the recipe as directed, substituting 1 pound trimmed sugar snap peas for haricots verts in Step 3 and cooking until almost tender, about 5 minutes.

Chicken-and-Rice Bake with Broccolini

ACTIVE 20 MIN. · TOTAL 45 MIN.

SERVES 6

- 1 lb. boneless, skinless chicken breasts, cut into 1-inch pieces
- 8 oz. fresh Broccolini, trimmed and cut into 2-inch pieces
- 3 Tbsp. olive oil, divided
- 1 tsp. kosher salt, divided
- ¾ tsp. black pepper, divided
- 1 small sweet onion, chopped (⅔ cup)
- 3 garlic cloves, minced (1 Tbsp.)
- 2 Tbsp. all-purpose flour
- 2 cups whole milk
- 8 oz. fontina cheese, shredded (about 2 cups), divided
- 1 (8.8-oz.) pkg. microwave-ready white rice, uncooked
- ½ cup panko breadcrumbs
- 1 tsp. chopped fresh thyme leaves, plus more for garnish

1. Preheat oven to 400°F. Stir together chicken, Broccolini, 1 tablespoon of the oil, ½ teaspoon of the salt, and ¼ teaspoon of the pepper in an 11- x 7-inch (2-quart) baking dish until evenly coated. Bake, uncovered, until chicken and Broccolini are partially cooked, about 10 minutes.

2. Meanwhile, heat 1 tablespoon of the oil in a large skillet over medium-high. Add onion; cook, stirring often, until tender, about 3 minutes. Add garlic; cook until fragrant, about 30 seconds. Reduce heat to medium, and stir in flour; cook, stirring constantly, until incorporated, about 30 seconds. Gradually whisk in milk until smooth; bring to a simmer over medium. Cook, whisking often, until slightly thickened, 5 to 8 minutes. Remove from heat, and whisk in 1½ cups of the cheese, remaining ½ teaspoon salt, and remaining ½ teaspoon pepper until smooth.

3. Transfer chicken and Broccolini to sauce in skillet, discarding any juices in baking dish. Add rice to skillet; stir until just coated. Spoon mixture into baking dish.

4. Stir together panko, thyme, remaining 1 tablespoon oil, and remaining ½ cup cheese in a small bowl; sprinkle evenly over chicken mixture. Bake, uncovered, in preheated oven until top is golden brown, 25 to 30 minutes. Garnish with additional thyme.

KNOW YOUR OPTIONS

No Broccolini at your market? Prepare the recipe as directed, substituting 4 cups broccoli florets.

Quiche for a Crowd

Store-bought piecrusts make short work of this breakfast favorite

PRESS & GO
Crimp the dough into the sides of the pan to help it hold its shape.

Spring-Vegetable Sheet Pan Quiche

ACTIVE 20 MIN. - TOTAL 1 HOUR, PLUS 30 MIN. COOLING

SERVES 10 TO 12

- 1   (14.1-oz.) pkg. refrigerated piecrusts (2 piecrusts)
-     All-purpose flour, for surface
- 1   Tbsp. unsalted butter
- 1   lb. fresh asparagus, cut into 1½-inch-long pieces
- 4   cups fresh baby spinach
- 1¾ tsp. kosher salt, divided
- ½   tsp. black pepper, divided
- 6   oz. Gruyère cheese, shredded (about 1½ cups)
- 12 large eggs
- 2   cups half-and-half
- 3   Tbsp. chopped fresh chives
- 2   tsp. chopped fresh dill
- ½   cup fresh or frozen sweet peas

1. Preheat oven to 375°F. Coat a 15- x 10-inch rimmed baking sheet with cooking spray.

2. Stack 2 crusts on top of each other on a lightly floured surface, and roll into a 17- x 12-inch rectangle. Transfer crust to prepared baking sheet, pressing into bottom and up sides. Tuck edges of crust under, and crimp as desired. Top crust with a piece of parchment paper; fill with pie weights or dried beans. Freeze, uncovered, 10 minutes. Bake in preheated oven until crust is set and edges are browned, about 20 minutes. Remove parchment paper and weights, and let cool 10 minutes.

3. While crust is cooling, melt butter in a large skillet over medium-high. Add asparagus, and cook, stirring often, until tender-crisp, about 4 minutes. Stir in spinach, ½ teaspoon of the salt, and ¼ teaspoon of the pepper. Cook, stirring often, until spinach is just wilted, about 1 minute. Remove skillet from heat.

4. Sprinkle 1 cup of the cheese evenly in bottom of baked crust. Whisk together eggs, half-and-half, chives, dill, remaining 1¼ teaspoons salt, and remaining ¼ teaspoon pepper in a large bowl until combined. Pour egg mixture over cheese in crust. Top evenly with asparagus and spinach mixture; sprinkle with peas and remaining ½ cup cheese.

5. Bake in preheated oven until filling is set, 25 to 30 minutes. Let cool at least 20 minutes before slicing as desired.

WHIP IT UP
If you're not keeping kosher for Passover, beat
3 cups heavy whipping cream with ¼ cup
powdered sugar and ½ teaspoon vanilla
using an electric mixer until stiff peaks form,
about 3 minutes. Use in place of the nondairy
whipped topping as directed in the recipe.

BERRY-AND-BASIL
PAVLOVA

Pretty Pavlovas

Three simple sheet-pan desserts for Passover or any special gathering

Berry-and-Basil Pavlova

ACTIVE 30 MIN. · TOTAL 2 HOURS, 30 MIN.,
PLUS 3 HOURS COOLING

SERVES 16

- 1½ cups packed light brown sugar
- 1 cup granulated sugar, divided
- 9 large egg whites, at room temperature
- ¼ tsp. cream of tartar (optional)
  Pinch of kosher salt
- 1 lb. fresh strawberries, hulled and quartered
- 1 (6-oz.) pkg. fresh raspberries
- 6 cups thawed frozen nondairy whipped topping (from 2 [8-oz.] containers)
- ¼ cup loosely packed fresh baby basil leaves

1. Preheat oven to 250°F. Line a large rimmed baking sheet with parchment paper. Whisk together brown sugar and ¾ cup of the granulated sugar until no lumps remain. Set sugar mixture aside.
2. Beat egg whites, cream of tartar (if using), and salt with a stand mixer fitted with a whisk attachment on medium-high speed until foamy, about 1 minute. Increase speed to high, and gradually add sugar mixture. Beat until stiff peaks form, 8 to 10 minutes. (The meringue should be glossy, and sugar should be dissolved completely.)
3. Spread the meringue almost to the edges of the prepared baking sheet using an offset spatula. Bake in preheated oven until pale off-white, about 2 hours. Turn off oven, and let meringue cool, undisturbed, inside oven with door closed, at least 3 hours or up to 12 hours.
4. During the last 30 minutes of cooling, toss together the strawberries, raspberries, and remaining ¼ cup granulated sugar in a medium bowl until combined. Set aside.
5. Transfer cooled meringue to a platter. Spread whipped topping evenly over meringue, leaving a 1½-inch border. Spoon berry mixture over whipped topping, and top with basil leaves. Serve immediately.

LEMON-PISTACHIO PAVLOVA

COCONUT MACAROON PAVLOVA

Lemon-Pistachio Pavlova

Prepare recipe as directed, omitting berry mixture and basil. Drop spoonfuls of lemon curd (1 cup) over whipped topping on meringue in Step 5; swirl with a knife. Top with ½ cup chopped pistachios.

Coconut Macaroon Pavlova

Omit berry mixture and basil; sprinkle 1 cup toasted coconut over whipped topping on meringue. Drizzle with 2 oz. melted dark chocolate.

Pickled Perfection

Inspired by a beloved Southern appetizer, this pasta salad is just
the ticket for a porch party or weekend brunch

THERE'S JUST SOMETHING about pickled shrimp that makes me giddy. It's a beautiful dish with plump, pink shrimp nestled among vibrant vegetables and herbs—all tossed together in a light vinaigrette studded with whole pickling spices. This old-school Southern classic, known to many as "Sea Island shrimp," still feels like a modern luxury to me. Every time I eat it, I vow to make it more often—which is how this delicious new recipe came to be. It's a fresh twist that has all the flavors and textures of pickled shrimp plus crunchy sugar snap peas and lots of tender herbs. And thanks to the pasta, it's filling enough to serve as a meal. I like to make it ahead (it gets better the longer it sits) and then enjoy it with a glass of sweet tea in my outdoor kitchen, which is where you'll find me all season long.

Southern Shrimp Pasta Salad

As the seasons change, swap out the vegetables and herbs listed here for whatever looks good at your local farmers market.

ACTIVE 30 MIN. - TOTAL 45 MIN.

SERVES 6

Ice

3 Tbsp. plus ¼ tsp. kosher salt, divided

12 oz. uncooked orecchiette pasta

3 Tbsp. plus ¾ tsp. lower-sodium Old Bay seasoning, divided

1 lb. medium-size raw shrimp, peeled and deveined

¼ cup fresh lemon juice (from 2 lemons)

1 Tbsp. coarse-grain Dijon mustard

1 Tbsp. honey

1 cup extra-virgin olive oil

1 tsp. minced garlic (from 2 garlic cloves)

½ tsp. crushed red pepper

¼ tsp. black pepper

2 cups fresh sugar snap peas, sliced

2 medium shallots, thinly sliced (about ½ cup)

½ cup thinly sliced celery (from 2 stalks)

1 cup roughly chopped fresh dill

½ cup roughly chopped fresh flat-leaf parsley

1. Fill a large bowl with ice and water; set aside. Bring 12 cups water and 3 tablespoons of the salt to a boil in a large stockpot over medium-high. Add pasta, and cook, stirring occasionally, until al dente, about 12 minutes. Using a spider skimmer or slotted spoon, transfer pasta from boiling water to a paper towel–lined baking sheet; let cool completely, about 10 minutes. Do not remove boiling water from heat.

2. Add 3 tablespoons of the Old Bay seasoning to boiling water, and boil 2 minutes. Add shrimp. Let cook until just pink and just cooked through, about 2 minutes; drain. Immediately transfer shrimp to ice water; let shrimp cool completely, about 7 minutes.

3. Meanwhile, whisk together lemon juice, mustard, and honey in a medium bowl. Gradually whisk in oil until smooth and combined. Whisk in garlic, crushed red pepper, black pepper, and remaining ¼ teaspoon salt and ¾ teaspoon Old Bay seasoning until combined.

4. Place pasta, shrimp, sugar snap peas, shallots, celery, dill, and parsley in a large bowl; add vinaigrette, and toss until well coated. Serve, or cover and store in refrigerator up to 24 hours.

Easter Feast

Make this roasted lamb the star of your holiday menu

ROMAINE SALAD
WITH ORANGES
AND RADISHES

ROASTED LAMB
WITH FRESH-HERB
SAUCE

GINGERY CARROTS

IN MANY PARTS of the world, lamb signifies spring. Perhaps it's the Paschal Lambs that are spit-roasted and served in villages throughout Greece at Easter. It may be the delicious and hearty Sunday roasts served in the U.K. My parents' house harked back to neither of those cultures but reflected the traditions of my mother's Virginia-bred family. There, the appearance of a leg of lamb on the Sunday table was a sure sign that spring had indeed arrived.

My mother was a lamb purist, preferring it to be seasoned with salt and pepper and served with good old-fashioned Day-Glo green mint jelly. I, on the other hand, love to change it up. I often make a basic dry spice mix that includes salt, pepper, dried garlic, and some herbes de Provence. Sometimes I ask the butcher to french the shank portion of the leg so I can hold the bone to carve it.

Preparing a leg of lamb gives me an excuse to use my manche à gigot, a utensil that I found at Lucullus Antiques, the curated culinary antiques store in New Orleans. It's a sterling silver claw that attaches to the exposed shank bone to allow the meat to be carved with elegance and panache. If you can find one in an antiques shop, it's a wonderfully esoteric piece of silverware that will dazzle your friends.

One of the things I love about lamb is that it's so versatile. If I want a more North African taste, I'll add cumin and caraway to the dry spice mix. In this recipe, the meat is flavored with garlic and Dijon and served with a sauce reminiscent of the mint jelly from my childhood holidays. –Jessica B. Harris

Roasted Lamb with Fresh-Herb Sauce

ACTIVE 35 MIN. · TOTAL 2 HOURS, 55 MIN.
SERVES 8 TO 10

- 1 (7- to 8-lb.) bone-in leg of lamb, trimmed and tied
- 1 large shallot, roughly chopped (about ½ cup)
- 1 tsp. Dijon mustard
- ¼ tsp. crushed red pepper
- 1 Tbsp. grated lemon zest plus 5 Tbsp. fresh juice (from 2 lemons), divided
- 8 garlic cloves, divided
- 1¾ tsp. kosher salt, divided
- 1¾ tsp. black pepper, divided
- 1¾ cups olive oil, divided
- 1 cup chopped fresh parsley, plus more for garnish
- 1 cup chopped fresh mint, plus more for garnish
- Lemon slices

1. Preheat oven to 450°F with rack 8 inches from heat source. Place a wire rack in a large roasting pan; top with lamb, and pat dry. Let stand at room temperature for 45 minutes.
2. Meanwhile, pulse shallot, mustard, red pepper, lemon zest, 3 tablespoons of the lemon juice, 4 of the garlic cloves, and 1 teaspoon each of the salt and black pepper in a food processor until roughly chopped, about 10 pulses. With processor running, gradually add 1 cup of the oil, processing until smooth. Transfer ½ cup of the shallot mixture to a small bowl, and set aside. Cover remaining shallot mixture in food processor bowl, and set aside.
3. Cut 1-inch slits all over lamb. Finely chop remaining 4 garlic cloves; stir into reserved ½ cup shallot mixture. Rub shallot-garlic mixture over lamb, and sprinkle with remaining ¾ teaspoon each salt and black pepper.
4. Bake lamb in preheated oven for 20 minutes. Reduce the oven temperature to 300°F, and bake until a thermometer inserted into thickest portion of lamb registers 130°F, 1 hour and 20 minutes to 1 hour and 30 minutes. Without removing lamb from oven, increase oven temperature to broil, and broil until well browned, 5 to

10 minutes. Remove lamb from oven, and cover loosely with aluminum foil. Let rest 20 minutes. (Temperature will continue to rise to 145°F.)
5. While lamb rests, add parsley and mint to shallot mixture in food processor; pulse until herbs are finely chopped and incorporated, about 20 pulses. With processor running, gradually add remaining ¾ cup oil and 2 tablespoons lemon juice, processing until incorporated. With processor running, gradually add 1 to 2 tablespoons water until sauce reaches desired consistency. Thinly slice lamb against the grain, discarding bone or reserving for another use. Serve sliced lamb with herb sauce. Garnish with lemon slices and herbs.

Romaine Salad with Oranges and Radishes

ACTIVE 15 MIN. · TOTAL 15 MIN.
SERVES 8

Whisk together 1½ Tbsp. **red wine vinegar,** 1 Tbsp. **fresh orange juice,** 1 tsp. **Dijon mustard,** 1 tsp. **honey,** ¼ tsp. **kosher salt,** and ⅛ tsp. **black pepper** in a large bowl. Gradually whisk in 5 Tbsp. **extra-virgin olive oil** until combined. Add 10 cups **baby romaine lettuce** leaves, 2 cups **orange segments,** and ¾ cup thinly sliced **radishes**; gently toss to combine.

Gingery Carrots

ACTIVE 35 MIN. · TOTAL 40 MIN.
SERVES 8

Bring 2 lb. **carrots,** peeled and cut into ½-inch-thick rounds; 1 cup **fresh orange juice;** and 2 Tbsp. minced **fresh ginger** to a simmer in a large high-sided skillet over medium-high. Reduce heat to medium; cover and cook, stirring occasionally, until fork-tender, 15 to 18 minutes. Stir in 2 Tbsp. **unsalted butter,** 1 Tbsp. **honey,** ¼ tsp. **kosher salt,** ¼ tsp. grated **fresh nutmeg,** and ⅛ tsp. **black pepper**; cook, stirring constantly, until butter is melted, about 1 minute. Top with **flaky sea salt,** chopped **fresh parsley,** and more grated fresh nutmeg and black pepper.

Southern Staple
Zatarain's Creole Mustard

Zatarain's Creole Mustard was one of the original products created by the famed Louisiana grocer and food entrepreneur Emile A. Zatarain in the late 1800s. Popular in everything from potato salad to po'boys, it is made of brown mustard seeds that are soaked in vinegar and then coarsely stone-ground. Here are three tasty ways to use the spicy condiment.

- Mix with mayonnaise for a zesty burger spread.

- Use as a rub on a pork tenderloin to create a beautiful crust.

- Add a kick to your favorite crab cake recipe.

Learn a New Instrument
Quicker than chopping, a mandoline makes wafer-thin slices of fruits and vegetables. Here's how to use one safely

GET IN POSITION
For the best control, place the mandoline perpendicular to your body with the slope facing away from you.

SAFETY FIRST
The blades are sharp; always use a hand guard or glove. Cut food into manageable pieces that fit within the slicing zone.

EASY DOES IT
Apply gentle, even pressure with each stroke. Stop near the end of the vegetable or fruit; discard scraps.

EDITORS' PICK

OXO V-Blade Mandoline Slicer *Simple to use and adjust, it comes with a hand guard and stand and has V-shape blades that produce uniform slices.*

May

Strawberry Sippers

Raise a glass to the glorious return of spring's juiciest fruit

STRAWBERRY
SPRITZERS

Strawberry Shrub
ACTIVE 10 MIN. - TOTAL 10 MIN.,
PLUS 2 DAYS CHILLING
SERVES 8

Place 1 qt. **fresh strawberries** (hulled and sliced), 2 cups **unfiltered apple cider vinegar,** 1½ cups **granulated sugar,** 2 Tbsp. sliced **fresh ginger,** and 2 tsp. grated **lemon zest** in a large bowl or resealable container. Stir until sugar is dissolved, about 2 minutes. Cover and refrigerate until flavors have infused, about 2 days. Pour mixture through a fine mesh strainer into a 1-qt. glass jar with a lid, discarding solids. Secure lid, and refrigerate shrub for up to 3 months.

Strawberry Spritzers
ACTIVE 5 MIN. - TOTAL 5 MIN.
SERVES 8

Pour 3 Tbsp. **Strawberry Shrub** into each of 8 glasses filled with **ice;** top with ½ to ¾ cup **seltzer water** per glass (or desired amount). Garnish with **fresh strawberries.**

Strawberry-Infused Tequila
ACTIVE 5 MIN. - TOTAL 10 MIN.,
PLUS 2 DAYS STANDING
MAKES 3 CUPS

Place 1 qt. **fresh strawberries** (hulled and sliced) in a large glass jar with lid. Pour 1 (750-milliliter) bottle **blanco tequila** over strawberries; seal lid on jar. Reserve tequila bottle. Let tequila mixture stand in a cool, dark place, shaking twice a day, until tequila turns red and strawberry flavor is pronounced, about 2 days. Using a funnel, pour mixture through a fine mesh strainer or coffee filter into reserved bottle; discard strawberries.

Strawberry Ranch Water

ACTIVE 5 MIN. - TOTAL 5 MIN.
SERVES 1

Fill a glass with **ice**. Pour in 6 Tbsp.
Strawberry-Infused Tequila and
2 Tbsp. **fresh lime juice**. Top with
½ cup **sparkling mineral water**.
Garnish with a **lime wedge** and **fresh
strawberry halves**.

Strawberry Simple Syrup

ACTIVE 10 MIN. - TOTAL 30 MIN.,
PLUS 1 HOUR COOLING
MAKES 3 CUPS

Bring 1 qt. **fresh strawberries** (hulled
and quartered) and 2½ cups **water** to
a boil in a saucepan over high. Reduce
heat to low; simmer until mixture is
slightly reduced, about 20 minutes.
Skim off any foam from surface. Pour
strawberry mixture through a fine mesh
strainer; discard solids. Stir in 2½ cups
granulated sugar until dissolved,
about 2 minutes. Let cool to room
temperature, about 1 hour. Store in an
airtight container in refrigerator for up
to 3 weeks.

Strawberry Mojito

ACTIVE 5 MIN. - TOTAL 5 MIN.
SERVES 1

Muddle 4 **fresh mint leaves** with 2 Tbsp.
Strawberry Simple Syrup in a cocktail
shaker. Add ¼ cup
white rum, 2 Tbsp.
lime juice, and
ice to fill shaker;
shake 15 seconds.
Strain into a glass
filled with **ice**. Top
with **club soda**,
mint, **lime**, and
strawberries.

STRAWBERRY
RANCH WATER

The Universal Language of Chicken Salad

This beloved Southern dish can contain a multitude of cultures

PERSIAN SALAD
OLIVIEH

IF THERE'S A SINGLE REGRET my parents have about raising my brother and me, it's that they didn't teach us their native languages. My mom, who emigrated from Malaysia in the early eighties, speaks Chinese. My dad, who arrived from Iran a few years before, speaks Farsi. English was their common ground. When they made the move from Illinois to Alabama in time to start a family, it was a foregone conclusion. Other than the few memorized phrases we dusted off for long-distance phone calls with relatives, my brother and I spoke English. Years later, while applying to colleges, we joined our parents in lamenting that "trilingual" wouldn't join our lists of academic accomplishments.

While I'm not fluent, or even functional, in Mandarin or Farsi, my parents made sure I was proficient in another language. Like many first-generation Americans, my strongest tether to culture is food. I grew up eating the cuisines of my parents' home countries. Slippery stir-fried noodles and salty, soy-glazed short ribs from my mom. Herbaceous beef stew and nutty lentil rice from my dad. Hamburger Helper and Kraft Macaroni & Cheese were rare delicacies.

One of the first dishes my mom learned after moving to the South was chicken salad. She had begun swapping recipes with two other mothers who lived in our apartment building. One, who'd emigrated from South Korea, shared dak kalguksu (Korean chicken-and-zucchini noodle soup). The other, who had Kentucky roots, introduced her to chicken salad, plus a fruitcake starter that most likely still lurks in the depths of my mom's freezer. Twenty-five years later, the friendships and recipes live on.

Part of what makes chicken salad so beloved is its adaptability. Scour your pantry, and throw in whatever is on hand—pecans, dried cranberries, grapes, herbs. My mom's version calls for curry powder. To this day, hers is the only one that my mayonnaise-averse 10th-generation-Southern husband is excited to eat.

In the South, chicken salad is synonymous with bridal showers, family potlucks, and church picnics. In Iran, the same is true for a dish called salad olivieh. Despite its Russian roots, salad olivieh–a combo of chicken, potato, and egg salads–is Southern at heart.

In Iran, it is the unofficial dish of Sizdah Bedar, the final day of the Persian New Year celebration (Nowruz) that begins on the first day of spring and lasts for two weeks. On Sizdah Bedar, also known as Nature's Day, it's bad luck to stay indoors, so everyone heads to a park for an all-day picnic with family and friends. Salad olivieh is always there in abundance. And just like Southerners comparing pound cakes at a potluck, there's always whispering about whose version is best. I'll go to the grave saying my dad's is far and away the winner.

When we were growing up, our parents loved to remind us that we're 50% Chinese, 50% Iranian, and 100% American. Sometimes it worked. Other times, it was decidedly hard to be a mixed-race kid growing up in the Deep South. During those times, I remember thinking the phrase was cheesy and that my parents must not have been so great at math.

I see now that they were doing their best with what they had–drawing parallels where they could and putting things in a perspective that might make us feel whole. Chicken salad was a surprising connection point. Its ability to transcend cuisine and culture spoke volumes, affirming I didn't have to be fluent in three languages to belong– because if something as simple as a combination of chicken and mayonnaise could be many things at once, maybe I could too. –Tara Massouleh McCay

Persian Salad Olivieh

I wasn't overly interested in cooking when I was growing up, but I always jumped at the opportunity to help prepare salad olivieh. My dad would boil the potatoes, chicken, and eggs, then lay out a vinyl tablecloth on the floor of our living room. If it was a warm spring day, he would open the windows, letting the breeze in as we sat cross-legged, peeling potatoes and shredding the chicken with our bare hands.

ACTIVE 20 MIN. - TOTAL 55 MIN.

SERVES 14

- 4 medium (about 2 lb. total) russet potatoes, scrubbed
- 1¼ cups frozen sweet peas
- 3 cups shredded cooked chicken breast (about 1 lb.)
- 1⅓ cups grated baby dill pickles (about 13 pickles)
- 1¼ cups mayonnaise
- 4 hard-cooked eggs, peeled and chopped (about ¾ cup)
- 1½ tsp. kosher salt
- ½ tsp. black pepper
  Garnishes: thinly sliced radishes, thinly sliced cucumber, fresh flat-leaf parsley sprigs, chopped fresh dill

1. Bring a large pot of water to a boil over high. Add potatoes to pot; cook until fork-tender, 20 to 25 minutes. Drain potatoes, and place in a medium bowl. Let stand until cool enough to handle, about 15 minutes. Peel potatoes, discarding skins; set flesh aside in bowl.
2. While potatoes are cooking, place peas in a small microwavable bowl. Microwave on HIGH for 2 minutes. Remove from microwave; set aside, and let cool 5 minutes.
3. Using a fork or a potato masher, mash cooked, cooled potatoes in bowl until mostly smooth. Add chicken, pickles, mayonnaise, eggs, salt, pepper, and 1 cup of the peas to mashed potatoes, stirring with a rubber spatula until evenly combined.
4. Spoon chicken mixture into an 11- x 7-inch baking dish or a large bowl. Sprinkle with remaining ¼ cup peas. Garnish salad as desired with radishes, cucumber, and herbs. Refrigerate until chilled.

Curry Chicken Salad

Because no gathering of Southern women is complete without chicken salad, my mom served this dish to my bridesmaids on my wedding day. (We also had Sonic hot dogs, but that is neither here nor there.) Worrying that not everyone would welcome her twist on the classic salad, she supplemented with a store-bought tub. Hers was the unanimous favorite. As someone who vividly remembers fretting about what foreign dish her parents might serve on sleepover nights, I was moved to tears by the sight of the empty Tupperware.

ACTIVE 15 MIN. - TOTAL 15 MIN., PLUS 1 HOUR CHILLING

SERVES 4

Place 2 cups **chopped cooked chicken breast** (from 1 large [4-lb.] rotisserie chicken) in a medium bowl. Add ¾ cup **finely chopped celery** (from about 3 small stalks), ½ cup **mayonnaise**, 2 Tbsp. finely chopped **white onion**, 1 Tbsp. **curry powder**, ½ tsp. **kosher salt**, and ½ tsp. **black pepper** to chicken; stir to combine. Cover and refrigerate until chilled, about 1 hour. Garnish with chopped fresh **cilantro**, and serve in **Bibb lettuce leaves** or with **bread and crackers**.

CURRY CHICKEN SALAD

Preserving Traditions

In a small North Carolina town, Gabrielle Eitienne uses
food to marry the past and present, with delicious results

PORK CHOPS WITH
CAROLINA BARBECUE
SAUCE, SMOKED BUTTER,
AND BRAISED ONIONS

AS A CHILD GROWING UP on her family's land in the Central North Carolina community of St. Mary's, Gabrielle Eitienne knew that a special event was taking shape by the aroma of barbecue sauce simmering in the kitchen. The recipe, passed down from her great-grandfather Andrew J. Woodard, is no ordinary sauce. "It is part of my family's story and spirit," explains Eitienne. "It's not something that we make every day, and it remains one of the most tangible and tasty reminders of the man he was."

Made from an apple cider vinegar base, the sauce is a legacy from one of the most principled and pioneering members of her clan. Woodard earned substantive money by smoking and barbecuing the hogs of his neighbors and friends. As a little girl, Eitienne heard the bright and bombastic stories of her great-grandfather's businesses (he had a day job at a lumber mill and also ran a wildly popular juke joint for some time) from her mother and other relatives who had a front-row seat to his culinary enterprises. "People brought their whole hogs over to my great-granddad, and he would give the meat the star treatment," she says. "That was his specialty, and this sauce sings with how skilled he was."

Passing down these anecdotes and recipes isn't just a personal project for Eitienne; it has become her life's work. As a cultural preservationist, she has made it her mission to uphold and amplify culinary traditions and knowledge from the past, specifically Black foodways. "There's so much practical wisdom to discover from how our ancestors lived and from their contributions to society," she says. "I find a strong sense of my identity and purpose from learning about them, their entrepreneurship, land stewardship, and unfailing sense of community." In Wake County, North Carolina, where she now resides, her direct connection to the place is at least four generations deep. And the presence of all the people who came before her remains her North Star.

Eitienne spent nearly a decade living away from North Carolina, studying film and communications in San Francisco and then working in the fashion industry in New York, but cooking—especially with Southern ingredients—was her passion. She returned home in 2018, looking for a way to unite her love of food with her interest in her family's rich history and ties to the land. Spending time with her grandfather, Mayfield Woodard; her great-uncles; and other elders, Eitienne delved into gardening, food preservation, seedkeeping, and winemaking. She has been unearthing a deeper understanding of her past and documenting the stories along the way.

These experiences blossomed into a broad range of projects—including a short film, recipe development, cooking classes, and community dinners (one of which was featured on the award-winning Netflix series *High on the Hog*). Then during the pandemic, she cofounded a community-supported agriculture (CSA) model called Tall Grass Food Box. The organization supports Black farmers in North Carolina by offering their produce and products in biweekly food subscription boxes for local consumers and businesses to purchase.

Eitienne's annual outdoor farm-to-table equinox suppers, hosted when summer is slowly turning into fall, are another approach she uses to build community. "Preserving Black foodways manifests itself in many different forms," she says. "These suppers serve to protect and propel dreams as well as foster discussions and action."

Around 100 people are seated at long, candlelit communal tables, where the work of farmers, fishers, and vintners is acknowledged and appreciated. Each dish tells a story about her rural Afro-Carolina heritage, a term coined by her friend, folklorist Michelle Lanier. Menus from past meals have included fried porgy with goldenrod hot sauce, hibiscus chowchow, and smoked cantaloupe-buttermilk pie with a cornmeal crust.

And at the heart of each spread is her adapted version of that famous family barbecue sauce: She uses a sorghum syrup to cut down on refined sugar and give it a deeper, naturally sweet profile. In addition to serving it with pork, one of her favorite preparations is to use it to make a smoky mignonette to crown both raw and roasted oysters. "There are a lot of great, happy memories around this sauce," she says.

It's quite common, especially in the South, for families to have a collection of beloved dishes that hold the weight and gaze of their history. For Eitienne, those recipes come alive most when they are anchored to the place and people who have steadfastly shaped and continue to define her course.

Pork Chops with Carolina Barbecue Sauce, Smoked Butter, and Braised Onions

ACTIVE 1 HOUR, 25 MIN. - TOTAL 2 HOURS, 40 MIN., PLUS 12 HOURS MARINATING

SERVES 4

2	Tbsp. black peppercorns
1½	cups apple cider vinegar
¼	cup whole-grain mustard
¾	cup unsalted butter, divided
¾	cup sorghum syrup or light brown sugar
½	cup ketchup or tomato paste
2	Tbsp. crushed red pepper
5	(5-inch) fresh thyme sprigs
1	fresh bay leaf
1	large shallot, grated (1½ Tbsp.)
¼	tsp. grated garlic
1½	Tbsp. kosher salt, divided
4	(1-lb., 2-inch-thick) double-cut bone-in pork chops
¼	tsp. black pepper
½	cup hickory chips
	Braised Onions (recipe follows)

Continued on page 102

> "There's so much practical wisdom to discover from how our ancestors lived and from their contributions to society."

Continued from page 101

1. Heat a medium saucepan over medium. Add black peppercorns; cook, shaking pan occasionally, until toasted and fragrant, about 2 minutes. Transfer to a spice grinder, and let cool slightly, about 5 minutes. Process peppercorns until finely ground, about 15 seconds.

2. Return ground pepper to pan. Add vinegar, mustard, and ¼ cup of the butter. Bring vinegar mixture to a simmer over medium, whisking occasionally. Whisk in sorghum syrup, ketchup, crushed red pepper, thyme, bay leaf, shallot, garlic, and 1 tablespoon of the salt. Cook over medium, whisking constantly, 1 minute. Cover, reduce heat to low, and simmer, stirring occasionally, until flavors meld, about 20 minutes. Uncover; remove from heat. Remove and discard bay leaf. Let sauce cool to room temperature. Reserve ½ cup barbecue sauce in a small bowl for basting. Refrigerate sauce until ready to use.

3. Place pork chops in a baking dish, and add remaining cooled barbecue sauce from pan; turn to coat. Cover; marinate in refrigerator for 12 hours.

4. Remove pork from marinade; discard remaining marinade. Rinse pork under cold water; pat dry, and place on a large plate. Let stand at room temperature 30 minutes. Sprinkle evenly with black pepper and remaining 1½ teaspoons salt.

5. While pork stands, open bottom vent of charcoal grill completely. Light charcoal chimney starter filled with briquettes. When the briquettes are covered with gray ash, pour them onto the bottom grate of the grill, and then push to 1 side of the grill. Coat top grate with oil; place on grill. Cover, and preheat grill for 10 minutes.

6. Place pork chops on oiled grates directly over coals. Grill, uncovered, until pork just begins to brown around edges and along the bones, about 2 minutes per side. Transfer pork to oiled grates over the side without the coals; arrange pork along edges of grill with bones facing coals. Grill, covered, until a thermometer inserted into thickest portion of pork registers 140°F, 25 to 30 minutes, flipping halfway through cook time. During final 5 minutes of cook time, baste pork with reserved barbecue sauce. Transfer pork to a cutting board, and brush with any remaining barbecue sauce. Loosely tent pork with aluminum foil, and let rest 10 minutes. Temperature will continue to rise to 145°F.

7. While pork rests, sprinkle hickory chips over coals. (Chips will flare up for a few minutes.) Place remaining ½ cup butter in a small cast-iron skillet. Place skillet on the grates over the side without the coals. Grill, covered, until butter is melted, foamy, and perfumed with smoke, about 10 minutes. Carefully pour smoked butter into a small heatproof bowl. Serve pork chops with smoked butter and Braised Onions.

Braised Onions
ACTIVE 55 MIN. - TOTAL 55 MIN.
MAKES 3 CUPS

Heat a small Dutch oven over medium. Add 3 large **Vidalia onions** (trimmed and quartered), 1½ Tbsp. **olive oil**, 2 tsp. **kosher salt**, 1½ tsp. **ground nutmeg**, and 1 tsp. **black pepper.** Cook, stirring constantly, until nutmeg is fragrant, about 1 minute. Stir in 1¾ cups **muscadine wine**, 1 Tbsp. **fish sauce**, and 1 Tbsp. **dark molasses.** Bring to a simmer over medium-high. Simmer, stirring occasionally, until onions are tender and wine mixture is reduced and glazes onions, 40 to 45 minutes. Remove from heat. Store, covered, in refrigerator up to 3 days.

Millet Salad with Butter Beans, Okra, and Garlicky Marinated Tomatoes
ACTIVE 45 MIN. - TOTAL 1 HOUR, 20 MIN., PLUS 8 HOURS SOAKING BEANS
SERVES 6 TO 8

- ½ cup dried butter beans
- 1 medium-size red onion, unpeeled
- 3 Tbsp. kosher salt, plus more for salting water
- 1 fresh bay leaf
- 1 cup uncooked millet
- ¼ cup olive oil
- ¼ cup sherry vinegar
- 1 Tbsp. chopped fresh dill, plus fronds for garnish
- 2 tsp. whole-grain mustard
- 2 tsp. honey
- 1 tsp. fresh thyme leaves
- 1 tsp. grated fresh ginger
- ¼ tsp. black pepper
- ¼ tsp. grated garlic
- ½ tsp. fine sea salt, divided
- 1 fresh small Scotch bonnet chile, halved and unseeded
- 4 tomatoes, cored and cut into wedges
- 8 oz. fresh okra, sliced lengthwise (2½ cups)
- Pinch of ground nutmeg

1. Place beans in a medium bowl. Add cold water to cover by 2 inches. Soak 8 to 12 hours; drain and set aside.

2. Cut unpeeled onion in half. Place 1 onion half in a large pot. Add 12 cups water, soaked beans, kosher salt, and bay leaf to onion in pot. Bring to a boil over high. Boil until beans are tender but slightly al dente, 25 to 30 minutes. Drain beans, discarding onion half and bay leaf. Line a baking sheet with parchment paper. Set aside.

3. While bean mixture cooks, bring a large saucepan of lightly salted water to a boil over high. Stir millet into boiling water. Reduce heat to medium, and simmer, stirring occasionally, until millet is tender but slightly al dente, 15 to 20 minutes. Drain millet, and spread evenly over prepared baking sheet. Chill, uncovered, until millet is cold and dry, about 30 minutes. Fluff with a fork.

4. While millet cools, whisk together olive oil, vinegar, chopped fresh dill, mustard, honey, thyme, ginger, black pepper, garlic, and ¼ teaspoon of the fine sea salt in a medium bowl. Add 1 Scotch bonnet chile half, and press on chile with back of spoon to release oils; reserve remaining half for another use. Add tomatoes, and toss to coat. Let marinate at room temperature 20 minutes.

5. Peel and thinly slice remaining onion half; transfer to a large bowl. Stir in beans, millet, okra, and remaining ¼ teaspoon fine sea salt. Using a slotted spoon, add tomatoes to millet; toss to coat. Drizzle evenly with tomato-marinating liquid. Garnish with nutmeg and dill fronds.

MILLET SALAD WITH
BUTTER BEANS,
OKRA, AND GARLICKY
MARINATED TOMATOES

Survival of the Sweetest

For more than a century, the family-run honey business L.L. Lanier and Son's has kept bees, which derive this prized delicacy from Florida's tupelo trees

THE SMALL WHITE BLOSSOMS of the tupelo trees blow in the breeze along the Chipola River, a tributary of the Apalachicola in the swamps of Northwest Florida. This river valley (not Elvis' hometown of Tupelo, Mississippi) is the hub for production of the rare honey, the sweetness of which you might recall from a Van Morrison song.

Tupelo honey has a reputation that precedes it. Known to sell for more than $13 per pound, it has graced the shelves of Neiman Marcus and even inspired the film *Ulee's Gold*, starring Peter Fonda as a beekeeper in the region. This isn't your ordinary honey—it is lauded around the world for its buttery richness and mild floral taste, which some say has hints of cinnamon and citrus. Pale gold with a greenish tinge, it has a special chemistry that prevents it from crystallizing, which is one way you can tell whether it is genuine.

In Wewahitchka, Florida, a small town of about 2,000 people that borders the Chipola River, the Lanier family has been harvesting tupelo honey for 125 years. The business is now in the hands of the fifth generation, Ben Lanier and his wife, Glynnis, who served as

consultants on the movie and lent their land to Hollywood for filming. Their son, Heath, is training to take over soon, but this is a fickle business. From the strength of the beehives to the weather, which oscillates between too wet and too dry, the harvest fluctuates. "You're at the mercy of everything," says Glynnis. "And then you don't get another chance for 365 days," adds Ben.

Much like the fragile tupelo blossoms, the ecosystem required to make the precious honey is delicate. Around 2 million tupelo tree flowers are needed for just 1 pound of the honey, and a single bee produces only about $\frac{1}{12}$ teaspoon in its lifetime. Both the bees and the trees have faced many hurdles. In 2018, Hurricane Michael devastated swaths of tupelo trees (including those of the Laniers), which are still recuperating. Glynnis hopes that within the next two years the trees will return to normal.

The region's growth is also providing its own challenges. Corporate developers seeking to convert the land into prime real estate have contributed to the draining of the wetlands, which has also impacted the oyster industry. Pesticides, many of which kill bees,

are increasingly sprayed to keep the mosquitoes at bay as temperatures climb and more people move to this part of the state.

Then there's the labor—both human and insect—required to make tupelo honey. Bees feed off the short-lived flowers that bloom for around two weeks, maybe two and a half if they're lucky, and then deposit nectar in wooden boxes that are filled with frames lined with a honeycomb interior. The Laniers later extract the frames to harvest the honey. When it's bottled, it appears clear except for a few black flecks (remnants of beeswax and pollen), which indicate that the honey is unprocessed—it gets strained but never heated.

Extracting this rare sweetener is a tenuous act, as the honey stores must be stripped at the first sign of tupelo blossoms to prevent cross contamination. Beekeepers must closely monitor the blooms to minimize the chance of other flowers' nectars mixing in. "I clean my hives out twice before I let the bees fill them up with tupelo

Continued on page 106

Golden Nectar

Order from these Southern producers, and savor one of the most sought-after honeys in the world

L.L. Lanier & Son's Tupelo Honey
The Lanier family has been producing honey since the late 1800s. From $9; lltupelohoney.com

Savannah Bee Company
Founder Ted Dennard was introduced to beekeeping at just 12 years old, leading to a lifelong passion for cultivating rare honeys. From $10; savannahbee.com

Smiley Honey
In 1989, Donald Smiley started this operation in a humble garage. Since then, it has grown into a renowned source for tupelo honey. From $3; smileyhoney.com

HONEYBEE
CUPCAKES (PAGE 109)

Continued from page 104

nectar. That means they make less honey, but it's a purer product," says Ben. Like his father and grandfather before him, he focuses on quality and not quantity.

To ensure the highest caliber, Ben's grandfather Lavernor Laveon Lanier Sr. helped develop tupelo honey certification, but over time, the standards have relaxed. Today, any product that contains at least 50% tupelo pollen can be labeled as tupelo honey. That percentage is determined through a pollen analysis, but that still leaves room for less-than-pure options to hit the market. "Do you want to buy 50% of anything? I don't think so," says Glynnis.

Producing true tupelo honey is akin to mining for gold. Much like the precious metal, it's laborious to extract and its quality varies. "The salvation is, if people ever taste our honey, they'll know the difference. They won't be fooled," says Ben. If you're lucky enough to get your hands on the good stuff, savor it and use it wisely. These dessert recipes can be made with any type of honey, but they become truly incredible when drizzled with a little bit of the tupelo kind.

Salted Honey Pie

This dessert is similar to a chess pie in texture and has a buttery sweetness that's balanced by a sprinkling of flaky sea salt. A light-color honey, such as clover or orange blossom, gives the filling a beautiful golden color.

ACTIVE 20 MIN. - TOTAL 1 HOUR, 35 MIN., PLUS 2 HOURS COOLING

SERVES 8

CRUST

- 1¼ cups all-purpose flour, plus more for work surface
- 1 tsp. honey
- 1 tsp. kosher salt
- ½ cup cold unsalted butter, cubed
- 2-3 Tbsp. ice water

FILLING

- 1 cup honey
- ½ cup unsalted butter, melted
- ½ cup granulated sugar
- 2 Tbsp. all-purpose flour
- 2 Tbsp. plain yellow cornmeal
- ½ tsp. kosher salt
- 4 large eggs
- ½ cup heavy whipping cream
- 1 Tbsp. white vinegar

ADDITIONAL INGREDIENTS

- Unsweetened whipped cream
- Tupelo honey
- Flaky sea salt

1. Prepare the Crust: Preheat oven to 350°F. Pulse together flour, honey, and salt in a food processor until combined, about 5 pulses. Add butter, and pulse until texture is similar to coarse meal, about 10 pulses. With processor running, drizzle in ice water, 1 tablespoon at a time, through food chute until dough just begins to clump together. Transfer to a floured work surface, and knead dough until it just comes together. Form into a disk, and tightly wrap in plastic wrap. Refrigerate until firm, about 30 minutes.
2. Roll out chilled dough on a lightly floured work surface into a 12-inch round. Place in an ungreased 9-inch pie plate, pressing dough into bottom and sides of pie plate; fold excess dough under edges, and crimp as desired. Freeze until ready to use.
3. Prepare the Filling: Whisk together honey, butter, sugar, flour, cornmeal, and salt in a large bowl until combined. Add eggs, whisking until smooth. Add cream and vinegar, whisking until combined. Pour Filling into frozen Crust.
4. Bake in preheated oven until edges are puffed and center jiggles slightly, 45 to 55 minutes, tenting edges with aluminum foil to prevent excess browning, if needed. Let cool to room temperature on a wire rack, about 2 hours. Garnish with whipped cream, tupelo honey, and flaky sea salt.

> "I clean my hives out twice before I let the bees fill them up with tupelo nectar. That means they make less honey, but it's a purer product."—Ben Lanier

NO-BAKE
HONEY
CHEESECAKE

No-Bake Honey Cheesecake

To create an extra-pretty presentation, use a small offset spatula or butter knife to swirl the top of the cheesecake. Drizzle on the tupelo honey, if desired, just before serving. (The extra moisture can make the top of the cheesecake crack.)

ACTIVE 20 MIN. - TOTAL 1 HOUR, 20 MIN., PLUS 3 HOURS CHILLING

SERVES 12

CRUST
- 2 cups cinnamon graham cracker crumbs (from 14 graham cracker sheets)
- ½ cup butter, melted
- ¼ cup firmly packed light brown sugar

FILLING
- 1 cup honey
- 1¼ cups heavy whipping cream
- 3 (8-oz.) pkg. cream cheese, at room temperature
- ¼ cup sour cream
- 1 Tbsp. fresh lemon juice (from 1 lemon)

ADDITIONAL INGREDIENT
Tupelo honey (optional)

1. Prepare the Crust: Coat a 9-inch springform pan with cooking spray. Stir together graham cracker crumbs, butter, and brown sugar in a medium bowl until combined. Press into bottom and sides of prepared springform pan. Freeze until firm and ready to use, at least 30 minutes.
2. Prepare the Filling: Bring honey to a boil in a medium saucepan over medium. Cook, stirring constantly, until honey is a medium-brown color, 3 to 4 minutes. Remove from heat. Let cool to room temperature, about 1 hour.
3. Beat cream in a medium bowl with an electric mixer on high speed until stiff peaks form, 2 to 3 minutes. Set aside.
4. Beat cream cheese in a large bowl with an electric mixer on medium speed until smooth and creamy, about 2 minutes. Add sour cream, lemon juice, and cooled honey; beat until smooth, about 30 seconds. Fold in whipped cream. Spoon mixture into chilled Crust. Cover with plastic wrap, and refrigerate until firm, at least 3 hours or up to 12 hours. Serve slices cold; drizzle with tupelo honey, if desired.

Honeybee Cupcakes

(Photo, page 105)

When topped with edible flowers and a light drizzle of honey, these cupcakes make a special treat for spring birthdays or other celebrations.

ACTIVE 20 MIN. - TOTAL 40 MIN., PLUS 1 HOUR COOLING

SERVES 12

CUPCAKES
- 1¾ cups all-purpose flour
- 1½ tsp. baking powder
- ½ tsp. kosher salt
- ½ cup granulated sugar
- ½ cup butter, softened
- 2 large eggs
- ½ cup honey
- 1 Tbsp. grated lemon zest (from 2 large lemons)
- ½ cup whole milk

BUTTERCREAM
- ¾ cup butter, softened
- 1½ cups powdered sugar
- ¼ cup plus 2 Tbsp. tupelo honey
- ¼ cup plus 2 Tbsp. heavy whipping cream

ADDITIONAL INGREDIENT
Edible flowers

1. Prepare the Cupcakes: Preheat oven to 350°F. Line a 12-cup muffin tray with 12 paper liners.
2. Stir together flour, baking powder, and salt in a medium bowl until combined. Beat sugar and butter in a large bowl with an electric mixer until light and fluffy, 3 to 4 minutes. Add eggs, 1 at a time, beating well after each addition. Add honey and lemon zest, beating until combined. With mixer on low speed, add flour mixture, alternately with whole milk, beating well after each addition. Spoon evenly into prepared paper liners.
3. Bake in preheated oven until a wooden pick inserted into centers of Cupcakes comes out clean, 18 to 20 minutes. Transfer to a wire rack, and let cool completely, about 1 hour.
4. Prepare the Buttercream: Beat butter in a large bowl with an electric mixer on high speed until creamy, about 2 minutes. With mixer on low speed, gradually add powdered sugar, tupelo honey, and heavy cream. Increase mixer speed to high, and beat until fluffy, 2 to 3 minutes. Pipe or spoon onto cooled Cupcakes. Garnish with edible flowers.

Chill & Grill

Dinners are a breeze with make-ahead marinades and flavor-packed dry rubs

Sweet-and-Smoky Grilled Pork Tenderloins

ACTIVE 30 MIN. - TOTAL 1 HOUR, 15 MIN., PLUS 8 HOURS CHILLING

SERVES 4

- ⅓ cup packed brown sugar
- 2 Tbsp. kosher salt
- 1 tsp. smoked paprika
- ½ tsp. onion powder
- ½ tsp. garlic powder
- ½ tsp. ground mustard
- 2 (1-lb.) pork tenderloins
- 1 Tbsp. canola oil

1. Place a wire rack inside a rimmed baking sheet, and set aside. Whisk together brown sugar, salt, smoked paprika, onion powder, garlic powder, and ground mustard in a small bowl. Pour sugar mixture into a gallon-size zip-top plastic bag, add pork, and seal well. Shake bag until pork is coated. Let stand 5 minutes; shake bag again to coat pork. Remove pork from bag, and transfer to prepared rack; discard sugar mixture. Refrigerate, uncovered, 8 to 12 hours.
2. Remove pork from refrigerator; let stand at room temperature 30 minutes. Gently brush pork with oil (do not brush off dry rub). Preheat grill to medium-high heat (400˚F to 450˚F).
3. Place pork on oiled grates; grill, uncovered, turning occasionally, until charred in spots and an instant-read thermometer inserted into thickest portion of pork registers 140˚F, 15 to 20 minutes. Remove from grill; let stand 15 minutes. (Temperature will rise to 145˚F.) Slice and serve with Corn-and-Tomato Salad.

Corn-and-Tomato Salad

ACTIVE 15 MIN. - TOTAL 15 MIN.
SERVES 4

Whisk together 1 Tbsp. each **extra-virgin olive oil**, **lime juice**, and **mayonnaise** and ¾ tsp. **kosher salt** in a medium bowl. Remove kernels from 4 ears **yellow corn**, and add to bowl with dressing. Add 1 cup halved **cherry tomatoes**, ¾ cup crumbled **Cotija cheese**, and 2 Tbsp. chopped **fresh cilantro**. Toss to combine.

Cheesy Mushroom Sliders

ACTIVE 30 MIN. · TOTAL 30 MIN.,
PLUS 8 HOURS CHILLING

SERVES 4

16 large (1 oz. each) cremini
   (baby portobello) mushrooms,
   stemmed and gills removed
1 tsp. adobo seasoning
½ cup mayonnaise
1 Tbsp. adobo sauce plus 1 tsp.
   finely chopped chipotle chile
   (from 1 [7-oz.] can chipotle chile in
   adobo sauce)
½ tsp. garlic powder
2 Swiss cheese slices, quartered
8 slider buns, split
8 dill pickle chips

1. Place mushrooms on a large rimmed
baking sheet, and season both sides
evenly with adobo seasoning. Refrigerate,
uncovered, cavity sides up, 8 to 12 hours.
2. Stir together mayonnaise, adobo
sauce and chopped chipotle chile, and
garlic powder in a bowl; cover and
refrigerate until ready to use.

3. Preheat a grill to medium-high (400°F
to 450°F). Gently pat mushrooms dry with
paper towels (do not remove seasoning).
Place mushrooms, cap sides down, on
oiled grates. Grill, uncovered, turning
occasionally, until tender and charred in
spots, 4 to 6 minutes. Flip all mushrooms
so caps are facing up. Top half of
mushrooms with 1 cheese slice quarter.
Cover grill, and cook, undisturbed, until
cheese melts, about 30 seconds. Set
mushrooms aside; turn off grill.
4. Place slider buns, cut sides down,
on grill, and toast with residual heat
for 1 minute. Remove from grill. Stack
2 mushrooms on each bun bottom;
top each with 1 pickle. Spread about
½ tablespoon reserved chipotle
mayonnaise onto cut sides of bun tops.
Place bun tops on sliders. Serve with
Spiced-Up Shoestring Fries.

Spiced-Up
Shoestring Fries

ACTIVE 10 MIN. · TOTAL 30 MIN.
SERVES 4

Whisk together ½ tsp. each ground
cumin, chili powder, garlic powder,
and **kosher salt** in a large bowl. Spread
14 oz. frozen **shoestring fries** evenly on
a large baking sheet. Bake at 450°F until
browned and crispy, about 20 minutes,
tossing halfway through with 1 tsp. of
the spice mixture. Remove fries from
oven; coat with **cooking spray.** Add fries
to remaining spice mixture, and toss
to coat. Serve with additional **chipotle
mayonnaise,** if desired.

Grilled Flank Steak with Chimichurri

ACTIVE 40 MIN. - TOTAL 1 HOUR, 25 MIN.,
PLUS 4 HOURS CHILLING

SERVES 4

- 1½ cups packed fresh cilantro leaves and stems
- 1 cup packed fresh flat-leaf parsley leaves and stems
- 3 Tbsp. red wine vinegar
- 2 Tbsp. chopped fresh oregano
- 6 medium garlic cloves, chopped (2 Tbsp.)
- 5 drained anchovy fillets, chopped (about 2 tsp., optional)
- 1 medium-size red Fresno chile, stemmed, seeded, and chopped (1½ Tbsp.)
- 1¾ tsp. kosher salt, divided
- ½ cup extra-virgin olive oil, divided
- 1 (1½-lb.) flank steak (¾ to 1 inch thick)

1. Place cilantro, parsley, vinegar, oregano, garlic, anchovies (if using), chile, and 1 teaspoon of the salt in a food processor; pulse until very finely chopped, 10 to 15 pulses, stopping to scrape down sides. With processor running, gradually pour 6 tablespoons of the oil through food chute; process until smooth, about 10 seconds. Spoon ¼ cup of the chimichurri into a large zip-top plastic bag. Refrigerate remaining chimichurri in an airtight container up to 1 day.

2. Add steak and remaining 2 tablespoons oil to bag with chimichurri. Seal bag, and massage to distribute marinade. Refrigerate 4 to 12 hours.

3. Let steak stand at room temperature 30 minutes. Preheat grill to high (450°F to 500°F). Remove steak from bag, and discard marinade. Sprinkle evenly with remaining ¾ teaspoon salt.

4. Place steak on oiled grates, and grill, uncovered, turning occasionally, until an instant-read thermometer inserted into thickest portion of steak registers 125°F, 10 to 12 minutes. Transfer to a cutting board; let rest 15 minutes. Slice steak against the grain, and serve with reserved chimichurri and Heirloom-Tomato Salad.

Heirloom-Tomato Salad

ACTIVE 10 MIN. - TOTAL 10 MIN.

SERVES 4

Whisk together 2 Tbsp. **apple cider vinegar**, 2 tsp. **Dijon mustard**, 1 tsp. **kosher salt**, and ½ tsp. each **black pepper** and **honey** in a small bowl. Gradually whisk in 2 Tbsp. **extra-virgin olive oil**. Stir in 1 finely chopped **shallot**. Cut 4 small **heirloom tomatoes** into wedges, and arrange on a serving platter. Spoon dressing over tomatoes; top with **fresh basil leaves**.

Bourbon- and Cola-Glazed Steak Kebabs

ACTIVE 45 MIN. - TOTAL 45 MIN., PLUS 4 HOURS CHILLING

SERVES 4

- 1 cup cola soft drink
- ¾ cup bourbon
- 2 Tbsp. brown sugar
- 2 Tbsp. Worcestershire sauce
- 2 tsp. balsamic vinegar
- 2 tsp. kosher salt, divided
- 2 lb. boneless rib-eye steaks, trimmed and cut into 1-inch pieces
- ½ tsp. black pepper
- 1½ Tbsp. cold unsalted butter

1. Whisk together cola, bourbon, brown sugar, Worcestershire sauce, balsamic vinegar, and 1 teaspoon of the kosher salt in a medium bowl until sugar has dissolved. Place steak pieces in a large zip-top plastic freezer bag. Pour 1 cup of the cola mixture over steak; seal bag, and refrigerate 4 to 12 hours. Refrigerate remaining cola mixture in an airtight container until ready to use.

2. Remove steak from refrigerator; let stand at room temperature 30 minutes. Preheat grill to high (450°F to 500°F). Remove steak from marinade, and place on a paper towel–lined plate; discard marinade. Thread steak onto 8 skewers. Pat kebabs dry with paper towels, and sprinkle with pepper and remaining 1 teaspoon kosher salt. Place kebabs on oiled grates. Grill, uncovered, turning every 2 minutes, until steak is medium-rare and charred on all sides, about 8 minutes. Remove to a plate, and cover loosely with aluminum foil. Let rest 15 minutes.

3. Meanwhile, pour reserved cola mixture into a small saucepan, and bring to a boil over medium-high. Reduce heat to medium, and simmer, stirring occasionally, until mixture is reduced to about ¼ cup, 10 to 12 minutes. Stir in butter, and continue to cook over medium, stirring often, until sauce thickens slightly and lightly coats the back of a spoon, 1 to 2 minutes. Drizzle sauce over kebabs. Serve with Smashed-Cucumber Salad.

Smashed-Cucumber Salad

ACTIVE 10 MIN. - TOTAL 25 MIN.
SERVES 4

Cut 6 **Persian cucumbers** in half lengthwise. Place cucumbers cut sides down; smash with a rolling pin until slightly flattened but still intact. Cut into 1-inch pieces; place in a large bowl with ¼ cup thinly sliced **red onion**, 1 tsp. **kosher salt,** and ½ tsp. **sugar;** toss to coat. Let stand 15 minutes. Pour off any liquid and discard. Add 2 Tbsp. each **olive oil** and **whole-grain mustard** and 1 Tbsp. **sherry vinegar;** toss to coat.

Grilled Chicken Legs with White Barbecue Sauce

ACTIVE 40 MIN. - TOTAL 1 HOUR, 25 MIN., PLUS 12 HOURS CHILLING

SERVES 4

- 1 cup mayonnaise
- 3 Tbsp. dill pickle brine
- 1½ Tbsp. white vinegar
- 1½ Tbsp. Worcestershire sauce
- 1 tsp. garlic powder
- ½ tsp. granulated sugar
- ¼ tsp. smoked paprika
- 2 tsp. kosher salt, divided
- 1 tsp. black pepper, divided
- 4 (12-oz.) chicken-leg quarters

1. Whisk mayonnaise, pickle brine, vinegar, Worcestershire sauce, 1 tablespoon water, garlic powder, sugar, smoked paprika, 1 teaspoon of the salt, and ½ teaspoon of the pepper together in a small bowl until smooth. Transfer ½ cup of the sauce to a large zip-top plastic freezer bag, and add chicken. Seal bag; massage to distribute marinade. Chill 12 to 24 hours. Refrigerate remaining sauce in an airtight container up to 4 days.
2. Remove chicken from refrigerator; let stand at room temperature 30 minutes. Preheat grill to high (450°F to 500°F). Remove chicken from marinade, letting excess drip off; discard marinade. Sprinkle both sides of chicken with remaining 1 teaspoon salt and ½ teaspoon pepper. Place chicken, skin sides down, on oiled grates; grill, uncovered, until grill marks appear and skin starts to turn golden, about 4 minutes. Flip chicken; close grill. Reduce heat to medium (350°F to 400°F), and cook, undisturbed, until a thermometer inserted into thickest portion of thigh registers 155°F, 15 to 20 minutes.
3. Spoon 2 tablespoons of reserved sauce into a small bowl, and brush over skin sides of chicken. Flip chicken, and continue to cook until a thermometer inserted into thickest portion of thigh registers 165°F, 2 to 4 minutes. Remove chicken from grill, and let rest 15 minutes. Serve with reserved sauce and Sweet Potato-and-Cabbage Slaw.

Sweet Potato-and-Cabbage Slaw

ACTIVE 15 MIN. - TOTAL 15 MIN.
SERVES 4

Whisk together ¼ cup **lime juice**, 3 Tbsp. **olive oil**, ½ Tbsp. **pure maple syrup**, and 1 tsp. **kosher salt** in a large bowl. Peel 1 medium-size **sweet potato**, and grate on large holes of a box grater; place in bowl with dressing. Add 2 cups shredded **red cabbage**, ½ cup thinly sliced **scallions**, and ½ cup **roasted salted pepitas**; toss to combine.

Better Beans

A wholesome take on the potluck staple

Smoky-Sweet Baked Beans

Thanks to grated sweet potato, this side has far less refined sugar than traditional recipes.

ACTIVE 30 MIN. - TOTAL 1 HOUR, 40 MIN.

SERVES 8

- 3 slices center-cut bacon
- 1½ cups finely chopped sweet onion (from 1 medium onion)
- 3 tsp. kosher salt, divided
- 1 cup grated peeled sweet potato (from 1 small sweet potato)
- 1 (15-oz.) can no-salt-added tomato sauce
- 4 tsp. Dijon mustard
- 2 tsp. smoked paprika
- 4 (15-oz.) cans no-salt-added navy beans, drained and rinsed
- 2 cups unsalted chicken stock
- ¼ cup unsulphured molasses
- 3 Tbsp. apple cider vinegar
- 2 Tbsp. lower-sodium Worcestershire sauce
- 1 Tbsp. unsalted butter

1. Preheat oven to 350°F. Place bacon in a large ovenproof saucepan or Dutch oven. Cook over medium, turning occasionally, until fat has rendered and bacon is crisp, 5 to 7 minutes. Transfer bacon to a paper towel–lined plate; discard drippings in pan.

2. Add onion and ½ teaspoon of the salt to pan. Cook over medium-low, stirring occasionally, until golden brown and caramelized, 15 to 20 minutes, adding 1 to 2 tablespoons water at a time, as needed, if onion starts to stick to bottom of pan. Add sweet potato, and increase heat to medium-high; cook, stirring frequently, until sweet potato is softened, 5 minutes. Add tomato sauce, mustard, paprika, and remaining 2½ teaspoons salt; cook over medium-high, stirring frequently, until sauce thickens slightly, about 3 minutes. Add beans, chicken stock, molasses, vinegar, Worcestershire sauce, and butter; stir until combined.

3. Cover pan, and bake in preheated oven until beans are just starting to bubble around edges, about 35 minutes. Uncover, and bake until caramelized on top and around edges, 25 to 30 minutes. Let stand 10 minutes; transfer to a serving dish, if desired. Crumble bacon, and sprinkle over beans. Store leftovers in an airtight container in refrigerator up to 3 days.

GOOD FOR YOU!
Rich in vitamins A and C, sweet potatoes are also high in potassium and fiber, which can improve blood pressure and gut health, respectively.

Before Recipe Makeover:

CALORIES: **357** – SUGAR: **28 G** – FAT: **7 G**

After Recipe Makeover:

CALORIES: **285** – SUGAR: **11 G** – FAT: **3 G**

You're So Sweet!

An impressively simple Danish for Mother's Day

Quick and Easy Cream Cheese Danish

ACTIVE 50 MIN. - TOTAL 1 HOUR, 55 MIN.

SERVES 8

- 1 (8-oz.) pkg. cream cheese, at room temperature
- 3 Tbsp. granulated sugar
- 1 tsp. vanilla extract
- ½ tsp. grated lemon zest
- 3 Tbsp. apple jelly
- ½ tsp. warm water, if needed
- 1 (17.3-oz.) pkg. frozen puff pastry sheets, thawed
  All-purpose flour, for surface
- 2 (6-oz.) pkg. fresh raspberries or blackberries or 2 thinly sliced plums or peaches
- 1 large egg, lightly beaten
- 1½ cups powdered sugar
- 2½ Tbsp. fresh lemon juice, divided (from 2 medium lemons)
- ¼ cup toasted sliced almonds or chopped pecans

PLAY IT COOL
Puff pastry is much easier to handle when it's cold. Use one sheet at a time, and keep the other refrigerated while you work.

1. Preheat oven to 400°F. Stir together cream cheese, granulated sugar, vanilla, and lemon zest in a medium bowl until smooth, and set aside. Whisk apple jelly in a separate medium bowl until mostly smooth, adding ½ teaspoon warm water, if needed. Set aside.

2. Unfold 1 puff pastry sheet on a lightly floured surface. Roll into a 10- x 11-inch rectangle; cut into quarters. Place pastry rectangles ½ inch apart on a parchment paper–lined rimmed baking sheet.

3. Prick centers of dough rectangles with a fork several times, leaving a ½-inch border. Spread half of the cream cheese mixture within the border (about 2 tablespoons per rectangle).

4. Arrange half of your desired fruit over the cream cheese–topped dough rectangles. Spoon half of apple jelly over fruit. Brush pastry edges with beaten egg.

5. Bake in preheated oven until edges and bottoms are golden brown, 22 to 30 minutes, covering loosely with foil during last 5 minutes of baking to prevent overbrowning, if needed. Let cool on pan 10 minutes. Repeat with the remaining puff pastry sheet, cream cheese mixture, fruit, apple jelly, and beaten egg.

6. Add powdered sugar to a medium bowl; gradually stir in 2 tablespoons of the lemon juice, adding remaining ½ tablespoon lemon juice as needed until smooth. Drizzle glaze over pastries; sprinkle with almonds or pecans.

PICK A FAVORITE
Customize these pretty pastries with the fruit Mom likes best.

Road Trip Ready

Delicious mixes for all your upcoming travels

Chocolate-Coconut-Pretzel Granola

ACTIVE 5 MIN. - TOTAL 50 MIN.
SERVES 8

Stir together 3 cups **oats-and-honey granola clusters**, 2 cups **miniature pretzels**, ¼ cup **light brown sugar**, and ¼ cup melted **coconut oil** in a large bowl. Whisk 1 **large egg white** until frothy; stir into granola mixture. Spread mixture in an even layer on a parchment paper-lined rimmed baking sheet; bake at 300°F until crisp, about 25 minutes, stirring once. Remove from oven; sprinkle 1 cup **coconut chips** and 1 cup **dark chocolate chips** over granola mixture; do not stir. Let cool completely; break into clusters.

Cheese Lover's Snack Mix

ACTIVE 5 MIN. - TOTAL 30 MIN.
SERVES 6

Stir together 3 cups **bite-size Cheddar cheese crackers**, 2 cups **fish-shape Cheddar cheese crackers**, 1 cup **miniature saltine crackers**, ½ cup **canola oil**, 1 Tbsp. **ranch dressing mix**, 2 tsp. **smoked paprika**, 1 tsp. **garlic powder**, and 1 tsp. **cayenne pepper** in a large bowl. Spread mixture in an even layer on a rimmed baking sheet; bake at 250°F until crisp, about 15 minutes. Let cool 10 minutes.

Charcuterie-Board Snack Mix

ACTIVE 5 MIN. - TOTAL 25 MIN.
SERVES 8

Place 6 **prosciutto slices** on a parchment paper-lined baking sheet, spacing evenly apart. Bake at 375°F until crisp, 10 to 15 minutes. Let cool completely; break into bite-size pieces. Stir together prosciutto; 2 cups broken **cranberry-hazelnut gourmet crackers** (such as Lesley Stowe Raincoast Crisps); 1 cup **smoked almonds;** 1 cup **salted, roasted shelled pistachios;** and 1 cup halved **dried Mission figs** in a large bowl. Stir in 1 cup broken **Parmesan cheese crisps** just before serving.

Easy-Peasy Lemon Bars

Our simplest (and best) recipe ever, plus two new flavor ideas

Get Fancy

For the neatest bars, wipe the knife's blade with a damp paper towel after each slice.

Pistachio Lemon Bars

Prepare recipe as directed through Step 5. After cutting in Step 6, top bars evenly with ¼ cup chopped **pistachios** and 1 Tbsp. **lemon zest.** Dust lightly with **powdered sugar.**

Blackberry-Mint Lemon Bars

Prepare recipe as directed through Step 5. While bars cool, combine 2 cups **blackberries**, 2 Tbsp. **granulated sugar,** 1 Tbsp. **lemon juice,** and a pinch of **salt** in a small saucepan. Cook over medium-high, stirring often, until berries are jammy, about 20 minutes. Let cool to room temperature, 20 to 30 minutes. After cutting bars in Step 6, spoon berries over top, omitting powdered sugar. Garnish with **fresh mint leaves.**

Classic Lemon Bars

ACTIVE 20 MIN. - TOTAL 1 HOUR, 10 MIN., PLUS 1 HOUR, 30 MIN. CHILLING

MAKES 16

- 1½ cups all-purpose flour, divided
- 1 cup granulated sugar, divided
- ½ cup butter, cubed and softened
- ¼ tsp. kosher salt
- 6 large eggs, at room temperature
- 1 cup fresh lemon juice (from 6 large lemons)
- 1 Tbsp. grated lemon zest
-   Powdered sugar

1. Preheat oven to 350°F with rack in center position. Coat an 8-inch square baking pan with cooking spray; line bottom and sides with parchment paper, leaving a 1-inch overhang.
2. Stir together 1 cup of the flour and ¼ cup of the granulated sugar in a medium bowl. Add butter. Work butter into flour mixture, using your fingers, until a shaggy dough forms and no large chunks remain, about 1 minute. (Mixture should hold together when squeezed.)

Press evenly into bottom and about ½ inch up sides of prepared pan. Bake, uncovered, in preheated oven until lightly browned, 20 to 25 minutes.
3. Meanwhile, whisk together remaining ½ cup flour, ¾ cup granulated sugar, and salt in a large bowl. Add eggs and lemon juice, whisking mixture just until combined. Pour through a fine mesh strainer into a large bowl, using a spatula to press mixture through strainer. Discard solids. Whisk in grated lemon zest.
4. Reduce oven temperature to 300°F. Carefully pour filling over crust. Bake, uncovered, until filling is set around edges and jiggles slightly in center, 20 to 25 minutes.
5. Transfer to a wire rack, and let cool 20 minutes. Cover with plastic wrap, and refrigerate until filling is completely set, 1 hour, 30 minutes to 3 hours.
6. Carefully lift bars up and out of baking pan, using parchment paper as handles. Transfer to a cutting board. Cut into squares. Sprinkle lemon bars with powdered sugar just before serving.

COOKING SCHOOL

Super Soakers

Kick up your grilling game by pairing these bold marinades with just about any protein

Orange Shallot

The citrus notes taste great with shrimp, chicken, and pork.

MAKES 1¼ CUPS

Whisk 1 cup **orange juice**, ¼ cup finely chopped **shallot**, 2½ Tbsp. **chile-lime seasoning** (such as Tajín), 1 Tbsp. **honey mustard**, and 1 tsp. **salt** in a medium bowl until blended.

Hot Pepper Jelly

Reserve ½ cup to use as a finishing glaze or sauce.

MAKES 1½ CUPS

Whisk together 1 cup **hot pepper jelly**, ¼ cup **apple cider vinegar**, 3 Tbsp. **oil**, 2 tsp. each **smoked paprika** and **salt**, and 1 tsp. **cayenne pepper** in a medium microwave-safe bowl. Microwave on HIGH until melted and smooth, whisking halfway through, about 1 minute.

Scallion Herb

Double this recipe, and save half for serving.

MAKES 1¼ CUPS

Stir together ⅓ cup sliced **scallions**, ½ cup each **olive oil** and chopped **mixed fresh herbs** (such as parsley, oregano, thyme, and/or cilantro), ⅓ cup **rice vinegar**, 2 tsp. grated **lime zest**, 3 Tbsp. **fresh lime juice**, 2 tsp. **kosher salt**, and ½ tsp. **black pepper** in a medium bowl until blended.

Soy Lime

Add a zippy teriyaki flavor to steak, salmon, or chicken.

MAKES 1¼ CUPS

Whisk together ½ cup **soy sauce**; ¼ cup each packed **light brown sugar, fresh lime juice,** and **olive oil**; and 3 Tbsp. **Sriracha chile sauce** in a medium bowl until blended.

TIMING IS EVERYTHING

Follow these guidelines to never under- or over-marinate food again

SHELLFISH
15 minutes

FISH
20 to 30 minutes

PORK
3 to 12 hours

CHICKEN
3 to 12 hours

BEEF AND LAMB
3 to 24 hours

June–July

Crunch Time

Slathered with spicy mayo, this decadent sandwich is the best way to celebrate soft-shell crab season

QUICK START
Although you can clean live soft-shell crabs yourself, it's not a job for the faint of heart. We recommend buying them freshly cleaned and cooking them within two hours of purchase.

Cornmeal-Crusted Soft-Shell Crab Sandwiches

ACTIVE 20 MIN. · TOTAL 30 MIN.
SERVES 4

Whisk together 1 **large egg**, 1 cup **whole buttermilk**, 1 Tbsp. **hot sauce**, and ½ tsp. **kosher salt** in a large shallow bowl. Add 4 cleaned **soft-shell crabs** (about ¾ lb. total). Turn to coat; set aside. Stir together ½ cup **mayonnaise**; ¼ cup chopped **pepperoncini**; and 1 Tbsp. each **pepperoncini pickling liquid**, chopped fresh **chives**, and chopped fresh **dill** in a medium bowl. Set aside. Stir together 1 cup **fine yellow cornmeal**, ½ cup **all-purpose flour**, and ½ tsp. **kosher salt** in a shallow dish; set aside. Heat ½ cup **canola oil** in a large cast-iron skillet over medium-high until shimmering. Remove 1 crab from buttermilk mixture, letting excess drip off. Transfer to cornmeal mixture; turn to fully coat. Gently place in hot oil. Repeat with the remaining crabs. Cook until golden and crispy, 6 to 8 minutes, turning once halfway through cook time. Transfer fried crabs to a paper towel-lined baking sheet. Sprinkle evenly with ¼ tsp. **kosher salt**. Spread cut sides of 4 split **brioche burger buns** with mayonnaise mixture. Top bottom bun halves with 1 cup **shredded iceberg lettuce**, sliced **beefsteak tomato**, and fried crabs. Replace top bun halves. Serve immediately.

Thrill of the Grill

Sliced, stuffed, or skewered, flank steak is a secret weapon for summer entertaining

Spice-Rubbed Flank Steak with Corn-Chile Relish

ACTIVE 40 MIN. - TOTAL 40 MIN.
SERVES 4

- 3 ears fresh corn
- 1 large poblano chile
- 3 large scallions
- 2 tsp. light brown sugar
- 2 tsp. ancho chile powder
- ½ tsp. ground cumin
- ¼ tsp. ground coriander
- 2¾ tsp. kosher salt, divided
- 1 (1½-lb.) flank steak (¾ inch thick), excess fat trimmed
- 3 Tbsp. olive oil, divided
- 3 Tbsp. fresh lime juice (from 2 limes)
- 1 Tbsp. seeded and finely chopped jalapeño chile (from 1 small chile)
- ½ tsp. black pepper

1. Preheat grill to high (450°F to 500°F). Place corn, poblano chile, and scallions on oiled grates. Grill, uncovered, turning occasionally, until corn kernels and scallions are tender and charred in spots and chile is charred all over, about 3 minutes for scallions and about 15 minutes for chile and corn. Transfer grilled chile to a small bowl, and cover tightly with plastic wrap. Let stand 15 minutes.
2. While chile cools, stir together brown sugar, chile powder, cumin, coriander, and 2 teaspoons of the salt in a small bowl. Rub mixture evenly over steak, pressing to adhere. Drizzle 2 tablespoons of the oil evenly over steak. Place on oiled grates; grill, uncovered, until charred and a thermometer inserted into thickest portion registers 130°F to 135°F (medium-rare), about 5 minutes per side, or to desired degree of doneness.
3. Remove steak from grill, and let rest 10 minutes. Meanwhile, cut grilled corn kernels from cobs and transfer to a medium bowl. Chop grilled scallions, and add to corn. Remove and discard skin, stem, and seeds from grilled poblano chile. Chop chile, and add to corn mixture. Add lime juice, jalapeño, black pepper, and remaining ¾ teaspoon salt and 1 tablespoon oil; stir to combine.
4. Cut steak against the grain into ½-inch-thick slices, and arrange on a platter. Spoon 1 cup Corn-Chile Relish over steak. Serve with remaining relish.

ROLL WITH IT
For a pretty and symmetrical spiral, roll up the stuffed steak gradually, tightening the cylinder as you go.

Pepper-Stuffed Grilled Flank Steak

ACTIVE 50 MIN. - TOTAL 1 HOUR

SERVES 4

- 1 (2-lb.) flank steak (¾ inch thick), excess fat trimmed
- 1 Tbsp. minced garlic (from 4 garlic cloves)
- 2½ tsp. kosher salt, divided
- 1 tsp. black pepper, divided
- ½ cup chopped fresh basil
- 1 (12-oz.) jar roasted red bell peppers, drained, patted dry, and chopped (about 1 cup)
- ½ cup seeded and chopped pickled hot or sweet cherry bell peppers
- 4 sharp provolone cheese slices
- 1 Tbsp. olive oil

1. Preheat a gas grill to high (450°F to 500°F) on 1 side, or push hot coals to 1 side of a charcoal grill. To butterfly the steak, place steak on a cutting board with 1 long side facing you. Trim short edges as needed to form a rough rectangle. Press 1 hand flat on steak to steady it. Holding knife parallel to cutting board and starting on one short side, slice horizontally to within ¾ inch of the opposite side. Open cut steak like a book.

2. Sprinkle cut sides of steak evenly with garlic, 1½ teaspoons of the salt, and ½ teaspoon of the black pepper. Top with basil, leaving a 1-inch border on all sides. Arrange bell peppers and cherry bell peppers evenly over basil, leaving a 1-inch border on all sides. Overlap cheese slices on top of peppers, leaving a 1-inch border on all sides. Roll up steak away from you into a tight cylinder.

3. Tie cylinder crosswise at about 1½-inch intervals starting from center and working out toward the ends using kitchen twine. Rub with oil. Sprinkle with remaining 1 teaspoon salt and ½ teaspoon black pepper.

4. Place steak on oiled grates over lit side of grill. Cook, uncovered, turning occasionally, until grill marks appear all over, about 10 minutes. Transfer to unlit side. Grill, covered, turning occasionally, until a thermometer inserted into thickest portion of steak registers 130°F to 135°F (medium-rare), 30 to 40 minutes, or to desired degree of doneness. Transfer steak to a clean cutting board. Let rest 10 minutes. Remove and discard kitchen twine. Cut crosswise into 8 slices.

Chile-Lime Steak Skewers with Coconut-Cilantro Sauce

ACTIVE 20 MIN. · TOTAL 35 MIN.,
PLUS 4 HOURS CHILLING

SERVES 4

- 2 garlic cloves
- 1 small red Fresno chile, stemmed and unseeded
- 3 cups packed fresh cilantro leaves and tender stems (from 2 bunches), divided
- ⅓ cup plus ¼ cup canned unsweetened coconut cream, divided
- ¼ cup, plus 2 Tbsp. fresh lime juice (from 3 limes), divided, plus lime wedges for serving
- ¼ cup granulated sugar, divided
- 3 Tbsp. plus 2 tsp. fish sauce, divided
- 1 (1½-lb.) flank steak (¾ inch thick), cut into 1-inch-wide strips
- ½ cup packed fresh basil leaves
- 4 (10-inch) wooden skewers
- ¾ tsp. kosher salt

1. Process garlic, Fresno chile, 1½ cups of the cilantro, ⅓ cup of the coconut cream, 2 tablespoons of the lime juice, 3 tablespoons of the sugar, and 3 tablespoons of the fish sauce in a blender or food processor until smooth, about 25 seconds. Transfer marinade to a large zip-top plastic bag. Add steak; seal bag. Massage bag to coat steak with marinade. Refrigerate 4 to 12 hours.

2. Preheat grill to high (450˚F to 500˚F). Process basil and remaining 1½ cups cilantro, ¼ cup coconut cream, ¼ cup lime juice, 1 tablespoon sugar, and 2 teaspoons fish sauce in a blender until smooth, about 30 seconds. Transfer Coconut-Cilantro Sauce to a small bowl.

3. Remove steak strips from bag, and discard marinade. Pat dry; discard excess marinade. Thread strips evenly onto wooden skewers. Sprinkle evenly with salt. Place skewers on oiled grates, and grill, uncovered, turning occasionally, until steak is charred in some spots and a meat thermometer inserted into thickest portion registers 130˚F to 135˚F (medium-rare), 9 to 11 minutes, or to desired degree of doneness. Transfer skewers to a cutting board, and let rest 5 minutes.

4. Arrange skewers on a serving platter. Drizzle evenly with Coconut-Cilantro Sauce, and serve immediately with lime wedges and remaining sauce.

SHAKE IT UP
Before opening the can of coconut cream, give it a vigorous jostle to recombine its contents.

SOUTHERN
FRIED SHRIMP WITH
TARTAR SAUCE

PEEL 'N' EAT
SHRIMP

Beach Eats

Bring vacation vibes to the dinner table with dishes inspired by our favorite seafood spots

Peel 'n' Eat Shrimp

Snip the shrimps' shells before you cook them so they soak up more flavor and are easier to peel. Barbecue sauce tames the punchy horseradish in the tangy dip.
ACTIVE 20 MIN. - TOTAL 50 MIN.
SERVES 6

- 2 lb. large unpeeled raw shrimp
- ½ cup pickling spice
- ¼ cup kosher salt
- 2 Tbsp. seafood seasoning
- 2 medium lemons, halved crosswise
- 6 medium garlic cloves, smashed
- ½ cup ketchup
- ½ cup barbecue sauce
- 4 tsp. prepared horseradish
- 1 Tbsp. fresh lemon juice
- 1 Tbsp. Worcestershire sauce
  Additional lemon halves, for serving

1. Use small scissors to cut the shell along the back of each shrimp, leaving shell and tail attached, if desired. Remove and discard vein. Set aside shrimp.
2. Stir together 8 cups water, pickling spice, salt, seafood seasoning, lemons, and garlic in a large pot; bring to a boil over high. Boil, uncovered, 5 minutes. Meanwhile, stir together ketchup, barbecue sauce, horseradish, lemon juice, and Worcestershire sauce in a medium bowl. Cover and refrigerate dipping sauce until ready to use.
3. Add shrimp to boiling water mixture; cook, stirring occasionally, until shrimp turn opaque, 3 to 4 minutes. Using a spider skimmer or slotted spoon, transfer shrimp to a rimmed baking sheet. Spread in an even layer, and let stand until cool enough to handle, 20 to 30 minutes. Serve with dipping sauce and lemon halves. Shrimp and sauce can be refrigerated in separate airtight containers until ready to serve, up to 3 days.

Southern Fried Shrimp with Tartar Sauce

A double dredge in flour yields super-crunchy shrimp that are a perfect match for this irresistible dipping sauce studded with chives, pickles, and capers. To ensure the crispiest results, dredge and fry the shrimp in several batches and keep an eye on the oil's temperature.
ACTIVE 45 MIN. - TOTAL 45 MIN.
SERVES 6

-   Canola oil
- 1 cup mayonnaise
- ¼ cup minced sweet onion
- 2 Tbsp. finely chopped dill pickles plus 1 tsp. pickle juice
- 1 Tbsp. chopped capers
- 1 Tbsp. chopped fresh chives, plus more for garnish
- 2 tsp. stone-ground mustard
- 2¼ tsp. kosher salt, divided
- 2¼ cups self-rising flour
- 3 Tbsp. Creole seasoning
- ¾ tsp. black pepper
- 1 cup whole milk
- 1 Tbsp. hot sauce (such as Tabasco)
- 2 large eggs, lightly beaten
- 2 lb. large peeled, deveined raw shrimp, tail-on

1. Pour oil to a depth of 2 inches in a large Dutch oven; heat over medium-high to 350°F to 375°F.
2. Stir together mayonnaise, onion, pickles and pickle juice, capers, chives, mustard, and ¾ teaspoon of the salt in a medium bowl until combined. Set Tartar Sauce aside.
3. Stir together flour, Creole seasoning, pepper, and 1 teaspoon of the salt in a shallow bowl. Whisk together milk, hot sauce, eggs, and remaining ½ teaspoon salt in a medium bowl until combined.
4. Working in batches, add a handful of shrimp to flour mixture, and toss to coat. Transfer to milk mixture, submerging shrimp completely. Remove from milk mixture; let excess drip off. Return shrimp to flour mixture, tossing to coat. Transfer to a baking sheet; repeat with remaining shrimp.
5. Working in batches, add shrimp to hot oil and cook, turning occasionally, until golden brown and cooked through, about 3 minutes per batch. Remove from oil using a spider skimmer or slotted spoon, and transfer to a wire rack set over a rimmed baking sheet. Repeat with remaining shrimp. Serve with Tartar Sauce and additional chopped chives.

BLACKENED FISH TACOS
(PAGE 131)

FRIED FISH SANDWICHES

Fried Fish Sandwiches

The tangy chowchow-infused mayonnaise revs up this slaw-topped sandwich. Faintly sweet, buttery brioche buns are ideal for this crunchy fish and Spicy Slaw.

ACTIVE 30 MIN. · TOTAL 30 MIN.

SERVES 4

- 4 (6-oz., 4- x 2-inch) skinless grouper or mahi-mahi fillets (about ¾ to 1 inch thick)
- 1¾ tsp. kosher salt, divided
  Canola oil
- ¾ cup all-purpose flour
- ¾ cup finely ground yellow cornmeal
- ¾ tsp. black pepper
- 1 cup whole buttermilk
- 1 Tbsp. hot sauce
- ½ cup mayonnaise
- ½ cup chopped chowchow
- 4 brioche hamburger buns, split
  Spicy Slaw (recipe at right)

1. Pat fillets dry with paper towels; sprinkle evenly with ½ teaspoon of the salt. Pour oil to a depth of 2 inches in a large Dutch oven; heat over medium-high to 350°F to 375°F. While oil heats, stir together flour, cornmeal, pepper, and ¾ teaspoon of the salt in a large shallow bowl until combined. Whisk together buttermilk, hot sauce, and remaining ½ teaspoon salt in a separate large shallow bowl until combined.
2. Place 1 fillet into cornmeal mixture, turning to coat. Dip in buttermilk mixture, turning to coat; let excess drip off. Return fillet to cornmeal mixture, turning to coat. Transfer to a plate, and repeat with remaining fillets.
3. Gently add 2 breaded fillets to hot oil; cook, gently turning occasionally, until golden brown and a thermometer inserted in thickest portion registers 145°F, 6 to 8 minutes. Remove from oil using a spider skimmer or slotted spoon, and place on a wire rack set over a large rimmed baking sheet. Repeat with remaining fillets.
4. Stir together mayonnaise and chowchow in a bowl. Spread mixture onto cut sides of buns. Place fillets on bun bottoms; add Spicy Slaw and bun tops.

Blackened Fish Tacos

(Photo, page 128)

Boldly flavored but only mildly spicy, these fast-fix tacos make a family-friendly supper. While fresh fish is best, thawed frozen fillets work just fine for this recipe.

ACTIVE 35 MIN. · TOTAL 35 MIN.

SERVES 4

- 2 tsp. hot paprika
- 1½ tsp. kosher salt
- 1 tsp. onion powder
- 1 tsp. garlic powder
- 1 tsp. black pepper
- ½ tsp. dried thyme
- ½ tsp. dried oregano
- 4 (5-oz.) grouper or mahi-mahi fillets (¾ to 1 inch thick)
- 1 Tbsp. canola oil
- ½ cup sour cream
- ¼ cup chopped mild green chiles, drained (from 1 [4-oz.] can)
- 8 (4- to 5-inch) flour tortillas, toasted
  Spicy Slaw (recipe follows)
  Garnishes: fresh cilantro leaves, sliced radishes, sliced avocado, and lime wedges

1. Stir together paprika, salt, onion powder, garlic powder, pepper, thyme, and oregano in a small bowl until combined. Pat fish dry with paper towels; generously coat with spice mix on all sides.
2. Heat oil in a large nonstick skillet over medium-high until shimmering. Add fish; cook, turning occasionally, until well browned and a thermometer inserted in thickest portion registers 145°F, 8 to 12 minutes, adjusting heat as needed to prevent overbrowning. Remove fish from skillet. Let cool slightly; use a fork to break fish into bite-size pieces.
3. Stir together sour cream and green chiles in a medium bowl until combined. Spread sour cream mixture evenly onto center of tortillas; top with Spicy Slaw and fish. Serve immediately with cilantro, radishes, avocado slices, and lime wedges.

Spicy Slaw

Top tacos and fish sandwiches with this quick-to-make, versatile side.

ACTIVE 15 MIN. · TOTAL 15 MIN.

SERVES 4

Stir together 4 cups thinly sliced **red or green cabbage**, 1 cup thinly sliced **sweet onion**, ¼ cup chopped **pickled jalapeños**, 2 Tbsp. **fresh lime juice,** and 1 tsp. **kosher salt** in a large bowl until combined. Lightly massage mixture using hands until cabbage softens slightly. Use immediately, or refrigerate in an airtight container up to 3 days.

CRAB CAKES WITH KEY LIME MAYONNAISE

Mango Salsa

Save this recipe—you'll want to spoon the zippy salsa over crab cakes, tacos, seared fish, or even grilled chicken.
ACTIVE 20 MIN. · TOTAL 40 MIN.
SERVES 4 TO 6

Stir together 3 cups diced **ripe mangoes**, ¼ cup each finely chopped **red onion**, **red bell pepper**, and **fresh cilantro**; ¼ cup **fresh lime juice**; 1 tsp. **kosher salt**; and ½ tsp. **black pepper** in a medium bowl until combined. Let stand at room temperature for 20 minutes to let flavors meld.

Heavenly Key Lime Pie

A longtime reader favorite, this classic recipe is blissfully simple to make. It's the ideal crescendo to a Southern seafood supper. Can't find Key limes? This pie will taste good using any fresh limes available at your local grocery store.
ACTIVE 15 MIN. · TOTAL 30 MIN., PLUS 1 HOUR COOLING AND 1 HOUR CHILLING
SERVES 6 TO 8

- 1 (14-oz.) can sweetened condensed milk
- 3 large egg yolks
- 2 tsp. Key lime zest
- ½ cup Key lime juice
- 1 (9-inch) graham cracker piecrust
- 1 cup heavy whipping cream
- 3 Tbsp. powdered sugar
  Key lime slices, for garnish (optional)

1. Preheat oven to 350°F. Whisk together condensed milk, egg yolks, and lime zest and juice until well blended. Pour mixture into piecrust.
2. Bake in preheated oven for 15 minutes or until pie is set. Let cool completely on a wire rack, about 1 hour. Chill 1 hour before serving.
3. Beat whipping cream at high speed with an electric mixer, gradually adding powdered sugar, until soft peaks form, 2 to 3 minutes. Top pie with whipped cream. Garnish with lime slices, if desired.

Crab Cakes with Key Lime Mayonnaise

Citrus mayo and mango salsa balance the richness of these tender, buttery crab cakes. When combining the crab cake ingredients, fold them together gently with a spatula for the most tender results.
ACTIVE 30 MIN. · TOTAL 30 MIN.
SERVES 4

- ¾ cup finely crushed saltine cracker crumbs (from about 20 crackers)
- ¼ cup finely chopped red bell pepper (from 1 small pepper)
- ¼ cup finely chopped scallions (from 2 scallions), plus more for garnish
- 2 large egg yolks
- ¾ tsp. kosher salt
- ½ tsp. seafood seasoning
- ½ tsp. Worcestershire sauce
- ¼ cup plus ⅓ cup mayonnaise, divided
- 1 lb. fresh lump crabmeat, drained and picked over
- ½ tsp. Key lime zest plus 1 Tbsp. fresh juice (from 1 Key lime)
- 2 Tbsp. unsalted butter
  Mango Salsa (recipe follows)
  Mixed greens (optional)
  Key lime slices, for garnish (optional)

1. Stir together cracker crumbs, bell pepper, scallions, egg yolks, salt, seafood seasoning, Worcestershire, and ¼ cup of the mayonnaise in a medium bowl until combined. Gently fold in crab until combined. Form crab mixture into 4 (3- to 3½-inch-wide) patties.
2. Whisk together lime zest and juice with remaining ⅓ cup mayonnaise in a small bowl until combined. Set aside.
3. Heat butter in a large cast-iron skillet over medium-high until foamy. Add crab cakes to pan; cook until golden brown and cooked through, 3 to 5 minutes per side, adjusting heat as needed to prevent overbrowning. Remove from heat.
4. Serve crab cakes with Mango Salsa, mayo mixture, and mixed greens, if desired. Garnish with scallions and Key lime slices, if desired.

HEAVENLY
KEY LIME PIE

Summer Jams

Celebrated Savannah baker Cheryl Day has launched a small-batch line inspired by the women in her family

SOUTHERNERS are nothing if not resourceful, and business owner Cheryl Day is no exception. As COVID-19 swept the country, she was forced to temporarily shut the doors of her nationally praised and locally beloved Back in the Day Bakery. Undeterred, she turned the space into a part-time cannery, offering the world a small slice of Savannah by selling her homemade jams online.

"I have always been inspired by what my grandmother called 'the craft of putting up,' saving and preserving the bounty of the season," says Day. Making jam was a hobby and a topic she wrote about in her cookbooks before it became her pandemic pivot. She officially launched Janie Q Provisions in August 2021, debuting with three flavors: Strawberry-Chamomile, Blueberry-Rose, and Peach-Lavender. Day named the business after her mother, Janie Queen, who taught her how to bake.

She was one of three "queens" in a line of industrious matriarchs, including Day's great-great-grandmother Hannah Queen Grubbs, who was an enslaved pastry chef renowned for her biscuits and cakes. The addition of botanicals is a nod to Day's grandmother Hannah Marie Hanson, who infused her preserves and baked goods with plants from her garden.

She was a true devotee of the saying "What grows together, goes together."

Much like Day's homestyle pastries, the jams have a handcrafted feel. The labels, designed by artist Emily Isabella, feature whimsical sketches of each jar's namesake fruit. The textures of the products are looser than the store-bought kinds, as they are low in sugar and made without commercial pectin. Day even simmers her jams in an old-school copper pot, making only 24 jars per batch.

Naturally, these spreads are great on baked goods, but Day loves using them in savory dishes, too, pairing the peach one with shrimp and the strawberry one with chicken or pork. Her favorite combo is the Blueberry-Rose flavor on a sausage biscuit.

Since the launch, she has added a Sweet Heat Pepper Jelly and a Buttermilk Biscuit Mix to the lineup, with more items to come. Despite all of her delicious offerings, Day encourages everyone to try making their own jams. Her advice? Lean into the craft, take your time, and—above all—have fun.

Strawberry Jam

ACTIVE 1 HOUR, 5 MIN. · TOTAL 1 HOUR, 5 MIN., PLUS 3 HOURS COOLING
MAKES ABOUT 5 CUPS

- 1 medium lemon
  Cheesecloth bag
- 4 lb. fresh strawberries, hulled and quartered (10 cups)
- 3 cups granulated sugar

1. Place a large plate and a metal spoon in freezer until ready to use. Grate lemon to equal 2 teaspoons zest. Cut lemon in half; juice lemon to equal 2 tablespoons juice. Place juiced lemon halves in a cheesecloth bag; close bag.
2. Place strawberries, sugar, lemon zest, lemon juice, and cheesecloth bag in a medium-size heavy-bottomed nonreactive pot. Bring to a boil over medium-high, mashing the strawberries

with a potato masher until chunky. Reduce heat to medium, and gently boil, stirring often and scraping bottom of pot to prevent sticking, until mixture thickens and looks dark and syrupy, 45 to 50 minutes, skimming and discarding any foam from surface. Remove from heat.
3. Remove plate and spoon from freezer. Using spoon, scoop a small amount of jam onto plate. Return plate to freezer for 1 minute. Remove plate; pull a finger through jam and across plate. It should leave a clean trail. (If it is runny and does not leave a clean trail, return jam in pot to a boil over medium-high and return plate and spoon to freezer. Boil, stirring often, for 3 minutes. Remove from heat, and retest thickness using spoon and plate; repeat process if necessary until jam reaches desired thickness.)
4. Remove cheesecloth bag. Using tongs, carefully squeeze lemon halves to release any juices into jam; discard. If desired, mash strawberries with a potato masher until jam reaches preferred consistency.
5. Carefully pour jam evenly into 5 (½-pint) canning jars. Let cool to room temperature, uncovered, about 3 hours. Seal jars. Store in refrigerator up to 2 weeks.

Strawberry-Chamomile Jam

Prepare the recipe as directed, adding 1 Tbsp. **edible dried chamomile flowers** to the ingredients in the nonreactive pot in Step 2.

Blueberry Jam

Prepare recipe as directed, substituting 3 lb. **fresh blueberries** for strawberries in Step 2.

Blueberry-Rose Jam

Prepare recipe as directed, substituting 3 lb. **fresh blueberries** for strawberries and adding 1 tsp. rose water to the ingredients in the nonreactive pot in Step 2.

No-Bake Bliss

One simple recipe, three dreamy icebox desserts, no oven required

Any-Berry No-Bake Cheesecake

ACTIVE 35 MIN. · TOTAL 50 MIN., PLUS 4 HOURS CHILLING

SERVES 10 TO 12

- 2 cups graham cracker crumbs (from about 15 graham cracker sheets)
- ⅓ cup packed light brown sugar
- ½ cup butter, melted
- 3 (8-oz.) pkg. cream cheese, at room temperature
- ¾ cup powdered sugar plus ¼ cup (if desired), sifted
- ¼ cup sour cream, at room temperature
- 1 Tbsp. grated lemon zest plus 2 tsp. fresh lemon juice (from 2 lemons)
- 2 tsp. vanilla extract
  Pinch of salt
- 1 cup heavy whipping cream
- 2 cups assorted fresh berries (such as strawberries, blackberries, raspberries, and blueberries)
  Edible fresh flowers (optional)
  Fresh mint leaves (optional)

1. Coat a 9-inch springform pan with cooking spray. Stir together graham cracker crumbs and brown sugar in a large bowl; add melted butter, and stir until well combined. Press graham cracker mixture into bottom and about ¾ inch up sides of prepared pan. Freeze, uncovered, while preparing filling, about 15 minutes.
2. Beat cream cheese and ¾ cup of the powdered sugar in a stand mixer fitted with a paddle attachment on low speed just until combined, 30 seconds to 1 minute; scrape down sides. Add additional ¼ cup powdered sugar, if desired. Increase mixer speed to medium; beat until smooth and fluffy, 1 to 2 minutes. Add sour cream, lemon zest and juice, vanilla, and salt; beat on medium speed until well combined, about 1 minute. Set aside.
3. Whisk heavy whipping cream in a large bowl by hand until stiff peaks form, 1 to 2 minutes. Fold whipped cream into cream cheese mixture just until combined. Spoon cream cheese mixture into chilled crust, smoothing top. Chill, covered, until set, at least 4 hours or up to 24 hours.
4. To serve, carefully remove sides of springform pan, and place cheesecake on a plate. Top with berries; garnish with flowers and mint, if desired.

Chocolate-Cherry No-Bake Cheesecake

Prepare recipe as directed, substituting 2 cups crushed **chocolate wafer cookies** for graham cracker crumbs in Step 1. Swirl ¼ cup **cherry preserves** into cream cheese mixture in chilled crust in Step 3. Substitute 1 cup **fresh** or **jarred pitted Bing cherries** for berries in Step 4; omit flowers and mint.

Peach-Ginger No-Bake Cheesecake

Prepare recipe as directed, substituting 2 cups crushed **gingersnaps** for graham cracker crumbs in Step 1. While cheesecake chills, stir together 2 Tbsp. **honey** and 1 pitted and thinly sliced **large (8-oz.) fresh peach** in a medium bowl; let stand for 30 minutes. Substitute peach mixture for berries in Step 4; omit flowers and mint, and garnish with chopped **candied ginger**.

Figging Out

Enjoying summer's sweetest and most fleeting delights

A HARDY FIG might be the most generous tree to grace our yards each summer. Covered in deep-lobed, brilliant green leaves that look hand carved, it's a beautiful feature for both its looks and its bounty of fruit. The full-grown trees can tower over us, rising up to 30 feet tall, with branches stretching even wider, making them enviable shade trees that gift us with something tasty. When laden with ripe fruit, the heavy boughs dip down closer to the ground, as if trying to make picking easier. Although we consider a fig a fruit, botanists clarify that it is actually the stem of an inflorescence—a cluster of many flowers. Celeste and Brown Turkey are the most prevalent types in our region, but given that there are about 470 common fig varieties in the Southeast, including in spots where no other fruit trees can flourish, we're sure to find something pretty to grow and delicious to eat.

Fig trees can have two harvest seasons. The first arrives in early- to midsummer and is small, like a dress rehearsal. A month or so later, during the peak heat of summer, we get a much larger show. People who cultivate figs eagerly keep watch when the first ones of the season appear. The fruits pop out like tiny water balloons that fill very slowly. It can feel like forever before the first one is ready to be picked, but then things kick into high gear.

Weather affects annual yield, but in a good year, figs ripen at a fast and furious pace. Keeping up with them can seem overwhelming at times, no matter how wonderful they are. Neighbors with brimming trees encourage—even beg—us to come share in the bounty. Farmers market tables spill over with baskets of figs so ripe that they sometimes split open to reveal their jammy centers. The harvest seems boundless, but it's only a surge, so we should make the most of the fresh produce while we can. Dried figs are available in stores year-round, but they are as different from fresh as raisins are from grapes.

Choose fruit that is plump and shapely with smooth skin. Underripe figs that

are picked too soon will stay hard and not ripen further. Overripe ones are quite soft and might have split skins, which can make them good for cooking but not the best for eating raw. If they turn mushy and emit a sour smell, they should be discarded. The entire fruit is edible, though most people do remove the stems, which can be tough and fibrous. (Don't get the sap on your hands, because it can cause irritation.)

Rinse uncut figs just before using them. Since they are fragile when fully ripe, with exteriors as delicate and thin as flower petals, they rarely withstand shipping or storage. This is why, despite their popularity, fresh figs have never been a viable commercial crop in the South. The upside is that local ones, with droplets of sweet syrup peeking through their split skins, are available nearby, where they feel right at home.

Fresh Fig Cake with Lemon and Rosemary

ACTIVE 15 MIN. · TOTAL 1 HOUR, 10 MIN., PLUS 1 HOUR COOLING

SERVES 8

CAKE

- 1 cup all-purpose flour, plus more for pan
- ¾ cup fine yellow cornmeal
- 1½ tsp. baking powder
- ½ tsp. kosher salt
- ¼ tsp. baking soda
- ½ cup unsalted butter, at room temperature
- ¾ cup granulated sugar
- 3 large eggs, at room temperature
- ¾ cup sour cream, at room temperature
- 2 tsp. vanilla extract
- 4 tsp. grated lemon zest (from 2 lemons), divided
- 4 tsp. finely chopped fresh rosemary, divided
- 12 oz. fresh figs, stemmed and chopped, plus more fig halves for garnish
- ¼ cup turbinado sugar

WHIPPED CREAM

- 1 cup heavy whipping cream, chilled
- ¼ cup powdered sugar
- ¼ cup sour cream

1. Prepare the Cake: Preheat oven to 350°F. Grease and flour a 9-inch springform pan.
2. Whisk together flour, cornmeal, baking powder, salt, and baking soda in a medium-size bowl. Set aside.
3. Beat butter in a large bowl with an electric mixer on low speed until smooth and creamy, about 1 minute. Add granulated sugar, and beat on high speed until light and fluffy, about 3 minutes. Add eggs, 1 at a time, beating only until incorporated after each addition. Beat in half of the flour mixture on low speed until just combined, about 1 minute. Beat in sour cream, vanilla extract, 2 teaspoons of the lemon zest, and 2 teaspoons of the rosemary until just combined, about 1 minute. Add remaining flour mixture; beat only until batter is smooth and combined, about 1 minute (it will be very thick). Gently fold in figs. Pour into prepared pan, and smooth top with a spatula.
4. Combine turbinado sugar, remaining 2 teaspoons lemon zest, and remaining 2 teaspoons rosemary in a small bowl, and rub sugar mixture with fingertips until sugar is shiny and fragrant. Sprinkle evenly over batter.
5. Bake in a preheated oven until a wooden pick inserted into center of Cake comes out clean, 45 to 55 minutes. Let cool in pan on a wire rack for 10 minutes. Loosen sides of pan, and remove; let Cake cool to room temperature, about 1 hour. (If making in advance, cover cooled Cake with plastic wrap and chill up to 3 days.)
6. Prepare the Whipped Cream: Beat heavy cream and powdered sugar in a large bowl with an electric mixer on high speed until soft peaks form, about 2 minutes. Add sour cream, and beat on high speed to medium peaks, 30 seconds to 1 minute. (If Whipped Cream is made more than 4 hours ahead, whisk vigorously to restore volume before topping Cake.)
7. Top Cake with Whipped Cream and additional fresh figs as desired, and serve immediately.

Fresh Fig, Pecan, and Orange Crostata

(Photo, page 141)

ACTIVE 20 MIN. · TOTAL 1 HOUR, 20 MIN., PLUS 1 HOUR CHILLING

SERVES 8

- 1 lb. fresh figs, stemmed and halved or quartered, depending on their size
- 2 Tbsp. (1 oz.) orange liqueur (such as Grand Marnier)
- ¼ cup packed dark brown sugar
- 2 Tbsp. cornstarch
- ¼ tsp. kosher salt
  All-purpose flour, for work surface
- ½ (14.1-oz.) pkg. refrigerated piecrusts (1 piecrust)
- ½ cup cream cheese, at room temperature
- 1 large egg, separated
- 2 tsp. fresh thyme leaves, plus more for garnish
- ½ cup pecan pieces
- 1 Tbsp. coarse or granulated sugar
  Grated orange zest

1. Stir together figs and liqueur in a large bowl. Whisk together brown sugar, cornstarch, and salt in a small bowl until smooth; sprinkle over figs, and stir to coat. Let stand until ready to use.
2. On a lightly floured work surface, roll out piecrust into a 12-inch round. Transfer pastry to a parchment paper-lined rimmed baking sheet.
3. Whisk together cream cheese and egg yolk in a small bowl until smooth. Using an offset spatula, spread cream cheese mixture over pastry round, leaving a 2-inch border around edge. Sprinkle evenly with thyme leaves.
4. Gently stir pecan pieces into fig mixture; spoon over cream cheese mixture, mounding fig-pecan mixture in center.
5. Fold edge of pastry dough over edge of filling, pinching folds closed. Whisk egg white until frothy, and brush over pastry. Sprinkle pastry with coarse or granulated sugar. Cover with plastic wrap, and refrigerate until pastry is chilled and firm, about 1 hour.
6. Preheat oven to 375°F. Bake crostata until pastry is a deep golden brown and juices are bubbling, 40 to 45 minutes. Let cool for at least 20 minutes. Serve warm or at room temperature, and garnish with grated orange zest and additional fresh thyme leaves.

Honey-Balsamic Fig Compote

(Photo, page 140)

ACTIVE 10 MIN. · TOTAL 30 MIN., PLUS 1 HOUR COOLING

SERVES 4

- 1 lb. fresh figs, stemmed and cut into ½-inch pieces (about 3 cups)
- ¼ cup light, floral honey
- 2 Tbsp. fresh lemon juice (from 1 lemon)
- 2 tsp. aged balsamic vinegar
  Vanilla ice cream, for serving
  Flaky sea salt, for serving

1. Preheat oven to 400°F. Stir together fig pieces and honey in an 8-inch square baking dish.
2. Bake fig mixture in preheated oven until juices bubble around edges of baking dish, about 20 minutes. Let stand until cool, about 1 hour. Mixture will thicken slightly as it cools. Stir in lemon juice and balsamic vinegar.
3. Serve compote over scoops of vanilla ice cream, and garnish with flaky sea salt. Store compote in an airtight container in refrigerator up to 3 weeks.

HONEY-BALSAMIC
FIG COMPOTE
(PAGE 139)

FRESH FIG, PECAN,
AND ORANGE CROSTATA
(PAGE 139)

Taste the Rainbow

Brighten up dinner with these colorful, plant-forward recipes

Ultimate Veggie Kebabs with Smoked Sausage

ACTIVE 35 MIN. - TOTAL 55 MIN.
SERVES 6

- 12 (12-inch) metal or bamboo skewers
- 1 medium yellow squash, sliced into ½-inch-thick half-moons (about 2 cups)
- 1 medium zucchini, sliced into ½-inch-thick half-moons (about 2 cups)
- 1 large red onion, cut into 1-inch pieces (about 1½ cups)
- 8 oz. sweet mini peppers (about 3 cups)
- 2 cups fresh okra, trimmed and halved crosswise
- 1 lb. smoked sausage, cut into 1-inch pieces
- 1½ tsp. kosher salt, divided
- ¾ tsp. black pepper, divided
- ½ cup extra-virgin olive oil
- ½ cup balsamic vinegar
- 3 garlic cloves, grated (about ¾ tsp.)
- ¼ cup finely chopped fresh flat-leaf parsley
- 3 Tbsp. fresh oregano, chopped

1. If using bamboo skewers, soak them in water for at least 15 minutes or up to overnight. While skewers soak, place squash, zucchini, onion, sweet peppers, okra, and smoked sausage in a large bowl. Sprinkle with ½ teaspoon each of the kosher salt and black pepper; toss to coat evenly.

2. Stir together oil, vinegar, garlic, parsley, oregano, and remaining 1 teaspoon kosher salt and ¼ teaspoon black pepper until combined. Drizzle half of herb mixture over vegetable mixture in bowl, tossing to coat. Reserve remaining herb mixture for serving. Let vegetable mixture marinate at room temperature, stirring occasionally, 20 minutes. Thread marinated vegetables and sausage evenly onto skewers.

3. Preheat grill to high (450°F to 500°F). Place kebabs on oiled grates; grill, covered, turning often, until vegetables are browned and softened, 6 to 8 minutes. Transfer kebabs to a large platter, and drizzle with reserved herb mixture. Serve immediately.

PRECIOUS METAL
Invest in stainless steel skewers for grilling this summer; they're sturdy, sustainable, and don't require soaking.

Creamed Corn Pasta

ACTIVE 40 MIN. - TOTAL 40 MIN.

SERVES 4

- 6 ears fresh corn, shucked
- ½ cup heavy whipping cream
- 4 thick-cut bacon slices, chopped
- 1 medium yellow onion, finely chopped (about 1½ cups)
- 3 large garlic cloves, minced (about 1 Tbsp.)
- 2 oz. Parmesan cheese, grated (about ½ cup), plus more for serving
- 1 lb. casarecce or penne pasta
- 1 Tbsp. chopped fresh thyme
- 1½ tsp. kosher salt, plus more for salting water

1. Place 1 ear of corn over a large bowl. Using a peeler, shave the edges of the kernels off into the bowl. Scrape remaining corn kernels and milk from cob with a spoon into bowl with corn kernel tops, reserving cobs. Repeat with remaining corn (yield should be about 1½ cups kernels and milk). Stir in whipping cream; set aside. Add cobs to a large pot, and cover with water; salt generously. Bring pot with corn cobs to a boil over high; let boil 20 minutes.

2. Meanwhile, place chopped bacon in a large skillet; cook over medium-high, stirring often, until crisp, about 10 minutes. Transfer bacon to a paper towel-lined plate, reserving drippings in skillet. Add yellow onion and garlic to skillet; cook over medium, stirring often, until tender, about 5 minutes. Stir in corn kernel mixture, and reduce to medium-low. Cook, stirring often, until slightly reduced, about 5 minutes. Stir in Parmesan cheese until melted. Remove from heat.

3. Add pasta to pot with corn cobs and boiling water, and cook according to package directions for al dente, about 10 minutes. Drain pasta, reserving 1 cup cooking liquid. Discard corn cobs.

4. Transfer cooked pasta to skillet with corn mixture. Cook over medium, stirring constantly and adding reserved cooking liquid ¼ cup at a time, as needed, until sauce clings to pasta, about 3 minutes. Remove from heat, and stir in fresh thyme and salt. Top with bacon, and serve with additional Parmesan cheese.

MAKING THE CUT
A Y-shaped vegetable peeler is handy for shaving corn kernels from the cobs, but a good sharp knife will work fine.

Skillet Stuffed Peppers

ACTIVE 15 MIN. - TOTAL 1 HOUR
SERVES 6

- 6 medium multicolor bell peppers
- 1½ tsp. kosher salt, divided
- 1 Tbsp. extra-virgin olive oil
- 1 lb. mild Italian sausage, casings removed
- 1 medium yellow onion, chopped (1¼ cups)
- 3 large garlic cloves, minced (1 Tbsp.)
- 2 cups cooked long-grain white rice
- 4 oz. Parmesan cheese, grated (about 1 cup)
- ½ cup chopped fresh flat-leaf parsley
- ¼ cup chopped fresh basil, plus more for garnish
- 1 (24-oz.) jar marinara sauce (such as Rao's)

1. Preheat oven to 450°F. Cut top off each pepper, and reserve; remove and discard seeds. Sprinkle insides of peppers evenly with ¾ teaspoon of the salt; set aside.

2. Heat oil in a large enamel-coated cast-iron skillet. Add Italian sausage, onion, and garlic; cook, stirring often and breaking up sausage with a wooden spoon, until sausage is browned and almost cooked through, 4 to 5 minutes. Remove from heat; stir in rice, Parmesan cheese, parsley, basil, and remaining ¾ teaspoon salt. Spoon rice mixture evenly into each pepper. Top each filled pepper with a reserved pepper top. Pour marinara in bottom of same skillet. Add filled peppers to skillet, and cover tightly with aluminum foil.

3. Bake in preheated oven until peppers are fork-tender, 35 to 45 minutes. Remove foil, and bake until tops of peppers are slightly browned, about 10 minutes. Sprinkle with additional basil.

THE BRIGHT STUFF
Make this dish using any color bell peppers you like. Red ones are the sweetest, but green ones are the most affordable.

READY, SET, DOUGH
Let the pizza dough rest on the counter for an hour to make it easier to stretch and shape.

Sheet Pan Veggie Supreme Pizza

ACTIVE 20 MIN. - TOTAL 45 MIN.

SERVES 6

- ¼ cup plus 2 tsp. extra-virgin olive oil, divided
- 1 Tbsp. plain yellow cornmeal
- 1 lb. pizza dough, at room temperature
- All-purpose flour, for work surface
- 1 large tomato, sliced
- ½ medium zucchini, very thinly sliced lengthwise (about ¾ cup)
- ¾ cup sliced fresh wild mushrooms
- 1 tsp. dried oregano, divided
- 1 tsp. garlic salt, divided
- ¼ cup heavy whipping cream
- 8 oz. low-moisture part-skim mozzarella cheese, shredded (about 2 cups), divided
- ¾ cup fresh yellow corn kernels (from 2 ears)
- ½ small red onion, sliced (about ½ cup)
- ¾ cup packed baby arugula
- Fresh basil leaves

1. Preheat oven to 500°F with rack in center position. Rub a 15- x 10-inch rimmed baking sheet with ¼ cup of the oil until evenly coated. Sprinkle pan with cornmeal.

2. Roll and stretch pizza dough on a lightly floured work surface to a 14- x 9-inch rectangle. Transfer to prepared pan. Cover with a clean kitchen towel, and let rest 10 minutes. Using your fingertips, make small dimples about 1 inch apart in dough, gently stretching and pushing dough toward edges to fill bottom of pan. Cover with kitchen towel until ready to use.

3. Place tomato slices on a paper towel-lined plate; let stand at least 5 minutes or up to 15 minutes to remove any excess water. While tomato slices drain, take zucchini ribbons and gently twist them into loose spirals. Set aside on paper towel-lined plate with tomato slices.

4. Toss together wild mushrooms and ¼ teaspoon each oregano and garlic salt in a small bowl; set aside. Drizzle cream over dough, leaving a ¼-inch perimeter around the edges. Sprinkle with remaining ¾ teaspoon each oregano and garlic salt. Top with three-fourths of the shredded cheese (1½ cups), corn kernels, red onion, twisted zucchini ribbons, mushrooms, and drained tomato slices. Sprinkle with remaining one-fourth of the shredded cheese (½ cup).

5. Bake pizza in preheated oven until edges are puffed and golden brown, 13 to 15 minutes, rotating pan halfway through. Toss together arugula and remaining 2 teaspoons oil; sprinkle over pizza. Top with fresh basil.

Barbecue Jackfruit Sandwiches

ACTIVE 50 MIN. - TOTAL 50 MIN.
SERVES 6

- 2 cups thinly sliced red cabbage (from ½ small [1½-lb.] head cabbage)
- 1 cup matchstick-cut carrots
- ½ small red onion, thinly sliced (about ½ cup)
- ¼ cup apple cider vinegar
- ¼ cup granulated sugar
- 1 tsp. celery seeds
- 2 Tbsp. plus ½ cup canola oil, divided
- 2½ tsp. kosher salt, divided
- ¾ tsp. black pepper, divided
- 1 cup chopped fresh cilantro
- 4 (14-oz.) cans young green jackfruit in water, drained, rinsed, and squeezed dry
- 3 Tbsp. light brown sugar
- 2½ tsp. smoked paprika
- 1 tsp. garlic powder
  Mayonnaise
- 6 hamburger buns, toasted
  Barbecue sauce

1. Place cabbage, carrots, and onion in a large heatproof bowl. Bring vinegar, sugar, celery seeds, 2 tablespoons of the canola oil, 1½ teaspoons of the salt, and ¼ teaspoon of the pepper to a boil in a small saucepan over medium-high. Pour boiling mixture over cabbage mixture in bowl; stir gently to combine. Stir in cilantro, and set aside.
2. Using a knife, remove the solid core from shreddable outer parts of jackfruit pieces; set aside. Remove any seedpods from outer parts, and set aside with cores. Place remaining shreddable jackfruit parts in a medium bowl, and pull apart into small pieces. Finely chop cores and seedpods until they are similar in size to the shredded jackfruit, and place in bowl with shredded jackfruit. Add the remaining ½ cup oil, remaining 1 teaspoon salt, and remaining ½ teaspoon pepper; toss to combine.
3. Heat a large cast-iron skillet over medium-high. Add jackfruit mixture, and press into an even layer with a spatula. Cook over medium-high, turning and pressing occasionally, until seared and golden brown, 25 to 35 minutes. Remove from heat; stir in brown sugar, paprika, and garlic powder.
4. Spread mayonnaise on bottom bun halves, and top evenly with jackfruit. Drizzle with barbecue sauce, and top evenly with slaw. Cover with top bun halves.

SIMPLE SWAP
Neutrally flavored like a mushroom, jackfruit is beloved by many vegetarians as a substitute for shredded pork.

Farm Fresh

Slice into this hearty frittata that's packed with peak-season produce and cheese

Farmers Market Frittata

ACTIVE 20 MIN. - TOTAL 50 MIN.
SERVES 8

- 12 large eggs, lightly beaten
- 8 oz. sharp Cheddar cheese, shredded (about 2 cups)
- 1 cup heavy whipping cream
- 1 Tbsp. chopped fresh chives, plus more for garnish
- 1½ tsp. kosher salt
- ½ tsp. black pepper
- 2 Tbsp. olive oil, divided
- ¾ cup thinly sliced red onion (from 1 small onion)
- 2 red sweet mini peppers, thinly sliced crosswise (½ cup)
- 4 cups roughly chopped curly kale leaves (from 1 bunch)
- 1 large garlic clove, grated
- Chopped fresh dill

1. Preheat oven to 400°F. Whisk together eggs, cheese, cream, chives, salt, and black pepper in a large bowl until combined. Set aside.
2. Heat 1 tablespoon of the olive oil in a 10-inch cast-iron skillet over medium. Add sliced red onion and sweet peppers; cook, stirring occasionally, until softened, 4 to 6 minutes. Transfer to a plate.
3. Heat remaining 1 tablespoon olive oil in skillet. Add kale and garlic; cook, stirring often, until kale is wilted, 1 to 2 minutes. Transfer half of kale mixture to a plate, and set aside. Return half of onion and peppers to skillet; stir to combine. Pour egg mixture over vegetables; sprinkle with reserved kale mixture, onion, and peppers. Cook on medium-low until edges are set, 1 to 2 minutes.
4. Transfer to preheated oven, and bake until center is set, about 20 minutes. Let stand 10 minutes before serving. Garnish with additional chives and dill.

A Superior Sandwich

Before you grab the white bread, you'll need to head to Louisiana

I HAVE A FRIEND who owns a suit with red velvet tails. No, not Santa Claus. It's Louis Costa, who for a time was the head of the French Market in New Orleans. He would don the suit annually to lead the Creole Tomato Festival parade. I'd never heard of Creole tomatoes until I started visiting New Orleans regularly. I learned that they are firm, juicy globes of summer-ripe flavor that come into season around June. At the festival, which is now in its 37th year, vendors sell them stuffed with shrimp pasta, topped with crabmeat and rémoulade, and pureed in all different kinds of Bloody Marys.

As I asked more about them, I was astonished to find out that they're a local delight that's a result of combining tomatoes and terroir. The Creole type is not one specific variety but rather a red tomato that's grown in the rich alluvial soil of South Louisiana and allowed to vine-ripen to achieve the intense flavor some of us remember from childhood as a true summer tomato.

I am a total fanatic about them and soon discovered that if I bought them slightly underripe and swaddled each one like baby Jesus, I could get them back North and continue to indulge. I now transport them across state lines every year and love to astonish friends with the most delicious salads and—my hands-down favorite—sandwiches. They are classically simple, basically a BLT without the B and L. To make them, I place a slice or two of ripe Creole tomato between two pieces of store-bought white bread that have been thinly spread with mayonnaise. From there, I can ring in the changes.

If I'm feeling a bit frisky, I might jazz up the mayonnaise with anchovies or anchovy paste, swap out the jarred mayo for the homemade kind (see recipe right), or even add a thin slice of sweet onion for crunch. Some folks like to get fancy about the bread, but I prefer to use the pillowy loaves of my youth. Smoosh your sandwich together, and enjoy—trying not to drip too much of those wonderful tomato juices.
–Jessica B. Harris

Creole Tomato Sandwich
ACTIVE 15 MIN. - TOTAL 15 MIN.
SERVES 4

- 8 white bread slices
- ¾ cup Homemade Mayonnaise (recipe follows)
- 1 lb. Creole tomatoes, cored and sliced crosswise into ¼-inch-thick rounds
- ¼ tsp. kosher salt
- ¼ tsp. black pepper

1. Spread 1 side of each bread slice with 1½ tablespoons Homemade Mayonnaise.
2. Arrange tomato slices in an even layer on a large plate, and sprinkle with salt and pepper. Evenly place tomato slices on mayonnaise side of 4 bread slices. Top tomatoes with remaining 4 bread slices, mayonnaise side down. Cut sandwiches in half, if desired, and serve immediately.

Homemade Mayonnaise
ACTIVE 10 MIN. - TOTAL 10 MIN.
MAKES ABOUT 2 CUPS

- 2 large egg yolks
- 2 Tbsp. fresh lemon juice
- 1½ tsp. Dijon mustard

- 1 tsp. anchovy paste
- ½ tsp. kosher salt
- ¼ tsp. granulated sugar
- ¼ tsp. cayenne pepper
- 1½ cups canola oil
- ½ cup extra-virgin olive oil

1. Process egg yolks, lemon juice, 1½ tablespoons water, mustard, anchovy paste, salt, sugar, and cayenne pepper in a food processor or blender until thoroughly blended, about 10 seconds.
2. With processor or blender running, gradually pour canola oil and extra-virgin olive oil through food chute in a thin, steady stream, processing until thickened and creamy looking, 1 minute, 30 seconds to 2 minutes. Store in an airtight container in refrigerator up to 2 weeks.

Attack of the Killer Tomatoes?

AT ONE POINT, it would have been considered dangerous to eat a tomato, as those perfect orbs were once deemed to be deadly. (They even earned the nickname "poison apple.") This fruit, obtained in Mesoamerica by Europeans in the 16th century, is a member of the nightshade family. Its acidity reacted with the lead used in making many early eating and cooking utensils, resulting in numerous deaths that caused the tomatoes to be feared. This fruit came into common use in the United States only in the mid-19th century. Originally published in 1824, *The Virginia Housewife*, one of the first American cookbooks, includes recipes for "eggs and tomatos," "scollop tomatos," and "tomato catsup." Thankfully, tomato season is now something we can celebrate, especially in the South.

Cracker Packed

Saltines make a tasty crust in this healthier take on Southern tomato pie

Cracker-Crust Tomato Pie

Trading the traditional pastry for cracker crumbs trims down the calories, fat, and carbs in this classic dish.

ACTIVE 25 MIN. · TOTAL 1 HOUR, 20 MIN.

SERVES 8

- 2 cups halved cherry tomatoes
- 4 small heirloom tomatoes, thinly sliced
- 1 tsp. black pepper, divided
- ¾ tsp. kosher salt, divided
- 2 sleeves saltine crackers (about 72 crackers), broken into pieces (about 4 cups)
- 2 large eggs, beaten
- ½ cup melted butter
- 2 oz. Parmesan cheese, grated (about ½ cup)
- ½ cup olive oil mayonnaise
- ¼ cup diced pimientos, drained and patted dry
- ½ tsp. smoked paprika
- ⅛ tsp. cayenne pepper
- 1½ cups shredded sharp white Cheddar cheese, divided
- Fresh basil leaves (optional)

1. Place tomatoes on a paper towel-lined baking sheet, and sprinkle both sides evenly with ½ teaspoon each of the pepper and salt. Cover with more paper towels, and press lightly. Let stand 15 minutes.

2. Meanwhile, preheat oven to 350°F. Pulse crackers in a food processor into coarse crumbs, about 15 pulses. Add beaten eggs, melted butter, Parmesan cheese, and remaining ½ teaspoon pepper and ¼ teaspoon salt; pulse until combined, about 20 pulses.

3. Lightly coat a 12-inch ceramic or metal tart pan with cooking spray. Firmly press cracker-crumb mixture evenly into bottom and up sides of pan. Bake in preheated oven until toasted, 15 to 20 minutes. Let cool 10 minutes.

4. Increase oven temperature to 425°F. Stir together mayonnaise, pimientos, paprika, cayenne pepper, and 1¼ cups of the Cheddar cheese in a medium bowl.

Spread evenly on bottom of crust, and arrange tomatoes in a single, even layer over top. Sprinkle with the remaining ¼ cup Cheddar cheese.

5. Bake at 425°F until golden brown, 25 to 30 minutes. Let stand 10 minutes before slicing. Garnish with basil, if desired.

Before Recipe Makeover:

CALORIES: **662** – CARB: **39 G** – FAT: **48 G**

After Recipe Makeover:

CALORIES: **471** – CARB: **26 G** – FAT: **36 G**

Gotta Try This Guac

Grilled corn, onion, and chiles level up your favorite dip

Charred-Vegetable Guacamole

ACTIVE 30 MIN. - TOTAL 30 MIN.
SERVES 10

- 4 ears fresh corn, husks removed
- 1 medium red onion, cut crosswise into ½-inch-thick slices (about 1 cup)
- 2 medium jalapeño chiles
- 1½ Tbsp. olive oil
- 3 medium avocados, cut into small cubes (about 3 cups)
- ¼ cup fresh lime juice (from 2 limes), divided
- 2 tsp. kosher salt, divided
- ¼ cup chopped fresh cilantro, plus more for garnish
- 1 oz. crumbled queso fresco (fresh Mexican cheese, about ¼ cup)
- Tortilla chips, for serving

1. Preheat grill to high (450°F to 500°F). Toss together corn, onion, jalapeños, and oil on a baking sheet. Place vegetables on oiled grates; grill, uncovered, turning occasionally, until charred on all sides, 8 to 10 minutes. Remove from grill, and let cool 10 minutes.

2. Meanwhile, place avocados, 2 tablespoons of the lime juice, and 1 teaspoon of the salt in a medium bowl, and mash using a fork until mostly smooth with some chunks remaining. Set aside.

3. Cut kernels from grilled corn, place in a medium bowl, and discard cobs. Coarsely chop grilled onion and jalapeños (removing seeds from jalapeños, if desired), and add to corn. Stir in cilantro and remaining 2 tablespoons lime juice and 1 teaspoon salt. Stir 1 cup grilled-corn mixture into avocado mixture. Transfer guacamole to a bowl. Top with remaining grilled-corn mixture, and sprinkle evenly with crumbled queso fresco. Garnish dip with additional cilantro; serve with chips.

WATERMELON-BASIL
SWEET TEA

WATERMELON
FROSÉ

WATERMELON
SANGRÍA

Pretty in Pink

Senior Test Kitchen Pro Ivy Odom brightens summer drinks
with a splash of homemade watermelon syrup

GROWING UP, I spent many summer afternoons on our back porch eating thick slices of fresh watermelon. With the sticky juice dripping from my chin, I would spit the seeds as far as I could and hope that a vine would soon start growing there. My parents have since moved from my childhood home, upgrading to a house that has a pool and a garden—with that watermelon vine I always wanted. During the summer of 2020, I spent a lot of time there making drinks poolside. My favorite was a margarita that inspired one of our first *Southern Living* TikTok videos and the Watermelon Simple Syrup used in these three easy drinks at right. While I still can't resist a seed-spitting contest, sipping the sweet juice is a lot like my parents' pool—a major upgrade. –Ivy Odom

Watermelon Simple Syrup

Add some fruity flavor to your favorite beverages.
ACTIVE 10 MIN. · TOTAL 10 MIN.,
PLUS 45 MIN. COOLING
MAKES ABOUT 2⅓ CUPS

Process 5 cups (1 lb., 10 oz.) cubed **watermelon** in a blender on medium-high speed until smooth, about 10 seconds. Pour through a fine mesh strainer into a medium bowl; discard solids. Measure out 2 cups juice; add to a medium saucepan with 1 cup **granulated sugar.** Reserve any remaining juice for another use. Cook watermelon mixture over medium-high, stirring occasionally, until sugar is completely dissolved, about 5 minutes. Pour syrup into a medium-size heatproof bowl, and let cool at room temperature for 45 minutes. Use immediately, or store in an airtight container in refrigerator up to 5 days.

Watermelon-Basil Sweet Tea

Fragrant basil adds a refreshing herbal taste to watermelon tea. Or use fresh mint for a more traditional version.
ACTIVE 20 MIN. · TOTAL 40 MIN.,
PLUS 1 HOUR CHILLING
SERVES 4

Place 2 **family-size tea bags,** ¼ cup loosely packed **fresh basil leaves,** and ¼ tsp. **baking soda** in a large glass jar or pitcher. Pour 4 cups **boiling water** over tea bags and basil, stirring to submerge. Steep for 15 minutes. Remove basil and tea bags, gently squeezing with kitchen tongs; discard. Stir in ¾ cup **Watermelon Simple Syrup** (recipe above) and 1½ cups water; add more simple syrup to taste, if desired. Chill, uncovered, until cold, 2 hours. Serve over **ice**; garnish with **fresh basil sprigs, watermelon** cubes, and lime slices. Store in refrigerator up to 2 days.

Watermelon Frosé

If you've never tried this grown-up slushy featuring wine, summer is the perfect time. Choose a dry rosé so the sweetness stays in check.
ACTIVE 5 MIN. · TOTAL 5 MIN.,
PLUS 3 HOURS FREEZING
SERVES 8

Process 5 cups (1 lb., 5 oz.) frozen **watermelon chunks,** 1 (750-milliliter) bottle chilled **rosé** (preferably from Pinot Noir grapes), and ¾ cup chilled **Watermelon Simple Syrup** (recipe at left) in a blender on medium-high speed until smooth, about 30 seconds. Pour watermelon mixture into a metal 13- x 9-inch baking pan. Freeze, covered, until mixture becomes icy and slushy, 3 to 4 hours. Spoon mixture into 8 glasses, and garnish with **fresh watermelon** slices or spears, if desired. Serve immediately.

Watermelon Sangría

Keep this sangría extra cold (and undiluted!) by freezing additional fresh watermelon balls, strawberry slices, and peach slices. Divide the frozen fruit among the glasses just before serving.
ACTIVE 15 MIN. · TOTAL 15 MIN.,
PLUS 30 MIN. CHILLING
SERVES 6

Combine 1 (750-milliliter) bottle chilled **Grenache Blanc** or other dry white Spanish wine; ¾ cup **Watermelon Simple Syrup** (recipe above left); 1 cup **watermelon balls** (from 1 small seedless watermelon); 4 **strawberries,** trimmed and sliced; 1 **small peach,** sliced into thin wedges; and 1 **small lemon,** thinly sliced and seeded, in a glass jar or pitcher, and stir. Chill sangría 30 minutes. Pour over **ice.** Garnish each serving with a **fresh mint sprig.** Serve immediately.

You Don't Know Jack?

Turn jackfruit into barbecue that might fool even die-hard meat lovers

DRAIN

Pour the canned jackfruit into a colander; rinse and drain. Squeeze to remove any excess moisture.

CORE

With a knife, cut off the solid core from shreddable outer parts of jackfruit pieces. Set aside. Remove any seedpods from outer parts; set aside with cores.

SHRED

Using your hands, gently pull each chunk of jackfruit into strands. Chop cores and seedpods until they are similar in size to shreds. Toss the pieces in oil, salt, and pepper.

SAUTÉ

Heat a large skillet over medium-high. Add jackfruit; press into an even layer with a spatula. Cook, turning and pressing occasionally, until golden brown, 25 to 35 minutes. Season as desired. Serve with barbecue sauce.

WHAT IS JACKFRUIT?

A large tropical fruit native to Asia, it has a spiky exterior and bulbs with large seeds inside. When unripe, the skin is green and the flesh takes on the taste of whatever it's flavored with. The texture is similar to shredded pork, which is why it's a popular meat alternative.

HOW TO BUY

Although jackfruit is sold both fresh and frozen, the canned option is often easiest to find. Look for it in Asian grocery stores, in the international-foods aisle, or online. Canned jackfruit comes in a brine or syrup solution; rinse before using. Avoid the kind sold in syrup when making savory dishes.

Reader Taste Test

"Honestly, it **tasted like pulled pork.** I will definitely make it again so the vegetarians in our family have a main-course option."
—Kathy Starling, Keller, Texas

"I did not like it, but **my husband did.** He ate his and mine. If one of my vegetarian or vegan friends asked about it, I'd tell them to try it."
—Jan Perez, League City, Texas

August

Aubergine Dreams

Three easy recipes to make the most of eggplants, which are incredibly versatile fruits (they're actually not vegetables!)

STIR-FRIED SESAME
EGGPLANT WITH
BASIL

Stir-Fried Sesame Eggplant with Basil

ACTIVE 20 MIN. · TOTAL 20 MIN.
SERVES 4

Stir together 3 Tbsp. **oyster sauce,** 2 Tbsp. **toasted sesame oil,** 1 Tbsp. **rice vinegar,** and ½ tsp. **salt** in a small bowl. Cut 4 large **Japanese eggplants** lengthwise into quarters; cut into 3-inch pieces. Heat 2 Tbsp. **canola oil** in a large cast-iron skillet over high until a wisp of smoke rises from skillet. Add half of the eggplant; cook, stirring occasionally, until tender-crisp and deeply browned in spots, about 5 minutes. Transfer to a large bowl; do not wipe skillet clean. Repeat process with 2 Tbsp. **canola oil** and remaining eggplant; do not wipe skillet clean. Heat 1½ teaspoons **canola oil** in same skillet over medium. Add 1 Tbsp. each minced **garlic,** minced **ginger,** and finely chopped seeded **serrano chiles;** cook, stirring often, until fragrant, about 30 seconds. Return eggplant to skillet. Add oyster sauce mixture; stir to coat eggplant. Remove from heat. Stir in 1 cup loosely packed **fresh basil leaves** until wilted, about 30 seconds. Garnish with **sesame seeds** and additional **basil leaves.**

Unless a recipe calls for a specific shape, most eggplants can be used interchangeably.

Grilled Baby Eggplants with Tomato-Corn Relish

ACTIVE 30 MIN. · TOTAL 30 MIN.

SERVES 4

Stir together 1 cup each **fresh corn kernels** and chopped **tomato**, ¼ cup finely chopped **shallot**, 2 Tbsp. **olive oil**, 1½ Tbsp. **lime juice**, 1 Tbsp. seeded finely chopped **serrano chiles**, 1 tsp. **honey**, ½ tsp. **salt**, and ¼ tsp. **cumin** in a bowl; set aside. Cut 8 **small round eggplants** (such as Indian eggplants) in half lengthwise, and score cut sides ½ inch deep in a crosshatch pattern using the tip of a paring knife. Stir together ¼ cup **olive oil**, 2 tsp. **chili powder**, and 1 tsp. each grated **garlic** and **cumin** in a small bowl. Rub mixture into scored eggplant flesh. Sprinkle with 1 tsp. **salt**. Grill eggplant halves, cut sides down, on oiled grates over medium-high (400°F to 450°F), covered, until tender and charred in spots, 4 to 6 minutes per side. Transfer to a large platter. Top each eggplant half with about 1 Tbsp. corn mixture along with juices in bowl. Serve with remaining corn mixture.

Spicy Eggplant Dip

ACTIVE 40 MIN. · TOTAL 40 MIN.

SERVES 6

Peel 2 large (2 lb. total) **eggplants**, and cut into 1-inch pieces. Heat ½ cup **extra-virgin olive oil** in a large saucepan over medium. Stir in eggplant, 8 smashed **garlic cloves**, ½ cup **spicy or mild harissa** (hot chile paste), 1¾ tsp. **salt**, and ¾ tsp. **ground coriander**. Cover; cook, stirring often to prevent sticking, until eggplant is very tender and broken down, about 30 minutes. Remove from heat. Using a potato masher, mash eggplant mixture until smooth. Stir in ½ cup finely chopped **mixed fresh herbs** (such as mint, cilantro, and/or parsley) and 1½ Tbsp. **fresh lemon juice**. Garnish dip with additional **mixed fresh herbs**. Serve warm or at room temperature with **pita chips** or assorted sliced **vegetables**, such as carrots, celery, and peppers.

GRILLED BABY EGGPLANTS WITH TOMATO-CORN RELISH

SPICY EGGPLANT DIP

SHAGADELIC

Stirring Curiosity

Mixologist Joseph Stinchcomb leans on his roots and unique
local ingredients to craft cocktails that suit the season

"I FELL IN LOVE with bartending because I could be culinarily experimental and engage with people," says Joseph Stinchcomb, mixologist and co-owner of Bar Muse in Oxford, Mississippi. When he was young, his father exposed him to many different flavors and foods, instilling in him a "don't knock it till you try it" mindset. He brought this approach to his first restaurant job in college at Proud Larry's, also in Oxford, where his role evolved from being a dishwasher to a bartender–and there he discovered his love of mixology. In 2016, he joined the team at another local restaurant, Saint Leo, where he went on to serve as the beverage director and earned a James Beard Award semifinalist nod for Outstanding Bar Program.

Today, just around the corner in Stinchcomb's establishment, Bar Muse, you'll rarely find the same ingredient twice on the curated menu of classics that have been reinvented with new techniques. "I'm on an endless quest to make the perfect cocktail," he says. "It's something I'll explore for the rest of my life because I don't think there is one–my palate constantly develops and changes." Here, he uses that imaginative approach to create drinks with exciting flavors that celebrate the end of summer.

Shagadelic
ACTIVE 10 MIN. - TOTAL 40 MIN.
SERVES 1

Place 3 Tbsp. **Lillet Blanc,** 1½ Tbsp. **botanical gin** (such as Uncle Val's), 1½ Tbsp. **Grapefruit Shrub** (recipe follows), and 1 Tbsp. **Honey Syrup** (recipe right) in a cocktail shaker, and fill shaker with **ice.** Cover tightly with lid, and shake until blended, about 30 seconds. Pour through cocktail strainer over **ice** in a collins glass. Garnish with a strip of **lemon peel.**

Grapefruit Shrub
Stir together 3 Tbsp. grated **grapefruit zest,** 1¼ cups **granulated sugar,** ¾ tsp. **citric acid,** and ¼ tsp. **malic acid** in a bowl. Cover and refrigerate at least 8 hours or up to 24 hours. Add 2 cups **fresh grapefruit juice** and 1 cup **apple cider vinegar** to zest mixture. Transfer grapefruit mixture to a blender, and process on medium-high speed until frothy and bright pink, about 1 minute. Pour through a fine mesh strainer into a bowl, and discard solids. Use immediately, or refrigerate in an airtight container up to 2 weeks.

Honey Syrup
Add 1 cup **honey** and ¼ cup **water** to a medium saucepan, and stir to combine. Bring to a simmer over medium. Remove from heat; let cool completely, about 30 minutes. Use immediately, or refrigerate in an airtight container up to 2 weeks.

The Dark Knight
ACTIVE 5 MIN. - TOTAL 20 MIN.
SERVES 1

Place 2 Tbsp. **bourbon,** 1½ Tbsp. **Amaro Montenegro,** 1½ Tbsp. **fresh lime juice,** and 1 Tbsp. **Cinnamon Syrup** (recipe follows) in a cocktail shaker; fill shaker with **ice.** Cover tightly with lid; shake until blended, about 30 seconds. Pour through cocktail strainer into a fine mesh strainer set over a rocks glass with a **large ice cube.** Garnish with **ground cinnamon.**

Cinnamon Syrup
Place 2 cups **water** and 4 **cinnamon sticks** in a saucepan; boil over high. Remove from heat, and add 2 cups **granulated sugar.** Stir until sugar dissolves, about 2 minutes. Cool completely. Remove and discard cinnamon sticks.

LYRIC VICTORY

Lyric Victory
ACTIVE 5 MIN. - TOTAL 5 MIN.
SERVES 1

Pour 1 Tbsp. **mezcal (or tequila blanco),** 1 Tbsp. **simple syrup,** and 2 dashes of **lemon bitters** in a mixing glass; add **ice** to fill. Stir for 30 seconds. Pour through a fine mesh strainer into a wineglass; discard ice. Add 6 Tbsp. of **still or sparkling white wine;** garnish with a **lemon peel twist.**

THE DARK KNIGHT

KEY LIME-COCONUT
ICEBOX CAKE

Think Outside the Icebox

Three delicious twists on summer's coolest cakes

Key Lime-Coconut Icebox Cake

ACTIVE 30 MIN. - TOTAL 30 MIN., PLUS 8 HOURS CHILLING

SERVES 8

- 3½ cups heavy whipping cream, divided
- ⅔ cup plus 4 Tbsp. powdered sugar, divided
- ¼ tsp. kosher salt
- 2 Tbsp. grated Key lime zest or regular lime zest (from 3 Key limes or 1 regular lime), plus more for garnish
- ¼ cup fresh Key lime juice or regular lime juice (from 5 Key limes or 2 regular limes)
- 50 vanilla wafers or other thin, crispy vanilla cookies (about 8 oz. total, from 1 [11-oz.] pkg.)
- 1½ tsp. coconut extract
- 2 Tbsp. toasted shredded coconut, for garnish

1. Beat 2 cups of the cream, ⅔ cup of the powdered sugar, and the salt with an electric mixer fitted with a whisk attachment on medium speed until soft peaks form, about 2 minutes. Beat in Key lime zest and juice on medium-high speed until medium-to-stiff peaks form, about 1 minute.

2. Layer about one-third of the cookies on the bottom of a 9-inch pie plate coated with cooking spray. Break up about 8 cookies, and use as many pieces as necessary to fill in any gaps to form a solid layer of cookies. Spread half of the Key lime whipped cream over cookies. Repeat with one-third of the cookies and remaining whipped cream. Top with remaining cookies. Cover tightly with plastic wrap, and chill 8 hours.

3. When ready to serve icebox cake, beat remaining 1½ cups cream, remaining 4 tablespoons powdered sugar, and the coconut extract in a large bowl with an electric mixer on medium speed until medium peaks form, about 2 minutes.

4. Pipe or spread the coconut whipped cream over the top of the cake. Sprinkle with toasted coconut and Key lime zest. Slice as desired, and serve immediately.

Test Your Icebox IQ

Simple tricks for serving success

PREP PROPERLY If you're planning to remove the dessert from its pan, sprinkle the interior with a little water before lining it with plastic wrap to help the plastic stay in place.

WORK AHEAD You can make the Key Lime-Coconut and Chocolate-Peanut Butter icebox cakes up to three days in advance and refrigerate them. The Berry Tiramisu Icebox Cake is best if it's prepared on the day it's eaten.

KEEP IT CLEAN When you're ready to serve the cake, a large chef's knife will yield the neatest slices. Dip the blade in warm water between cuts.

Chocolate-Peanut Butter Icebox Cake

(Photo, page 5)

ACTIVE 50 MIN. - TOTAL 1 HOUR, 20 MIN., PLUS 6 HOURS CHILLING

SERVES 8

- 4⅔ cups heavy whipping cream, divided
- 1 cup sweetened creamy peanut butter (not natural peanut butter)
- ½ cup powdered sugar
- ¼ cup marshmallow creme
- 2 tsp. vanilla extract
- 1 (9-oz.) pkg. chocolate wafer cookies
- 6 oz. (1 cup) semisweet chocolate chips
- 1 Tbsp. plus 1 tsp. light corn syrup

1. Sprinkle about 2 teaspoons water in an 8½- x 4½-inch loaf pan (water will help plastic wrap stick to the sides and bottom). Line pan with 2 long pieces of plastic wrap, overhanging about 2 inches on sides and ends of pan (it should be long enough so it can be stretched to cover the cake once the pan is full).

2. Beat 3½ cups of the heavy cream, the peanut butter, powdered sugar, marshmallow creme, and vanilla with an electric mixer fitted with a whisk attachment on low speed until mixture begins to thicken, about 1 minute. Scrape down sides of bowl. Gradually increase speed to medium, and beat until medium-to-stiff peaks form, about 1 to 2 minutes.

3. Fill prepared pan two-thirds full with peanut butter whipped cream. Position the pan with 1 of the long sides facing you, and begin wedging cookies upright in horizontal rows of 16 to 17 (like dominoes), starting at the long side facing you and continuing until you reach the other end. You will have room for 4 rows of upright cookies.

4. Top with additional peanut butter whipped cream until pan is full (there may be some left over). Smooth with a spoon or an offset spatula; cover top of cake with plastic wrap overhang. Chill for 6 hours, or freeze for 4 hours for a firmer cake, if desired.

5. When you're ready to serve, microwave chocolate chips, ⅔ cup of the heavy cream, and corn syrup on HIGH in a medium-size microwavable bowl until thick and glossy, about 90 seconds, stirring every 30 seconds. Let cool to room temperature, about 30 minutes. Remove and reserve 1 tablespoon of the ganache; set aside.

6. Invert chilled cake onto a serving plate, and remove plastic wrap. Carefully pour ganache over cake, allowing it to run down the sides. Use a spoon or offset spatula to smooth ganache over entire top and sides of cake. Return cake to refrigerator to let the ganache set while making the topping.

7. Beat remaining ½ cup heavy cream in a large bowl with an electric mixer on medium speed until soft-to-medium peaks form, about 1 minute. Remove bowl from mixer. Add 1 to 2 teaspoons of the reserved ganache, gently stirring with a small spoon or offset spatula to create streaks. Spoon topping over the top of the cake. Slice and serve immediately.

Berry Tiramisu Icebox Cake

ACTIVE 45 MIN. - TOTAL 1 HOUR, 45 MIN., PLUS 4 HOURS CHILLING

SERVES 8

- 1 (16-oz.) container (about 3 cups) fresh strawberries, hulled and coarsely chopped, plus more for garnish
- 2 (6-oz.) containers fresh raspberries (about 1½ cups), plus more for garnish
- ¼ cup granulated sugar
- 2 Tbsp. fresh lemon juice
- 2-4 Tbsp. fruit-flavor liqueur (such as Chambord, Grand Marnier, or limoncello) or orange juice, as needed
- 2 cups mascarpone cheese (from 2 [8-oz.] pkg.), at room temperature
- 2 cups heavy whipping cream
- ½ cup powdered sugar
- 2 tsp. vanilla extract
- ¾ tsp. kosher salt
- 1 (7-oz.) pkg. crisp ladyfingers

1. Stir together strawberries, raspberries, granulated sugar, and lemon juice in a large bowl, and let stand at room temperature 1 hour. Line the bottom of a 9-inch springform pan with plastic wrap. Coat sides of pan with cooking spray, and line sides with a 3-inch-wide strip of parchment paper. Set aside.

2. Drain berry mixture over a shallow bowl, reserving juice. Pour juice into a measuring cup (you should have about ½ cup), and add liqueur or orange juice to yield ⅔ cup liquid. Set aside.

3. Place mascarpone in a large bowl, and beat briefly with an electric mixer on low speed to loosen. Add cream, powdered sugar, vanilla, and salt; beat on medium-high speed until medium peaks form, about 2 minutes, stopping to scrape down sides of bowl as needed.

4. Dip 1 ladyfinger in berry liquid for about 3 seconds, and place in prepared pan. Repeat with remaining ladyfingers and berry liquid, breaking ladyfingers as necessary to fit snugly and create a solid layer. Evenly cover with half of the drained berries (about 2 cups), and spread half of the mascarpone whipped cream (about 3 cups) over berries. Repeat with another layer of ladyfingers, berries, and mascarpone whipped cream. Cover tightly with plastic wrap, and refrigerate until icebox cake is firm, about 4 hours.

5. When ready to serve, remove sides of pan, and peel away parchment paper. Remove springform bottom and plastic wrap. Using a large spatula or cake lifter, carefully transfer to a serving platter. Garnish with additional strawberries and raspberries. Slice and serve cake immediately.

BERRY TIRAMISU
ICEBOX CAKE

Pockets Full of Sunshine

Celebrate the return of stone fruit season with jammy, buttery hand pies

Cherry-Lime Hand Pies

ACTIVE 25 MIN. · TOTAL 3 HOURS

MAKES 10

DOUGH

- 2¼ cups all-purpose flour, plus more for work surface
- 1 Tbsp. granulated sugar
- 1 tsp. kosher salt
- 1 cup cold unsalted butter, cubed
- 6-8 Tbsp. ice water, as needed

FILLING

- 2 cups pitted stemmed fresh cherries (from 10 oz. whole cherries), halved lengthwise
- ⅓ cup granulated sugar
- 1 Tbsp. cornstarch
- 1 tsp. grated lime zest plus 1 Tbsp. fresh juice (from 1 lime)

ADDITIONAL INGREDIENTS

- 1 large egg, beaten
- 2 Tbsp. turbinado sugar or sparkling sugar

1. Prepare the Dough: Pulse together flour, sugar, and salt in a food processor until combined, about 5 pulses. Add butter cubes; pulse until texture resembles coarse meal, about 10 pulses. Sprinkle mixture with 6 tablespoons ice water; pulse mixture 4 pulses. Add up to 2 additional tablespoons ice water as needed, using 1 tablespoon at a time and pulsing after each addition, until Dough just begins to clump together. Transfer to a lightly floured work surface, and knead until it just comes together, about 30 seconds. Shape Dough into a disk, and wrap tightly in plastic wrap. Chill until firm, about 30 minutes.

2. Unwrap chilled Dough, and roll out on a lightly floured work surface to ⅛-inch thickness. Using a 3-inch round cutter, cut out as many rounds as you can. Reroll scraps up to 2 times to make 20 Dough rounds total. Place rounds on a parchment paper–lined baking sheet, and refrigerate, uncovered, until ready to use.

3. Prepare the Filling: Stir together cherries, sugar, cornstarch, and lime zest and juice in a medium saucepan. Bring to boil over medium-high; boil, stirring often, until thickened, 3 to 4 minutes. Remove from heat. Transfer saucepan to refrigerator; chill until room temperature, about 1 hour.

4. Preheat oven to 350°F with racks in upper third and center positions. Place 1 heaping tablespoon Filling on center of each of 10 Dough rounds. Brush edges of the Filling-topped rounds with some of the beaten egg. Top with remaining rounds. Press Dough edges to seal, and crimp using a fork. Cut 4 small (about ½-inch-long) slits into the top of each pie.

5. Arrange pies 2 inches apart on 2 baking sheets lined with parchment paper. Brush tops of pies evenly with remaining beaten egg; sprinkle evenly with turbinado sugar. Bake in preheated oven until browned, 25 to 28 minutes, rotating baking sheets between top and middle racks halfway through bake time. Let cool completely on baking sheets, about 30 minutes.

CHERRY-LIME
HAND PIES

FRIED PEACH HAND
PIES (PAGE 168)

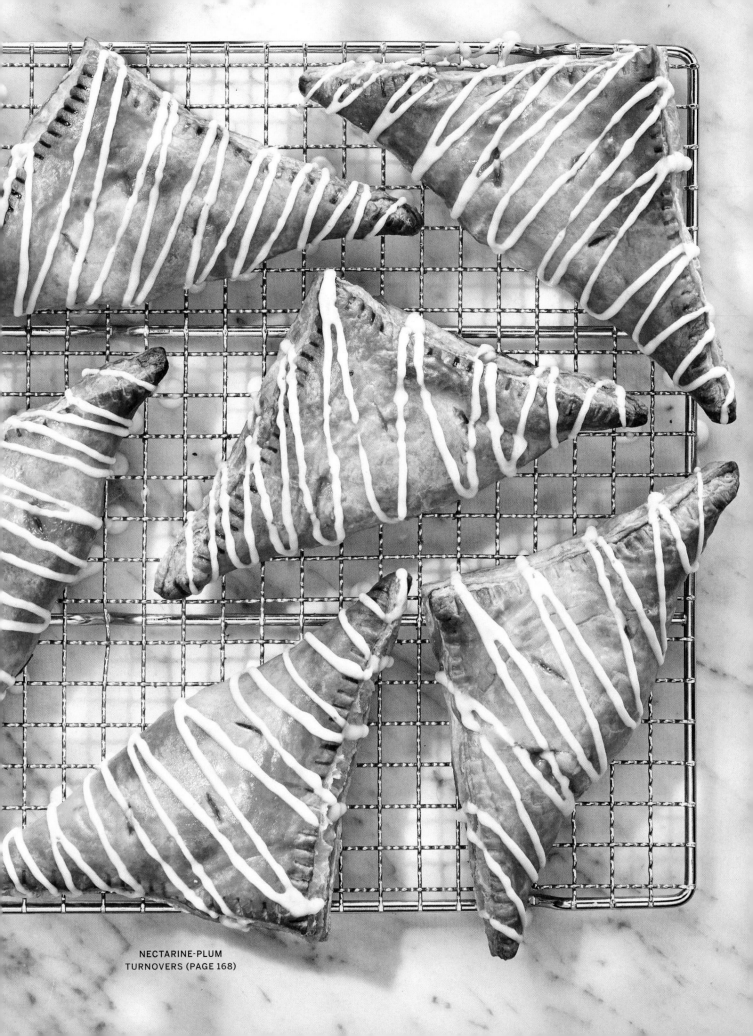

NECTARINE-PLUM
TURNOVERS (PAGE 168)

Nectarine-Plum Turnovers

(Photo, page 167)

ACTIVE 20 MIN. · TOTAL 1 HOUR, 10 MIN.

MAKES 8

- 3 large nectarines, unpeeled and thinly sliced (about 2½ cups)
- 3 red or black plums, unpeeled and thinly sliced (about 1½ cups)
- 3 Tbsp. light brown sugar
- 3 tsp. cornstarch
- ½ tsp. ground cinnamon
-    Pinch of kosher salt
- 1 (17.3-oz.) pkg. frozen puff pastry sheets (2 sheets), thawed but cold
-    All-purpose flour, for work surface
- 1 large egg, beaten
- 1½ cups powdered sugar

- ½ tsp. vanilla extract
- 2-3 Tbsp. whole milk, as needed

1. Preheat oven to 400°F. Line a large baking sheet with parchment paper; set aside. Stir together nectarines, plums, brown sugar, cornstarch, cinnamon, and salt in a bowl until combined. Set aside.
2. Roll each sheet of puff pastry into a 12-inch square on a lightly floured work surface. Cut each square into 4 (6-inch) squares (you will have 8 squares total). Place about ⅓ cup nectarine mixture on center of each square. Brush edges of filled dough with beaten egg. Fold dough in half over filling to form triangles. Press edges to seal, and crimp with a fork. Refrigerate until firm, about 15 minutes.
3. Brush top of each chilled pastry with some of the beaten egg. Cut 3 (¾-inch) slits into the top of each pastry. Bake in preheated oven until golden brown, 22 to 25 minutes. Remove from oven; let cool slightly on baking sheet, about 10 minutes.
4. Whisk together powdered sugar, vanilla, and 2 tablespoons of the milk in a small bowl until smooth, adding up to 1 tablespoon remaining milk, 1 teaspoon at a time, until desired consistency. Drizzle glaze over slightly cooled turnovers.

Fried Peach Hand Pies

(Photo, page 166)

ACTIVE 45 MIN. · TOTAL 2 HOURS

MAKES 8

DOUGH

- 3 cups all-purpose flour, plus more for work surface
- 3 Tbsp. granulated sugar
- 1 tsp. kosher salt
- ½ cup vegetable shortening, cut into cubes
- 1 large egg, beaten
- 1 cup whole buttermilk

FILLING

- 4 large peaches, peeled and chopped (about 2½ cups)
- ¼ cup packed light brown sugar
- 2 Tbsp. unsalted butter
- 2 tsp. cornstarch

- 1 tsp. grated fresh ginger
- ¼ tsp. ground cinnamon
-    Pinch of kosher salt

ADDITIONAL INGREDIENTS

- 1 large egg, beaten
-    Canola oil, for frying
-    Powdered sugar, for topping

1. Prepare the Dough: Stir together flour, sugar, and salt in a large bowl until combined. Using your fingers or a pastry cutter, cut shortening into flour mixture until small pea-size pieces remain. Stir in beaten egg and buttermilk until Dough just comes together. Shape into a rectangle (about 1 inch thick), and wrap tightly in plastic wrap. Refrigerate until firm, about 1 hour.
2. Meanwhile, prepare the Filling: Stir together peaches, brown sugar, butter, cornstarch, ginger, cinnamon, and salt in a medium saucepan. Bring to boil over medium-high; boil, stirring often, until peaches are tender and mixture is thickened, 4 to 5 minutes. Remove from heat; let cool to room temperature, about 1 hour.
3. Roll chilled Dough out on a lightly floured work surface to ⅛-inch thickness. Cut evenly into 16 (4-inch) squares, rerolling scraps up to 2 times as needed. Place Dough squares on a baking sheet lined with parchment paper, and place in refrigerator until ready to use.
4. Place 1 Dough square in palm of your hand, making a cup shape with your hand and the Dough. Place 2 tablespoons Filling on center of square. Brush edges of filled Dough lightly with beaten egg. Top with another square. Press edges to seal. Return to parchment-lined baking sheet; if desired, crimp with a fork. Repeat process with remaining Dough squares and Filling. Freeze until firm, about 15 minutes.
5. Meanwhile, fill a large Dutch oven two-thirds deep with oil. Heat over medium-high until a thermometer registers 350°F, about 10 minutes.
6. Working in batches, fry pies, 2 at a time, until golden brown, 4 to 5 minutes per batch. Drain on paper towels. Dust fried pies with powdered sugar.

Spice Up Breakfast

Start your day right with this quick Mexican-style skillet dish

HAVE IT YOUR WAY
Make this meal vegetarian with plant-based sausage, bump up the heat with hot sauce, or top servings with fried eggs.

Loaded Chilaquiles

ACTIVE 20 MIN. - TOTAL 20 MIN.
SERVES 4

- 1 cup plus 1 Tbsp. vegetable oil, divided
- 12 (6-inch) corn tortillas, cut into 6 wedges each
- ¾ tsp. kosher salt
- 12 oz. fresh Mexican chorizo, casings removed
- 1 cup red enchilada sauce
- 1 large tomato, chopped (¾ cup)
- 1 large avocado, diced (¾ cup)
- 4 oz. queso fresco (fresh Mexican cheese), crumbled (about 1 cup)
- 1 medium jalapeño chile, unseeded and thinly sliced (2 Tbsp.)
- ½ cup finely chopped red onion (from 1 onion)
  Fresh cilantro leaves

1. Heat 1 cup of the oil in a large skillet over medium-high. Working in 4 batches, fry tortilla wedges until lightly brown and crisp, 1 to 2 minutes per side. Drain tortilla chips on a paper towel-lined baking sheet. Sprinkle evenly with salt. Discard oil from skillet, and carefully wipe clean.

2. Heat remaining 1 tablespoon oil in skillet over medium-high. Add chorizo; cook, stirring often and breaking up using a wooden spoon, until cooked through, about 5 minutes. Transfer chorizo to a plate using a slotted spoon; reserve drippings in skillet. Cover chorizo with foil to keep warm.

3. Drain excess oil, reserving 1 tablespoon in skillet. Add enchilada sauce, and cook over medium until simmering, about 1 minute. Add tortilla chips; stir gently to coat. Remove skillet from heat. Top with chorizo, tomato, avocado, queso fresco, jalapeño, and red onion. Garnish with cilantro.

Make It Easy

Your no-sweat guide to the last party of the season

IT'S BEEN A LONG, HOT SUMMER, RIGHT?
After three months of hosting, you may be experiencing entertainer's burnout. Common symptoms of this might include the following: menu malaise, vague feelings of martyrdom, inspiration dysfunction, dishpan hands, and occasional delusions of grandeur. If you have these problems, you're not alone. Thousands of Southerners just like you are currently facing August with empty tanks—but we're here to help.

Give yourself a break, and use this menu of make-ahead recipes to celebrate the end of summer with one more delicious blast.

Tomato-Sandwich Toasts

Cut the tomatoes a few hours before serving if you like. Store them at room temperature for the best flavor.
ACTIVE 15 MIN. - TOTAL 15 MIN.
SERVES 8

Divide ¼ cup **mayonnaise** evenly among 4 (¾-inch-thick) toasted **brioche bread** slices, spreading in an even layer on one side of bread. Cut each slice in quarters diagonally, forming 16 triangle toast points. Divide 1 cup halved or quartered **cherry tomatoes** among toast points, and sprinkle with ⅛ tsp. each **kosher salt** and **black pepper**. Garnish with **fresh basil leaves**.

Pimiento Cheese-Stuffed Peppers

You can stuff these peppers up to three days ahead. Refrigerate in an airtight container, and garnish just before serving.
ACTIVE 20 MIN. - TOTAL 20 MIN.
SERVES 8

Drain 1 (14-oz.) jar of **Peppadew peppers**, and pat dry. Place ¾ cup softened **pimiento cheese** in a zip-top plastic bag, cutting a ¾-inch hole in one corner. Pipe cheese into peppers until slightly overstuffed; place on a plate. Garnish with chopped **fresh chives** and **black pepper**.

Cucumber-and-Onion Dip

Scratch this dip off your to-do list early. Refrigerate it in your chosen serving bowl up to three days in advance.
ACTIVE 15 MIN. - TOTAL 15 MIN.,
PLUS 30 MIN. CHILLING
SERVES 8

Stir together 1½ cups **sour cream**, 1 cup chopped peeled **English cucumber**, ½ cup **mayonnaise**, ¼ cup chopped **red onion**, 2 tsp. **ranch dressing mix**, and ¼ tsp. each **kosher salt** and **black pepper** in a bowl until well combined. Cover and refrigerate at least 30 minutes or up to 36 hours. Garnish with chopped **fresh parsley**, chopped **cucumber**, and chopped **red onion**; serve with **wavy potato chips**.

Pepper Sauce Watermelon Wedges

To save time, you can slice the watermelon the night before and refrigerate it in an airtight container. Drizzle, sprinkle, and garnish just before serving.
ACTIVE 10 MIN. - TOTAL 10 MIN.
SERVES 8

Place 16 (¾-inch-thick) **watermelon** wedges in an even layer on a platter. Drizzle both sides of wedges with 1 Tbsp. **liquid from a bottle of hot peppers in vinegar** (such as Texas Pete Pepper Sauce). Sprinkle with ½ tsp. **flaky sea salt** and ¼ tsp. **coarsely ground black pepper**. Garnish with 1 tsp. sliced **peppers from bottle of hot peppers in vinegar**.

> **START SIMPLE**
> Parties have a lot of moving parts, so make it easier whenever you can. All of these low-effort, big-flavor appetizers come together in minutes.

PIMIENTO CHEESE-STUFFED PEPPERS

CUCUMBER-AND-
ONION DIP

PEPPER SAUCE
WATERMELON
WEDGES

TOMATO-
SANDWICH
TOASTS

BAIL ON BARTENDING
Set up a beverage station so guests can serve themselves and you can relax. Give this punch a kick with a little bourbon, or serve it as is—it's wonderful either way.

BLACKBERRY-LIME
PORCH PUNCH
(PAGE 174)

ZESTY CORN-AND-
SQUASH SALAD
(PAGE 174)

ROASTED PEPPER-TOMATO
SALAD WITH CRISPY BLACK-
EYED PEAS (PAGE 174)

ACCEPT HELP
Don't be a party martyr. Let
a few guests bring sides.
Recruit a friend to be your
grill buddy. Allow people to
assist with cleanup. You'll
get a break, and they'll have
fun in the process.

THREE-PICKLE
POTATO SALAD
(PAGE 174)

Blackberry-Lime Porch Punch

(Photo, page 172)

Lighten your load by preparing the blackberry juice and combining it with the sweet tea, water, and fresh lime juice one day ahead. Just before serving, add the ginger beer and frozen berries. Stir in 1½ cups bourbon, if desired.

ACTIVE 20 MIN. - TOTAL 20 MIN.
SERVES 12

- 3 cups fresh blackberries
- 4 cups chilled sweet tea
- 2 cups cold water
- ½ cup fresh lime juice (from 5 limes)
- 4 (12-oz.) cans chilled nonalcoholic ginger beer
- 1 (16-oz.) bag frozen blackberries
  Ice
  Lime slices
  Fresh mint sprigs

1. Place fresh blackberries in a large bowl; mash with a potato masher until fully broken. Pour through a fine mesh strainer into a measuring cup or bowl, pressing pulp to release juice. Discard solids.
2. Pour blackberry juice into a large (4- to 6-qt.) punch bowl. Stir in sweet tea, water, and lime juice until well combined. Gently stir in ginger beer and frozen blackberries until just combined. Serve over ice. Garnish with lime slices and mint sprigs.

Zesty Corn-and-Squash Salad

(Photo, page 173)

The trick to making this ahead is layering. Prepare the dressing, and then add the corn. Top with zucchini and squash—without stirring—to help keep them fresh. Stir everything together just before serving.

ACTIVE 20 MIN. - TOTAL 20 MIN., PLUS 2 HOURS CHILLING
SERVES 6 TO 8

- 2 Tbsp. fresh lime juice (from 2 limes)
- 2 Tbsp. chopped fresh cilantro, plus more for garnish
- 1 tsp. Dijon mustard
- ¼ tsp. black pepper
- ⅛ tsp. cayenne pepper
- 1½ tsp. kosher salt, divided
- 2 Tbsp. extra-virgin olive oil
- 1¾ cups fresh corn kernels (from 2 ears)
- 1 medium zucchini, thinly sliced (about 1¾ cups)
- 1 medium yellow squash, thinly sliced (about 1¾ cups)
- ¼ cup chopped smoked almonds

1. Whisk together lime juice, cilantro, mustard, black pepper, cayenne pepper, and 1 teaspoon of the salt in a large bowl until combined. Gradually whisk in oil until emulsified, about 30 seconds.
2. Sprinkle corn evenly over lime juice mixture (do not stir). Top with sliced zucchini and squash (do not stir). Cover and refrigerate at least 2 hours or up to 24 hours.
3. Toss together vegetables and dressing with remaining ½ teaspoon salt. Sprinkle with smoked almonds, and garnish with remaining cilantro just before serving.

Roasted Pepper-Tomato Salad with Crispy Black-Eyed Peas

(Photo, page 173)

These crunchy black-eyed peas are great for snacking and can be made up to three days in advance. Shake up the dressing right in the bell pepper jar, and drizzle it over the salad just before serving.

ACTIVE 30 MIN. - TOTAL 1 HOUR, 30 MIN.
SERVES 6 TO 8

- 1 (15½-oz.) can black-eyed peas, drained and rinsed
- 1 tsp. kosher salt, divided
- ½ tsp. black pepper, divided, plus more for garnish
- 1½ lb. assorted heirloom tomatoes, cored
- 1 pt. multicolor cherry tomatoes
- 1 cup drained jarred roasted red bell peppers, sliced, plus 2 Tbsp. juice reserved in jar (from 1 [12-oz.] jar)
- 2 Tbsp. balsamic vinegar
- 2 Tbsp. extra-virgin olive oil
- 1 Tbsp. chopped fresh flat-leaf parsley, plus more for garnish
- 2 tsp. country-style Dijon mustard
- 1 garlic clove, thinly sliced (1 tsp.)
- 3¼ oz. crumbled goat cheese (about 3 Tbsp.)
  Flaky sea salt

1. Preheat oven to 375°F. Line a large rimmed baking sheet with aluminum foil, coat with cooking spray, and set aside. Stir together black-eyed peas, ½ teaspoon of the kosher salt, and

¼ teaspoon of the black pepper in a small bowl until fully coated. Arrange in an even layer on prepared baking sheet. Bake, stirring occasionally, until golden brown and crispy, about 40 minutes. Let cool completely, about 20 minutes.
2. Cut heirloom tomatoes into slices, wedges, or chunks, as desired. Cut larger cherry tomatoes in half, leaving smaller remaining tomatoes whole. Arrange all tomatoes and red bell pepper slices on a platter.
3. Add vinegar, oil, parsley, mustard, garlic, remaining ½ teaspoon kosher salt, and remaining ¼ teaspoon black pepper to reserved 2 tablespoons juice in jar. Cover with lid, and shake until fully combined, about 30 seconds. Drizzle evenly over tomato mixture. Sprinkle with goat cheese and about ¼ cup of the Crispy Black-Eyed Peas. (Reserve remaining black-eyed peas for another use.) Garnish with flaky sea salt, parsley, and black pepper.

Three-Pickle Potato Salad

(Photo, page 173)

This side will hold overnight in the fridge if well covered. Combine the ingredients in the serving bowl so you can grab and go when it's cookout time.

ACTIVE 25 MIN. - TOTAL 1 HOUR
SERVES 8

- 3 lb. petite red potatoes, scrubbed and cut into eighths
- 3 Tbsp. plus 1 tsp. kosher salt, divided
- ⅓ cup mayonnaise
- 2 Tbsp. dill pickle relish
- 1 Tbsp. chopped fresh dill, plus more for garnish
- ½ tsp. black pepper, plus more for garnish
- ½ cup chopped spicy pickled okra plus 1 Tbsp. juice from jar, and more okra for garnish
- ½ cup bread-and-butter pickle chips, plus more for garnish

1. Add potatoes, 3 tablespoons of the salt, and cold water to cover potatoes by 1 inch in a medium Dutch oven. Bring to a boil over high; reduce heat to medium-low. Cook, stirring occasionally, until fork-tender, 10 to 15 minutes. Drain well, and rinse with cold water. Let cool slightly in colander, about 15 minutes.

2. Meanwhile, whisk together mayonnaise, relish, dill, black pepper, 1 tablespoon pickled okra juice, and remaining 1 teaspoon salt in a large bowl. Add cooled potatoes, chopped okra, and pickle chips; stir together until combined. Serve immediately, or store, covered, in refrigerator up to 24 hours. Garnish with dill, black pepper, and more pickled okra and pickle chips.

Grilled Kebabs with Pickled-Peach Marinade

(Photo, page 176)

If you're planning to include chicken as one of the options, marinate those kebabs in a separate dish because the chicken has to cook to a higher temperature than the steak, pork, and shrimp.

ACTIVE 30 MIN. · TOTAL 1 HOUR

SERVES 8

- 4 lb. large peeled, deveined raw shrimp, or top sirloin steak, pork tenderloin, or boneless, skinless chicken breasts (cut into 1½-inch pieces)
- 3 medium peaches, peeled and pitted
- ¾ cup apple cider vinegar
- ½ cup extra-virgin olive oil
- ½ cup chopped red onion
- 2 Tbsp. chopped fresh dill
- 1 Tbsp. kosher salt, plus more to taste
- 1 tsp. smoked paprika
- ½ tsp. black pepper, plus more to taste
- ¼ tsp. crushed red pepper
- 1 small red onion, halved lengthwise
- 2 medium unpeeled peaches, halved and pitted
  Fresh mint sprigs

1. Thread desired meat onto each of 8 (12-inch) skewers. Place in an even layer in 2 glass or ceramic 13- x 9-inch baking dishes, and set aside. Place peeled and pitted peaches, vinegar, oil, chopped red onion, dill, salt, smoked paprika, black pepper, and crushed red pepper in a blender; process until smooth, about 30 seconds. Pour evenly over meat, turning skewers to coat. Cover and refrigerate at least 30 minutes for all meats (up to 1 hour for shrimp, up to 2 hours for pork, up to 4 hours for chicken, or up to 12 hours for steak).

2. Preheat grill to high (450°F to 500°F). Remove skewers from marinade (discard marinade). Place skewers, halved red onion, and unpeeled halved peaches on oiled grates. Grill, covered, turning halfway through cook time, until red onion and peaches are charred and just tender and a thermometer inserted into thickest portion of shrimp, pork, or steak registers 145°F and chicken registers 165°F (8 to 12 minutes for onion and peaches, 2 to 3 minutes for shrimp, 10 to 12 minutes for pork or steak, and 10 to 15 minutes for chicken).

3. Sprinkle skewers with additional salt and black pepper to taste, and place on a platter. Cut onion and peaches into wedges; place around skewers. Garnish with mint.

Peaches-and-Cream Icebox Pies

(Photo, page 177)

No special pans are required to make these easy desserts—all you need are jumbo muffin liners. Assemble the mini icebox pies up to three days ahead of time, and pull them out of the refrigerator just before serving. Top with a drizzle of warm Bourbon Caramel.

ACTIVE 50 MIN. · TOTAL 50 MIN., PLUS 4 HOURS CHILLING

SERVES 12

- 12 jumbo foil and 12 jumbo paper muffin liners
- 24 shortbread cookies
- ⅓ cup pecans
- 3 Tbsp. unsalted butter, melted
- ½ tsp. ground cinnamon
- 1½ cups heavy whipping cream
- 3 (8-oz.) pkg. cream cheese, softened
- ½ cup granulated sugar
- 1½ tsp. grated lemon zest
- ¼ tsp. kosher salt
- 1 medium peach, peeled and chopped (about ¾ cup)
- 2 medium peaches, sliced (about 2 cups)
  Bourbon Caramel (recipe follows)

1. Place 12 jumbo foil muffin liners on a large rimmed baking sheet. Place 12 jumbo paper liners inside foil liners; set aside. Pulse cookies and pecans in food processor until fine crumbs form, 15 to 20 pulses. Stir in melted butter and cinnamon until mixture resembles wet sand. Divide evenly among liners, about 4 teaspoons in each, pressing gently into bottom of the liner using your thumb. Refrigerate, uncovered, while preparing the peaches-and-cream filling.

2. Beat whipping cream in a large bowl with a hand mixer on medium-high speed until stiff peaks form, 2 to 3 minutes; set aside. Beat cream cheese, sugar, lemon zest, and salt in a large bowl with a hand mixer on medium-high speed until fluffy and creamy, 2 to 3 minutes. Gently fold whipped cream and chopped peach into cream cheese mixture until combined. Using a ½-cup measuring cup, divide mixture evenly among crust-filled liners. Refrigerate, uncovered, until firm, at least 4 hours (or, covered, up to 3 days).

3. Just before serving, divide peach slices evenly among pies; top each with 1 tablespoon warm Bourbon Caramel.

Bourbon Caramel

ACTIVE 10 MIN. · TOTAL 10 MIN., PLUS 1 HOUR CHILLING

MAKES ¾ CUP

- ½ cup granulated sugar
- ½ cup heavy whipping cream
- 1 vanilla bean pod, halved lengthwise
- 1 Tbsp. (½ oz.) bourbon
- ⅛ tsp. kosher salt

Heat sugar and 2 tablespoons water in a small saucepan over medium, swirling occasionally, until golden amber in color, 6 to 8 minutes. Remove from heat, slowly stirring in whipping cream until fully combined. Scrape vanilla seeds from pod. Whisk vanilla seeds, bourbon, and salt into sugar mixture until combined. Transfer to a heatproof jar; cover and refrigerate at least 1 hour or until ready to use. Just before serving, microwave on HIGH in 15-second intervals until warm.

SHOW OFF…JUST A SMIDGE
You can take it easy and still make a big impression. Adding a drizzle of warm caramel over a cold icebox dessert is a finishing touch your crowd won't soon forget.

GRILL GENEROUSLY
Kebabs are a great choice for a get-together. Use a versatile marinade to flavor a variety of proteins—chicken, shrimp, beef, and pork—so everyone can get what they want.

GRILLED KEBABS
WITH PICKLED-PEACH
MARINADE (PAGE 175)

PEACHES-AND-CREAM
ICEBOX PIES (PAGE 175)

Bowls of Plenty

Light on lettuce, these main-dish salads make hearty dinners

Barbecue-Pork Bowls

ACTIVE 30 MIN. - TOTAL 40 MIN.

SERVES 6

- 2 cups cubed cornbread
- 3 Tbsp. olive oil, divided
- ¼ cup stone-ground mustard
- 2½ Tbsp. honey
- 2 tsp. kosher salt
- 2 tsp. dry mustard
- ¾ cup plus 1 Tbsp. apple cider vinegar, divided
- 1½ tsp. grated garlic, divided (from 3 cloves)
- 2 (16-oz.) pkg. shredded tricolor coleslaw mix
- ¾ cup barbecue sauce
- 1½ lb. pulled smoked pork, warmed
- 1½ cups dill pickle chips

1. Preheat oven to 350°F. Toss cubed cornbread and 1 tablespoon of the oil on a rimmed baking sheet until well coated. Bake until lightly toasted, 10 to 15 minutes, stirring once halfway through bake time. Let cornbread croutons cool slightly, about 5 minutes.
2. Meanwhile, whisk together stone-ground mustard, honey, kosher salt, dry mustard, ¾ cup of the apple cider vinegar, 1 teaspoon of the garlic, and remaining 2 tablespoons oil in a medium saucepan; bring to a boil over medium-high, whisking occasionally. Pour mustard mixture into a large heatproof bowl. Stir in coleslaw mix until well combined.
3. Whisk together barbecue sauce and remaining 1 tablespoon apple cider vinegar and ½ teaspoon garlic in a medium bowl until combined. Divide coleslaw mixture, pulled pork, and pickles among 6 bowls. Drizzle pork with barbecue dressing, and top with reserved cornbread croutons.

MEAT OR THREE
Swap out the pulled pork for an equal amount of another smoked meat (like brisket or chicken), or use a combination of your favorites.

Steak Taco Salad

ACTIVE 45 MIN. - TOTAL 55 MIN.
SERVES 4

- 1 (8-oz.) container sour cream
- 2/3 cup smooth mild salsa
- 1/2 cup plus 1 Tbsp. chopped fresh cilantro, divided, plus more for garnish
- 3 tsp. kosher salt, divided
- 1 (1-oz.) envelope taco seasoning mix, divided
- 2 Tbsp. canola oil
- 3 ears (about 1 lb. total) fresh yellow corn
- 1 (1½-lb.) top sirloin steak (1 to 1½ inches thick)
- 1 (5-oz.) pkg. spring mix salad greens (about 7 cups)
- 1 (7-oz.) pkg. shredded Mexican 3-cheese blend (about 1¾ cups)
- 1½ cups roughly crushed tortilla chips
- 1½ cups diced plum tomatoes (from 3 medium tomatoes)
- 1½ cups thinly sliced pickled red onions (from 1 [16-oz.] jar)
- 2 medium avocados, chopped

1. Whisk together sour cream, salsa, 1 tablespoon of the cilantro, 1½ teaspoons of the salt, and 1½ teaspoons of the taco seasoning mix until smooth; set dressing aside.
2. Preheat grill to high (450°F to 500°F). Whisk together oil and remaining taco seasoning mix in a small bowl. Brush corn with 1½ teaspoons oil mixture; set remaining oil mixture aside. Pat steak dry using paper towels; sprinkle evenly with remaining 1½ teaspoons salt.
3. Place corn and steak on oiled grates. Grill corn, covered, until slightly charred and tender, 10 to 12 minutes, turning occasionally. Grill steak, covered, until a thermometer inserted into thickest portion registers 135°F to 145°F (medium), 8 to 11 minutes, or to desired degree of doneness, brushing both sides with reserved oil mixture halfway through grill time. Transfer steak to a cutting board. Cover with aluminum foil, and let rest 10 minutes.
4. When corn is cool enough to handle, cut kernels from cobs. Thinly slice steak against the grain; cut slices into 1-inch pieces. Divide lettuce and remaining ½ cup cilantro among 4 bowls. Top with steak, corn, cheese, chips, tomatoes, onions, and avocados. Drizzle as desired with dressing. Garnish with additional cilantro, and serve with remaining dressing.

DIY PICKLED ONIONS
Microwave ½ cup each vinegar and water in a heatproof jar for 3 minutes. Stir in 1 tsp. sugar, ½ tsp. salt, and 1 sliced red onion. Let stand 20 minutes.

PASTA POINTER
Toss the cooked, drained noodles with a little bit of olive oil to prevent sticking.

BLT Pasta Salad

ACTIVE 35 MIN. - TOTAL 35 MIN.
SERVES 8

- 1 Tbsp. garlic-and-herb butter
- ½ cup panko breadcrumbs
- 1 cup mayonnaise
- ⅓ cup whole milk
- 1 (1-oz.) envelope ranch dressing mix
- 4 tsp. Dijon mustard
- 1 (16-oz.) pkg. farfalle pasta, cooked al dente and cooled

- ½ cup thinly sliced scallions, plus more for garnish
- 2½ cups thinly sliced romaine lettuce (from 1 romaine heart)
- 1 lb. thick-cut bacon, cooked and chopped
- 2 cups assorted grape tomatoes, halved

1. Heat butter in a small skillet over medium until melted and bubbly. Add panko, and cook, stirring often, until toasted, 3 to 5 minutes. Transfer to a small bowl, and set aside.

2. Whisk together mayonnaise, milk, ranch dressing mix, and Dijon mustard in a large bowl. Add cooked pasta, scallions, lettuce, bacon, and tomatoes; toss gently until combined and coated with dressing. Sprinkle with toasted panko and additional sliced scallions just before serving.

RICE ADVICE
For fluffy results, place uncooked grains in a bowl. Then add water to cover. Gently swish with your fingers; drain and repeat until water is mostly clear.

Shrimp-and-Herb Rice Bowls

ACTIVE 30 MIN. · TOTAL 45 MIN.

SERVES 6

- 4 Tbsp. unsalted butter, divided
- ½ cup fresh vegetable trinity mix (onions, celery, and bell peppers, from 1 [8-oz.] pkg.)
- 2 cups uncooked long-grain white rice, rinsed well
- 1²/₃ cups vegetable broth
- 2½ tsp. kosher salt, divided, plus more to taste
- 2 lb. jumbo peeled, deveined raw shrimp, patted dry
- 3 Tbsp. olive oil
- 2 Tbsp. minced fresh garlic (from 6 cloves)
- ½ tsp. grated lemon zest plus 2 tsp. fresh juice (from 1 lemon), divided
- 2 Tbsp. finely chopped fresh herbs (such as thyme, chives, and parsley), plus more for garnish
- Seafood seasoning, for garnish
- Lemon wedges

1. Melt 2 tablespoons of the butter in a large Dutch oven over medium. Add vegetable trinity mix; cook, stirring constantly, until vegetables are just softened, 3 to 4 minutes. Stir in rice, broth, 1⅓ cups water, and ½ teaspoon of the salt; bring to a boil over medium-high. Reduce heat to low. Cover and cook, undisturbed, until rice is tender and liquid has absorbed, about 15 minutes. Remove from heat; let stand, covered, 5 minutes.

2. While rice cooks, stir together shrimp, olive oil, garlic, and remaining 2 teaspoons salt in a large bowl until combined. Heat a large skillet over medium-high. Working in batches, add shrimp mixture to skillet. Cook until shrimp turn pink and are cooked through, 2 to 3 minutes, turning shrimp halfway through cook time. Transfer cooked shrimp to a large serving bowl, and stir in fresh lemon juice until combined.

3. Fluff rice using a fork. Add to bowl with shrimp. Gently stir in herbs, lemon zest, and remaining 2 tablespoons butter until combined. Season with salt to taste. Sprinkle individual servings with seafood seasoning and additional chopped fresh herbs. Serve with lemon wedges.

Greek Chicken Bowls

ACTIVE 30 MIN. · TOTAL 30 MIN.

SERVES 6

- ½ cup tahini (ground sesame seeds)
- ½ tsp. grated lemon zest plus ¼ cup fresh juice (from 2 lemons)
- 1 Tbsp. honey
- 2 tsp. Greek seasoning, plus more to taste
- ¼ tsp. smoked paprika
- 1 medium garlic clove, grated
- ⅓ cup warm water, plus more if needed
- 3 cups pulled rotisserie chicken
- 1 medium cucumber, thinly sliced (about 2¼ cups)
- 4 cups torn butter lettuce leaves (from 1 head)
- 2 cups roughly chopped Kalamata olives
- 1 cup sliced roasted red bell peppers (from 1 [12-oz.] jar)
- ¼ cup chopped tender fresh herbs (such as parsley and mint)
- 2 cups broken pita chips

1. Whisk together tahini, lemon zest and juice, honey, Greek seasoning, paprika, and garlic until combined. Gradually whisk in water, a little at a time, until dressing is smooth and pourable, adding more water, if needed. Set aside.

2. Add chicken and cucumber to a large bowl; lightly season to taste with Greek seasoning. Stir in lettuce, olives, peppers, and herbs until combined. When ready to serve, stir in pita chips. Transfer to a platter or serving bowls; drizzle with dressing just before serving.

DRESS FOR SUCCESS

Lemon juice causes tahini to seize up when first combined; gradually whisk in warm water to loosen the dressing.

Aw, Shucks

You won't miss the extra sugar and fat in this healthier side

"Creamed" Corn with Basil

ACTIVE 25 MIN. · TOTAL 25 MIN.
SERVES 6

- 8 medium ears fresh corn, shucked
- 3 Tbsp. unsalted butter, divided
- 1 small yellow onion, chopped (about ¾ cup)
- 1 tsp. kosher salt
- ⅛ tsp. cayenne pepper
- ¼ to ½ cup vegetable broth
   Small fresh basil leaves
   Black pepper

1. Cut kernels from corn cobs using a sharp knife; transfer kernels to a large bowl. Place cobs over a bowl; use back of a knife to scrape cobs, releasing as much corn milk as possible.
2. Melt 2 tablespoons of the butter in a large skillet over medium. Add onion, salt, and cayenne pepper; cook, stirring often, until onion is tender, about 5 minutes. Stir in reserved corn kernels and corn milk; cook, stirring often, until corn is tender, 4 to 6 minutes.
3. Reduce heat to low; transfer half of corn mixture to a blender. Secure lid on blender, and remove center piece to allow steam to escape. Add ¼ cup of the vegetable broth, and place a kitchen towel over opening. Process until mostly smooth, about 30 seconds, adding up to ¼ cup additional broth as needed to reach desired consistency.
4. Return corn mixture to skillet, and stir in remaining 1 tablespoon butter. Cook over medium, stirring constantly, until mixture thickens, about 2 minutes. Remove from heat; garnish with basil and black pepper.

Before Recipe Makeover:

CALORIES: **338** – ADDED SUGAR: **3 G** – FAT: **27 G**

After Recipe Makeover:

CALORIES: **177** – ADDED SUGAR: **0 G** – FAT: **8 G**

GOOD FOR YOU!
Fresh basil is a great way to showcase the flavor of sweet summer corn without adding sugar, salt, or fat.

Ice Capades

Cool down with simple frozen desserts made with fresh fruits

Watermelon Granita

ACTIVE 15 MIN. - TOTAL 15 MIN., PLUS 3 HOURS
FREEZING
SERVES 4

1½	lb. seedless watermelon, cubed (about 3 cups)
¼	cup granulated sugar
1	Tbsp. lime zest plus 3 Tbsp. fresh juice (from 2 limes)
¼	tsp. kosher salt

Garnishes: lime zest twists, lime slices, and watermelon cubes

1. Combine watermelon, sugar, lime zest and juice, and salt in a blender. Process until smooth, 1 minute.
2. Pour mixture into a 13- x 9-inch baking pan. Freeze for 1 hour.
3. Remove pan from freezer (sides of mixture should be frozen, but center will not be set). Using a fork, lightly scrape sides of granita. Freeze for 1 hour. Repeat process every hour until granita is fully frozen and flaky, about 3 hours total.
4. Divide granita evenly into 4 glasses. Garnish with lime zest twists, lime slices, and watermelon cubes; serve immediately.

Peach Granita
SERVES 4

In Step 1, substitute 3 cups peeled and sliced **fresh peaches** for watermelon. Proceed with recipe as directed. In Step 4, garnish with **lime zest** twists, **lime** slices, and **peach** slices.

Blackberry Granita
SERVES 4

Skip Step 1. Then process 3 cups **fresh blackberries** and 1 cup water in a food processor until smooth. Pour mixture through a fine mesh strainer into a large bowl. Stir in ½ cup **sugar**, 1 Tbsp. **lime zest**, 3 Tbsp. **lime juice**, and ¼ tsp. **salt**. Proceed with Steps 2 and 3 as directed. In Step 4, garnish with **lime zest** twists, **lime** slices, and **fresh blackberries**.

Add some zing: For an adults-only version, serve the granita with a splash of tequila, rum, vodka, or sparkling rosé.

BLACKBERRY GRANITA

PEACH GRANITA

WATERMELON GRANITA

Faux-caccia

Combine pimientos, cheese, and deli pizza dough for an easy-bake bread

Pimiento Cheese Flatbread

ACTIVE 30 MIN. - TOTAL 35 MIN.

SERVES 10

- 7 Tbsp. mayonnaise, divided
- 10 oz. shredded sharp Cheddar cheese (about 2½ cups), divided
- 1 lb. fresh pizza dough, at room temperature
- 1 (4-oz.) jar diced pimientos, drained and divided (about ⅓ cup)
- ¼ cup diced yellow onion (from 1 small onion), divided
- ½ tsp. smoked paprika, divided
- ½ tsp. cayenne pepper, divided
- ½ tsp. black pepper, divided
- Flaky sea salt

SECRET SWAP

In this Southern spin on focaccia, mayo stands in for the olive oil that's typically used to grease the baking pan and drizzle over the dough.

1. Preheat oven to 425°F. Spread 1 tablespoon of the mayonnaise to grease a 13- x 9-inch rectangle in center of a rimmed baking sheet; sprinkle ½ cup of the cheese evenly over mayonnaise. Using your hands, stretch pizza dough into a 13- x 9-inch oval or rectangle; place on top of cheese on prepared pan. Brush 2 tablespoons of the mayonnaise over dough; press fingers deeply into dough to create dimples.

2. Sprinkle dough with 1 cup of the cheese; half of the pimientos; 2 tablespoons of the onion; and ¼ teaspoon each of the paprika, cayenne, and black pepper. Bake in preheated oven until top is golden brown and bread is baked all the way through, about 20 minutes.

3. While bread bakes, stir together remaining 1 cup cheese; 4 tablespoons mayonnaise; half of the pimientos; 2 tablespoons onion; and ¼ teaspoon each paprika, cayenne, and black pepper in a small bowl. Set aside.

4. Remove bread from oven; let cool about 5 minutes. Slice bread, garnish with flaky sea salt, and serve warm with additional pimiento cheese.

COOKING SCHOOL

TIPS AND TRICKS FROM THE SOUTH'S MOST TRUSTED KITCHEN

All the Fixings
We combed the South for charcuterie inspiration

Finocchiona Salami from Salume Beddu
MADE IN ST. LOUIS, MO
Featuring toasted fennel, red wine, and pork from heritage-breed hogs, this small-batch salami has a mild sweetness that plays well with nutty cheeses. *salumebeddu.com*

Apple & Horseradish Jam from Terrapin Ridge Farms
MADE IN CLEARWATER, FL
Sweet apple juice is blended with spicy horseradish to create an excellent companion for salty cured meats and cheeses. It also doubles as a glaze for grilled chicken or pork. *terrapinridge.com*

Rosemary Olive Oil Crackers from Georgia Sourdough Co.
MADE IN ATLANTA, GA
With tangy sourdough and fragrant rosemary, these crackers are extra crunchy. *georgia sourdoughco.com*

Mango Wood Rectangle Paddle Serving Board from the *Southern Living* Collection at Dillard's
Made of strong and durable mango wood, it has ample space to hold all your favorite snacks, comes in two colors, and includes a jute rope for hanging. *dillards.com*

Thomasville Tomme from Sweet Grass Dairy
MADE IN THOMASVILLE, GA
This semisoft French farmhouse-style cheese is extremely versatile. It has subtle grassy undertones and a lovely buttery texture that pairs well with just about anything. *sweetgrassdairy.com*

Pickled Okra from Lowcountry Produce
MADE IN BEAUFORT, SC
The heat and acidity of this okra cuts through the richness of soft cheeses. It also makes a great stand-in for olives in dirty martinis. *lowcountryproduce.com*

September

Make It Snappy

Sweet and juicy, the best-tasting pole beans are here

SKILLET-
CHARRED POLE
BEANS WITH
BACON

Skillet-Charred
Pole Beans with Bacon

ACTIVE 25 MIN. - TOTAL 25 MIN.

SERVES 6

Stir together 3½ Tbsp. **red wine vinegar,** 1 Tbsp. **olive oil,** 2 tsp. **granulated sugar,** 1 tsp. minced **fresh garlic,** and 1 tsp. **kosher salt** in a medium bowl. Heat a 12-inch skillet over medium. Add 4 **center-cut bacon slices;** cook, turning occasionally, until crispy, about 6 minutes. Transfer bacon to a paper towel-lined plate, reserving drippings in skillet. Let bacon cool 5 minutes; crumble. Add 1 lb. **fresh green pole beans** (trimmed) to drippings in skillet; cook over medium, using tongs to toss beans occasionally, until charred in spots, about 8 minutes. Remove skillet from heat, and drizzle vinegar mixture over beans. Toss beans until well coated and vinegar mixture is mostly evaporated, about 30 seconds. Top with crumbled bacon just before serving.

New-Fashioned
Two-Bean Salad

ACTIVE 20 MIN. - TOTAL 20 MIN.

SERVES 6

Fill a large bowl with **ice water;** set aside. Bring a large pot of **salted water** to a boil over high. Add 16 oz. **fresh green and yellow pole beans** (trimmed) to boiling water, and cook until tender-crisp, about 3 minutes. Transfer beans to ice water; let cool 1 minute. Drain, and pat dry with paper towels. Whisk together ½ cup **mayonnaise,** 3 Tbsp. **whole buttermilk,** 1 Tbsp. minced **shallot,** 1 Tbsp. chopped **fresh dill,** 1 Tbsp. finely chopped **fresh chives,** 1 tsp. **fresh lemon juice,** ½ tsp. **Dijon mustard,** ¼ tsp. **kosher salt,** and ¼ tsp. **black pepper** in a medium bowl. Place beans on a platter; top evenly with ½ cup thinly sliced **radish.** Drizzle desired amount of dressing over bean mixture. Garnish with **fresh dill fronds** and grated **lemon zest.** Serve with remaining dressing.

NEW-FASHIONED
TWO-BEAN
SALAD

Beer-Battered Green Bean
Fries with Spicy Dipping Sauce

ACTIVE 25 MIN. - TOTAL 35 MIN.

SERVES 6

Stir together ½ cup **mayonnaise,** 2 Tbsp. **ketchup,** and 1 Tbsp. **hot sauce** in a small bowl; set aside. Whisk together 1 cup **all-purpose flour,** 2 tsp. **kosher salt,** 2 tsp. **paprika,** and 1 tsp. **garlic powder** in a large bowl. Add 1 lightly beaten **large egg** to bowl; whisk in 1½ cups cold **light beer** until combined. Add **vegetable oil** to a large Dutch oven, filling to a depth of 2 inches; heat over medium to 360°F. Working in 3 batches, dip 12 oz. **fresh green pole beans** (trimmed), 1 at a time, into batter to fully coat, letting excess drip off. Add beans (1 at a time) to hot oil, and fry until crust is golden brown, 3 to 4 minutes per batch. Transfer cooked beans to a paper towel-lined baking sheet. Serve with dipping sauce.

The Beauty of an Ordinary Biscuit

Returning to the humble roots of this beloved Southern pastry

MICAH'S BUTTERMILK
BISCUITS (PAGE 192)

NOT LONG AGO, my ego stood almost as tall as my biscuits. At a bakery in South Carolina, I feigned humility when coworkers called me "the biscuit master," but deep down, I felt a little too much pride over my flaky creations. Nowadays, my biscuits are short and without any distinct layers—and that's okay with me.

Many modern recipes promise to deliver "perfect" results. From shredding frozen butter to folding the dough in a pattern rivaling origami, these techniques often work, but they can also convince people that they need to be a pastry chef or have learned from a Southern-born grandma to achieve blue-ribbon results.

As an actual pastry chef from the South, I had fixed ideas about biscuits. Then I learned the truth: There is no perfect recipe. Working in restaurants and bakeries didn't afford me this lesson. Instead, the knowledge I held close was completely undone in one afternoon spent in a sunny kitchen in Marion, Alabama.

In this tiny town, chef and Alabama native Scott Peacock has made a home for himself and created a space for the craft of biscuit making. For the past four years, he has shared his wisdom in intimate classes he calls The Black Belt Biscuit Experience. Part history lesson and part workshop, they take place in a Greek Revival mansion that has been outfitted with a modern-day kitchen.

Following his James Beard Award-winning tenure at Watershed in Decatur, Georgia, and the passing of his beloved friend and mentor, chef Edna Lewis, Peacock began a research project interviewing some of the oldest Alabamians about their early food memories. In a conversation with a 100-year-old woman from his hometown of Hartford, Peacock learned that biscuits were once considered a luxury compared to cornbread. The high cost of flour in the South before the increased industrialization of wheat production meant that they were not eaten every day. Both practical and precious, a good batch would feed a crowd and make the most out of flour, butter or lard, and buttermilk.

That changed with the rise of the "synthetic biscuit," as Peacock calls the canned and frozen varieties, which he grew up eating. Large in size and homogeneous in color and shape, they were so foolproof to make that you could enjoy them at any meal of the day. Over the years, biscuits in advertisements, cookbooks, and magazines (including this one) grew higher, flakier, and more golden—almost engineered for their close-ups.

Using some of the oldest recipes he could find, Peacock fine-tuned a process that respects the generations of hands that made delicious ones without concerns about appearances. This method is no secret. At The Black Belt Biscuit Experience I attended, he baked a few dozen and explained each ingredient and technique in detail. Every step left me less certain that I knew what I was doing.

Words of Wisdom

Helpful tips for biscuits (and life)

Keep Watch
These bake at a very hot 500°F. Because oven temperatures can vary, monitor them after 10 minutes to make sure they don't overbrown.

Practice Doesn't Make Perfect
Each batch offers a chance to learn something new. Don't aim for perfection; the "ideal" biscuit is one that makes you smile with each bite.

Don't Skimp
There are few ingredients in biscuits, so each one counts. Use whole (not low-fat) buttermilk when possible. If you can find it, small-batch buttermilk from a local dairy may have more flavor than the commercial kinds.

Flour Power
Make sure your hands, surfaces, and cooking tools are lightly floured. This is a very wet dough, so have extra flour on hand for dusting in case things get sticky.

Before, I had always taken care to cube frozen butter to just the right size so the dough would transform into those coveted layers (what pastry chefs call "lamination"). During the class, I tried to hold back my surprise as Peacock plopped an entire block of butter into the flour. He methodically pressed the flour into the butter with his fingers, creating elongated pieces that he compared to flower petals. Then he added an alarming amount of buttermilk, stirred the mixture with a wooden spoon, and turned the wet mass onto a floury surface. I'd never made a biscuit that could hold that much liquid. However, these were short and baked at an almost unbelievable 500°F, so they could handle a higher proportion of buttermilk, which created an extra-crusty exterior and a soft, tangy inside.

He gathered the dough together several times—with no kneading, cutting, or stacking—before rolling it to a thinness that would raise eyebrows in many bakeries. He punched out the shape with a round cutter and lined them up on the baking sheet. Finally, he cut the remaining dough into uneven segments to cook alongside the biscuits. These "leavings" can act as a barometer to help you determine just how browned you like your biscuits.

My anticipation mounted for the 10 minutes they spent in the oven, as wafts of toasting flour and evaporating buttermilk filled the kitchen. When they emerged, they were plain and small. My inner critic noticed patches of uneven brown blanketing the surface. I easily pulled one apart, and with my first taste experienced an unmistakable rush of joy. A crusty bite dissolved into a tender center that surpassed any fancy version I'd tried. I polished off two more, feeling humbled.

Even after baking countless trays, Peacock still marvels at the slight differences from batch to batch and says each one teaches him something new. I left Marion that day with a newfound belief in something he says about biscuits and life in the South: "There really is nothing ordinary about the ordinary." –Micah A. Leal

Micah's Buttermilk Biscuits

(Photo, page 190)

Inspired by chef Scott Peacock's class, this recipe produces tender biscuits that are not tall and layered.

ACTIVE 20 MIN. · TOTAL 35 MIN.

MAKES 14 BISCUITS, PLUS SCRAPS

- 4 cups unbleached all-purpose flour, plus more for folding, rolling, and cutting
- 1 Tbsp. cream of tartar
- 2 tsp. fine sea salt
- 1½ tsp. baking soda
- 10 Tbsp. unsalted butter, chilled and cut into 1-Tbsp. pieces
- 2¼ cups whole buttermilk

1. Preheat oven to 500°F with rack in top third position. Line 1 large (about 18- x 13-inch) rimmed heavy baking sheet with parchment paper; set aside.

2. Whisk together flour, cream of tartar, sea salt, and baking soda in a large bowl until combined, about 30 seconds.

3. Toss butter pieces in flour mixture to coat. Using hands, pull out each piece of butter with some flour, and press between fingertips to flatten, pressing flour into butter. Continue to break butter into smaller pieces, flattening with fingertips until pieces are thin and long, resembling flower petals. Stir buttermilk into flour-butter mixture with a large spoon until all liquid is absorbed. Mixture will be very wet.

4. Transfer dough to a generously floured work surface; press together into a mound. Sprinkle surface of dough with additional flour to prevent sticking, and press into a 2-inch-thick round. Lift 1 edge of round; fold it over opposite side, forming a semicircle. Gently press dough into a 2-inch-thick round, flouring as needed to prevent sticking. Repeat folding process 2 more times, gently pressing dough into a 1½-inch-thick round after last fold. Using a lightly floured rolling pin, roll dough out to ¾-inch thickness, moving from center of dough outward but not back and forth.

5. Flour a 2½-inch round pastry cutter, and tap to knock off excess. Cut out biscuits by pressing down on edges of cutter (do not twist), flouring and tapping cutter between biscuits. Transfer to prepared baking sheet, placing 1 inch apart. Using a knife, cut remaining dough scraps into irregular shapes. Transfer as many as will fit onto prepared baking sheet, placing about ¾ inch apart. Discard any remaining scraps.

6. Bake in preheated oven until lightly browned on top and smelling of toasted flour, 10 to 12 minutes. Cool slightly on baking sheet, about 5 minutes. Serve warm.

A Sweet New Year

Atlanta TV host Skye Estroff and her grandmother celebrate Rosh Hashanah with cherished family desserts

ON ROSH HASHANAH, it's customary for Jewish people to wish one another a "sweet" New Year. Anita Estroff, however, takes it a bit more literally. Although brisket is usually the star of the holiday on most menus, Anita's legendary dessert buffet takes the cake, with up to 15 treats displayed on elegant plates and statuesque stands.

For Anita's granddaughter Skye Estroff, these family-famous recipes sparked her lifelong love of food. When she was growing up, Skye spent a lot of time in Vidalia, Georgia, baking with her grandmother, "Nini." Now a TV, radio, and podcast host covering the Atlanta culinary scene on shows like Foodie Road Trip and The Georgia Foodcast, Skye fondly recalls her early days cooking with her grandmother when she wasn't even tall enough to see over the counter. "Some of my oldest memories are being in Nini's kitchen and making sugar cookies," Skye says. "She was pretty strict with the baking, and it had to be done the right way."

The "right way," Anita says, means being precise, but it's also just what tastes delicious. For her, this often translates to forgoing chocolate in favor of locally grown pecans and a hefty glug of vanilla.

"There are certain ingredients that I always look for in a recipe," Anita says. "If a recipe has butter, sour cream or cream cheese, and pecans in it, then I know it has got to be good—and it has to have a lot of vanilla."

Among those lucky enough to receive a seat at Anita's table are members of the only temple in Vidalia, of which she is a founding member. Beth Israel Synagogue doesn't have an official rabbi; instead, Friday prayers are led by "the sisterhood," a group of four female temple members. On the first Friday of each month, they come together in Anita's home for a proper supper before services, followed by a bountiful array of sweets that reflect their shared Southern-Jewish heritage, like gooey Chocolate Meringue Cookies, crumbly Party Coffee Cake, and biscotti-like Mandel Bread.

"Jewish and Southern cultures both focus on making people feel welcome— and having huge portions of food," Skye says. "In our family, those concepts are done to the next level. You're going to be welcomed to Nini's house like family, and you're never going to leave hungry."

Mandel Bread

ACTIVE 35 MIN. - TOTAL 1 HOUR, 45 MIN., PLUS 3 HOURS CHILLING AND 1 HOUR COOLING

MAKES ABOUT 40 COOKIES

6	large eggs
1½	cups granulated sugar
1½	cups vegetable oil
1½	tsp. almond extract
1	tsp. vanilla extract
1	tsp. lemon extract
1	tsp. orange extract
4½	cups all-purpose flour, sifted
1	tsp. baking powder
¼	tsp. kosher salt
3	cups semisweet chocolate chips or chopped pecans

1. Beat eggs in a large bowl with an electric mixer on medium speed until smooth, about 30 seconds. Increase

Continued on page 194

Continued from page 193

mixer speed to high, and gradually add sugar; beat on high speed until mixture has doubled in volume and is pale yellow in color, 4 to 5 minutes. Reduce mixer speed to medium; gradually beat in oil and almond, vanilla, lemon, and orange extracts until combined.

2. Whisk together flour, baking powder, and salt in a medium bowl. Gradually add flour mixture to egg mixture, beating on low speed just until combined. Add chocolate chips or nuts; fold by hand with a rubber spatula until combined. Cover and chill until dough is firm, at least 3 hours or up to 24 hours.

3. Preheat oven to 350°F. Shape one-fourth of the dough (about 1¾ cups) into an 8- x 4-inch rectangle (about ¾ inch thick) on 1 half of a parchment paper–lined baking sheet. Repeat process with another one-fourth of the dough, spacing rectangles 3 inches apart. Cover and refrigerate remaining dough until ready to use.

4. Bake in preheated oven until edges are lightly golden and tops bounce back when pressed, about 20 minutes. (Dough rectangles will spread significantly in oven.) Let cool on baking sheet on a wire rack 10 minutes. Reduce oven temperature to 300°F.

5. Carefully place 1 cooled rectangle on a cutting board. Cut crosswise into about 10 (¾-inch) slices, wiping knife clean between cuts. Return slices to parchment paper–lined baking sheet, cut side up, spacing ¼ inch apart. Repeat with second rectangle.

6. Bake at 300°F until lightly golden around edges and toasted, 20 to 25 minutes, carefully turning cookies once halfway through baking.

7. Increase oven temperature to 350°F. Let cookies cool completely on baking sheet on a wire rack, 30 to 45 minutes. While cookies cool, repeat shaping and baking process with remaining chilled dough. Store in an airtight container for up to 5 days.

Party Coffee Cake

ACTIVE 25 MIN. - TOTAL 1 HOUR, 25 MIN.
SERVES 12

TOPPING
- 1 cup chopped pecans
- ½ cup granulated sugar
- 1 tsp. ground cinnamon

BATTER
- 1 cup unsalted butter, softened
- 1 cup granulated sugar
- 3 large eggs, at room temperature
- 1 cup sour cream, at room temperature
- 2½ cups all-purpose flour, sifted
- 2 tsp. baking powder
- 1 tsp. baking soda
- 1 tsp. grated lemon zest
- 1 tsp. vanilla extract
- ¼ tsp. kosher salt
  Baking spray with flour

1. Preheat oven to 375°F. Prepare the Topping: Stir together pecans, sugar, and cinnamon in a small bowl until well combined. Set aside.

2. Prepare the Batter: Beat butter and sugar in a large bowl with an electric mixer on medium speed until fluffy, 3 to 4 minutes, stopping to scrape down sides of bowl as needed. Add eggs, 1 at a time, beating on medium speed just until combined after each addition. Add sour cream; beat on medium speed until incorporated, about 15 seconds. Whisk together flour, baking powder, and baking soda in a medium bowl until combined. With mixer on low speed, gradually add flour mixture to butter mixture, beating just until nearly combined and stopping to scrape down sides of bowl as needed. Add lemon zest, vanilla, and salt; beat on low speed just until combined, about 15 seconds. (Batter will be thick.)

3. Coat a 13- x 9-inch baking pan with baking spray. Spread half of the Batter (about 2½ cups) evenly in bottom of prepared pan with a small offset spatula or the back of a spoon. Sprinkle evenly with half of the Topping. Spoon small dollops of remaining Batter all over top; spread into an even layer. Sprinkle remaining Topping evenly over top.

4. Bake in preheated oven until a wooden pick inserted in the center comes out clean, 20 to 25 minutes. Let cool in pan on a wire rack 40 minutes. Serve warm or at room temperature.

Chocolate Meringue Cookies

ACTIVE 30 MIN. - TOTAL 1 HOUR, 15 MIN.
MAKES 20 COOKIES

- 1 cup finely chopped semisweet chocolate (from 2 [4-oz.] 56% cacao semisweet chocolate bars)
- 2 large egg whites, at room temperature
- ¼ tsp. cream of tartar
- ½ cup granulated sugar
- ¾ cup chopped pecans
- ¼ tsp. vanilla extract
- ⅛ tsp. table salt

1. Preheat oven to 350°F. Fill a medium saucepan with water to a depth of 1 inch. Bring to a boil over medium-high, then reduce heat to a simmer over medium-low. Place chocolate in a medium-size heatproof bowl, and place over simmering water in pan. (Make sure bottom of bowl does not touch water.) Cook, stirring occasionally and adjusting heat as needed to maintain a simmer, until chocolate is melted and smooth, 2 to 3 minutes. Remove from heat, and set aside.

2. Beat egg whites and cream of tartar in a stand mixer fitted with a whisk attachment on medium speed until foamy, about 1 minute. With mixer on medium speed, gradually add sugar in a slow, steady stream; increase mixer speed to high, and beat until stiff peaks form, 1 to 2 minutes, stopping to scrape down sides as needed. Fold in melted chocolate, pecans, vanilla, and salt by hand with a spatula until combined.

3. Drop tablespoonfuls of egg white mixture 1 to 1½ inches apart on a large parchment paper–lined baking sheet. Bake in preheated oven until tops are shiny and cracked, edges are set, and centers still feel slightly soft to the touch, 8 to 10 minutes. Remove immediately from oven; let cool completely on baking sheet on a wire rack, 30 minutes to 1 hour. Serve, or store in an airtight container at room temperature for up to 5 days.

PARTY
COFFEE
CAKE

KEEP YOUR COOL
Resist the urge to eat
one of these meringues
right out of the oven;
they need to stand for at
least 30 minutes.

CHOCOLATE
MERINGUE
COOKIES

PEANUT BUTTER-
BANANA BLONDIES

MAYO MAKES IT TENDER
If you've ever had a slice of chocolate
cake made with mayonnaise, you won't
be surprised by how well it works in other
baked goods. Because it's a mixture of
oil and eggs, mayo gives these blondies
an incredibly moist and delicate crumb.
The hint of vinegar highlights the peanut
butter and banana flavors and then
vanishes into the background.

The Magic of Mayo

Surprising new ways to love the South's favorite condiment

I HAVE A CONFESSION TO MAKE: I never liked mayo. When I was 5 years old, my sweet grandfather made me a ham-and-cheese sandwich slathered with the stuff, prompting a calamitous meltdown my family will never let me forget. While they love mayo in everything—including their mashed potatoes—I was haunted by the sight of a jar for years.

In the South, a dislike of mayo can make life a treacherous journey. Potlucks and picnics require a sort of hopscotch through the side dishes. Casseroles are often off-limits. Even desserts can be difficult. I can't deny that my aversion, though well-founded and honest, leaves me short a wealth of fascinating foods. That's why recently, begrudgingly, I've had a change of heart.

The truth is...mayonnaise is magical. It's like alchemy how the combination of oil, egg yolks, and vinegar creates a kind of saucy sorcery that can render cakes more tender, meat juicier, and crusts crispier. With that spirit of wonder, we tasked our Test Kitchen with finding uses for this condiment that reveal just how versatile it can be. Mayonnaise works in baffling ways that few ingredients can—making it the South's closest thing to a superfood. Even I am learning to keep an open mind—and a jar in the fridge. –Kimberly Holland

Peanut Butter-Banana Blondies

ACTIVE 15 MIN. - TOTAL 45 MIN., PLUS 2 HOURS COOLING
SERVES 12

- 2 cups all-purpose flour
- 1½ tsp. baking powder
- 1 tsp. kosher salt
- 2 large eggs, lightly beaten
- 1 cup dark brown sugar
- ½ cup granulated sugar
- ½ cup mashed ripe bananas (from 2 bananas)
- ½ cup creamy peanut butter
- ½ cup mayonnaise
- 3 Tbsp. unsalted butter, melted
- ¼ cup dry-roasted peanuts, roughly chopped and divided
- ¼ tsp. flaky sea salt

1. Preheat oven to 350°F. Grease a 9-inch square baking dish with cooking spray, and line with parchment paper, letting parchment overhang on 2 sides by at least 1 inch.
2. Whisk together flour, baking powder, and kosher salt in a medium bowl. Place eggs, brown sugar, granulated sugar, bananas, peanut butter, mayonnaise, and butter in a large bowl; whisk until mostly smooth. Add flour mixture to egg mixture, and stir until just combined. Fold in 3 tablespoons of the peanuts. Pour batter into prepared pan, spreading evenly to edges. Top with remaining 1 tablespoon peanuts.
3. Bake in preheated oven until lightly browned and a wooden pick inserted in center comes out with a few moist crumbs attached, about 30 minutes. Place pan on a wire rack, and sprinkle top with flaky sea salt. Let cool completely, about 2 hours. Remove from pan using parchment overhang, and transfer to a cutting board. Cut into 12 pieces; serve.

Skillet-Seared Strip Steaks

(Photo, page 198)
ACTIVE 15 MIN. - TOTAL 1 HOUR
SERVES 2

- 1 tsp. flaky sea salt
- 1 tsp. black pepper
- ½ tsp. granulated garlic
- ½ tsp. onion powder
- ½ tsp. ground cumin
- ¼ tsp. crushed red pepper
- 2 (12-oz.) beef strip steaks (1½ inches thick)
- ½ cup mayonnaise
- 2 tsp. kosher salt

1. Combine sea salt, black pepper, granulated garlic, onion powder, cumin, and crushed red pepper in a small bowl; set aside.
2. Remove steaks from refrigerator 30 minutes before cooking, and let come to room temperature. Stir together mayonnaise and 1 tablespoon of the spice mix in a small bowl. (Reserve any remaining spice mix for another use.)
3. Pat steaks dry with a paper towel, and sprinkle both sides evenly with kosher salt. Heat a large cast-iron skillet over medium-high until hot. Brush one side of each steak with some of the mayonnaise mixture, and place steaks, mayonnaise mixture sides down, in hot skillet. Brush opposite side of steaks (side facing up) with some of the mayonnaise mixture.
4. Cook steaks, turning occasionally and spreading with remaining mayonnaise mixture using a butter knife or offset spatula, until medium-rare and deeply browned on both sides, about 12 minutes. Flip steaks, and cook until edges on both sides are seared, about 1 minute. Transfer to a cutting board, and let rest at least 15 minutes before serving.

MAYO MAKES IT JUICY
Brushing steaks with mayo is an ingenious idea. Because mayonnaise is made of tiny droplets of oil bound together by protein from eggs, it creates a buffer between the heat of the skillet and the seasonings and surface of the meat. The result is tender beef with a gorgeous crust and spices that are toasted just right.

SKILLET-SEARED STRIP STEAKS (PAGE 197)

TARTAR SAUCE-
BATTERED FRIED FISH
(PAGE 200)

MAYO MAKES IT CRISPY

Sometimes the best tricks are the most obvious. Fried fish tastes great with tartar sauce, so why not use it in the crust? When mixed with rice flour, eggy mayonnaise creates an easy one-dip batter that fries up golden, locks in moisture, and flavors the fish.

Tartar Sauce-Battered Fried Fish

(Photo, page 199)
ACTIVE 30 MIN. - TOTAL 40 MIN.
SERVES 6

- 1 cup mayonnaise
- 2 Tbsp. chopped fresh dill
- 2 Tbsp. chopped dill pickles
- 1 Tbsp. chopped capers
- 2 tsp. Dijon mustard
- ¾ tsp. granulated sugar
- ½ tsp. Worcestershire sauce
- 1 tsp. garlic powder, divided
- 1 tsp. onion powder, divided
  Canola oil
- ⅔ cup stone-ground white rice flour
- ⅔ cup ice-cold tap water
- 1½ tsp. kosher salt, divided
- 6 (5- to 6-oz.) skinless catfish fillets (about 2 lb. total)
  Lemon wedges

1. Stir together mayonnaise, dill, pickles, capers, Dijon mustard, sugar, Worcestershire sauce, and ½ teaspoon each garlic powder and onion powder in a medium bowl. Cover and refrigerate.
2. Add oil to a Dutch oven, filling to a depth of 2 inches. Heat over medium until oil reaches 360°F. Whisk together rice flour, water, remaining ½ teaspoon each garlic powder and onion powder, 3 tablespoons of the mayonnaise mixture, and 1 teaspoon of the salt in a medium bowl. Working in 3 batches, dip catfish pieces, 1 at a time, into batter. Remove each piece from batter, letting excess drain into bowl. Add 2 catfish pieces, 1 at a time, to hot oil; cook, turning occasionally, until golden brown and crispy, about 4 minutes. Transfer fried fish to a wire rack set over a rimmed baking sheet. Repeat with remaining batter and catfish.
3. Sprinkle fried fish with remaining ½ teaspoon salt. Serve with lemon wedges and remaining mayonnaise mixture.

Potato, Leek, and Roasted Garlic Soup

ACTIVE 45 MIN. - TOTAL 1 HOUR
SERVES 8

- 3 small garlic heads
- 1 Tbsp. olive oil
- 1½ tsp. kosher salt, divided
- 2 Tbsp. unsalted butter
- 3 medium leeks, trimmed, washed, and thinly sliced (3 cups)
- 3 large Yukon Gold potatoes, peeled and chopped (3 cups)
- 6 cups chicken broth
- ½ cup mayonnaise
  Freshly ground black pepper, fresh thyme leaves, and croutons, for topping

1. Preheat oven to 450°F. Trim tops of garlic heads so that tops of cloves are exposed. Place on a large piece of aluminum foil; drizzle with olive oil. Sprinkle with ½ teaspoon of the salt; wrap garlic in foil and seal tightly. Place on a baking sheet. Bake until garlic is soft, about 45 minutes. Remove from oven; open foil, and let stand 5 minutes. Squeeze garlic cloves from heads into a small bowl; set aside.
2. While garlic cools, melt butter in a large saucepan over medium. Add leeks, and cook, stirring occasionally, until starting to soften, about 3 minutes. Add potatoes and ½ teaspoon of the salt, and cook, stirring occasionally, about 2 minutes. Add chicken broth; bring to a boil over medium-high. Reduce heat to medium, and vigorously simmer, stirring occasionally, until potatoes are very soft, about 18 minutes.
3. Transfer potato mixture and roasted garlic to a blender. Secure lid on blender, and remove center piece to allow steam to escape. Place a clean towel over opening. Process until smooth, about 30 seconds.
4. Place mayonnaise in a medium bowl, and gradually pour 1 cup of the potato mixture into bowl, whisking constantly until smooth. Pour mayonnaise mixture into blender along with remaining ½ teaspoon salt; blend until smooth. Top with pepper, thyme, and croutons, and serve immediately.

Caramelized Onion-and-Mushroom Quiche

ACTIVE 50 MIN. - TOTAL 2 HOURS
SERVES 6

- ½ (14.1-oz.) pkg. refrigerated piecrusts (1 piecrust)
  All-purpose flour, for work surface
- 3 Tbsp. olive oil, divided
- ¾ cup chopped yellow onion
- 1½ tsp. kosher salt, divided
- 4 oz. sliced shiitake mushrooms
- 6 large eggs
- 1¼ cups heavy whipping cream
- ½ cup mayonnaise
- 1 tsp. dry mustard
- 5 oz. fontina cheese, shredded (about 1¼ cups), divided
- 1 Tbsp. thinly sliced fresh chives

POTATO, LEEK, AND ROASTED GARLIC SOUP

MAYO MAKES IT CREAMY

The notion of mayonnaise in soup might give you pause, but hear us out: Our Test Kitchen tried this recipe with cream and with mayo, and the latter was better by far. Our best guess is the mayonnaise coated the tiny grains of potato, yielding a velvety smooth texture. Or maybe...it was magic.

CARAMELIZED ONION-AND-MUSHROOM QUICHE

MAYO MAKES IT SILKY
Adding heavy cream or milk to savory baked-egg dishes like quiches and frittatas results in a tender texture, but too much can deliver runny results. Enter mayonnaise, and—ta-da—the thick, already emulsified mixture creates a custardy filling that sets and slices like a dream.

1. Preheat oven to 400°F. Unroll piecrust on a lightly floured work surface; roll into a 12-inch round. Fit into a 9-inch deep-dish pie plate, folding edges under and crimping as desired. Cover with parchment paper, and fill with pie weights or dried beans. Bake until edges are golden brown and bottom is set and looks dry, 12 to 15 minutes. Remove from oven, and carefully remove parchment paper and pie weights. Return piecrust to oven; bake until bottom of piecrust is golden brown, about 5 minutes. Remove from oven; let cool on a wire rack while preparing filling. Decrease oven temperature to 325°F.
2. While piecrust bakes and cools, heat 1 tablespoon of the oil in a large skillet over medium. Add onion and ½ teaspoon of the salt; cook, stirring occasionally, until caramelized and deep golden brown, 15 to 18 minutes, adding 2 tablespoons water at a time if onion darkens too quickly. Transfer from skillet to a medium bowl, and wipe skillet clean.
3. Return skillet to medium-high. Add remaining 2 tablespoons oil; heat until shimmering. Add mushrooms, and cook, stirring occasionally, until tender and browned, about 8 minutes. Transfer to bowl with onions, and set aside.
4. Whisk together eggs, cream, mayonnaise, dry mustard, and remaining 1 teaspoon salt in a large bowl. Place piecrust on a baking sheet, and pour egg mixture into piecrust. Evenly sprinkle half of the fontina over egg mixture; lightly tap pan to submerge fontina. Bake at 325°F until edges are set and center is starting to set, about 35 minutes. Remove from oven.
5. Stir together caramelized onions, mushrooms, and remaining fontina. Gently spoon onion mixture evenly over egg mixture. Bake until center is just set and edges are golden brown, about 25 minutes. Remove from oven; let cool at least 15 minutes. Top with chives before serving.

That's My Chicken Fry

Oklahoma stakes its claim on this regional icon

OKLAHOMANS might scoff at tornadoes, but they take chicken-fried steak seriously. Stand outside to watch the twister form, sure, but don't you dare try to put brown gravy on an Okie's beloved chicken fry. The wrong preparation will have you laughed out of the state by anyone who has ever had that red dirt stuck in the soles of their shoes. This dish is more of an icon there than buffalo, oil derricks, or college football—and that's saying something.

When I was 4 years old, my parents moved us from Oklahoma City to Memphis and broke a chain of Oklahomans going back at least four generations. Instead of Woody Guthrie and windswept plains, the hallmarks of my childhood were Elvis Presley and the mighty Mississippi River. But whenever my mom broke out the electric skillet and fried up thin, tender pieces of beef covered in seasoned flour, I might as well have been Ado Annie.

Chicken-fried steak was the thing I was most excited to eat when we visited Oklahoma. If the craving struck me in Tennessee, I would have only been able to find its less exciting cousin, country-fried steak. But back in the land of my forebears, the coating is mostly flour and maybe crushed crackers or cornflakes, the dredging process includes eggs, and the gravy is always white. If Rodgers and Hammerstein hadn't been New Yorkers, they might've known to include chicken-fried steak in their famous musical named after the state.

This dish most likely originated in Texas from Germans and Austrians who adapted it from the schnitzel of their homelands. Over the years, veal and breadcrumbs were traded for beef and flour, but the shared DNA between these meals is evident. The chicken-fried version stands as a distinctly American take on the nearly global breaded-and-fried-cutlet phenomenon—Japanese tonkatsu is another well-known relative.

And though this statement may not be historically accurate, here is where I plant my flag: Chicken-fried steak belongs to Oklahoma.

This may make me persona non grata in the Lone Star State, but I'm standing firm. Texans, you have so much: bluebonnets, Tex-Mex, ten-gallon hats, chili, a coastline, and even the stars at night! Oklahoma, ever the afterthought, should get dibs on this one thing. From Idabel to Enid, in restaurants and in homes, this humble entrée is elevated to legendary status. And I'm not alone in this opinion. In 1988, the Oklahoma Legislature named chicken-fried steak part of the official state meal. (This smorgasbord includes 11 items—never accuse Okies of skimping.) Texas can keep their international name recognition—just leave us the chicken fry. –Katie Akin

Chicken-Fried Steak with Cream Gravy

ACTIVE 45 MIN. - TOTAL 45 MIN.
SERVES 4

- 1 tsp. garlic powder
- 4½ tsp. kosher salt, divided, plus more to taste
- 2 tsp. black pepper, divided, plus more for garnish
- 4 (6-oz.) cube steaks (see note at bottom right)
- ⅔ cup finely crushed round buttery crackers (such as Ritz, from 16 to 18 crackers)
- 1½ cups plus 3 Tbsp. all-purpose flour, divided
- 2 large eggs
- 2½ cups plus 2 Tbsp. whole milk, divided
- 3 cups vegetable oil

1. Preheat oven to 200°F. Stir together garlic powder, 3 teaspoons of the salt, and 1½ teaspoons of the pepper in a small bowl. Sprinkle 2½ teaspoons seasoning mix evenly over both sides of all steaks. Stir together crushed crackers, 1½ cups of the flour, and remaining 3 teaspoons seasoning mix in a shallow bowl. Whisk together eggs and 2 tablespoons of the milk in another shallow bowl until well combined.

2. Heat oil in a large (12-inch) cast-iron skillet over medium to 325°F. Working with 1 at a time, dredge steaks in flour mixture to coat; shake off excess. Dip into egg mixture; let excess drip off. Press in flour mixture again to coat both sides completely.

3. Carefully place 2 steaks in hot oil, and fry until evenly golden brown, 3 to 5 minutes per side. (Adjust heat as needed to maintain oil temperature of 325°F.) Place on a paper towel-lined plate, and sprinkle with salt to taste. Transfer to a wire rack set on a baking sheet, and keep warm in preheated oven. Repeat procedure with remaining 2 steaks.

4. Drain fat from skillet, reserving ¼ cup drippings mixture and as much of the solids as possible. Return reserved ¼ cup drippings mixture and solids to skillet, and heat over medium-low. Whisk remaining 3 tablespoons flour into drippings mixture. Cook, stirring constantly, until mixture is bubbling and smells toasty, about 1 minute. Gradually whisk in remaining 2½ cups milk. Bring gravy to a simmer over medium. Reduce heat to medium-low, and cook, stirring often, until thickened, 6 to 7 minutes. Stir in remaining 1½ teaspoons salt and ½ teaspoon pepper.

5. Transfer steaks to a serving platter; serve immediately with warm gravy. Garnish with additional black pepper.

NOTE: Cube steak is a cut of beef (usually top round or sirloin) that has been pounded with a meat mallet until tender and flattened.

Food for Thought

Chef and author Bryant Terry's Memphis roots are the inspiration
behind his meaningful work in the culinary world

FOR BRYANT TERRY, food is more than a way to fuel our bodies. "It's about history, memory, and culture," he says. Over the past two decades, it has been the connecting thread in his efforts to create a more just, sustainable, and healthy world. He has taught kids cooking skills; acted as the chef in residence at San Francisco's Museum of the African Diaspora; authored cookbooks like *Vegetable Kingdom*; and published *Black Food*, a colorful collection of recipes, stories, and art. This son of the South never stands still.

Terry lives in the Bay Area of California with his wife and two daughters, but he was born and raised in Tennessee. "Everything I do and everything I am is because of Memphis and the local heroes and heroines who inspired me through their activism and bravery." There's a great deal of joy in his Bluff City roots, anchored by his family, many of whom were in the musical community. His uncle Don Bryant was a staff songwriter for Hi Records, Memphis' legendary label, and is a member of the Memphis Music Hall of Fame. (He cowrote Ann Peebles' 1973 song "I Can't Stand the Rain.") "My Uncle Don would be playing the piano, his brothers would be crooning, and my mom and her sisters would be singing," Terry remembers. "There wasn't a family gathering without some kind of art, talent show, or cultural component. And it all revolved around food; we harvested fresh produce from the kitchen garden or the mini orchard in the backyard."

Memphis is at the heart of his work, yet his relationship with the city and the wider Southeast is complicated. "There have been so many historic moments when Black people could have had the chance to thrive and have access to economic and political opportunities, but they've been constantly crushed because those with power have been unwilling to share it," he says.

A passion for justice has fueled Terry's career, and it all comes back to that basic human need to eat. Promoting recipes centered in African American and diasporic culture is one way he spurs change. "There are so many structural realities that prevent communities across this country from succeeding and being able to live joyful lives. I'm committed to doing whatever I can to help change those realities," he says.

Smashed Fried Potatoes with Field Peas and Corn

This recipe was inspired by irio (a Kenyan staple of seasoned pureed white potatoes, green peas, and corn—sometimes with greens) and tostones (a popular snack throughout Latin America in which green plantains are sliced crosswise, fried, smashed flat, and then fried again until crispy and golden).

ACTIVE 55 MIN. · TOTAL 55 MIN.

SERVES 4

CHILE-GARLIC OIL
- 4 tsp. crushed red pepper
- ⅓ cup peanut oil
- 1 large garlic clove, minced

SMASHED FRIED POTATOES
- 16 small (2-inch) new potatoes (1 lb. total), scrubbed
- ¼ cup peanut oil
- ½ tsp. kosher salt, divided

FIELD PEAS AND CORN
- 1½ tsp. coarsely ground sea salt, divided
- 1¼ cups shelled fresh field peas (6 oz. total)
- 1¼ cups fresh corn kernels
- 2 Tbsp. chopped fresh flat-leaf parsley
- 2 tsp. white vinegar
- 1 tsp. extra-virgin olive oil
  Freshly ground white pepper

1. Prepare the Chile-Garlic Oil: Place crushed red pepper in a small heatproof bowl. Heat peanut oil in a small skillet over medium. Add garlic, and cook, stirring often, until garlic is fragrant and starting to turn golden, 2 to 3 minutes. Pour garlic oil over red pepper in bowl. Let stand, stirring occasionally, until cooled to room temperature, about 20 minutes.

2. Meanwhile, prepare the Smashed Fried Potatoes: Fit a large pot with a steamer insert or heatproof colander; fill with water to a depth of 2 inches. Add potatoes to pot; cover and cook over medium until fork-tender, 20 to 25 minutes, adding more water to pot as necessary. Drain potatoes, and let stand until cool enough to handle, about 5 minutes. Transfer to a clean surface; gently press each potato with the bottom of a small bowl to flatten to about ½ inch thick. Set aside. Line a baking sheet with paper towels.

3. While potatoes cook, prepare the Field Peas and Corn: Fill a large pot with 6 cups water; bring to a boil over high. Add 1 teaspoon of the sea salt; stir in field peas. Bring to a boil over high, and boil, uncovered, until just barely tender, 15 to 20 minutes. Stir in corn; boil until tender-crisp, 1 minute. Drain; transfer to a large bowl. Add parsley, vinegar, olive oil, and remaining ½ teaspoon sea salt; toss together.

4. To cook potatoes, heat peanut oil in a large skillet over medium-high. Add half of the potatoes to skillet; cook, undisturbed, until crispy and browned, 3 to 5 minutes. Sprinkle with ⅛ teaspoon of the kosher salt; turn over in skillet. Cook, undisturbed, until crispy and browned, 4 to 5 minutes. Sprinkle with ⅛ teaspoon of the kosher salt; transfer to prepared baking sheet. Repeat process with remaining potatoes and salt.

5. Top each of the Smashed Fried Potatoes with 1 heaping tablespoon of Field Peas and Corn, a drizzle of Chile-Garlic Oil, and 1 or 2 grinds of white pepper.

Mac Memories

This treasured dish provides comfort and warmth in more ways than one

THE MACARONI AND CHEESE would come to the table piping hot alongside the other sides on holidays and special Sundays. It usually arrived last in an old-fashioned round Pyrex dish that was set into a metal holder with Bakelite handles. I wasn't overly fond of it (the beets and rutabagas were always my favorites), but I would always take a spoon or two of the mac and cheese just to get some of the crispy, crunchy, brown edge–that was the highlight. Over time, it gradually won me over. The creamy, cheesy béchamel played on my taste buds with hints of the three different cheeses my mother included: the tang of extra-sharp Cheddar, the bite of chiles in the pepper Jack, and the complexity of the Parmesan. Eventually, mac and cheese came to mean the meal was extra special.

Back in those childhood days, I'd never heard of James Hemings, Thomas Jefferson's enslaved chef, who helped popularize the European dish in the United States. During his tenure in France, Jefferson brought Hemings along with him to Paris. Hemings apprenticed under the finest chefs and mastered French cooking, pastry making, and the art of haute cuisine. Macaroni pie, as the dish was then known (and is still called in parts of the Caribbean), was one such specialty. It became a favorite of Jefferson, who ordered the pasta and Parmesan cheese from Europe regularly.

Unlike Hemings' simple recipe, my mother's version was so distinctive and filled with memories that I have given up eating mac and cheese since her passing–for the most part. I do manage to sneak one small bite each year. After my mother died and I cleaned out her refrigerator, I found a container of her mac and cheese stashed in the freezer. For the past 23 years, I have annually risked ptomaine poisoning, E. coli, and Lord knows what other maladies to eat it. I'll take a small forkful, heat it up, and enjoy it, savoring the recollections of family dinners past. –Jessica B. Harris

Mom's Mac and Cheese

ACTIVE 30 MIN. - TOTAL 1 HOUR
SERVES 4

- 6 Tbsp. unsalted butter, divided, plus more for greasing baking dish
- 2½ cups uncooked medium-size elbow macaroni
- ¼ cup fine dry breadcrumbs
- 3 Tbsp. all-purpose flour
- 2½ cups whole milk, at room temperature
- 6 oz. extra-sharp Cheddar cheese, grated (about 2 cups), divided
- 4 oz. pepper Jack cheese, grated (about 1¼ cups), divided
- 2 oz. Parmesan cheese, grated (about ½ cup), divided
- 1 tsp. hot sauce, or to taste (optional)
- 1 tsp. kosher salt
- ¼ tsp. black pepper
  Sliced scallions, for garnish

1. Lightly grease an 11- x 7-inch baking dish with butter; set aside. Cook pasta according to package directions for al dente. Drain pasta, and transfer to prepared baking dish. Set aside.
2. Microwave 2 tablespoons of the butter in a microwavable bowl on HIGH in 30-second intervals until melted, about 90 seconds. Add breadcrumbs; stir to coat, and set aside.
3. Preheat oven to 350°F. Melt remaining 4 tablespoons butter in a small saucepan over medium. Whisk in flour; cook, whisking constantly, until mixture is smooth and forms a loose paste, about 2 minutes. Gradually drizzle in milk, whisking constantly, and bring to a gentle simmer over medium. Simmer, whisking constantly, until sauce has reduced slightly and thickened enough to drizzle off a spoon, 3 to 5 minutes. Remove white sauce from heat, and cover to keep warm.
4. Add 1½ cups of the Cheddar, 1 cup of the pepper Jack, and ¼ cup of the Parmesan to white sauce in saucepan; stir until smooth. Stir in hot sauce (if using), salt, and pepper.
5. Pour cheese mixture over pasta in baking dish; stir until well incorporated. Stir together breadcrumbs and remaining ½ cup Cheddar, ¼ cup pepper Jack, and ¼ cup Parmesan in a small bowl; sprinkle mixture over top of pasta. Bake in preheated oven until hot, bubbly, and lightly browned on top, 25 to 30 minutes. Garnish with scallions just before serving.

Any Cheese You Please

MOM'S MAC AND CHEESE originated after she discovered she didn't have enough Cheddar and mixed in what she had in the fridge. The recipe is a forgiving one, and you, too, can play around with whatever kinds of cheese you may have on hand. Try a bit of Manchego or Asiago, or (when you're feeling frisky) add a bit of smoked Gouda. If you like the flavor of any cheese on its own, then you'll probably enjoy it in this dish.

Apple and Spice, Always Nice

Some seasonal flavors were just made for each other

Apple-and-Clove Spice Cake

ACTIVE 50 MIN. - TOTAL 2 HOURS, 10 MIN.,
PLUS 1 HOUR, 45 MIN. COOLING

SERVES 9

CAKE

- ¾ cup unsalted butter
- 1½ cups all-purpose flour
- 1 tsp. baking powder
- ¾ tsp. baking soda
- ½ tsp. ground cloves
- ¼ tsp. ground nutmeg, plus more for garnish
- ¼ tsp. kosher salt
- ½ cup granulated sugar
- ½ cup packed light brown sugar
- 1½ tsp. grated orange zest
- 3 large eggs, at room temperature
- 6 Tbsp. vegetable oil
- 1½ cups peeled, grated Fuji apples (from 3 apples)
- ½ cup toasted pecan pieces, plus more for garnish

FROSTING

- 1 (8-oz.) pkg. cream cheese, at room temperature
- 6 Tbsp. unsalted butter, at room temperature
- 2½ cups powdered sugar, sifted
- 1½ tsp. grated orange zest
- 1½ tsp. vanilla extract
- ¼ tsp. kosher salt

1. Prepare the Cake: Preheat oven to 325°F. Grease a 9-inch square baking pan with cooking spray; line with parchment paper, letting excess extend over sides of pan.
2. Melt butter in a medium saucepan over medium-high, stirring occasionally, until light brown in color and has a nutty aroma, 8 to 10 minutes. Pour brown butter into a medium bowl. Let stand until barely warm to the touch, 30 to 35 minutes.
3. Whisk together flour, baking powder, baking soda, cloves, nutmeg, and salt in a medium bowl; set aside. Stir together sugars and orange zest in a large bowl until combined; whisk eggs into sugar mixture until combined. Gradually whisk in vegetable oil and brown butter. Gradually whisk in flour mixture just until combined. Fold in apples and pecans.
4. Spread batter into prepared pan; tap pan on counter a few times to release any air bubbles. Bake in preheated oven until a wooden pick inserted in center comes out clean, 35 to 38 minutes, loosely covering with aluminum foil during last 10 minutes of baking to prevent excessive browning. Let Cake cool in pan on a wire rack 15 minutes. Using excess parchment paper as handles, remove Cake from pan, and let cool completely, about 1 hour, 30 minutes.
5. Prepare the Frosting: Add cream cheese and butter to bowl of a stand mixer fitted with the paddle attachment. Beat on medium speed until light and fluffy, about 3 minutes. Gradually add powdered sugar, ½ cup at a time, beating on low speed until all sugar is incorporated, scraping down sides of bowl between additions. Increase speed to medium-high; beat until frosting is fluffy, about 2 minutes. Add orange zest, vanilla, and salt; beat on low speed just until incorporated, about 30 seconds.
6. To assemble, place Cake on a plate or cake stand, and spread Frosting over top. Garnish with additional toasted pecans and a sprinkle of ground nutmeg.

Apple-Cardamom Babka Wreaths

(Photo, page 210)

ACTIVE 1 HOUR, 25 MIN. - TOTAL 2 HOURS, 5 MIN.,
PLUS 8 HOURS, 30 MIN. CHILLING AND 1 HOUR,
30 MIN. RISING

MAKES 2 (10-INCH) WREATHS

- 4½ cups all-purpose flour, plus more for dusting
- ⅓ cup granulated sugar
- 1 (¼-oz.) envelope active-dry yeast (2¼ tsp.)
- 3 tsp. ground cardamom, divided
- 1 cup whole milk
- 2 tsp. kosher salt
- 3 large eggs, divided
- 10 Tbsp. unsalted butter, cubed and at room temperature
- 1⅓ cups apple butter
- 2 cups finely chopped peeled Fuji apples (from 3 apples), divided
- 4 Tbsp. honey, divided, plus more for garnish

1. Add flour, sugar, yeast, and 2 teaspoons of the cardamom to the bowl of a stand mixer fitted with a dough hook attachment. Beat on low speed until well combined, 1 to 2 minutes. Add milk, salt, and 2 of the eggs to bowl. Beat on low speed until a dough forms, 2 to 3 minutes, stopping to scrape down sides as needed.
2. Increase mixer speed to medium-low. Gradually add butter, a few cubes at a time, beating until mostly incorporated into dough before next addition, stopping to scrape down sides of bowl as needed. (Dough will be soft and sticky; avoid adding extra flour.) Once all butter is added, beat on medium-low speed until dough is smooth and elastic, 8 to 10 minutes.
3. Place dough in a large bowl lightly greased with cooking spray; cover with plastic wrap. Chill, covered, at least 8 hours or up to 12 hours. Grease

Continued on page 212

APPLE-AND-CLOVE
SPICE CAKE

APPLE-CARDAMOM
BABKA WREATHS
(PAGE 208)

APPLE-CINNAMON
BUDINO (PAGE 212)

Continued from page 208

2 (10-inch) tube pans with cooking spray (see tip). Stir together apple butter and remaining 1 teaspoon cardamom. Set aside.

4. Remove dough from refrigerator; divide in half. Cover half of dough, and store in refrigerator until ready to use. Roll remaining half of dough into a 20- x 9-inch rectangle on a lightly floured surface. Use an offset spatula or spoon to spread half of apple butter mixture (about ⅔ cup) over dough, leaving a ½-inch border around all edges. Top evenly with 1 cup of the chopped apples.

5. Lightly brush 1 long side of dough with just enough water to moisten. Starting with dry long side, roll up dough, jelly roll style, gently lifting and tucking dough as you roll to avoid pushing out filling. (It's okay if some falls out.) Pinch seam to seal. Carefully place roll diagonally on a parchment paper-lined baking sheet, bending as needed to fit; chill, covered, in refrigerator until slightly firm, 30 minutes. Repeat with remaining dough, apple butter mixture, and apples.

6. Remove 1 roll from refrigerator. Straighten roll (if needed). Using a serrated knife, cut roll in half lengthwise into two long pieces. With cut sides up, press top ends of each half together; twist pieces, right over left, to create a twist. Pinch together bottom ends of dough pieces to seal.

7. Gently transfer twist to 1 prepared tube pan, tucking and gently pressing ends under dough to secure. Repeat with remaining rolled dough and prepared pan. Cover pans with clean kitchen towels; let rise in a warm, draft-free place until dough is puffed, 1½ hours. (Wreaths will not double in size but should grow 10% to 20%.) During last 30 minutes of rising, preheat oven to 375˚F.

8. Whisk together 1 Tbsp. water with remaining egg; brush wreaths with egg mixture. Bake in preheated oven until golden brown, 28 to 34 minutes.

9. Let cool in pans on wire racks for 8 minutes. Loosen edges with a small offset spatula or a butter knife; remove from pans, and place each wreath, twisted side up, on a platter.

Brush 1 tablespoon of the honey over each wreath. Serve warm or at room temperature. Brush with remaining 2 tablespoons honey just before serving. Garnish with a drizzle of additional honey.

PRO TIP: If you have only one tube pan, keep half of the dough covered and refrigerated, punching down if necessary, until your pan can be cooled and cleaned to bake the second babka.

Apple-Cinnamon Budino

(Photo, page 211)
ACTIVE 1 HOUR, 10 MIN. - TOTAL 1 HOUR, 10 MIN., PLUS 3 HOURS COOLING
SERVES 4

CINNAMON BUDINO
2½ Tbsp. cornstarch
⅛ tsp. kosher salt
8 Tbsp. granulated sugar, divided
2 large egg yolks
1½ cups half-and-half
¾ cup heavy whipping cream
1 (2½-inch) cinnamon stick
2½ Tbsp. unsalted butter, cubed and softened
1½ tsp. vanilla extract

APPLE-CINNAMON BUTTERSCOTCH
1 cup apple cider
½ cup unsalted butter
¾ cup packed light brown sugar
¼ cup heavy whipping cream
½ tsp. ground cinnamon
½ tsp. vanilla extract
¼ tsp. kosher salt

TOPPINGS
Sweetened whipped cream
Thinly sliced unpeeled Fuji apples

1. Prepare the Cinnamon Budino: Whisk together cornstarch, salt, and 2 tablespoons of the sugar in a medium bowl. Add egg yolks, and stir until well combined. Set egg yolk mixture aside.
2. Add half-and-half, cream, cinnamon stick, and the remaining 6 tablespoons sugar to a medium saucepan; bring to a simmer over medium, stirring occasionally. Remove pan from heat.
3. Gradually add about ¼ cup of the hot cream mixture to egg yolk mixture, whisking constantly until

well combined. Repeat 3 more times until about half of the cream mixture is combined with egg yolk mixture. Whisk all of egg yolk mixture into cream mixture in saucepan; bring to a boil over medium, whisking constantly, 5 to 6 minutes. Boil, whisking constantly, 1 minute. Remove from heat; whisk in butter and vanilla until well combined.
4. Pour mixture through a fine mesh strainer into a medium bowl, discarding cinnamon stick and any solids. Divide mixture evenly among 4 (6- to 8-oz.) widemouthed glass jars or ramekins, spreading into an even layer with the back of a spoon. Wipe rims clean, if necessary. Cover with plastic wrap, pressing it directly onto surface of custard to prevent a skin from forming. Chill, covered, until set, about 2 hours.
5. Prepare the Apple-Cinnamon Butterscotch: Bring apple cider to a boil in a small saucepan over medium-high, 4 to 5 minutes. Boil, stirring occasionally, until reduced to ¼ cup, about 20 to 25 minutes.
6. Add butter to reduced cider; cook, stirring often, until completely melted, about 2 minutes. Add brown sugar; cook, stirring occasionally, until sugar has dissolved and entire mixture is bubbling, about 2 minutes. Whisk in heavy cream; cook, whisking constantly, 1 minute. Remove from heat; add cinnamon, vanilla, and salt. (Mixture will thicken as it cools.) Transfer butterscotch mixture to a medium heatproof bowl, and let cool until room temperature, about 3 hours (see tip below).
7. Spoon 3 to 5 tablespoons butterscotch over each chilled budino, spreading as needed. (If butterscotch becomes too thick, microwave on HIGH for 10- to 15-second intervals, stirring after each interval, until butterscotch becomes slightly looser.) Just before serving, top each budino with whipped cream and an apple slice.

PRO TIP: To cool butterscotch faster, add warm mixture to a medium-size heatproof bowl (preferably metal); place in a larger bowl filled with ice water. Stir warm butterscotch until cooled and thickened.

Party Peppers

Fire up your next get-together with colorful appetizers made
with a bounty of spicy and sweet late-summer varieties

TEX-MEX SKILLET
POBLANO DIP
(PAGE 215)

CREAMY CORN
JALAPEÑO POPPERS

Sweet and Fiery Pepper Bruschetta

(Photo, page 216)

A generous glug of honey tames the hot serrano and Fresno chiles, while tangy red wine vinegar and briny capers tip the flavor scale back into balance. Spooned over crusty baguette slices that are spread with creamy goat cheese, this spicy-sweet relish is something your guests won't soon forget.

ACTIVE 20 MIN. · TOTAL 35 MIN.

MAKES 20

- 5 Tbsp. extra-virgin olive oil, divided
- 20 (⅓-inch-thick) diagonally cut baguette slices
- 1 orange or red bell pepper, trimmed and cut into thin strips (about 1½ cups)
- 2 red Fresno chiles, unseeded and thinly sliced into rings (about ⅓ cup)
- 1 medium shallot, thinly sliced (about ¼ cup)
- 1 serrano chile, unseeded and thinly sliced into rings (about 2 Tbsp.)
- 2 small garlic cloves, minced (about 1 tsp.)
- ⅓ cup red wine vinegar
- 3 Tbsp. honey
- ¼ tsp. kosher salt
- 2 Tbsp. drained nonpareil capers
- 1 (4-oz.) plain goat cheese log, softened

1. Preheat oven to 350°F. Line a baking sheet with parchment paper.
2. Brush 3 tablespoons of the oil evenly over both sides of baguette slices. Arrange slices on prepared baking sheet. Bake in preheated oven until crisp and lightly browned around edges, 10 to 12 minutes, flipping slices halfway through baking, if desired. Set aside, or store in an airtight container up to 1 day.
3. Meanwhile, heat the remaining 2 tablespoons oil in a medium saucepan over medium. Add bell pepper, Fresno chiles, shallot, serrano chile, and garlic; cook, stirring occasionally, until softened, 3 to 5 minutes. Stir in vinegar, honey, and salt. Cook, stirring occasionally, over medium until almost all liquid has evaporated and mixture is syrupy, 10 to 12 minutes.
4. Remove pepper mixture from heat, and stir in capers until combined. (If making ahead, let mixture cool and refrigerate in an airtight container up to 3 days. Let the mixture come to room temperature, and reheat it over medium heat in a medium saucepan, if desired.)
5. To serve, spread softened goat cheese evenly over one side of each baguette slice. Top each with about 1½ teaspoons warm pepper-vinegar mixture. Serve bruschetta warm or at room temperature.

Creamy Corn Jalapeño Poppers

You've never tasted a jalapeño popper this good. Sweet summer corn joins forces with mozzarella and sharp Cheddar to temper the heat of the chiles; white miso brings a subtle savoriness to the filling. Look for miso in the refrigerated section of the produce department; it's often sold in tubs like sour cream.

ACTIVE 20 MIN. · TOTAL 40 MIN.

MAKES 24

- 12 large (3½- to 4-inch-long) jalapeño chiles
- ⅓ cup mayonnaise
- 1 Tbsp. white miso
- ¼ tsp. kosher salt
- 1 cup fresh corn kernels (from about 2 ears)
- 3 oz. preshredded whole-milk mozzarella cheese (about ¾ cup)
- 2 oz. preshredded sharp Cheddar cheese (about ½ cup)
- ¼ cup chopped scallions (from 2 scallions), plus more for garnish

1. Preheat oven to 375°F. Line a rimmed baking sheet with aluminum foil or parchment paper.
2. Cut chiles in half lengthwise; scrape out seeds and membranes with a spoon or melon baller. (Discard seeds and membranes.) Arrange chile halves on prepared baking sheet.
3. Whisk together mayonnaise, miso, and salt in a medium bowl until smooth. Stir in corn, mozzarella, Cheddar, and scallions. Stuff corn mixture evenly into chile halves. Bake in preheated oven until filling is gooey and bubbly, 18 to 20 minutes. Garnish with additional scallions, if desired. Serve warm.

Tex-Mex Skillet Poblano Dip

(Photo, page 213)

This queso-inspired appetizer can be assembled up to three days ahead. Cover and store the unbaked dip in the fridge; then put it in the oven just before guests arrive, adding five minutes to the bake time. Serve with sturdy chips to scoop up all the cheesy goodness.

ACTIVE 15 MIN. · TOTAL 1 HOUR

SERVES 8

- 5 medium poblano chiles (about 1 lb. total)
- 2 (8-oz.) pkg. cream cheese, softened
- ½ cup chopped scallions (from 4 medium scallions)
- ¼ cup sour cream
- 1 tsp. ground cumin
- ¾ tsp. kosher salt
- 1 large garlic clove, grated (about ½ tsp.)
- 8 oz. Monterey Jack cheese, shredded and divided (about 2 cups)
  Tortilla chips

1. Preheat oven to broil with oven rack about 7 inches from heat source. Coat a medium (10-inch) cast-iron or other ovenproof skillet with cooking spray; set aside. Line a large rimmed baking sheet with aluminum foil.
2. Arrange chiles on prepared baking sheet. Broil, turning occasionally, until blackened all over, about 10 minutes. Remove baking sheet from oven; reduce oven temperature to 350°F. Wrap foil tightly around chiles, and let stand 10 minutes.
3. Unwrap chiles. Rub off skins; cut stems from chiles. Slice chiles in half lengthwise; scrape out seeds. (Discard skins, stems, and seeds.) Cut halves lengthwise into thin strips; cut strips into 1-inch pieces.
4. Stir together cream cheese, scallions, sour cream, cumin, salt, and grated garlic in a bowl. Stir in chiles and 1½ cups of the Monterey Jack. Spread dip into prepared skillet. Sprinkle remaining ½ cup Monterey Jack over dip. Bake, uncovered, at 350°F until bubbly, about 25 minutes. Serve warm with tortilla chips.

SWEET AND FIERY
PEPPER BRUSCHETTA
(PAGE 215)

SAUSAGE-AND-
PEPPER MINI SUBS
(PAGE 219)

PEPPER
LOVER'S
SHEET PAN
PIZZA

Pepper Lover's Sheet Pan Pizza

Spicy Fresno chiles, tangy banana peppers, sweet bell peppers, and a dash of crushed red pepper team up with an easy no-knead dough in this party-worthy pie.

ACTIVE 25 MIN. - TOTAL 50 MIN.,
PLUS 4 HOURS RISING

SERVES 12

- 8 thick-cut bacon slices, chopped
- ¼ cup extra-virgin olive oil, divided
- 1⅓ cups warm water (100°F to 110°F)
- 1 Tbsp. granulated sugar
- 1½ tsp. active dry yeast (from 1 [¼-oz.] envelope)
- 2 tsp. kosher salt
- 3¾ cups all-purpose flour
- 1½ cups marinara sauce (from 1 [24-oz.] jar)
- ½ tsp. crushed red pepper
- 8 oz. preshredded whole-milk mozzarella cheese (about 2 cups)
- 4 oz. fontina cheese, shredded (about 1 cup)
- 1 yellow bell pepper, trimmed and thinly sliced into rings
- 1 red bell pepper, trimmed and thinly sliced into rings
- 4 orange sweet mini peppers, thinly sliced into rings
- 3 red Fresno chiles, unseeded and thinly sliced into rings
- ½ cup drained mild banana pepper rings (from 1 [12-oz.] jar)

1. Cook bacon in a large skillet, stirring occasionally, over medium until crisp, 12 to 15 minutes. Transfer bacon from skillet with a slotted spoon to a paper towel–lined plate, and set aside. Remove 2 tablespoons bacon drippings from skillet; pour onto an 18- x 13-inch rimmed baking sheet. Add 2 tablespoons of the olive oil to the baking sheet, tilting to coat the bottom of the baking sheet. (Reserve remaining bacon drippings for another use.)
2. Pour warm water into a food processor bowl. Stir in sugar and yeast; let stand until mixture looks cloudy or bubbly, about 5 minutes. (If mixture does not become cloudy or bubbly, yeast is not active. Start over with new yeast.) Add remaining 2 tablespoons olive oil to water mixture in processor bowl; add salt, and stir gently to combine. Add flour; process until dough forms, about 1 minute. Process until fully incorporated, about 30 seconds.

3. Transfer dough (it will be sticky) to prepared baking sheet, turning to coat with bacon drippings. Pat dough into a rectangle. (Dough will not cover sheet.) Cover with plastic wrap. Let rise in a warm place (85°F), free from drafts, until puffy and slightly bubbly, 3 hours, 30 minutes to 4 hours.
4. Place a pizza stone in oven. Preheat oven to 500°F, leaving stone in oven as it preheats. Uncover dough. Pat dough to edges of baking sheet. Cover with plastic wrap, and let rise for 30 minutes.
5. Uncover dough. Spread marinara sauce evenly over dough, leaving a ½-inch border; sprinkle with crushed red pepper. Sprinkle pizza evenly with mozzarella and fontina. Top evenly with bell peppers, sweet mini peppers, and Fresno chiles; sprinkle with reserved bacon. Place pan on pizza stone, and bake in preheated oven until crust is browned on edges and cheese is bubbly and starting to brown, 18 to 20 minutes. Remove from oven, and sprinkle with banana pepper rings.

Sausage-and-Pepper Mini Subs

(Photo, page 217)

Use your cast-iron skillet on the grill to make these grab-and-go sandwiches. While the veggies soften in the pan, the hickory-smoked sausage gets a quick char before being tucked into mustard-slathered buns.

ACTIVE 45 MIN. - TOTAL 45 MIN.

MAKES 16

- ¼ cup extra-virgin olive oil
- 1 large yellow onion, thinly sliced vertically (2½ to 3 cups)
- 1 large red bell pepper, trimmed and cut lengthwise into thin strips (about 2 cups)
- 1 large yellow bell pepper, trimmed and cut lengthwise into thin strips (about 2 cups)
- 1 large orange bell pepper, trimmed and cut lengthwise into thin strips (about 2 cups)
- 5 large garlic cloves, thinly sliced (about 2 Tbsp.)
- 1 tsp. kosher salt
- 1 lb. hickory-smoked sausage (such as Conecuh), cut into 16 (2½- to 3-inch-long) pieces
- ⅓ cup Creole mustard
- 8 top-split hot dog buns, cut in half crosswise

1. Preheat grill to medium-high (400°F to 450°F). Heat a large cast-iron skillet over medium. Add oil to skillet; swirl to coat. Add onion, bell peppers, and garlic; cook, stirring occasionally, until onion and peppers are very tender and starting to brown, 15 to 20 minutes. Stir in salt. Remove from heat.
2. Meanwhile, place sausage pieces on oiled grates of grill; cook, uncovered, turning occasionally, until lightly charred, 6 to 8 minutes.
3. Spread 1 teaspoon mustard inside each bun half, and tuck 1 sausage piece into each. Divide bell pepper mixture evenly among subs. Serve immediately.

Pick a Pepper Like a Pro

From sweet to heat to eat

1
When shopping for peppers—whether sweet or hot—look for firm ones with shiny, unblemished skins. Skip past any that feel soft or look wrinkly.

- - - - - - - - - - - - - - - - -

2
Select bell peppers that have four sides. You'll get the best yield from these, and they're easiest to prep (cut off the four "walls" of the peppers, and discard the stems and seeds).

- - - - - - - - - - - - - - - - -

3
There are many myths about how to discern if jalapeños or other hot chiles are spicy or mild at the market, but the truth is you really won't know until you cut into them. To tone down the heat, cut or scrape out the seeds and any white membranes—that's where the capsaicin is most concentrated.

- - - - - - - - - - - - - - - - -

4
To store peppers, leave them unwashed and stash them in the crisper drawer in a loose (not sealed) plastic produce bag. They should keep for about a week, but check them periodically for freshness.

Do the Mashed Potato

Traditional mains to pair with everyone's favorite side

Easiest Mashed Potatoes

ACTIVE 15 MIN. · TOTAL 45 MIN.

SERVES 6

Bring 1½ lb. each **russet** and **Yukon Gold potatoes** or 3 lb. **sweet potatoes** (peeled and cut into 1½-inch pieces), 3 Tbsp. **salt**, and **water** to cover by 2 inches to a boil in a medium pot over high. Boil until tender, 10 to 12 minutes; drain. Return to pan; mash with a potato masher. For Mashed Potatoes: Stir in 1 cup warm **half-and-half**, ¾ cup melted **butter**, and ½ tsp. **salt** until smooth. For Mashed Sweet Potatoes: Stir in ½ cup warm **half-and-half**, ½ cup melted **butter**, and ¾ tsp. **salt** until smooth.

Sticky Honey-Garlic Chicken

ACTIVE 15 MIN. · TOTAL 40 MIN.

SERVES 4

- 1 Tbsp. olive oil
- 4 (8-oz.) bone-in, skin-on chicken thighs, excess skin and fat trimmed
- 1½ tsp. kosher salt
- ¼ cup honey
- 1 Tbsp. Asian chile-garlic sauce
- 1 Tbsp. lower-sodium soy sauce
- 1 tsp. grated garlic (from 2 garlic cloves)
- 1½ tsp. grated fresh ginger, divided
- 2 Tbsp. cold unsalted butter, cut into small pieces
- Thinly sliced scallions

1. Preheat oven to 425°F. Heat oil in a large cast-iron skillet over medium-high. Sprinkle chicken on both sides with salt. Place chicken, skin side down, in hot oil. Cook, undisturbed, until skin is golden brown, 10 to 12 minutes (chicken will not be fully cooked). Transfer chicken to a plate; reserve 1 tablespoon drippings in skillet.

2. While chicken cooks, whisk together honey, chile-garlic sauce, soy sauce, garlic, and 1 teaspoon of the ginger in a small bowl. Return chicken to skillet, skin side up, over medium-high. Pour honey mixture over chicken; add butter to skillet. Cook, basting chicken with honey mixture, until butter is melted, about 30 seconds.

3. Transfer the skillet to preheated oven, and bake until a thermometer inserted into thickest portion of chicken registers 165°F and honey mixture thickens, 12 to 15 minutes, stirring and basting chicken with honey mixture halfway through bake time.

4. Transfer chicken thighs to a large plate. Stir remaining ½ teaspoon ginger into sauce in skillet, and spoon sauce evenly over chicken. Garnish with scallions. Serve with Mashed Potatoes (recipe opposite) and Bacon-Balsamic Brussels Sprouts (recipe at right).

Bacon-Balsamic Brussels Sprouts

ACTIVE 25 MIN. · TOTAL 25 MIN.

SERVES 4

Cook 3 oz. (about 2½ slices) chopped **thick-cut bacon** in a large skillet over medium-high, stirring often, until bacon is crisp, about 7 minutes. Transfer bacon to a paper towel–lined plate, reserving drippings in skillet. Reduce heat to medium. Add 4½ cups trimmed and halved **fresh Brussels sprouts** to drippings in skillet. Cook, stirring occasionally, until Brussels sprouts are just tender and lightly charred in spots, about 8 minutes, adding a splash of **water** if the skillet is too dry. Stir in 2 Tbsp. **balsamic vinegar,** 1 Tbsp. **honey,** and ½ tsp. **kosher salt.** Remove from heat, and garnish with bacon and grated **Parmesan cheese.**

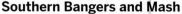

Southern Bangers and Mash

ACTIVE 25 MIN. - TOTAL 35 MIN.
SERVES 4

- 1½ Tbsp. canola oil
- 1 (1-lb.) pkg. hickory-smoked sausage, cut crosswise into 4 even pieces, and each piece halved lengthwise
- 1 medium yellow onion, finely chopped (about 1¾ cups)
- ½ tsp. kosher salt, divided
- 1 Tbsp. tomato paste
- ½ cup dry red wine
- 1½ cups beef stock
- 1 fresh rosemary sprig
- ¼ tsp. black pepper
- 1 Tbsp. cold unsalted butter
- 1 tsp. Dijon mustard

1. Preheat oven to 400°F. Heat oil in a large ovenproof skillet over medium-high. Add sausage; cook, turning once, until deeply browned on both sides, 2 to 3 minutes per side. Transfer sausage to a plate; do not wipe skillet clean. Stir onion and ¼ teaspoon of the salt into drippings. Return sausage to skillet.
2. Transfer skillet to preheated oven, and bake until onion softens and browns on the bottom and a thermometer inserted into thickest portion of sausage registers 165°F, about 10 minutes. Remove from oven, and transfer sausage to a plate. Cover tightly with aluminum foil to keep warm.
3. Heat skillet over medium-high, and cook onion, stirring occasionally, until lightly browned, about 5 minutes. Stir in tomato paste to coat. Add wine, scraping up any browned bits on bottom of skillet. Simmer over medium-high, stirring often, until wine has mostly evaporated, about 2 minutes. Add stock, rosemary, and pepper; bring to a simmer over medium-high. Cook, stirring occasionally, until thickened and reduced to about 1¼ cups, 8 to 10 minutes. Return sausages to skillet. Stir in butter, mustard, and remaining ¼ teaspoon salt; cook, stirring constantly, until butter is melted and sauce thickens and looks glossy, about 1 minute. Remove skillet from heat. Serve with Mashed Sweet Potatoes (recipe, page 220) and Speedy Sautéed Greens (recipe at right).

Speedy Sautéed Greens

ACTIVE 10 MIN. - TOTAL 10 MIN.
SERVES 4

Heat 3 Tbsp. **olive oil** in a large Dutch oven over medium-high. Add 2 Tbsp. thinly sliced **garlic cloves;** cook, stirring often, until browned around the edges, about 2 minutes. Add 12 packed cups (12 oz.) stemmed and chopped **mixed greens** (such as spinach, kale, and Swiss chard), 1 Tbsp. **hot sauce,** ½ tsp. **kosher salt,** and ¼ tsp. **smoked paprika.** Cook over medium-high, stirring constantly, until greens are tender-crisp, about 2 minutes.

Mini Meatloaves

ACTIVE 10 MIN. - TOTAL 40 MIN.

SERVES 4

- 1 large egg
- ⅔ cup panko breadcrumbs
- ½ cup half-and-half
- 2 Tbsp. Worcestershire sauce
- 2 tsp. chopped fresh thyme
- 2 tsp. kosher salt
- 3 garlic cloves, grated (about 1 tsp.)
- ½ cup plus 2 Tbsp. ketchup, divided
- 2 lb. 85/15 lean ground beef
- 2 Tbsp. dark brown sugar

1. Preheat oven to 375°F. Coat a 12-cup muffin tray with cooking spray. Stir together egg, panko, half-and-half, Worcestershire sauce, thyme, salt, garlic, and 2 tablespoons of the ketchup in a medium bowl. Let stand 5 minutes to moisten. Add ground beef to panko mixture; gently but thoroughly mix together using your hands.

2. Scoop a heaping ⅓ cup beef mixture into each prepared muffin well, and flatten tops. Stir together sugar and remaining ½ cup ketchup in a bowl until combined. Gently spread 2 teaspoons ketchup mixture over each meatloaf.

3. Bake in preheated oven until a thermometer inserted into thickest portion of one meatloaf registers 160°F, 20 to 22 minutes. Let cool 5 minutes. Serve with Mashed Sweet Potatoes (recipe, page 220) and Buttery Peas (recipe at right).

Buttery Peas

ACTIVE 10 MIN. - TOTAL 10 MIN.

SERVES 4

Melt 2 Tbsp. **unsalted butter** in a large skillet over medium-high. Add ¼ cup finely chopped **shallots**; cook, stirring often, until softened, about 2 minutes. Stir in 2 (10-oz.) pkg. **frozen green peas**, 3 tablespoons **unsalted butter**, and 2 tsp. grated **lemon zest**. Cook, covered, stirring occasionally, until peas are tender, about 5 minutes. Uncover and stir in 2 Tbsp. finely chopped fresh **chives**, 1 Tbsp. fresh **lemon juice**, and ¾ tsp. **kosher salt**.

Smothered Steaks with Mushroom Sauce

ACTIVE 30 MIN. - TOTAL 30 MIN.
SERVES 4

- 4 (6-oz.) beef tenderloin filets (1 inch thick)
- ½ tsp. black pepper
- 2½ tsp. kosher salt, divided
- 1 Tbsp. canola oil
- 1 cup beef stock
- 2 Tbsp. unsalted butter
- 8 oz. fresh wild mushrooms, chopped (about 4 cups)
- 1 medium shallot, finely chopped (2 Tbsp.)
- 3 garlic cloves, finely chopped (1 Tbsp.)
- ½ cup heavy whipping cream
- 2 tsp. Dijon mustard
- 2 tsp. Worcestershire sauce
- 1 Tbsp. chopped fresh tarragon
  Flaky sea salt

1. Sprinkle steaks with pepper and 2 teaspoons of the kosher salt. Heat oil in a large cast-iron skillet over high until smoking. Cook steaks, turning often, until a thermometer inserted into thickest portion registers 125°F, about 10 minutes. Transfer steaks to a plate, and loosely cover with aluminum foil. Wipe skillet clean.

2. Reduce heat to medium-high. Add stock; bring to a simmer. Cook until reduced to about ¼ cup, 3 to 5 minutes. Pour into a heatproof bowl.

3. Melt butter in same skillet over high. Add mushrooms; cook, stirring occasionally, until browned, about 5 minutes. Reduce heat to medium-high; add shallot and garlic. Cook, stirring often, until softened, 1 to 2 minutes. Return reduced stock mixture to skillet; add heavy cream, mustard, Worcestershire, and remaining ½ teaspoon kosher salt. Return steaks to skillet, and cook over medium-high until sauce thickens, 1 to 2 minutes, flipping steaks halfway through cook time. Remove from heat.

4. Spoon sauce over steaks; garnish with tarragon and flaky sea salt. Serve with Mashed Potatoes (recipe, page 220) and Roasted Cheddar Broccoli (recipe at right).

SWAP AND SAVE
Trade the filets for two (12-ounce) less expensive New York strip steaks; reduce the cook time to six to eight minutes.

Roasted Cheddar Broccoli

ACTIVE 5 MIN. - TOTAL 25 MIN.
SERVES 4

Preheat oven to 425°F. Stir together 2 Tbsp. **olive oil** and 2 tsp. **Dijon mustard** in a small bowl. Toss together 8 cups **fresh broccoli florets**, mustard mixture, and ½ tsp. **kosher salt** on a large rimmed baking sheet; spread in an even layer. Bake until broccoli is tender-crisp and florets are browned in spots, about 15 minutes, stirring once and sprinkling with 1 cup shredded **sharp Cheddar cheese** after 10 minutes of bake time. Sprinkle with **crushed red pepper**, if desired.

Mississippi-Style Pork Chops

ACTIVE 25 MIN. · TOTAL 35 MIN.
SERVES 4

- 4 (10-oz.) bone-in rib-cut pork chops (1 to 1¼ inches thick)
- 2 tsp. buttermilk ranch dressing mix (from 1 [1-oz.] envelope)
- 1 tsp. kosher salt
- ½ tsp. black pepper
- 2 Tbsp. canola oil
- ¼ cup unsalted butter
- 1 small red onion, thinly sliced (about 2 cups)
- 1 cup jarred pepperoncini salad peppers plus ½ cup liquid from jar, divided
- 2 tsp. jarred beef stock base
- 2 tsp. cornstarch
- ¼ cup finely chopped mixed fresh herbs (such as parsley, dill, and/or chives), plus more for topping

1. Preheat oven to 350°F. Sprinkle pork chops evenly on both sides with ranch dressing mix, salt, and black pepper. Heat oil in a large cast-iron skillet over high until smoking. Add pork chops, and cook, turning occasionally, until lightly browned around the edges, about 8 minutes. Transfer pork to a plate, reserving drippings in skillet; do not wipe skillet clean.

2. Reduce heat to medium-high. Melt butter in drippings in skillet. Add onion, and cook, stirring often and scraping up any browned bits on bottom of skillet, until onion softens slightly, about 4 minutes. Remove skillet from heat.

3. Whisk together pepperoncini liquid, beef stock base, and ½ cup water in a small bowl. Return pork to skillet; add pepperoncini peppers and liquid from jar mixture.

4. Bake in preheated oven until a thermometer inserted into thickest portion of pork registers 140°F, 10 to 12 minutes. Transfer pork to a large platter, reserving gravy mixture in skillet.

5. Bring gravy mixture to a simmer over medium-high. Whisk together cornstarch and ¼ cup water in a small bowl. Stir cornstarch mixture into gravy. Cook over medium-high, stirring often, until thickened, about 2 minutes. Stir in herbs. Spoon over pork chops; sprinkle with additional herbs. Serve with Mashed Sweet Potatoes (recipe, page 220) and Garlicky Green Beans (recipe below).

Garlicky Green Beans

ACTIVE 10 MIN. · TOTAL 10 MIN.
SERVES 4

Heat 2 Tbsp. each **unsalted butter** and **olive oil** in a large skillet over medium-high. Add 1 lb. trimmed **fresh green beans**, and cook, stirring often, until tender-crisp, about 4 minutes. Add 2 Tbsp. thinly sliced **garlic** and 1 tsp. **kosher salt**; cook, stirring often, until garlic is light golden brown, about 2 minutes.

Good to the Last Bite

A chocolate dessert that starts with half a cup of joe

One-Bowl Chocolate Cake with Salted Caramel Buttercream

ACTIVE 25 MIN. - TOTAL 55 MIN., PLUS 1 HOUR, 15 MIN. COOLING

SERVES 8

CHOCOLATE CAKE

- 1 large egg, at room temperature
- 1 cup granulated sugar
- ½ cup sour cream, at room temperature
- ¼ cup vegetable oil
- 1 tsp. vanilla extract
- ½ tsp. kosher salt
- ½ cup hot brewed coffee
- ¾ cup all-purpose flour
- ¼ cup Dutch-process cocoa
- ½ tsp. baking soda
- ½ tsp. baking powder

SALTED CARAMEL BUTTERCREAM

- ½ cup unsalted butter, at room temperature
- ½ cup jarred salted caramel topping, plus more for garnish
- 1½ cups powdered sugar, sifted

ADDITIONAL INGREDIENT

Flaky sea salt (optional)

1. Prepare the Chocolate Cake: Preheat oven to 350°F. Coat a 9-inch round cake pan with cooking spray; line bottom of pan with parchment paper. Set aside. Whisk together egg, granulated sugar, sour cream, oil, vanilla, and kosher salt in a large bowl until combined. Gradually add hot coffee, whisking constantly to combine.

2. Sift flour, cocoa, baking soda, and baking powder into egg mixture; whisk just until combined and no patches of flour remain, scraping down sides of bowl as needed.

3. Pour batter into prepared pan. Bake in preheated oven until a wooden pick inserted into center comes out clean, 30 to 35 minutes. Remove pan from oven, and transfer to a wire rack. Let cool in pan for 15 minutes. Invert cake onto wire rack; remove pan, and let cool completely, about 1 hour.

4. Prepare the Salted Caramel Buttercream: Beat butter and salted caramel topping in a large bowl with an electric mixer on medium speed until light and fluffy, about 2 minutes. Gradually beat in powdered sugar, ½ cup at a time. Beat on medium speed until smooth, about 30 seconds.

5. Spread frosting over top of cooled cake. Frosted cake may be covered and stored at room temperature up to 4 days. Just before serving, garnish with sea salt and additional salted caramel topping, if desired.

Tasty Twists

Switch up your sweets

Chocolate Cake with Tahini Buttercream

Prepare recipe as directed through Step 3. In Step 4, substitute ¼ cup **tahini** and ¼ tsp. **kosher salt** for salted caramel. In Step 5, omit caramel; sprinkle with sea salt and **sesame seeds.**

Chocolate Cake with Spiced Chocolate Buttercream

Prepare recipe as directed through Step 3. In Step 4, substitute 3 Tbsp. **unsweetened cocoa;** 1 tsp. **ground cinnamon;** and ¼ tsp. each **cayenne pepper, ancho chile powder,** and **kosher salt** for salted caramel. After beating in powdered sugar in Step 4, beat in 1 Tbsp. **heavy whipping cream.** In Step 5, omit sea salt and caramel; garnish with shaved **semisweet chocolate** and **cinnamon.**

BAKING TIP
The sea salt garnish helps balance out the sweetness of the frosting.

Butter Me Up

Whip up a batch of these Scottish-born biscuits for breakfast

Butter Pecan Scones

ACTIVE 20 MIN. - TOTAL 1 HOUR, 15 MIN.
SERVES 6

- 5 Tbsp. cold unsalted butter, divided
- 1 cup chopped pecans
- ⅓ cup plus ⅛ tsp. granulated sugar, divided
- ¾ tsp. kosher salt, divided
- 1½ cups all-purpose flour, plus more for surface
- 1½ tsp. baking powder
- ¼ tsp. plus a pinch of ground cinnamon, divided
- 1 large egg, cold
- 1 tsp. vanilla extract
- 9 Tbsp. cold heavy whipping cream, divided
- 1 cup powdered sugar
- 1 Tbsp. pure maple syrup

1. Preheat oven to 400°F with rack in top third position. Melt 1 tablespoon of the butter in a medium skillet over medium. Add pecans; cook, stirring occasionally, until nuts are toasted and fragrant, 2 to 3 minutes. Remove from heat, and transfer to a plate. Sprinkle pecans with ⅛ teaspoon each of the granulated sugar and the salt. Cool 10 minutes.

2. Whisk together flour, baking powder, ¼ teaspoon of the cinnamon, ½ teaspoon of the salt, and remaining ⅓ cup granulated sugar in a large bowl. Cut remaining 4 tablespoons cold butter into small cubes, and work the butter into the flour mixture using a pastry cutter or 2 forks until the mixture is crumbly but some larger pea-size pieces of butter remain.

3. Whisk together egg, vanilla, and 6 tablespoons of the cream in a medium bowl; add to flour mixture, and stir until almost combined, about 2 minutes. Add ¾ cup of the toasted pecans, and fold until just combined and a loose, crumbly dough comes together.

4. Turn dough out onto a lightly floured surface; shape into a 6-inch-diameter disk about ¾ inch thick. Use a sharp knife to cut disk into 6 wedges. Arrange wedges about ½ inch apart on a small rimmed baking sheet lined with parchment paper. Chill, uncovered, 20 minutes, or cover and chill for up to 12 hours.

5. Lightly brush tops of scones with 1 tablespoon of the cream. Bake in preheated oven until golden brown and edges are crisp, 18 to 20 minutes. Let cool on baking sheet 5 minutes.

6. While scones cool, whisk together powdered sugar; maple syrup; and remaining 2 tablespoons cream, ⅛ teaspoon salt, and pinch of cinnamon in a small saucepan over medium, stirring constantly, until sugar dissolves and mixture thickens, about 2 minutes. Drizzle icing over warm scones, and sprinkle with the remaining ¼ cup toasted pecans.

Cauliflower Power

Made with half the potatoes, this light and fluffy mash tastes like the real deal

GOOD FOR YOU!
Neutral in flavor, cauliflower boosts the nutrition of classic mashed potatoes by adding fiber and immunity-boosting vitamin C.

Cauliflower Mashed Potatoes

ACTIVE 20 MIN. · TOTAL 45 MIN.

SERVES 6

- 2 lb. Yukon Gold potatoes, peeled and cut into 1½-inch chunks (6 cups)
- 5 cups fresh cauliflower florets (from 1 head)
- 3 large garlic cloves, peeled and smashed
- 2 Tbsp. plus ½ tsp. kosher salt, divided
- ¼ cup butter, cut into pieces, plus 1½ tsp., divided
- ¼ cup whole buttermilk
- Chopped fresh chives
- Black pepper

1. Bring 8 cups water, the potatoes, cauliflower, garlic, and 2 tablespoons of the salt to a boil in a Dutch oven over medium-high. Reduce heat to medium; cover, and simmer until fork-tender, 15 to 20 minutes.
2. Drain; return to Dutch oven. Cook over medium until no liquid remains, about 1 minute. Remove from heat.

3. Gradually add ¼ cup butter pieces to Dutch oven; using a potato masher, mash until combined. Add buttermilk and remaining ½ teaspoon salt; fold until combined. Top with remaining 1½ teaspoons butter. Garnish with chives and pepper.

Before Recipe Makeover:

CALORIES: **356** – FIBER: **3 G** – FAT: **18 G**

After Recipe Makeover:

CALORIES: **217** – FIBER: **5 G** – FAT: **9 G**

Falling for Apples

Senior Test Kitchen Pro Ivy Odom adds some European flair to a Southern classic

WHEN TASKED WITH DREAMING UP a fall crowd-pleaser, I immediately thought of the food that makes me weak in the knees: fried apples. It's a side I can never turn down, often sharing the table with chicken and dumplings, green beans, and a pegboard game at a popular interstate country store. But to give it the proper dessert treatment, I had to look beyond family-vacation pit stops to my first jaunt overseas—my ninth-grade choir trip to Austria. In Vienna, I swooned over a Sacher torte and savored my first real schnitzel, but it was the flaky strudel I loved most. Surrounded by scenery straight out of *The Sound of Music*, I was singing about girls in white dresses with blue satin sashes after just one bite. This version takes my love of Southern-style fried apples and wraps it in the sweet memories of my European adventure. So now when people ask me for my go-to fall dish, I simply remember my favorite things...and give them a slice of crisp apple strudel.

Strudel with Fried Apples

ACTIVE 30 MIN. - TOTAL 1 HOUR, 10 MIN.
SERVES 8

- 2 lb. Honeycrisp apples (about 4 medium apples), peeled and cut into ¼-inch slices (about 6 cups)
- ¼ cup packed light brown sugar
- 1 Tbsp. bacon drippings
- ½ tsp. ground cinnamon
- ¼ tsp. kosher salt
- 1 tsp. all-purpose flour, plus more for work surface

- ½ (17.3-oz.) pkg. frozen puff pastry sheets (1 sheet), thawed
- 1 large egg
- 1 Tbsp. granulated sugar
- Vanilla ice cream (optional)

1. Cook apples, brown sugar, bacon drippings, cinnamon, and kosher salt in a large skillet over medium, stirring occasionally, until liquid has evaporated and apples soften, about 12 minutes. Add flour to mixture; toss to coat. Cook, stirring occasionally, for 1 minute. Remove from heat; let cool 20 minutes.

2. Meanwhile, preheat oven to 400°F. Line a large rimmed baking sheet with parchment paper; set aside. Roll thawed puff pastry sheet into a 14- x 9-inch rectangle on a lightly floured work surface. Transfer to prepared baking sheet. Whisk together egg and 1 teaspoon water in a small bowl; set aside.

3. Using scissors and starting at 1 long edge of pastry sheet, cut 2½-inch-long slits, going from the edge toward the center in 1-inch intervals to yield 14 strips. Repeat process on opposite side. Spoon the cooled apple mixture evenly down the center of the pastry sheet. Lightly brush some of the egg-water mixture over the strips on both sides.

4. Position the pan so that 1 short edge is facing you. Starting at the short edge farthest from you, fold the top left strip over the apples at a slight angle, slightly toward you. Repeat with right strip, overlapping the left strip. Repeat with remaining strips, going from left to right to enclose the apple filling. Brush with remaining egg-water mixture, and sprinkle with granulated sugar.

5. Bake in preheated oven until pastry is crisp and golden, 15 to 18 minutes. Let cool 5 minutes. Slice and serve with ice cream, if desired.

That's So Cheesy

Crispy wafers with a cayenne kick

Spicy Cheddar Crisps

ACTIVE 10 MIN. · TOTAL 40 MIN.

MAKES 20

- 8 oz. extra-sharp Cheddar cheese, finely shredded (about 2 cups)
- 2 oz. Parmigiano-Reggiano cheese, finely shredded (about ¾ cup)
- 2 oz. aged gouda cheese, finely shredded (about ½ cup)
- 2 Tbsp. nutritional yeast
- 2 tsp. garlic powder
- 2 tsp. onion powder
- ¾ tsp. dried thyme
- ¼ tsp. cayenne pepper

1. Preheat oven to 400°F. Line 2 large baking sheets with parchment paper, and set aside.
2. Place all ingredients in a medium bowl, and gently stir together until cheeses are evenly distributed and coated in spices. Using a tablespoon, scoop cheese mixture into 20 heaping mounds onto prepared baking sheets, leaving at least 2 inches between scoops.
3. Bake in batches in preheated oven until deepened in color and crispy, about 8 minutes. Let cool on baking sheets until set, about 2 minutes. Transfer to wire racks to cool completely, about 10 minutes.

SECRET INGREDIENT
Nutritional yeast (not the active dry kind) gives these gluten-free snacks a baked-cracker flavor. Look for it in the baking aisle.

The Meltdown

Chocolate can scorch quicker than you think–especially in the microwave. We recommend using a double boiler to melt it gently with the indirect heat of the steam. Simply bring a few inches of water to simmer in a saucepan, and then nestle a slightly wider heatproof bowl on top (the bottom of the bowl shouldn't touch the water). Add chopped chocolate to the bowl. Heat, stirring often with a spatula and scraping down the sides, until it's almost entirely melted. Remove the bowl from the saucepan, and stir the chocolate until it is liquid and smooth.

All the Chips On the Table
Get to know the different kinds of chocolate in the baking aisle

SEMISWEET VS. BITTERSWEET
There isn't an official distinction between these two types of dark chocolate, but both must have at least 35% cacao, although many have closer to 70%. No matter the name on the label, the higher the cacao percentage, the darker (less sweet) the chocolate will be, so keep that in mind when baking.

BARS VS. CHIPS
Contrary to popular belief, different forms of chocolate are not interchangeable. Chips are an easy mix-in option for baked goods like cookies because they retain their shape. Chopped bars are ideal for melting into ganaches or sauces since they typically don't contain stabilizers, which can impact the final product's smoothness.

WHAT ABOUT UNSWEETENED CHOCOLATE?
You won't like snacking on this kind—it's 100% cacao with no added milk or sugar. It's best used in desserts like cakes or brownies that call for a hefty amount of sugar to achieve their desired textures and structures.

COCOA POWDER
Cocoa powder is produced in two styles: natural and Dutch-process. The latter is made from chocolate treated with a neutralizing agent, yielding a darker version that's less bitter. Natural cocoa powders are more acidic and contain less fat, resulting in drier baked goods. In chocolate-forward recipes that use substantial amounts of cocoa powder, it pays to use Dutch-process.

CACAO NIBS
These crushed bits of roasted cacao beans haven't been mixed with sugar. Crunchy and slightly fruity, they are often used as a garnish for added texture. Their natural bitterness is their superpower, helping balance the sweetness of desserts. Try folding some nibs into granola or into your favorite banana or pumpkin bread batter.

October

The South's Most Treasured Desserts

Straight from the butter-stained recipe cards of our readers, these tried-and-true cakes, cookies, pies, and more celebrate the Southerners who made them with love

JEAN HOPE'S CHOCOLATE BROWNIE PIE (PAGE 241)

OUR MOTHERS AND GRANDMOTHERS
did it best, didn't they? In tight kitchens with simple ingredients and humble tools, they stirred together the desserts that we place on pedestals in our homes and hearts. The 15 recipes and stories that grace the following pages are just a few of the hundreds of cherished memories our readers have generously submitted. Each dish has been prepared in the *Southern Living* Test Kitchen and reviewed by our editors to preserve its integrity, intent, and personality. It's our privilege to share them with you and honor the cooks who brought them to life for generations.

Potato Cake

(Photo, page 236)

"The first memory I have of Christmas is Mama making her Potato Cake. I know she would be so honored that this recipe made it into the magazine." —Barbara Walden, Stockbridge, Georgia

ACTIVE 25 MIN. · TOTAL 1 HOUR, 5 MIN., PLUS 1 HOUR COOLING TIME

SERVES 12

- ¾ cup butter
- 1¾ cups sugar
- 2 egg yolks
- 1 cup warm mashed Irish (russet) potatoes
- 1½ Tbsp. cocoa powder
- 1 cup chopped pecans
- ½ cup whole milk
- 2 cups self-rising flour
- 2 tsp. cinnamon
- ½ tsp. nutmeg
- 2 egg whites, beaten until frothy
- 1 cup chopped raisins

Cream butter and sugar. Add egg yolks, mashed potatoes, cocoa powder, and pecans. Add milk, flour, cinnamon, and nutmeg. Fold in beaten egg whites, and then add raisins. Pour into a greased and floured Bundt pan. Bake 45 minutes at 350°F.

Test Kitchen Tip We peeled and cubed 1 large russet potato and then boiled it until it was tender to yield 1 cup of mashed potatoes for this recipe.

Oatmeal Cake

(Photo, page 236)

"My mom would make this on special occasions, like when my older sister and I had piano recitals. (We sure needed a treat after sitting through one of those!) I still have the pan she used to bake the cake. It was handed down from our grandma to her and now to me. It's an Ovenex that's probably almost 100 years old." —Pat Ynesta, Navarre, Florida

ACTIVE 15 MIN. · TOTAL 1 HOUR, 10 MIN.

SERVES 12

CAKE

- 1 cup quick-cooking oatmeal
- 1 tsp. baking soda
- 1¼ cups hot water
- ½ cup butter or margarine
- 1 cup brown sugar
- 1 cup granulated sugar
- 2 eggs
- 1 tsp. vanilla
- 1⅓ cups flour
- 1 tsp. cinnamon

TOPPING

- ½ cup butter or margarine
- 1 cup shredded coconut
- 1 cup brown sugar
- ½ cup chopped nuts (pecans)
- ¼ cup milk

1. For Cake: Combine oatmeal, baking soda, and water in a bowl. Let mix stand for 20 minutes. Cream butter and sugars in another bowl; add eggs, and beat thoroughly. Stir oatmeal and vanilla into creamed mixture. Gradually add flour and cinnamon; blend well, and pour into an oblong pan (13- x 9-inch baking dish). Bake at 375°F for 35 minutes.

2. For Topping: Combine all ingredients in a small saucepan; heat over low flame until melted. Spread over warm Cake. Place topped Cake in oven under broiler set to low heat until bubbles form in the Topping.

Test Kitchen Tip If your oven's broiler doesn't have a low setting, bake the topped cake at 450°F until bubbles form in the topping. Keep a close eye on it so the coconut doesn't burn.

How to Decode Vintage Recipes

When it comes to writing down instructions, seasoned cooks often make assumptions. Here are a few best practices your grandmother may have left out.

Start with a Hot Oven

Chances are the wording on your heirloom recipe cards doesn't begin with the instruction to preheat the oven. Unless the recipe specifies otherwise, always do this so that once the batter or dough is mixed, it can go right in.

Pay Attention to Temperature

Old-school recipes might not specify this, but the eggs, butter, and cream cheese should be at room temperature before you begin baking. This simple step will allow the ingredients to combine with others more easily.

Prepare Cake Pans

Before baking spray existed, folks would rub butter inside the pan, add a teaspoon or two of flour, and then tap the pan like a tambourine to help the flour stick. However you choose to do it, be sure you don't skip this step, which is rarely included in older recipes.

Fluff It Up

Many of these methods say to "cream the butter and sugar." Here's how to do it: Beat soft butter and sugar in a bowl with a mixer at medium speed until light and fluffy, about three minutes. Your grandmother probably used a hand mixer, but a stand one will work fine.

POTATO CAKE
(PAGE 235)

OATMEAL CAKE
(PAGE 235)

BANANA LAYER
CAKE WITH
CARAMEL ICING

Banana Layer Cake with Caramel Icing

"When I make this cake, I often think of my mom as well as my grandmother, who passed it down from her mother. It has created a thread of connection to many wonderful memories and stories with my own family. It's simple to make with ingredients on hand, especially if you have a ripe banana to use up." —Mary Vail-Grube, Allen, Texas

ACTIVE 20 MIN. - TOTAL 45 MIN.

SERVES 8

- 2 cups flour
- 1 tsp. baking powder
- 1 tsp. baking soda
- ½ tsp. salt
- ½ cup butter
- 1½ cups sugar
- 1 egg and 1 egg yolk, well beaten
- 1 cup mashed ripe banana
- ¾ cup buttermilk
- 1 tsp. vanilla
- Caramel Icing (recipe follows)

Sift dry ingredients together. Cream butter and sugar in a bowl until fluffy. Add egg and egg yolk, and beat well. Then add banana, and mix well. Alternate flour mixture with buttermilk, beating after each addition. Add vanilla, and mix well. Bake in 2 (8- or 9-inch) layer pans greased or lined with parchment at 350°F for 25 to 28 minutes. Let cool before frosting.

Test Kitchen Tip This recipe can also make a batch of cupcakes (put paper liners in tins; bake about 15 minutes) or a sheet cake (grease a 10- x 15-inch pan; bake about 18 minutes).

Caramel Icing

Melt ⅓ cup **butter**, 1 cup **brown sugar**, and ¼ cup **milk** in a 2-quart saucepan over very low heat. Stir and bring to boil for 1 minute. Don't cook too long, or icing will get hard and grainy. Cool slightly. Stir in 2 cups **powdered sugar** and 1 teaspoon **vanilla**. Beat until smooth and creamy either with a whisk or an electric mixer. If too thick, add 1 teaspoon milk at a time until spreadable. While icing is still warm, frost the cake.

BUTTERNUT
SQUASH CAKE

HARVEST
CAKE

DOROTHY POWE'S
TRIPLE-CHOCOLATE CAKE

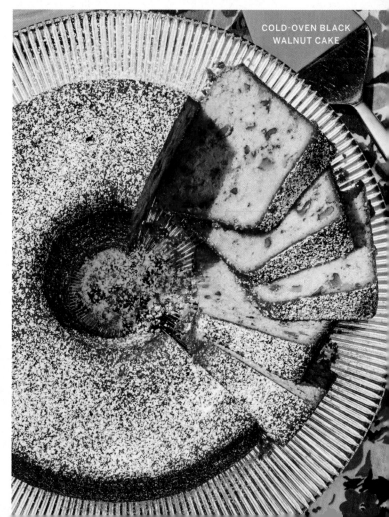

COLD-OVEN BLACK
WALNUT CAKE

Dorothy Powe's Triple-Chocolate Cake

"I recall my mother baking this cake in our kitchen as a much-anticipated treat. Her three daughters usually surrounded her and watched, helped, and learned from the hands of an expert." —Barbara Pachman, The Woodlands, Texas

ACTIVE 15 MIN. - TOTAL 3 HOURS, 10 MIN. (INCLUDES COOLING TIME)

SERVES 10

CAKE

- 1 (15.25-oz.) box devil's food cake mix
- 1 (3.9-oz.) pkg. instant chocolate pudding mix
- 1 cup sour cream
- ¼ cup canola oil
- ⅓ cup milk
- 1 large egg
- 3 large egg whites
- ⅓ cup amaretto
- 1 tsp. almond extract
- ⅓ cup chocolate chips

ALMOND GLAZE

- 1½ cups powdered sugar
- ¼ cup milk
- 1 tsp. almond extract

Preheat oven to 350°F. Combine all ingredients for the Cake except the chocolate chips in a large bowl. Beat with a mixer for 2 minutes. Add chocolate chips. Pour into a well-greased Bundt pan. Bake 40 to 45 minutes. Cool completely. Mix all Almond Glaze ingredients in a bowl until smooth. Drizzle over cooled Cake.

Test Kitchen Tip Stir ¼ teaspoon salt into cake batter to enhance the chocolate flavor. We tested with semisweet chips.

Butternut Squash Cake

"This was a favorite when we were kids. My mom made it in the fall and at other times with frozen butternut squash or even pumpkin. As her note on the back of the recipe card states, she usually dusted it with powdered sugar. Cream cheese icing was only for company or for a donated cake!" —Connie Taylor, Crossville, Tennessee

ACTIVE 15 MIN. - TOTAL 1 HOUR, 5 MIN., PLUS 1 HOUR COOLING TIME

SERVES 10

- 4 eggs
- 2 cups sugar
- 1 cup oil
- 2 cups flour

- ½ tsp. salt
- 2 tsp. baking soda
- 2 tsp. cinnamon
- 2 tsp. pumpkin pie spice
- 1 tsp. baking powder
- 2 cups cooked, drained, and mashed squash (See Test Kitchen Tip below)
- 8 oz. cream cheese, at room temperature
- 1 stick butter, at room temperature
- 1 (1-lb.) box powdered sugar
- 1 tsp. vanilla
  Nuts (optional)

1. Beat together eggs, sugar, and oil in a bowl until combined. Beat in flour, salt, baking soda, cinnamon, pumpkin pie spice, baking powder, and squash until smooth. Pour batter into a greased Bundt pan. Bake at 350°F until done, 50 minutes to 1 hour.

2. Beat cream cheese and butter until creamy. Beat in powdered sugar and vanilla until smooth. Spread on cooled cake. Sprinkle with nuts, if desired.

Test Kitchen Tip We tested this recipe with pecans and canned pumpkin puree. Don't buy pumpkin pie filling by mistake; it's made with added sugar and spices that will impact the flavor of this cake.

Harvest Cake

"When I was dating my husband, he told me about this cake his grandmother would make for Thanksgiving but said that no one made it anymore and he missed it. Well, I saw my chance to impress! I got the recipe from his mom—she had written it on a yellow legal pad—and then I got to work!" —Meghan Mays, Lynchburg, Virginia

ACTIVE 30 MIN. - TOTAL 3 HOURS, 30 MIN. (INCLUDES COOLING TIME)

SERVES 12

- 4 cups diced fresh apples
- 2 cups sugar
- 3 cups flour
- 1 tsp. cinnamon
- 1 tsp. nutmeg
- 1 tsp. salt
- 2 tsp. baking soda
- 2 eggs
- 1 cup vegetable oil
- 1 tsp. vanilla
- 1 cup chopped walnuts or pecans, plus more for garnish
  White Icing (See Test Kitchen Tip above right)

Mix apples and sugar together in a bowl; let stand for 1 hour. Sift flour, cinnamon, nutmeg, salt, and baking soda into a medium bowl. In another bowl, beat eggs, oil, and vanilla together. Add the apple mixture, then fold in flour mixture followed by the walnuts. Bake in a 10-inch tube pan in a 350°F oven for 1 hour and 10 minutes. Drizzle cooled cake with White Icing; garnish with more chopped nuts.

Test Kitchen Tip To make our version of White Icing, whisk together ⅔ cup powdered sugar, 1 to 2 tablespoons milk, and ½ teaspoon vanilla until smooth.

Cold-Oven Black Walnut Cake

"It wouldn't be the holidays without Mom Gee's cake—my four children and their families clamor for it every year. The recipe is in her handwriting—it's a small part of this very special woman that is with us to this day. Her direction at the end to not open the oven door, even to peek, instantly brings back the memories of baking together." —Susan Sartory, Juno Beach, Florida

ACTIVE 20 MIN. - TOTAL 2 HOURS, 40 MIN. (INCLUDES COOLING TIME)

SERVES 12

- ½ cup butter, plus more for greasing pan
- ½ cup margarine
- ½ cup shortening
- 3 cups sugar
- 6 eggs
- ½ tsp. baking powder
- 3 cups flour, plus more for prepping pan
- ½ lb. black walnuts, chopped
- 1 cup whole milk

Cream together the butter, margarine, and shortening in a large bowl. Add sugar, and beat until fluffy. Add eggs 1 at a time, and beat well. Add baking powder to flour. Toss walnuts in flour mixture. Add walnut-flour mixture and milk a little at a time to the butter mixture. Pour batter into a greased and floured large tube pan. Place in a cold oven. Heat oven to 350°F and bake for 1 hour and 15 minutes. Do not open the oven door until time is up.

Test Kitchen Tip We tested this recipe with 1 cup butter and ½ cup shortening but no margarine. Dust the cake with powdered sugar for some extra flair.

GOOGIE'S ROSABELLES

MOM'S BUTTERSCOTCH OATIES

MOMMA MILLIE'S POTATO CHIP COOKIES

Googie's Rosabelles

"My grandmother Googie always pulled out a cereal bowl to hold the white sugar to roll the balls of cookie dough in. I use the same bowl almost 50 years later. I can't imagine making them with any other vessel in my kitchen. Googie's Rosabelles have been enjoyed the world over—I've sent them to friends abroad!" —Kristin Stewart, Apex, North Carolina

ACTIVE 10 MIN. - TOTAL 45 MIN.

MAKES ABOUT 40 COOKIES

- 1 cup sugar, plus more for rolling
- ¾ cup shortening
- ¼ cup molasses
- 1 egg
- 2 cups flour
- 2 tsp. baking soda
- 1 tsp. ginger
- 1 tsp. cinnamon
- 1 tsp. cloves
- ½ tsp. salt

1. Cream together sugar and shortening in a bowl. Add molasses and egg. Sift together flour, baking soda, ginger, cinnamon, cloves, and salt; add to egg mixture. Spoon dough into balls, and roll in a bowl of sugar.

2. Place the dough balls on a baking sheet, and bake for 9 minutes at 350°F. These cookies should be crispy on the outside and soft on the inside. Don't overbake.

Momma Millie's Potato Chip Cookies

"Get ready for the best, buttery, melt-in-your-mouth, crunchy, and deliciously unique cookies you'll ever taste. This recipe has to be over 40 years old, and Mom was known for her baked goods. This was one of her most requested desserts." —Ruth Maicki, Tampa Bay, Florida

ACTIVE 15 MIN. - TOTAL 1 HOUR, 20 MIN.

MAKES ABOUT 60 COOKIES

- 2 sticks butter, at room temperature
- 2 sticks margarine
- 1 cup white sugar
- 2 tsp. vanilla extract
- 3 cups flour
- 1½ cups crushed potato chips, plus more for sprinkling
- Powdered sugar, for dusting

Cream butter, margarine, and white sugar. Add vanilla. Add flour, cream thoroughly, and then add crushed potato chips. Drop tablespoonfuls of dough on ungreased cookie sheet. Sprinkle with more crushed chips. Bake at 325°F for 13 to 14 minutes. When cool, sift powdered sugar over the tops.

Test Kitchen Tip We tested with four sticks of butter (2 cups) instead of using both butter and margarine.

Mom's Butterscotch Oaties

"This is a treat we had when we came home from school in the fall, and now the taste of them takes me right back to those days. My recipe box was my mother's when she first got married in the 1960s. She is 82 now and can still bake her way into my heart!" —Claire Killeen, Bedford, Texas

ACTIVE 15 MIN. - TOTAL 55 MIN.

MAKES ABOUT 60 COOKIES

- 1 cup butterscotch chips
- ¾ cup butter or margarine
- 2 Tbsp. boiling water
- 1 tsp. baking soda
- 2 cups rolled oats
- 1 cup flour
- ¾ cup sugar
- Generous pinch of salt

Preheat oven to 350°F. Melt butterscotch chips and butter in a saucepan over low heat. Mix boiling water and baking soda in a small bowl, and add to butterscotch mixture. Gradually blend in the remaining ingredients. Drop by slightly rounded teaspoons onto ungreased baking sheets. Bake for 10 minutes.

Test Kitchen Tip These cookies spread a good bit; bake on four baking sheets with 2 inches in between the dough balls. The recipe makes a lot; cut it in half, if desired.

Pineapple Juice Pie

(Photo, page 242)

"I cannot recall the first time I had this pie, but I am certain that it was a family dinner at my mother-in-law's home. She made sure that every meal included something that everyone liked. Mamie Ellis Casey of Gadsden, Alabama, created this dish as part of the Works Progress Administration effort to avoid waste. I was told that the leftover juice from the cans of pineapple rings is what she used. She shared this recipe with my mother-in-law, Marie Smith Casey, who then entrusted it to me. I will pass it down to my daughters and granddaughters." —Vicki Casey, Huntersville, North Carolina

ACTIVE 20 MIN. - TOTAL 5 HOURS, 20 MIN. (INCLUDES COOLING TIME)

SERVES 8

- 1 cup brown sugar
- 4 Tbsp. flour
- 3 eggs
- 1½ cups pineapple juice
- 1 tsp. vanilla
- ¼ tsp. salt
- 1 parbaked piecrust (see Test Kitchen Tip below)
- ⅓ cup granulated sugar
- ½ tsp. cream of tartar

1. Mix together brown sugar and flour in a saucepan. Separate eggs. Reserve whites. Beat yolks; whisk into sugar mixture. Add pineapple juice gradually, and cook until thick. Remove from heat, add vanilla and salt, cool slightly, and pour into parbaked piecrust.
2. Beat egg whites, granulated sugar, and cream of tartar until stiff peaks form. Spread meringue over filling. Bake at 350°F until browned, 10 to 12 minutes. Let stand at room temperature 1 hour before refrigerating until set, at least 4 hours.

Test Kitchen Tip To parbake a crust, top a preformed, frozen piecrust with a sheet of parchment paper; fill with pie weights, and bake at 400°F for 10 minutes. Remove parchment paper and pie weights; bake until crust is lightly browned, about 5 more minutes.

Jean Hope's Chocolate Brownie Pie

(Photo, page 234)

"Back in the day, my mom, Jean Hope, would prepare a whole pie for each of her grandsons as well as one for the Thanksgiving meal. Later, I would make them each one to take back to college after break—most of it was eaten while they were driving. Now I give them pies to carry home to their families." —Beth Lewis, Cary, North Carolina

ACTIVE 10 MIN. - TOTAL 2 HOURS, 10 MIN. (INCLUDES COOLING TIME)

SERVES 8

- 2 (½-oz.) squares unsweetened chocolate
- 2 Tbsp. butter or margarine
- 3 eggs
- ½ cup sugar
- ¾ cup dark corn syrup
- ¾ cup pecan halves
- 1 (9-inch) frozen piecrust

Melt chocolate and butter together in a saucepan over low heat, stirring until smooth. Beat together eggs, sugar, chocolate mixture, and corn syrup. Mix in pecan halves. Pour into piecrust. Bake at 375°F until just set, 40 to 50 minutes.

Sour Cream-Apple Pie

(Photo, page 243)

"I lost my mom, Neddy Nokes, six years ago. I make this pie when I am missing her. For as long as I can remember, this was her go-to dessert for holidays, bridge games, and my birthday. I love her little recipe card because it is in her handwriting." —Beverly Thompson, Willis, Texas

ACTIVE 20 MIN. - TOTAL 1 HOUR, 30 MIN., PLUS 1 HOUR COOLING TIME

SERVES 8

PIE
- ¾ cup sugar
- 2 Tbsp. flour
- 1 cup sour cream
- 1 egg
- ½ tsp. vanilla
- ¼ tsp. salt
- 1 cup fresh sliced apples or canned apples
- 1 parbaked piecrust (see Test Kitchen Tip left)

TOPPING
- ⅓ cup sugar
- 1 tsp. cinnamon
- ¼ cup flour
- 4 Tbsp. butter

1. Stir together sugar and flour in a large bowl. Stir in sour cream, egg, vanilla, and salt until combined. Then stir in apples. Pour into parbaked piecrust. Bake for 40 minutes at 350°F.
2. Stir together the Topping ingredients, and sprinkle evenly over Pie. Bake for 15 more minutes.

Know Your Ingredients

To preserve the authenticity of these special recipes, we've left them as untouched as possible. To clear up any questions you might encounter, here's a list of frequently used ingredients and a little more information about what to shop for.

Butter = Salted Butter

Flour = All-Purpose Flour

Eggs = Large Eggs

Milk = Whole Milk

Sugar = White Granulated Sugar

Chocolate Chips = Semisweet Chocolate Chips

Coconut = Sweetened Flaked Coconut

Spices = Ground Versions

PINEAPPLE
JUICE PIE
(PAGE 241)

SOUR CREAM-
APPLE PIE
(PAGE 241)

Wilma Tidwell's Chocolate Chip Pie

"I hope this recipe encourages you to take time to enjoy simple pleasures with your loved ones. With three small children of my own, I hope they'll think of me and smile, just as I think of my grandmother."
—Cassie Tidwell Tramel, Columbia, Tennessee

ACTIVE 10 MIN. · TOTAL 1 HOUR
SERVES 8

1	cup sugar
½	cup flour
½	cup butter or margarine, melted
1	cup nuts, chopped
1	cup chocolate chips
2	eggs, lightly beaten
1	unbaked deep-dish piecrust

Mix ingredients well in a large bowl. Pour into an unbaked piecrust, and bake at 350°F for 50 minutes.

Ozark Pudding

"This is my mother-in-law's Ozark Pudding recipe. She was a leader in the Democratic Party back in the 1950s. On her original card, there's a note that this dessert was President Truman's favorite. It's such a simple dish, but it's so tasty and wonderful after an apple-picking trip in the fall."
—Pat Meakin, Wilmington, North Carolina

ACTIVE 10 MIN. · TOTAL 40 MIN.
SERVES 8

¾	cup sugar
2	Tbsp. flour
1¼	tsp. baking powder
¼	tsp. salt
1	egg
½	cup pecans, chopped
1	medium apple, chopped
1	tsp. vanilla

Mix dry ingredients in a bowl. Add egg, nuts, apple, and vanilla. Bake in a well-greased pie plate at 350°F for 30 minutes.

WILMA TIDWELL'S CHOCOLATE CHIP PIE

OZARK PUDDING

Good Gourd!

Savory and sweet butternut squash takes fall's best comfort food to the next level

Butternut Squash Mac and Cheese

ACTIVE 30 MIN. · TOTAL 1 HOUR, 10 MIN.
SERVES 6

Toss together 6 cups cubed **butternut squash**, 1 Tbsp. **olive oil**, ¾ tsp. **kosher salt**, and ¼ tsp. **black pepper** on a large rimmed baking sheet until fully coated. Bake at 375°F until fork-tender and golden brown, about 30 minutes. Let cool at room temperature, about 5 minutes. Place cooled squash and 1¼ cups **lower-sodium chicken broth** in a blender, and process until smooth, about 30 seconds. Bring 1½ cups **whole milk** and ¼ cup **unsalted butter** to a simmer in a large Dutch oven over medium, stirring occasionally. Stir in squash puree, 1¼ tsp. **kosher salt**, and ½ tsp. **black pepper** until smooth. Remove from heat; gradually stir in 1½ cups shredded **extra-sharp Cheddar** and ½ cup shredded **fontina** until melted. Stir in 1 lb. **elbow macaroni** (cooked to al dente) until fully coated. Spoon into a 13- x 9-inch baking dish coated with **cooking spray**; sprinkle evenly with 1 cup shredded **Cheddar** and ½ cup shredded **fontina**. Bake at 375°F until cheese is melted and top is golden brown, about 25 minutes. Garnish with **fresh thyme leaves.**

MAKE IT WORK FOR YOU
Butternut squash thickens the sauce without flour. You can use gluten-free pasta and broth for a celiac-friendly meal.

Love Me Tender

Tasty new ways to enjoy pork tenderloin

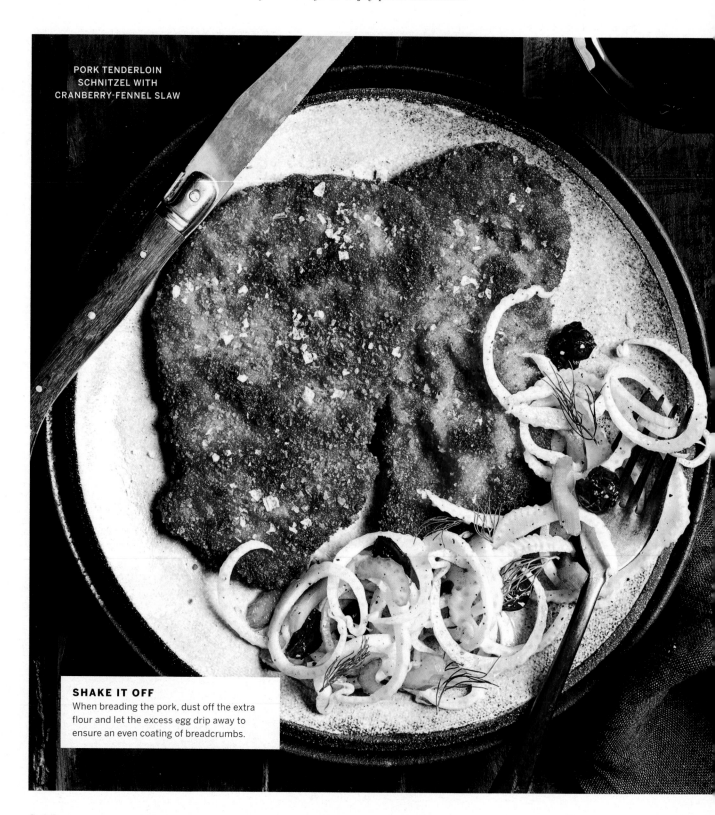

PORK TENDERLOIN
SCHNITZEL WITH
CRANBERRY-FENNEL SLAW

SHAKE IT OFF
When breading the pork, dust off the extra
flour and let the excess egg drip away to
ensure an even coating of breadcrumbs.

Pork Tenderloin Sliders with Tomato Chutney Aïoli

ACTIVE 25 MIN. · TOTAL 55 MIN.
SERVES 6

- 1 Tbsp. vegetable oil
- 2 garlic cloves, finely chopped (about 2 tsp.)
- ¼ tsp. crushed red pepper
- ¼ tsp. ground ginger
- 1 (14½-oz.) can fire-roasted diced tomatoes, drained
- ¼ cup raisins
- 1 Tbsp. red wine vinegar
- 1 Tbsp. dark brown sugar
- ½ cup mayonnaise
- ¾ tsp. kosher salt, divided
- 12 slider buns or dinner rolls (such as Pepperidge Farm), split
- 1 Roasted Pork Tenderloin (recipe, page 249), sliced ¼ inch thick
- 3 cups loosely packed baby arugula

1. Heat oil in a medium saucepan over medium. Add garlic, red pepper, and ginger; cook, stirring constantly, until fragrant, about 30 seconds. Add tomatoes, raisins, vinegar, and brown sugar; cook, stirring occasionally, until raisins are plump and tomatoes start to break down, 8 to 10 minutes. Remove from heat; let cool to room temperature, about 30 minutes, stirring occasionally.
2. Process tomato mixture, mayonnaise, and ¼ teaspoon of the kosher salt in a food processor until smooth, about 30 seconds, or less for a chunkier consistency.
3. Spread aïoli evenly over tops and bottoms of buns. Divide pork tenderloin slices among bottoms of buns, and sprinkle evenly with remaining ½ teaspoon salt and arugula. Cover with tops of buns. Aïoli can be made up to 1 week in advance; store in an airtight container in refrigerator.

Pork Tenderloin Schnitzel with Cranberry-Fennel Slaw

ACTIVE 45 MIN. · TOTAL 45 MIN.
SERVES 4

- 1 lb. pork tenderloin
- ¼ tsp. ground black pepper
- 2 tsp. kosher salt, divided
- 2 Tbsp. fresh lemon juice (from 1 lemon)
- ½ cup all-purpose flour

PORK TENDERLOIN SLIDERS WITH TOMATO CHUTNEY AÏOLI

- 2 large eggs
- 1 cup plain dry breadcrumbs
- ½ cup unsalted butter, divided
- ½ cup vegetable oil, divided
  Flaky sea salt
  Cranberry-Fennel Slaw (recipe follows)
  Lemon wedges (optional)

1. Preheat oven to 200°F. Place 2 wire racks on 2 large rimmed baking sheets; set aside.
2. Cut pork crosswise into 8 (1-inch) pieces. Working with 1 piece at a time, place between 2 sheets of plastic wrap. Using a meat mallet or rolling pin, pound until pork is about ⅛ inch thick. Remove and discard plastic wrap; set aside. Repeat with remaining pork. Sprinkle both sides of pork evenly with pepper and 1 teaspoon of the salt; drizzle both sides with lemon juice.
3. Whisk together flour and remaining 1 teaspoon salt in a shallow bowl. Beat eggs in a separate shallow bowl. Place breadcrumbs in a third shallow bowl. Working with 1 piece of pork at a time, place in flour mixture, turning to fully coat, and shake off excess. Place in beaten eggs, turning to fully coat; let excess drip off. Place in breadcrumbs, turning to fully coat and pressing gently so breadcrumbs adhere. Place coated pork on 1 prepared rack, and repeat process with remaining pork, flour mixture, and breadcrumbs.

4. Heat ¼ cup each of the butter and oil in a large skillet over medium until butter is melted, about 3 minutes. Increase heat to medium-high. Working in batches, add 2 breaded pork pieces to skillet; cook until browned and a thermometer inserted into thickest portion of pork registers 145°F, about 2 minutes per side. Transfer to remaining clean prepared rack; place in preheated oven to keep warm. Repeat process with 2 more breaded pork pieces. Carefully transfer oil from skillet to a medium heatproof bowl; let cool, and discard. Wipe skillet clean, and heat remaining ¼ cup butter and ¼ cup oil over medium-high. Repeat with remaining 4 breaded cutlets. Sprinkle schnitzel evenly with sea salt; serve with slaw and lemon wedges (if desired).

Cranberry-Fennel Slaw

Whisk together 3 Tbsp. **extra-virgin olive oil**, 2 Tbsp. **apple cider vinegar**, 2 tsp. **lemon juice**, 1 tsp. **honey**, ¾ tsp. **kosher salt**, and ½ tsp. **black pepper** in a large bowl. Add 3 cups thinly sliced **fennel**, 1 cup thinly sliced **celery**, and ½ cup **sweetened dried cranberries**; toss until coated. Cover and refrigerate until ready to serve. Garnish with **fennel fronds**. Slaw may be stored in refrigerator up to 24 hours.

Skillet Pork Tenderloin with Apples

ACTIVE 15 MIN. - TOTAL 50 MIN.

SERVES 4

- 1¼ tsp. kosher salt, divided
- ½ tsp. black pepper
- ½ tsp. ground fennel
- 1 lb. pork tenderloin, patted dry
- 4 Tbsp. butter, divided
- 2 large unpeeled Honeycrisp apples, sliced ½ inch thick (about 4 cups)
- 1 small shallot, thinly sliced (about ⅓ cup)
- ½ cup apple cider, divided
- 1 tsp. grated orange zest (from 1 orange)
- 1 tsp. fresh thyme leaves, plus more for garnish

1. Place a 12-inch cast-iron skillet in oven, and preheat oven to 450°F.
2. While oven is preheating, stir together 1 teaspoon of the salt with the pepper and ground fennel in a small bowl. Sprinkle pepper mixture over pork; let stand at room temperature until ready to cook.
3. Add 2 tablespoons of the butter to preheated skillet; carefully swirl to melt butter and coat bottom of skillet. Place pork tenderloin in center of skillet, and arrange sliced apples and shallot on both sides of pork. Bake for 10 minutes. Remove from oven; turn tenderloin. Stir apple mixture, and drizzle with ¼ cup of the apple cider. Return skillet to oven, and bake at 450°F until a thermometer inserted into thickest portion of pork registers 145°F, about 15 minutes. Transfer pork to a cutting board, reserving apple mixture in skillet, and let rest 10 minutes.
4. Meanwhile, heat apple mixture and remaining 2 tablespoons butter in skillet over medium until butter is melted, about 1 minute. Stir in zest, thyme, and remaining ¼ cup apple cider and ¼ teaspoon salt. Bring to a simmer over medium; simmer, stirring occasionally, until slightly reduced, about 2 minutes. Slice pork, and return to skillet, spooning pan sauce over pork. Garnish with additional thyme.

PRETTY IN PINK
Trust your meat thermometer, and embrace a slightly rosy hue—you'll be rewarded with tender pork.

Roasted Pork Tenderloin and Fall Harvest Salad

ACTIVE 30 MIN. - TOTAL 50 MIN.
SERVES 6

ROASTED PORK TENDERLOIN

- 1 lb. pork tenderloin, patted dry
- 1 Tbsp. olive oil
- 1 tsp. kosher salt
- ½ tsp. black pepper

FALL HARVEST SALAD

- 1 medium (about 2½-lb.) butternut squash, peeled, seeded, and cut into 1-inch cubes (about 5 cups)
- 5 Tbsp. olive oil, divided
- 1¼ tsp. kosher salt, divided
- ¾ tsp. black pepper, divided, plus more for garnish
- 2 Tbsp. white wine vinegar
- 2 tsp. whole-grain mustard
- 1 tsp. honey
- 2 medium bunches Lacinato kale, stemmed and roughly chopped (about 14 cups)
- 2 medium-size red Anjou pears, unpeeled and sliced (about 3 cups)
- 2 oz. Gorgonzola cheese, crumbled (about ½ cup), plus more for garnish
- ½ cup chopped toasted pecans

1. Prepare the Roasted Pork Tenderloin: Preheat oven to 425°F with racks in upper third and lower third positions. Line a rimmed baking sheet with aluminum foil; set a wire rack inside baking sheet, and set aside. Rub pork with oil; sprinkle with salt and pepper. Place on prepared wire rack on baking sheet, and bake on upper third oven rack until a thermometer inserted into thickest portion of pork registers 145°F, about 25 minutes, turning once. Let pork rest 10 minutes before cutting.
2. While pork tenderloin is baking, prepare the Fall Harvest Salad: Toss together squash, 1 tablespoon of the oil, 1 teaspoon of the salt, and ½ teaspoon of the pepper on a large rimmed baking sheet. Spread in an even layer. Bake at 425°F on lower third rack (below the pork), stirring once, until golden brown and fork-tender, about 25 minutes.
3. While pork is resting, whisk together the vinegar, whole-grain mustard, honey, and remaining ¼ teaspoon each salt and pepper in a large bowl. Gradually whisk in the remaining 4 tablespoons oil. Add kale, massaging with your hands until it is slightly tender, about 30 seconds; set aside. Add roasted squash, pears, Gorgonzola, and pecans, and gently toss to combine. Cut pork into ½-inch slices. Add to the Fall Harvest Salad, and gently toss to combine. Sprinkle with additional pepper and Gorgonzola.

Bacon-Wrapped Pork Tenderloin "Filets"

ACTIVE 25 MIN. - TOTAL 35 MIN.

SERVES 4

- 1 lb. pork tenderloin, patted dry
- 2 (1 oz. each) slices bacon, halved lengthwise
- 1 tsp. kosher salt
- ½ tsp. black pepper
- 1 Tbsp. unsalted butter
- ¼ cup (2 oz.) bourbon
- 2 Tbsp. apple cider vinegar
- 1 Tbsp. unsulphured molasses
- ½ tsp. Dijon mustard
- ½ tsp. chopped fresh rosemary

1. Preheat oven to 400°F. Cut pork tenderloin into 4 equal portions (about 2½ inches thick). Gently pat down to flatten to about 1¾ inches thick. Wrap 1 bacon half around outside edge of each pork filet, securing with a wooden pick. Sprinkle pork evenly with salt and pepper.
2. Melt butter in a medium (10-inch) cast-iron skillet over medium-high. Add the wrapped pork to skillet, bacon side down. Cook, turning occasionally, until bacon is browned, about 6 minutes. Turn filets cut side down; cook, undisturbed, until browned, about 4 minutes. Flip filets; transfer skillet to oven. Bake in preheated oven until a thermometer inserted into thickest portion of pork registers 145°F, 8 to 10 minutes. Remove from skillet, and place on a plate (do not wipe skillet clean); let rest 5 minutes.
3. Add bourbon to skillet; cook over medium-high about 30 seconds, scraping bottom of skillet to loosen any browned bits. Stir in apple cider vinegar, molasses, and Dijon mustard; cook, stirring often, until slightly thickened, 1 to 2 minutes. Remove from heat; stir in rosemary. Remove and discard wooden picks; return pork to skillet, and spoon sauce over pork.

TURN, TURN, TURN
Bacon makes this affordable take on filet mignon extra delicious. Use tongs to help each strip crisp up evenly.

Bread Winner

Leftover sourdough achieves star status in this one-pan breakfast casserole

STALE MATE
To dry out fresh bread, place torn pieces on a baking sheet; bake at 300°F until dried, about 25 minutes, stirring halfway through. Let cool 15 minutes.

Sausage-Kale Strata

ACTIVE 25 MIN. · TOTAL 1 HOUR, 30 MIN.,
PLUS 4 HOURS CHILLING
SERVES 6

- 1 Tbsp. olive oil
- ½ lb. ground mild Italian sausage
- 1 cup sliced red onion (from 1 medium onion)
- 1 medium bunch Lacinato kale, stemmed and coarsely chopped (3 packed cups)
- 5 large eggs
- 1½ cups half-and-half
- 1 Tbsp. Dijon mustard
- 1 tsp. kosher salt
- 8 oz. day-old sourdough bread loaf, torn into 1-inch pieces (about 6 cups)
- 4 oz. sharp white Cheddar cheese, shredded (about 1 cup)

1. Heat oil in a 10-inch cast-iron skillet over medium-high. Add sausage; cook, stirring frequently and breaking up meat into small pieces, until sausage begins to brown, 4 to 6 minutes. Add onion, and cook over medium-high, stirring occasionally, until softened, about 3 minutes. Add kale, and cook, stirring constantly, until just wilted, about 2 minutes. Remove from heat. Let cool 15 minutes.

2. While sausage mixture is cooling, whisk together eggs, half-and-half, mustard, and salt in a large bowl until thoroughly combined. Add bread, stirring to coat. Let stand 15 minutes, stirring occasionally.

3. Add sausage mixture to bread mixture in bowl; do not wipe skillet clean. Add cheese, and stir to combine. Spoon mixture into skillet. Cover with plastic wrap, pressing wrap directly on surface. Refrigerate at least 4 hours or up to 12 hours.

4. Preheat oven to 325°F. Uncover skillet, and let stand at room temperature while oven preheats. Bake until slightly puffed and center is set, 40 to 45 minutes. Let cool 10 minutes before serving.

PUMPKIN SLAB PIE
WITH CINNAMON-MAPLE
WHIPPED CREAM

Go Big Orange!

This fuss-free pumpkin dessert feeds a crowd

Pumpkin Slab Pie with Cinnamon-Maple Whipped Cream

ACTIVE 25 MIN. - TOTAL 1 HOUR, 50 MIN..
PLUS 2 HOURS COOLING

SERVES 18

PIE

- 3 (9-inch) refrigerated piecrusts, softened per pkg. directions (from 2 [14.1-oz.] pkg.)
  All-purpose flour, for surface
- 4 large eggs, at room temperature
- 2 (15-oz.) cans pumpkin
- 1 (14-oz.) can sweetened condensed milk
- ½ cup packed light brown sugar
- 1 Tbsp. pumpkin pie spice
- ½ tsp. kosher salt

WHIPPED CREAM

- 2 cups heavy whipping cream
- ¼ cup pure maple syrup
- 1 tsp. ground cinnamon, plus more for garnish
- ¼ tsp. kosher salt

1. Prepare the Pie: Stack 3 piecrusts on top of one another on a lightly floured surface; roll into a 22- x 17-inch rectangle. Transfer to an 18- x 13-inch rimmed baking sheet, pressing dough into bottom and sides of baking sheet. Fold excess dough under, leaving a ½-inch overhang. Crimp tightly, pressing over edges of baking sheet. Freeze until firm, about 30 minutes. Meanwhile, preheat oven to 425°F.
2. Remove piecrust from freezer, and top with a piece of parchment paper; fill to the rim with pie weights or dried beans. Bake in preheated oven until piecrust is set and edges are lightly browned, 18 to 20 minutes. Remove parchment paper and weights, and return to oven. Bake at 425°F until center is dry to the touch, 4 to 5 minutes. Let cool on a wire rack, about 30 minutes. Reduce oven temperature to 350°F.
3. Whisk eggs in a large bowl until whites and yolks are combined. Whisk in pumpkin, sweetened condensed milk, brown sugar, pumpkin pie spice, and salt until smooth. Pour pumpkin mixture into piecrust, and bake at 350°F until set, about 30 minutes. Transfer to a wire rack, and let cool completely, about 2 hours.
4. Prepare the Whipped Cream: Beat whipping cream, maple syrup, cinnamon, and salt in a large bowl with an electric hand mixer on medium speed until frothy, about 1 minute. Increase mixer speed to medium-high, and beat until stiff peaks form, 1 to 2 minutes. Serve Whipped Cream on top of cooled Pie; garnish with additional cinnamon.

Pumpkin Slab Pie with Pecan-Praline Sauce

Follow recipe as directed through Step 3; omit Step 4. In a saucepan, combine 1 cup packed **dark brown sugar**, ¾ cup **unsalted butter**, 6 Tbsp. **heavy whipping cream**, and ½ tsp. **kosher salt**. Bring to a boil over medium-high, stirring often; let boil for 1 minute. Remove from heat, and stir in 2 tsp. **vanilla extract** and 1½ cups chopped **pecans**. Let cool for 5 minutes. Spoon Pecan-Praline Sauce over slices of cooled Pie.

Pumpkin Slab Pie with Pumpkin Seed Brittle

Follow recipe as directed through Step 3; follow Step 4 if desired. Combine 1 cup raw **pumpkin seed kernels (pepitas)**, ¼ cup **pure maple syrup**, and ¾ tsp. **kosher salt** in a medium bowl; toss to coat. Transfer to a parchment paper-lined baking sheet, and bake at 400°F until toasted, 9 to 10 minutes, stirring halfway through baking time. Let cool 30 minutes. Break into clusters, and scatter over cooled Pie. Top with Whipped Cream, if desired.

A Better Bowl of Chili

Shh, don't tell your guests this hearty dish is healthier than traditional recipes

Three-Bean Beef Chili

ACTIVE 25 MIN. - TOTAL 45 MIN.

SERVES 8

- 2 Tbsp. olive oil
- 2 cups chopped yellow onion (from 1 large onion)
- 2 cups chopped poblano chiles (from 2 large chiles)
- 1½ lb. ground sirloin
- 3 Tbsp. ancho chile powder
- 2 Tbsp. ground cumin
- 2 tsp. smoked paprika
- 2 tsp. kosher salt
- 1 tsp. ground coriander
- 1 tsp. dried oregano
- 1 (6-oz.) can no-salt-added tomato paste (about ¾ cup)
- 2 Tbsp. finely chopped garlic (from 6 garlic cloves)
- 4 (15-oz.) cans no-salt-added beans (such as black, pinto, and dark red kidney beans), drained and rinsed
- 1 (28-oz.) can diced fire-roasted tomatoes

Toppings: plain whole-milk yogurt, shredded cheese, fresh cilantro leaves, sliced radish

Lime wedges, for serving

1. Heat oil in a large Dutch oven over medium-high. Add onion and chiles, and cook, stirring occasionally, until chiles are softened and onion is translucent, about 5 minutes.

2. Add ground sirloin to onion mixture in Dutch oven. Cook, stirring occasionally, until meat is crumbly, 4 to 5 minutes. Add chile powder, cumin, smoked paprika, kosher salt, coriander, and oregano. Cook, stirring constantly, until spices are toasted and fragrant, about 1 minute. Add tomato paste and chopped garlic; cook, stirring constantly, until tomato paste darkens and garlic is fragrant, about 1 minute more.

3. Stir beans, tomatoes, and 2 cups water into Dutch oven; bring mixture to a boil over medium-high. Reduce heat to medium-low; simmer, covered and undisturbed, until slightly thickened, about 15 minutes. Remove from heat; let cool slightly. Divide evenly among bowls; top as desired, and serve with lime wedges.

Before Recipe Makeover:

CALORIES: **659** – SODIUM: **1,480 MG** – FAT: **31 G**

After Recipe Makeover:

CALORIES: **424** – SODIUM: **882 MG** – FAT: **14 G**

Warm & Toasty

Sweet, spicy, and salty, these nuts are ready for company

CHIPOTLE-
MAPLE
ALMONDS

ROSEMARY-
BROWN BUTTER
PECANS

SPICED HONEY
CASHEWS

Chipotle-Maple Almonds

ACTIVE 5 MIN. · TOTAL 50 MIN.
SERVES 8

Line a large rimmed baking sheet with parchment paper. Whisk together ¼ cup **pure maple syrup,** 1½ Tbsp. **chipotle chile powder,** 1 tsp. **smoked paprika,** and 1 tsp. **kosher salt** in a medium bowl until combined. Stir in 3 cups **whole unsalted raw almonds.** Transfer to prepared baking sheet, spreading in an even layer. Bake at 300°F until almonds are toasted, 20 to 25 minutes, stirring halfway through baking time. Remove from oven, and let cool to room temperature, about 20 minutes.

Rosemary-Brown Butter Pecans

ACTIVE 10 MIN. · TOTAL 50 MIN.
SERVES 8

Line a large rimmed baking sheet with parchment paper. Melt ¼ cup **butter** in a small saucepan over medium. Cook, stirring occasionally, until butter starts to foam and turns brown, 4 to 5 minutes. Remove from heat, and stir in 2 Tbsp. **dark brown sugar** and 1 Tbsp. chopped **fresh rosemary.** Place 3 cups **unsalted raw pecan halves** on prepared baking sheet; pour brown butter mixture over pecans, and toss until fully coated. Bake at 300°F until pecans are toasted, 20 to 25 minutes, stirring halfway through baking time. Remove from oven; garnish with **flaky sea salt.** Let cool to room temperature, about 20 minutes.

Spiced Honey Cashews

ACTIVE 5 MIN. · TOTAL 55 MIN.
SERVES 8

Line a large rimmed baking sheet with parchment paper. Place 1 **large egg white** in a medium bowl, and whisk until foamy, about 1 to 2 minutes. Heat ¼ cup **honey,** 2 tsp. **ground cardamom,** 1½ tsp. **ground ginger,** and 1 tsp. **kosher salt** in a small saucepan over medium until runny, about 45 seconds. Pour honey mixture into egg white, whisking constantly, until combined. Stir in 3 cups **unsalted raw cashews.** Transfer to prepared baking sheet, spreading in an even layer. Bake at 300°F until cashews are toasted, about 25 minutes, stirring halfway through baking time. Remove from oven, and let cool to room temperature, about 20 minutes.

COOKING SCHOOL

Southern Staple
Jell-O

What the Heck Is Oleo?
And why do Grandma's recipes call for it?

WHAT IT IS: Oleo is another name for margarine, the hydrogenated-oil product developed to taste and look like butter. Oleo was originally invented in France in 1869 at the request of Emperor Napoleon III as a cheaper alternative. Early versions mimicked butter using beef fat, but today's margarines are made from plant oils, like canola.

WHAT TO USE INSTEAD: Although your grandma's beloved recipes may have specified oleo, our Test Kitchen generally feels that butter is the preferred option. Not only does it have more flavor, but it also helps baked goods brown better. When it comes to making cookies, butter-based ones are more crisp and spread less than those made with margarine.

The star ingredient of many a midcentury salad, Jell-O may not have originated in the South, but it's a go-to in our pantries nonetheless. The company was started in 1897 by Pearle Wait, a carpenter in LeRoy, New York, who experimented with cough remedies and teas made from powdered gelatin with added flavorings. Eventually, that tinkering resulted in a powder that contained natural fruit extracts and formed a jiggly, ready-to-eat food when added to boiling water and chilled. The rights to the product were purchased by the Genesee Pure Food Company, which grew its popularity with advertising, including free recipe books, a brand-new marketing strategy at the time. Jell-O was also one of the first companies to advertise on the radio.

INGREDIENTS THAT MADE HISTORY

SPRY
In the mid-1930s Lever Brothers launched Spry shortening. Iconic campaigns featuring their spokesperson "Aunt Jenny" helped the product reach about 75% of the sales of Crisco, its biggest rival. But by the 1970s, that momentum faded, and the product was discontinued.

HYDROX
Hydrox, the original cream-filled chocolate sandwich cookie, debuted in 1908, four years before the Oreo was introduced. First made by Sunshine Biscuits, they were discontinued in 1999. Leaf Brands recently brought the treats back and claim they taste just the same.

PET EVAPORATED MILK
What began in 1885 as a tiny canned-milk company in the small town of Highland, Illinois, was by 1898 supplying Teddy Roosevelt's Rough Riders with shelf-stable evaporated milk during the Spanish-American War. Now, almost 140 years later, it's a tried-and-true baking standby.

November

GINGER
LOAF CAKE

New Roots

Fresh ginger adds a spicy kick to these seasonal recipes

Ginger Loaf Cake

ACTIVE 35 MIN. - TOTAL 2 HOURS, 45 MIN.
SERVES 8

Baking spray with flour
2½ cups all-purpose flour
1 tsp. ground cinnamon
¾ tsp. baking soda
½ tsp. kosher salt
½ tsp. ground nutmeg
¾ cup unsalted butter, softened
¾ cup granulated sugar
2 large eggs, at room temperature
½ cup unsulphured molasses
½ cup plus 2 Tbsp. whole milk, divided
½ cup minced fresh ginger
1½ cups powdered sugar

1. Preheat oven to 350°F. Coat a 9- x 5-inch loaf pan with baking spray. Line with parchment paper, leaving a 2-inch overhang on long sides.
2. Whisk together flour, cinnamon, baking soda, salt, and nutmeg in a medium bowl until combined; set aside. Beat butter and sugar in a large bowl with an electric mixer on medium-low speed until just combined, 1 to 2 minutes. Increase to medium-high speed, and beat until fluffy, about 3 minutes, stopping to scrape down sides. Add eggs, 1 at a time, beating until well combined after each addition. With mixer on low speed, add flour mixture in thirds, alternating with molasses and ½ cup of the milk, beginning and ending with flour mixture. Fold in ginger. Spoon batter into prepared pan, smoothing top.
3. Bake in preheated oven until a wooden pick inserted in center comes out clean, about 1 hour, loosely covering with aluminum foil during final 15 minutes of bake time. Let cool in pan 10 minutes. Remove from pan, and let cool completely on a wire rack, 1 to 1½ hours.
4. Whisk together powdered sugar and remaining 2 tablespoons milk in a bowl until mixture is smooth. Drizzle over cooled cake.

GINGER ROGERS COCKTAIL

Gingered Cranberry Sauce

ACTIVE 15 MIN. - TOTAL 2 HOURS, 15 MIN.
SERVES 6

Place 1 lb. **fresh or frozen cranberries,** 1 cup **sugar,** 2 tsp. **orange zest,** 1 cup **orange juice,** 2 Tbsp. minced **fresh ginger,** and 1 **hibiscus tea bag** in a medium saucepan. Cook over medium-high, stirring often, until cranberries begin to pop and mixture thickens just slightly, 10 to 15 minutes. Remove from heat; let cool 2 hours. Discard tea bag. Garnish with **orange zest,** if desired.

Ginger Rogers Cocktail

ACTIVE 5 MIN. - TOTAL 5 MIN.
SERVES 1

Fill a cocktail shaker with **ice.** Add ¼ cup **gin,** 2 Tbsp. **grapefruit juice,** 2 Tbsp. **lime juice,** 2 Tbsp. **simple syrup,** and 1 tsp. grated **fresh ginger** to shaker. Shake until outside of shaker is frosty, 30 seconds to 1 minute. Strain into a glass filled halfway with **ice;** top with ¼ cup **club soda** and more **ice** as needed. Garnish with a **grapefruit** wedge and sliced **crystallized ginger.**

This Dip Is My Jam

Senior Test Kitchen Pro Ivy Odom's favorite snack will be your new go-to appetizer

BEFORE JOINING THE STAFF AT SOUTHERN LIVING, I worked as a cook at a well-known restaurant in Atlanta. We had an extremely popular menu item that featured a platter of buttery toast points for dipping into jars of savory goodies: egg salad topped with caviar, smoked fish dip with pickles, and the hands-down crowd favorite—pimiento cheese with bacon jam. Night after night, it felt like I never stopped preparing that dish. At the end of each shift, despite being nearly cross-eyed from making it for hours, I couldn't stop myself from scooping up a bite of the leftover jam with anything I could find, from potato chips to carrot sticks.

By the time my stint at the restaurant was over, I had eaten so much bacon jam that I should have never wanted to touch it again. Nope, not quite—I still crave it. This recipe for Whipped Goat Cheese with Smoky Bacon Jam (creamy, salty, crunchy, and entirely irresistible) is an homage to that beloved dip. While I enjoy this version spooned over goat cheese, it's perfectly acceptable to use the bacon jam as a topper for whatever you like—sandwiches, veggies, and more. However you decide to serve it, I hope it becomes something that you'll keep coming back to... just maybe not every evening.

Whipped Goat Cheese with Smoky Bacon Jam

ACTIVE 30 MIN. - TOTAL 30 MIN.
SERVES 8

- 8 oz. thick-cut bacon (about 6 slices), chopped
- 1 cup chopped yellow or sweet onion (from 1 small onion)
- 3 Tbsp. light brown sugar
- 1 tsp. smoked paprika
- ½ tsp. Worcestershire sauce
- 8 oz. goat cheese, softened
- 4 oz. cream cheese, softened
- 1 Tbsp. olive oil
- ½ tsp. kosher salt
  Fresh thyme leaves
  Easy Fried Crackers (recipe follows) or crostini

1. Cook bacon in a 10-inch skillet over medium, stirring occasionally, until fat renders and edges start to crisp, about 9 minutes. Remove from heat. Using a slotted spoon, transfer bacon to a paper towel–lined plate. Pour drippings into a heatproof measuring cup. Add 2 tablespoons drippings back to skillet; reserve remaining drippings for another use.
2. Add onion and cooked bacon to skillet; cook over medium, stirring often, until onion is golden brown, about 8 minutes.

3. Stir brown sugar, 1 tablespoon water, smoked paprika, and Worcestershire into bacon mixture; cook, stirring constantly, until syrupy and combined, 15 to 30 seconds. Remove from heat; transfer mixture to a heatproof measuring cup or bowl. Let cool slightly, about 5 minutes.
4. Beat goat cheese, cream cheese, oil, and salt with an electric mixer fitted with a whisk attachment on medium speed until smooth and creamy, about 30 seconds.
5. Spread goat cheese mixture inside a shallow bowl. Top with Smoky Bacon Jam, and garnish with thyme leaves. Serve with Easy Fried Crackers or crostini.

Easy Fried Crackers

Level up your snack board with these tasty bites. Heat 4 cups canola oil in a skillet over medium-high to 350°F. Working in batches, fry 1 sleeve of saltine crackers until golden brown, 2 to 3 minutes per batch. Let drain and dry on a wire rack. Store in an airtight container at room temperature up to 1 week.

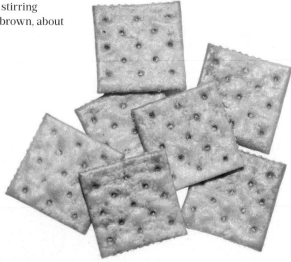

WHIPPED GOAT CHEESE
WITH SMOKY BACON JAM

Handsome Devils

Ready to impress? There are countless ways to dress up this Southern essential

CLOSE YOUR EYES, and picture your Thanksgiving table. What do you see? Turkey, of course. Cornbread dressing, surely. Casseroles aplenty, no doubt. But what about deviled eggs? If you're only serving them for Easter or at summer potlucks, you're definitely missing out.

In my family, holiday dinners never seem to start on time. Enter the perfect two-bite appetizer. Topped to the nines and convenient to make ahead, these savory delights can be served with nothing but a cocktail napkin—meaning you have fewer dishes to deal with later.

The filling for deviled eggs is endlessly customizable. While there's certainly no harm in playing the hits—mustard, mayonnaise, and relish are the usual suspects—why not mix things up a bit? Whether you decide to elevate the ingredients (by adding pimiento cheese, caramelized onions, or briny olives) or use fun garnishes (like a sprinkle of breadcrumbs, some crispy bacon, or a flurry of fresh herbs), they are easy to jazz up for company. If you're feeling extra fancy, pipe the filling using a star tip.

Change up your deviled-egg game by trying any of these creative twists; or make our classic recipe (at right), and set out a few bowls of add-ons so your guests can build their own personalized bites. As the saying goes, the devil's in the details—so why not make them delicious?

(1) Classic Deviled Eggs

ACTIVE 15 MIN. · TOTAL 40 MIN.

MAKES 12

6	large eggs
	Ice
2	Tbsp. mayonnaise
1½	Tbsp. sweet or dill pickle relish
1	tsp. yellow mustard
¼	tsp. kosher salt
⅛	tsp. black pepper
	Paprika (optional)

1. Fill a large pot with water; bring to a boil over high. Carefully lower eggs into boiling water; cook, undisturbed, for 11 minutes, 30 seconds.
2. Meanwhile, fill a large bowl halfway with ice; add water to cover. Set ice bath aside.
3. Using a slotted spoon, immediately transfer cooked eggs from boiling water to ice bath. Let stand until completely cooled, at least 5 minutes.
4. Working with 1 egg at a time, firmly tap on a flat surface until cracks form all over the shell. Peel under cold running water.
5. Cut eggs in half lengthwise; remove yolks. Set egg white halves aside. Using a fork, mash together yolks and mayonnaise in a medium bowl. Add relish, mustard, salt, and pepper; stir well to combine.
6. Spoon or pipe about 1 tablespoon filling into each egg white half. Garnish with paprika, if desired. Serve immediately, or store, covered, in refrigerator up to 3 days.

(2) Crispy Bacon Deviled Eggs

ACTIVE 30 MIN. · TOTAL 40 MIN.

MAKES 12

Cook 2 slices finely chopped **thick-cut applewood-smoked bacon** in a nonstick skillet over medium, stirring occasionally, until crispy, about 7 minutes; remove skillet from heat. Transfer cooked bacon to a paper towel-lined plate, and let drain; reserve drippings in skillet. Prepare Classic Deviled Eggs as directed through Step 4. Heat reserved drippings in skillet over medium. Before filling eggs in Step 5, place 6 of the egg white halves, cut sides down, in skillet. Cook until golden brown and crispy, 1 to 2 minutes per side. Transfer to a serving plate, and repeat with remaining halves. Sprinkle evenly with ⅛ tsp. **kosher salt.** Omit relish in filling, and stir in half of the cooked bacon. In Step 6, omit paprika and top eggs evenly with remaining cooked bacon.

(3) Caesar Salad Deviled Eggs

ACTIVE 20 MIN. · TOTAL 45 MIN.

MAKES 12

Heat 1 tsp. **olive oil** in a small nonstick skillet over medium. Add 1 Tbsp. **panko breadcrumbs;** cook, stirring often, until toasted, 2 to 3 minutes. Prepare Classic Deviled Eggs as directed through Step 4. In Step 5, omit relish and yellow mustard; reduce **salt** to ⅛ tsp.; increase **pepper** to ¼ tsp.; and add 2 tsp. finely grated **Parmesan cheese,** 1 tsp. **Dijon mustard,** 1 finely chopped **anchovy fillet,** and 3 finely chopped **roasted garlic cloves** to filling. In Step 6, omit paprika; top eggs with toasted panko, shaved **Parmesan cheese,** and **fresh tarragon leaves.**

(4) Green Goddess Deviled Eggs

ACTIVE 15 MIN. · TOTAL 35 MIN.

MAKES 12

Stir together 3 Tbsp. sliced **fresh chives,** 2 Tbsp. each chopped **fresh tarragon and parsley,** and ½ tsp. **lemon zest** in a small bowl. Prepare Classic Deviled Eggs as directed through Step 4. In Step 5, omit relish, yellow mustard, and pepper; add ¾ tsp. **Dijon mustard,** ½ **medium avocado,** 1½ Tbsp. **lemon juice,** and ¼ cup of the herb mixture to filling. In Step 6, omit paprika; top eggs evenly with remaining herb mixture.

Peel Like a Pro

Tips from the
Southern Living Test Kitchen

Many folks may claim to know "the secret" to perfect hard-cooked eggs, but the truth is, there's no master method that will work every single time. However, after preparing hundreds of eggs for this story, our Test Kitchen discovered that placing them directly in boiling water and then shocking them in an ice bath immediately after cooking made peeling much easier. Be sure to add the eggs to the hot water carefully; even a slight tap on the bottom of the pan can cause a crack to form, resulting in a less-than-picture-perfect look. Peel the cooled eggs under cold running water to help the shells slip away with ease.

8 Tasty Toppings

Crown Classic Deviled Eggs with
one of these simple toppings.

Barbecue Sauce
Use a tomato- or vinegar-based one.

Chimichurri or Pesto
Add a fresh, herbaceous zip.

Fried Chicken
Save some crispy bits from the fast-food bucket.

Smoked Salmon
Whip up this option for brunch.

White Barbecue Sauce
Try a tangy Alabama classic.

Olive Salad
Consider this for more than muffulettas, y'all.

Pickled Peppers
Slice some from a bottle of pepper sauce.

Chowchow
Punch up the flavor with pickled relish.

(5) Pimiento Cheese Deviled Eggs

(Photo, page 262)
ACTIVE 15 MIN. - TOTAL 35 MIN.
MAKES 12

Prepare Classic Deviled Eggs as directed through Step 4. In Step 5, omit relish and pepper; increase **mayonnaise** to 3 Tbsp.; add 3 Tbsp. shredded **extra-sharp Cheddar cheese**, 2 Tbsp. drained **diced pimientos** (from 1 [4-oz.] jar), and 1 tsp. **onion powder** to filling. In Step 6, top eggs with additional shredded **extra-sharp Cheddar cheese** and **smoked paprika**, if desired.

(6) Pickle-Packed Deviled Eggs

(Photo, page 262)
ACTIVE 15 MIN. - TOTAL 30 MIN.,
PLUS 24 HOURS CHILLING
MAKES 12

Cut 3 **pickled baby beets** (from 1 [16-oz.] jar) into small cubes; refrigerate until ready to use. Prepare Classic Deviled Eggs as directed through Step 4. Place peeled whole eggs in a large zip-top plastic bag. Pour 1 cup **pickled beet brine** (from jar) into bag. Add up to ½ cup **water** to bag as needed until eggs are submerged in liquid. Remove excess air from bag, and seal. Place bag in a large bowl, and refrigerate for 24 hours. Remove eggs from bag; discard brine. In Step 5, increase **pickle relish** to 2½ Tbsp. In Step 6, omit paprika; top eggs with thinly sliced **pickled okra**, reserved beet cubes, and thinly sliced **cornichons.**

(7) Pickled-Shrimp Deviled Eggs

(Photo, page 262)
ACTIVE 25 MIN. - TOTAL 1 HOUR, 15 MIN.,
PLUS 24 HOURS CHILLING
MAKES 12

Bring ½ cup each **apple cider vinegar** and **water** to a boil in a small skillet over high. Stir in 1 Tbsp. **kosher salt**, 2 tsp. **granulated sugar**, and 1 tsp. each **black peppercorns, mustard seeds,** and **coriander seeds**. Remove from heat; let cool completely, about 30 minutes. Pour into a pint-size jar; add ½ lb. peeled, deveined cooked **medium-size shrimp** and 2 **fresh dill sprigs**. Seal jar; refrigerate until shrimp absorb flavors,

at least 24 hours or up to 4 days. Prepare Classic Deviled Eggs as directed through Step 4. In Step 5, omit relish, reduce **salt** to ⅛ tsp., and add 1½ tsp. chopped **capers** to filling. Cut 6 pickled shrimp in half lengthwise; reserve remaining shrimp for another use. In Step 6, omit paprika; top eggs with shrimp and additional **fresh dill** and **whole capers.**

(8) French Onion Deviled Eggs

ACTIVE 50 MIN. - TOTAL 1 HOUR, 35 MIN.
MAKES 12

Heat 2 Tbsp. **olive oil** in a nonstick skillet over medium-low. Add 1 cup finely chopped **sweet onion** and ½ tsp. **kosher salt**. Cook, stirring occasionally, until caramelized, about 30 minutes, adding a splash of **water** if onion starts to stick. Remove from heat; stir in 1 tsp. **sherry vinegar**. Transfer to a bowl; let cool completely, about 20 minutes. Prepare Classic Deviled Eggs as directed through Step 4. In Step 5, omit relish, yellow mustard, and pepper; add 1 tsp. **Dijon mustard** and cooked onion to filling. In Step 6, omit paprika; top eggs with **Crispy Gruyère Onions** (recipe follows).

Crispy Gruyère Onions

ACTIVE 10 MIN. - TOTAL 25 MIN.
MAKES ¼ CUP

Preheat oven to 350°F. Toss together 2 Tbsp. each shredded **Gruyère cheese** and **crispy fried onions** (such as French's) in a small bowl. Spread on a parchment paper–lined baking sheet. Bake until golden brown and cheese is melted, 8 to 10 minutes. Cool 10 minutes; discard any burned bits. Break into small pieces. Use immediately, or store in an airtight container at room temperature up to 3 days.

(9) Tex-Mex Deviled Eggs

(Photo, page 265)
ACTIVE 20 MIN. - TOTAL 45 MIN.
MAKES 12

Heat a medium-size nonstick skillet over medium-high. Add 2 oz. (about ½ cup) **fresh Mexican chorizo** (casings removed); cook, stirring and breaking into pieces, until cooked through, about 3 minutes. Transfer chorizo to a paper towel-lined plate. Prepare Classic Deviled Eggs as directed through Step 4. In Step 5, omit relish and mustard, increase **mayonnaise** to 3 Tbsp., and add 1½ tsp. **hot sauce** and ¾ tsp. **lime juice** to filling. Stir together 2 Tbsp. chopped **avocado** and ½ tsp. **lime juice** in a small bowl. In Step 6, omit paprika; top eggs with cooked chorizo, avocado mixture, finely chopped **fresh cilantro**, and additional **hot sauce.**

(10) Greek Salad Deviled Eggs

(Photo, page 265)
ACTIVE 15 MIN. - TOTAL 40 MIN.
MAKES 12

Prepare Classic Deviled Eggs as directed through Step 4. In Step 5, omit relish and yellow mustard; reduce **salt** to ⅛ tsp.; and add 1 tsp. **Dijon mustard**, 1½ Tbsp. finely chopped **Kalamata olives**, 1 Tbsp. crumbled **feta cheese**, and ½ tsp. **red wine vinegar** to filling. In Step 6, omit paprika; top eggs with finely chopped **Persian cucumber**, thinly sliced **cherry tomatoes**, **fresh oregano leaves**, and additional crumbled **feta** and sliced **Kalamata olives.**

(11) Creole Deviled Eggs

(Photo, page 265)
ACTIVE 20 MIN. - TOTAL 55 MIN.
MAKES 12

Melt 1 Tbsp. **unsalted butter** in a skillet over medium. Add ¼ cup each finely chopped **yellow onion, celery,** and **green bell pepper** and ¼ tsp. **kosher salt**; cook, stirring occasionally, until softened, about 5 minutes. Remove from heat; let cool 10 minutes. Prepare Classic Deviled Eggs as directed through Step 4. In Step 5, omit relish and yellow mustard; add 2 tsp. **Creole mustard** and all but 2 Tbsp. of the cooked vegetable mixture to filling. In Step 6, omit paprika; top eggs evenly with a pinch of **cayenne pepper** and remaining 2 Tbsp. vegetable mixture.

(12) Crab Salad Deviled Eggs

(Photo, page 265)
ACTIVE 15 MIN. - TOTAL 2 HOURS, 45 MIN.
MAKES 12

Gently stir together 1 lb. **fresh lump crabmeat** (drained and picked over); 1 cup finely chopped **white onion**; and ½ tsp. each **kosher salt, black pepper,** and **Old Bay seasoning** in a bowl. Whisk together ⅓ cup each **rice vinegar, canola oil,** and **cold water**; pour over crab mixture, tossing to coat. Cover and refrigerate until flavors meld, at least 2 hours (up to 2 days). Prepare Classic Deviled Eggs as directed through Step 4. In Step 5, omit relish and reduce **mustard** to ½ tsp. In Step 6, omit paprika; top each egg with about 1 tsp. crab salad. Garnish with sliced **chives** and coarsely crushed **Buttered Old Bay Saltines** (recipe follows; you will have leftover crackers).

Buttered Old Bay Saltines

ACTIVE 10 MIN. - TOTAL 20 MIN.
MAKES 24

Preheat oven to 400°F. Line a baking sheet with aluminum foil, and place a piece of parchment paper on top. Arrange 24 **saltine crackers** on baking sheet in an even layer. Stir together ⅓ cup melted **unsalted butter** and ½ tsp. **Old Bay seasoning**; pour evenly over saltines. Bake until golden brown, 8 to 10 minutes. Remove from oven; sprinkle with ¼ tsp. **Old Bay.** Let cool slightly, about 5 minutes. Store in an airtight container at room temperature up to 3 days.

(13) Buffalo-Blue Cheese Deviled Eggs

(Photo, page 265)
ACTIVE 15 MIN. - TOTAL 40 MIN.
MAKES 12

Prepare Classic Deviled Eggs as directed through Step 4. In Step 5, omit relish and pepper, increase **mayonnaise** to 3 Tbsp., and add 2 tsp. **Buffalo sauce** to filling. In Step 6, omit paprika; top each egg with **crumbled blue cheese.** Garnish with **celery leaves** and additional **Buffalo sauce.**

(14) Curry-Cashew Deviled Eggs

(Photo, page 265)
ACTIVE 15 MIN. - TOTAL 35 MIN.
MAKES 12

Prepare Classic Deviled Eggs as directed through Step 4. In Step 5, omit relish, increase **mayonnaise** to 3 Tbsp., reduce **mustard** to ½ tsp., and add ½ tsp. **curry powder** to filling. In Step 6, omit paprika; top eggs with finely chopped **red Fresno chile**, chopped **roasted salted cashews**, and additional **curry powder.**

A Korean American Thanksgiving

A child of immigrants discovers the joy of Southern casseroles

CHEESY SCALLION STUFFING WITH SESAME SEEDS (PAGE 268)

GROWING UP IN ATLANTA, Eric Kim learned to make American food before his mother, Jean, did. Born to Korean immigrants, he was a fan of Food Network cooking shows from a young age. His fondness for this country's cuisine was stoked by Sunday trips to Ryan's Buffet, where he'd look forward to creamy macaroni and cheese with that Velveeta ooze. Naturally, Thanksgiving, the most quintessentially American holiday, became his favorite. But before he took over preparing the feast as a teenager, he learned the ropes from his extended family.

Kim's childhood Thanksgivings began on the road, with a two-hour trip to his Aunt Joy's house in Augusta. The journey would start at night after his parents got off work, so he always slept through the drive. When they'd arrive, he'd awaken to the sound of his cousins excitedly banging on the car windows. Aunt Joy was one of his first family members who were interested in cooking American food, and she happened to have a boyfriend from the U.S. "It just made sense that for an American-food holiday we'd go to our most American aunt's house," Kim says. On Thanksgiving Day, Aunt Joy and his mother would wake up at 4 a.m. to put the bird in the oven to roast it for (too) many hours. "The turkey was always incredibly dry, but I really cherish those early Thanksgivings in Augusta, because that was when we had green bean casserole for the first time," he says. Like many Americans, his aunt got her recipe from a can, and it instantly became a family staple; Kim still prefers the nostalgic taste of French's Crispy Fried Onions over homemade.

Aunt Joy also introduced him to sweet potato casserole. In his debut cookbook, *Korean American: Food That Tastes Like Home,* he created his own version with goguma (a yellow-fleshed Korean sweet potato) and turmeric. Sweet potato casserole was his mother's most-loved Thanksgiving dish, so she served as his taste tester, approving the tweaks along the way. He cuts the marshmallows in half for just the right amount of sweetness.

Stuffing has always been the side Kim likes best. (Yes, he calls it that instead of "dressing.") As a writer for *The New York Times,* he tested 20 variations in the name of research. "Laying the bread out to dry the night before is really the beginning of Thanksgiving; it signals you're making room—both literal space and setting aside time to lean into the cooking," Kim says.

Other recipes from his book could easily be welcome additions to your holiday menu. His creamed spinach is inspired by sigeumchi namul, a Korean dish in which this veggie is seasoned with soy sauce, garlic, and toasted sesame oil, one of his go-to ingredients.

Kim says these recipes were some of the simplest to develop for his cookbook, as he has spent almost his entire life training for Thanksgiving. By the time he was 13, he and his cousins had taken over the cooking while the parents sat back, drinking, gossiping, and playing cards in the living room. They were given a $100 budget and went shopping the night before Thanksgiving, stopping at a 24-hour grocery store around 2 a.m.—when only teenagers would go looking for a turkey. Sometimes they opted for a chicken (or two) instead, as a cost-cutting move. The cousins stayed up assembling casseroles while catching up. Versions of those dishes still grace Kim's holiday table, even if the whole family isn't gathering in Augusta anymore.

"These recipes have traveled through time, and it's sort of like a game of telephone. I imagine as they get passed down to readers, and to my future children, they'll be adapted even more," Kim says. He hopes you'll fold them into your holiday traditions too.

Cheesy Scallion Stuffing with Sesame Seeds

(Photo, page 267)

Inspired by the flavors of pajeon (Korean green onion pancakes), Kim's recipe uses 3 cups of scallions. You can prep this dish a day ahead; before baking, cover with foil and place in the refrigerator. You'll need to add a few minutes to the bake time because the stuffing will be colder when going in the oven.

ACTIVE 45 MIN. - TOTAL 1 HOUR, 45 MIN., PLUS 8 HOURS DRYING BREAD

SERVES 12 TO 15

1 (24-oz.) sourdough bread loaf
1 cup unsalted butter, plus more for greasing baking dish

- 2 medium-size red onions, halved and cut vertically into ⅓-inch-thick slices (4½ cups)
- 3 cups diagonally sliced scallions (from 8 to 10 large scallions)
- 3 cups sliced celery (from 4 large celery stalks)
- 2 Tbsp. granulated sugar
- 2 tsp. kosher salt
- 1 cup turkey or vegetable stock
- 4 large eggs
- ½ cup whole milk
- 2 tsp. toasted sesame oil
- 2 tsp. soy sauce
- 7 oz. Parmesan cheese, shredded (about 1¾ cups), plus more for topping
- 4 Tbsp. toasted sesame seeds, plus more for topping

1. The night before serving, tear bread into 1- to 2-inch pieces, removing crusts (you will have about 8 to 8½ cups). Spread bread pieces on a baking sheet, and let stand, covered with a clean dish towel, at room temperature until dry and slightly crisp (almost like a crouton), at least 8 hours or up to 1 day. (If making the same day, preheat oven to 300°F with racks in top third and lower third positions. Place bread pieces on 2 baking sheets, and bake until dried out, 30 to 50 minutes, stirring pieces and rotating baking sheets between top and bottom racks halfway through bake time.)
2. Preheat oven to 350°F, and grease a broiler-safe 13- x 9-inch baking dish with softened butter.
3. Heat 1 cup butter in a large 8-quart pot over medium-high until melted and bubbly. Add red onions, scallions, celery, sugar, and salt. Cover and cook, stirring occasionally, until vegetables begin to soften but are still vibrant and crunchy and scallions have infused the butter with their wonderful flavor, about 5 minutes.
4. Whisk together stock, eggs, milk, sesame oil, and soy sauce in a very large bowl until well combined. Add vegetable mixture, bread pieces, Parmesan, and sesame seeds; toss until well combined and bread is evenly coated. Let stand at room temperature, stirring occasionally, until bread has slightly soaked up egg mixture, about 10 minutes.
5. Transfer bread mixture to prepared baking dish; top with additional sesame seeds and Parmesan cheese, as desired.

6. Cover with aluminum foil, and place on a rimmed baking sheet. Bake in preheated oven until cooked through and an instant-read thermometer inserted in the center registers at least 165°F, 50 minutes to 1 hour. Remove baking sheet from oven, and uncover.
7. Increase oven temperature to broil. Broil, uncovered, on rack in center of oven until top is lightly browned, 3 to 6 minutes. Serve warm.

Honey-Buttered Goguma Casserole with Turmeric

(Photo, page 271)

If you can't find goguma (yellow-fleshed Korean sweet potatoes) at your local Asian grocery, any kind will work in this recipe. Ground turmeric gives the potatoes a pretty golden color, and the soy sauce balances the sweetness of the toasted marshmallows on top.

ACTIVE 30 MIN. · TOTAL 2 HOURS, 5 MIN.
SERVES 6 TO 8

- 1½ lb. goguma (Korean sweet potatoes)
- 1½ cups whole milk
- 3 large eggs
- 3 Tbsp. dark brown sugar
- 3 Tbsp. unsalted butter, cubed and at room temperature, plus more for greasing baking dish
- 3 Tbsp. honey
- 1½ tsp. ground cinnamon
- 1½ tsp. ground turmeric
- 1½ tsp. soy sauce
- ¼ tsp. kosher salt
- 15 to 18 large marshmallows, halved lengthwise

1. Preheat oven to 400°F with racks in top third and lower third positions.
2. Place goguma on a baking sheet, and roast in preheated oven on lower rack until tender, 45 minutes to 1 hour, turning each one halfway through roasting. Remove baking sheet from oven. Reduce oven temperature to 350°F.
3. Let goguma stand until cool enough to handle, 15 to 20 minutes. Peel, discarding skins, which should slip right off. Place peeled goguma in a large bowl. Mash using a potato masher or a fork; whisk in milk, eggs, brown sugar, butter, honey, cinnamon, turmeric, soy sauce, and salt until smooth. (Mixture will be quite liquid.)

4. Grease a broiler-safe 2-quart, 8-inch square baking dish with butter. Transfer goguma mixture to prepared baking dish.
5. Bake at 350°F on lower rack until set (a knife inserted into center should come out mostly clean), 35 to 42 minutes. Remove baking dish from oven, and increase oven temperature to broil.
6. Carefully arrange marshmallow halves, cut sides down, evenly over top of goguma mixture, covering as much of surface as possible (they will not cover entire top but will melt and spread once broiled).
7. Place baking dish on upper rack, and broil until each marshmallow is perfectly toasted, 30 seconds to 1 minute. (Watch carefully so they don't burn.) Serve warm.

Garlicky Creamed Spinach Namul

(Photo, page 270)

Squeeze out as much liquid as you can from the thawed spinach to prevent this dish from being watery. The sesame seeds add a nice crunch throughout.

ACTIVE 25 MIN. · TOTAL 1 HOUR
SERVES 4

- 4 (10-oz.) pkg. frozen chopped spinach, thawed
- 1¼ cups heavy whipping cream
- ⅔ cup toasted sesame seeds, plus more for garnish
- 5 Tbsp. soy sauce
- 2 Tbsp. finely grated garlic (about 10 large garlic cloves)
- 5 tsp. granulated sugar
- 5 tsp. toasted sesame oil

1. Preheat oven to 425°F. Working in batches, squeeze spinach with your hands over sink, wringing out as much liquid as possible. Place spinach in a medium bowl; add cream, sesame seeds, soy sauce, garlic, sugar, and sesame oil, stirring until well combined.
2. Spoon spinach mixture into a 1½-quart baking dish (about 2 inches deep). Cover with aluminum foil. Bake, covered, in preheated oven for 30 minutes. Uncover and bake until spinach mixture is bubbly and warmed through, 5 to 10 minutes. Garnish with more sesame seeds, and serve warm.

GARLICKY CREAMED
SPINACH NAMUL
(PAGE 269)

HONEY-BUTTERED
GOGUMA
CASSEROLE
WITH TURMERIC
(PAGE 269)

Surprise Pies

Take a break from the pecan and pumpkin mainstays, and wow company
with something deliciously different this year

APPLE CIDER
VINEGAR PIE

Apple Cider Vinegar Pie

Long ago, vinegar was often used in pie recipes instead of lemon juice, which could be expensive and hard to come by. In our version, the creamy filling gets its zing from a hint of cider vinegar, which balances out the layer of buttery, sweet Sautéed Apples on top.

ACTIVE 20 MIN. - TOTAL 2 HOURS, 10 MIN.

SERVES 8

PIE

- 4 large eggs
- 1¼ cups packed light brown sugar
- 6 Tbsp. unsalted butter, melted and cooled
- 2 Tbsp. apple cider vinegar
- 2 tsp. vanilla extract
- 2 Tbsp. all-purpose flour
- ¾ tsp. kosher salt
- 1 Cream Cheese Piecrust (recipe, page 279)

SAUTÉED APPLES

- 2 medium-size red apples, unpeeled and thinly sliced (about 2²/₃ cups)
- 2 Tbsp. granulated sugar
- 2 Tbsp. apple cider vinegar
- 1 tsp. vanilla extract
- ½ tsp. kosher salt
- ½ tsp. ground cinnamon
- 4 Tbsp. unsalted butter

1. Prepare the Pie: Preheat oven to 350°F. Whisk together eggs, brown sugar, melted butter, vinegar, and vanilla in a large bowl until combined. Whisk in flour and salt until combined. Pour mixture into prepared Cream Cheese Piecrust. Bake until filling is set, about 40 minutes, covering edges of crust with foil halfway through to prevent overbrowning. Transfer Pie to a wire rack, and let cool 1 hour.

2. Prepare the Sautéed Apples: Stir together apples, sugar, vinegar, vanilla, salt, and cinnamon in a large bowl until evenly coated. Set aside. Melt butter in a large skillet over medium-high; cook butter, swirling occasionally, until beginning to brown, about 3 minutes. Add apple mixture; cook, stirring often, until the apples are tender-crisp and caramel has thickened, about 5 minutes. Remove from heat, and let cool slightly, about 10 minutes.

3. Spoon Sautéed Apples and juices over cooled Pie. Serve immediately. To make ahead, cover untopped Pie and refrigerate up to 2 days; add apples just before serving.

Cranberry Chiffon Pie

(Photo, page 274)

Popularized during the 1920s and 1930s, chiffon pies have a custard or curd filling that is set with gelatin and combined with whipped egg whites to make them as light as air. In this pretty pink version, the tangy, mousse-like Cranberry Filling contrasts with the crispy, spicy Gingersnap Crust for a textural match made in heaven.

ACTIVE 1 HOUR, 20 MIN. - TOTAL 1 HOUR, 20 MIN., PLUS 4 HOURS CHILLING

SERVES 8

GINGERSNAP CRUST

- 1¾ cups (about 9¾ oz.) packed finely ground gingersnap cookie crumbs, such as Nabisco (from 1 [16-oz.] pkg.)
- ¼ cup granulated sugar
- ½ tsp. kosher salt
- 6 Tbsp. unsalted butter, melted

CRANBERRY FILLING

- 3 cups fresh or frozen cranberries
- ½ tsp. kosher salt
- 1 cup plus ²/₃ cup granulated sugar, divided
- 4 Tbsp. unsalted butter, cubed, at room temperature
- 1¼ tsp. unflavored gelatin (from 1 [¼-oz.] envelope)
- 4 large eggs, 2 separated
- ½ tsp. vanilla extract

GINGER WHIPPED CREAM

- ¾ cup heavy whipping cream
- 3 Tbsp. powdered sugar
- 1 tsp. vanilla extract
- ½ tsp. ground ginger

1. Prepare the Gingersnap Crust: Preheat oven to 350°F. Coat a 9-inch deep-dish pie plate with cooking spray, and set aside. Whisk together cookie crumbs, sugar, and salt in a medium bowl until well combined. Stir in butter until combined and mixture holds together when squeezed. Spoon into prepared pie plate; firmly press mixture into bottom and up sides of plate. Bake until golden brown, 10 to 12 minutes. Transfer Gingersnap Crust to a wire rack, and let cool to room temperature, about 45 minutes.

2. Meanwhile, prepare the Cranberry Filling: Bring cranberries, ½ cup water, salt, and 1 cup of the sugar to a boil in a medium saucepan over medium-high, stirring often. Reduce heat to medium, and cook, stirring often, until the berries have burst and mixture thickens slightly, 8 to 10 minutes (to yield a scant 2 cups). Pour mixture through a fine mesh strainer into a medium-size heatproof bowl (do not wipe pan clean), and use the back of a spoon to press cranberry solids to release as much juice as possible (about 1¾ cups). Discard solids, or save for another use. Add butter to strained juice, and whisk until butter is melted and combined. Return juice mixture to saucepan, and set aside.

3. Place 3 tablespoons cold water in a small bowl, and stir in gelatin. Let stand 5 minutes. Meanwhile, whisk 2 whole eggs and 2 egg yolks (reserve 2 whites; set aside) into cranberry juice mixture until combined. Cook over medium, whisking constantly, until slightly thickened, 4 to 5 minutes. Remove from heat, and whisk vanilla and gelatin into cranberry juice mixture until gelatin melts and mixture is smooth. Transfer to a large heatproof bowl, and let cool, whisking occasionally, until just warm to the touch, about 20 minutes.

4. Meanwhile, fill a small saucepan with water to a depth of 1 inch, and bring to a boil over medium-high. Whisk together reserved egg whites and remaining ²/₃ cup sugar in bowl of a stand mixer. Reduce heat under boiling water to medium, and place bowl over simmering water, making sure bottom of bowl does not touch water. Cook, whisking constantly, until an instant-read thermometer registers 160°F, about 4 minutes. Transfer bowl to stand mixer fitted with a whisk attachment, and beat on high speed until medium-stiff peaks form, about 10 minutes. Fold egg white mixture into cooled cranberry juice mixture in 3 additions, folding until combined each time. Pour into cooled Gingersnap Crust. Refrigerate, uncovered, until set, at least 4 hours or up to 12 hours.

5. Prepare the Ginger Whipped Cream: Whisk together cream, sugar, vanilla, and ginger in a medium bowl until medium-stiff peaks form, 1 to 2 minutes. Gently spoon the cream mixture into a piping bag fitted with a large open star tip. Pipe 8 large rosettes along edge of pie filling. (Alternatively, dollop heaping tablespoons of whipped cream over pie, or spread over pie, if desired.) Serve with remaining whipped cream. To make ahead, loosely cover undecorated pie with plastic wrap and refrigerate up to 2 days. Top with Ginger Whipped Cream just before serving.

CRANBERRY
CHIFFON PIE
(PAGE 273)

POSSUM PIE
(PAGE 276)

No-Bake Chocolate-Peanut Butter Pie

Every Thanksgiving host deserves an easy no-bake pie that frees up oven space on the busiest of cooking days. But the real beauty of this dessert (second to tasting like a chocolate-peanut butter cup) is that it can also be made a day in advance.

ACTIVE 45 MIN. - TOTAL 45 MIN., PLUS 6 HOURS CHILLING

SERVES 8

CHOCOLATE-PEANUT CRUST

- 1½ cups packed finely ground chocolate cookie crumbs (such as Teddy Grahams, from 1 [10-oz.] pkg.)
- ½ cup salted dry-roasted peanuts, plus chopped peanuts for garnish
- ¼ cup packed light brown sugar
- 7 Tbsp. unsalted butter, melted and cooled slightly
- ½ tsp. vanilla extract

GANACHE

- 1 cup semisweet chocolate chips
- ½ cup heavy whipping cream

PEANUT BUTTER PUDDING

- ¾ cup packed dark brown sugar
- ¼ cup cornstarch
- ½ tsp. kosher salt
- 2½ cups whole milk
- ¾ cup heavy whipping cream
- 1 large egg
- 1 cup creamy peanut butter (not the all-natural kind)
- 2 Tbsp. unsalted butter, at room temperature
- 2½ tsp. vanilla extract

1. Prepare the Chocolate-Peanut Crust: Lightly coat a 9-inch deep-dish pie plate with cooking spray, and set aside. Pulse together cookie crumbs, peanuts, and sugar in a food processor until peanuts are finely ground, 20 to 24 pulses. Add butter and vanilla; pulse until mixture holds together when squeezed, about 6 pulses. Spoon into prepared pie plate; firmly press into bottom and up sides of plate. Freeze for 5 minutes.

2. Prepare the Ganache: Place chocolate chips and cream in a small microwavable bowl; microwave on HIGH in 30-second intervals, stirring until chocolate is melted and smooth. Pour half of mixture evenly over bottom of crust; freeze crust until ready to use. Cover remaining Ganache, and refrigerate until ready to use.

3. Prepare the Peanut Butter Pudding: Whisk together sugar, cornstarch, and salt in a medium saucepan. Whisk in milk, cream, and egg until combined. Bring to a simmer over medium-high, whisking constantly. Reduce heat to medium; cook, whisking vigorously, until thickened, about 1 minute. Remove from heat; whisk in peanut butter, butter, and vanilla until smooth. Spoon mixture into a large bowl. Refrigerate until slightly cooled, whisking occasionally, about 20 minutes.

4. Remove crust from freezer. Using a small offset spatula, spread pudding evenly over Ganache layer in crust. Place plastic wrap directly on pudding to prevent a film from forming. Refrigerate until pudding is set, at least 6 hours or up to 12 hours.

5. Microwave remaining Ganache on HIGH in 30-second intervals, stirring until chocolate is melted and smooth. Using a small offset spatula, spread mixture over pie to evenly cover pudding layer. Garnish with chopped peanuts. Pie may be loosely covered with plastic wrap and stored in refrigerator up to 24 hours.

Possum Pie

(Photo, page 275)

One of the most popular desserts in Arkansas is Possum Pie. But don't worry; it's absolutely meat free. Possums are notorious for pretending to be dead—playing tricks—and that's exactly what this pie's cream cheese and chocolate layers do by hiding underneath a pile of fluffy whipped cream.

ACTIVE 55 MIN. - TOTAL 2 HOURS, 40 MIN., PLUS 6 HOURS CHILLING

SERVES 8

PECAN SHORTBREAD CRUST

- ⅓ cup toasted pecan halves, plus chopped pecans for garnish
- ¼ cup granulated sugar
- 1¼ cups all-purpose flour, plus more for hands
- ½ tsp. kosher salt
- 7 Tbsp. (3½ oz.) cold unsalted butter, cubed
- 1 Tbsp. ice water

CREAM CHEESE LAYER

- 6 oz. cream cheese, at room temperature
- ⅓ cup powdered sugar
- 2 Tbsp. heavy whipping cream

- 1 tsp. vanilla extract
- ¼ tsp. kosher salt

CHOCOLATE PUDDING

- ¾ cup granulated sugar
- ½ cup Dutch-process dark cocoa
- ¼ cup plus 1 Tbsp. cornstarch
- ¾ tsp. kosher salt
- 2¼ cups whole milk
- 1 cup heavy whipping cream
- 1 large egg
- 1 Tbsp. unsalted butter, at room temperature
- 2 tsp. vanilla extract

WHIPPED CREAM

- 1 cup heavy whipping cream
- ¼ cup powdered sugar
- 1 tsp. vanilla extract

1. Prepare the Pecan Shortbread Crust: Preheat oven to 375°F. Coat a 9-inch deep-dish pie plate with cooking spray, and set aside. Pulse pecan halves and sugar in a food processor until nuts are finely ground, 12 to 18 pulses. Add flour and salt; pulse until combined, about 3 pulses. Add butter; pulse until butter is pea size, about 6 pulses. Sprinkle ice water over flour mixture; pulse until mixture resembles coarse meal and holds together when squeezed, 6 to 8 pulses. Spoon mixture into prepared pie plate. Using floured fingers, press dough evenly into bottom and up sides of plate. Carefully prick bottom of dough all over with a fork. Freeze until firm, 30 to 45 minutes.

2. Lightly spray a piece of aluminum foil with cooking spray; place spray side down on chilled crust. Add pie weights or dried beans to completely fill crust. Bake in preheated oven until lightly browned around edges, 25 to 30 minutes. Remove and discard foil and weights. Return to oven, and bake until crust is golden brown and set, 10 to 15 minutes, loosely covering edges with foil to prevent overbrowning. Transfer to a wire rack, and let cool completely, about 45 minutes.

3. Prepare the Cream Cheese Layer: Stir together cream cheese, powdered sugar, cream, vanilla, and salt in a medium bowl until smooth, about 30 seconds. Spread evenly in bottom of cooled crust. Refrigerate until ready to use.

4. Prepare the Chocolate Pudding: Whisk together sugar, cocoa, cornstarch,

Continued on page 279

NO-BAKE CHOCOLATE-
PEANUT BUTTER PIE

GINGER-MAPLE
AMBER PIE

Continued from page 276

and salt in a medium saucepan until combined. Whisk in milk, cream, and egg until smooth. Bring mixture to a boil over medium, whisking constantly. Reduce heat to medium-low; cook, whisking vigorously, for 1 minute. Remove from heat; whisk in butter and vanilla until smooth. Whisk vigorously until thickened, about 1 minute. Spoon mixture into a large bowl; refrigerate, whisking frequently, until slightly cooled, about 20 minutes.

5. Spoon cooled Chocolate Pudding over Cream Cheese Layer in crust; spread in an even layer. Cover with plastic wrap, placing on surface of pudding to prevent a film from forming. Refrigerate until set, at least 6 hours or up to 12 hours.

6. Prepare the Whipped Cream: Whisk together cream, sugar, and vanilla in a large bowl until medium peaks form, about 2 minutes. Spoon on top of pudding; spread in an even layer over pie. Garnish with chopped pecans. Pie may be covered loosely with plastic wrap and stored in refrigerator up to 2 days.

Ginger-Maple Amber Pie

Traditional amber pie recipes typically call for a pastry crust filled with a thick ginger custard and topped with loads of billowy meringue. We've tweaked the classic by adding rich maple syrup; it's the perfect flavor partner with the gently spicy filling and Cinnamon Meringue topping.

ACTIVE 55 MIN. - TOTAL 1 HOUR, 15 MIN., PLUS 2 HOURS COOLING

SERVES 8

PIE
- 2½ cups whole milk
- ¾ cup packed light brown sugar
- 2 Tbsp. grated fresh ginger
- 1 tsp. ground ginger
- ½ tsp. ground cinnamon
- 4 large eggs, 3 separated, at room temperature
- ¾ cup pure maple syrup
- ⅓ cup cornstarch
- 2 tsp. vanilla extract
- ½ tsp. kosher salt
- 1 Deep-Dish Cream Cheese Piecrust (recipe at right)

CINNAMON MERINGUE
- 5 large egg whites, at room temperature
- 1 cup granulated sugar
- ¾ tsp. vanilla extract
- ½ tsp. ground cinnamon
- ¼ tsp. cream of tartar
- ¼ tsp. kosher salt

1. Prepare the Pie: Whisk together milk, sugar, grated ginger, ground ginger, and cinnamon in a medium saucepan. Cook, whisking constantly, until mixture just begins to bubble around edges, about 12 minutes. Remove from heat. Cover and let steep 20 minutes.

2. Whisk together 3 egg yolks (reserve whites for Cinnamon Meringue), 1 whole egg, maple syrup, and cornstarch in a medium bowl. Whisking constantly, gradually whisk in warm milk mixture to gently heat up eggs. Return milk-egg mixture to saucepan; bring to a simmer over medium, whisking constantly. Simmer, whisking constantly, until thickened, about 1 minute. Remove from heat; whisk in vanilla and salt. Pour custard into prepared Deep-Dish Cream Cheese Piecrust. Preheat oven to 350°F.

3. Prepare the Cinnamon Meringue: Fill a small saucepan with water to a depth of 1 inch. Bring to a boil over medium-high. Whisk together egg whites, sugar, vanilla, cinnamon, cream of tartar, and salt in the stainless-steel bowl of a stand mixer. Reduce heat to medium; place bowl over simmering water, making sure bottom of bowl doesn't touch water. Cook, whisking constantly, until an instant-read thermometer registers 160°F, about 4 minutes. Transfer bowl to stand mixer fitted with a whisk attachment; beat on high speed until stiff peaks form, about 7 minutes.

4. Spoon Cinnamon Meringue in an even layer over warm custard, spreading to crust edges and swirling decoratively. Bake in preheated oven until golden brown, about 15 minutes. Transfer to a wire rack, and let cool to room temperature, about 2 hours, before serving.

Cream Cheese Piecrust

ACTIVE 20 MIN. - TOTAL 2 HOURS, 30 MIN., PLUS 1 HOUR, 5 MIN. FREEZING

MAKES 1 (9-INCH) PIECRUST

- 2 oz. cold cream cheese, cubed
- 1⅓ cups all-purpose flour, plus more for work surface
- 1 Tbsp. granulated sugar
- ½ tsp. kosher salt
- ½ cup cold unsalted butter, cubed
- 1 Tbsp. ice water

1. Freeze cubed cream cheese until slightly firm and chilled, about 10 minutes. Pulse flour, sugar, and salt in a food processor until combined, 3 to 5 pulses. Add cold butter and cold cream cheese; pulse until butter and cream cheese are pea size, about 6 pulses. Sprinkle ice water over flour mixture; pulse until dough comes together in large clumps.

2. Transfer dough to a sheet of plastic wrap; shape into a 6-inch disk. Cover tightly with plastic wrap, massaging away any cracks with your fingers. Refrigerate at least 45 minutes or up to 12 hours. (Dough refrigerated for longer periods of time may need to stand at room temperature for 10 to 15 minutes to soften slightly before rolling.)

3. Lightly coat a 9-inch pie plate with cooking spray. Unwrap dough, and roll out on a lightly floured work surface into a 12½- to 13-inch round, about ⅛ inch thick. Carefully place dough inside prepared pie plate, pressing into bottom and up sides of plate. Trim excess dough, leaving a ¼- to ½-inch overhang. Fold overhang under itself, creating a thicker ring of crust around pie edge. Crimp edge as desired. Prick bottom all over with a fork. Freeze, uncovered, until firm, at least 1 hour or up to 12 hours.

4. Preheat oven to 425°F. Lightly coat a piece of parchment paper with cooking spray; place spray side down over chilled crust, pressing into bottom and sides. Add enough pie weights or dried beans to completely fill crust. Place filled crust on a large rimmed baking sheet. Bake until edges are golden and set, about 15 to 20 minutes. Transfer to a wire rack, and let cool 5 minutes. Remove parchment and weights. Let cool completely on wire rack, about 45 minutes. Crust may be stored, covered with plastic wrap, at room temperature up to 3 days.

Deep-Dish Cream Cheese Piecrust

Prepare Cream Cheese Piecrust as directed through Step 2. In Step 3, substitute a 9-inch deep-dish pie plate for the regular pie plate, and roll out dough to a 14-inch round. In Step 4, after removing parchment paper and weights from crust, return crust to oven and continue baking until inside is light golden brown, 12 to 15 minutes. Let cool completely on wire rack, about 45 minutes.

It's Turkey Time

Three easy ways to enjoy the holiday bird, whether you're feeding a crowd or just a few folks

Easiest Dry-Brined Turkey

ACTIVE 20 MIN. · TOTAL 3 HOURS, 25 MIN.,
PLUS 12 HOURS BRINING

SERVES 8 TO 10

- 1 (12- to 14-lb.) fresh (or thawed frozen) whole turkey, patted dry using paper towels, with giblets and neck removed
- 2 Tbsp. kosher salt
- 1 Tbsp. black pepper
- 1 medium-size yellow onion, unpeeled and quartered lengthwise
- 3 dried bay leaves
- 1 garlic head, halved crosswise
- 5 (5-inch) fresh thyme sprigs, plus more for garnish
- 5 (6-inch) fresh rosemary sprigs, plus more for garnish
- 2 Tbsp. olive oil

1. Line a large roasting pan with aluminum foil, and fit a roasting rack inside pan. Sprinkle turkey evenly with salt and pepper. Place turkey, breast side up, on prepared roasting rack. Chill, uncovered, at least 12 hours or up to 48 hours.
2. Remove turkey from refrigerator, and let stand at room temperature 20 to 30 minutes. Meanwhile, preheat oven to 450°F with rack in lower third position.
3. Place onion quarters, bay leaves, garlic halves, thyme sprigs, and rosemary sprigs inside turkey cavity. Tie legs together with kitchen twine; tuck wing tips under. Lightly brush turkey with oil, being careful not to brush off the seasoning from skin.
4. Bake on lower third rack of preheated oven until golden brown and crispy, about 45 minutes. Without removing from oven, carefully cover turkey loosely with foil; reduce oven temperature to 350°F. Bake until a thermometer inserted into thickest portion of thigh registers 165°F, 1 hour, 30 minutes to 2 hours, 30 minutes. Transfer turkey to a cutting board; let rest, loosely covered with foil, for 30 minutes.

5. Remove and discard mixture inside cavity. Carve turkey into 1-inch-thick slices. If desired, reserve pan drippings for making a gravy. Arrange carved turkey on a platter. Garnish with additional thyme and rosemary sprigs.

Dutch Oven Turkey Breast

(Photo, page 283)

ACTIVE 30 MIN. · TOTAL 3 HOURS

SERVES 4 TO 6

- 1 (5- to 6-lb.) bone-in, skin-on turkey breast, patted dry with paper towels
- 2 Tbsp. olive oil
- 3 tsp. kosher salt, divided, plus more to taste
- 1 tsp. black pepper, divided, plus more to taste and for garnish
- 1¾ lb. medium-size red potatoes, halved
- 4 medium carrots, peeled, halved lengthwise, and cut into 1-inch pieces (about 2 cups)
- 1 small sweet onion, cut lengthwise into eighths
- ¾ cup dry white wine
- 2 Tbsp. all-purpose flour
- 1 Tbsp. white wine vinegar
- 1½ tsp. chopped fresh sage, plus sage leaves for garnish

1. Preheat oven to 325°F with rack about 12 inches from heat source. Brush turkey with oil; sprinkle with 2 teaspoons of the salt and ½ teaspoon of the pepper. Place in a large broiler-safe Dutch oven. Bake, uncovered, until turkey is golden brown, about 1 hour. Do not turn oven off.
2. Remove pot from oven. Arrange potatoes, carrots, and onion around turkey; set aside. Whisk together wine, flour, vinegar, chopped sage, and remaining 1 teaspoon salt and ½ teaspoon pepper in a small bowl. Pour evenly over vegetables. Cover and bake at 325°F until vegetables are fork-tender and a thermometer inserted into thickest portion of meat registers 160°F, 1 hour, 10 minutes to 1 hour, 25 minutes.

3. Without removing pot from oven, carefully uncover; increase temperature to broil. Broil until turkey is golden brown, 8 to 10 minutes.
4. Remove pot from oven. Transfer turkey to a cutting board. Let rest 15 minutes; turkey temperature will continue to rise to 165°F. Season vegetables to taste with additional salt and pepper. Carve turkey into 1-inch-thick slices. Arrange meat and vegetables on a platter. Whisk gravy until combined; drizzle over sliced turkey and vegetables. Garnish with fresh sage leaves and additional pepper, if desired.

Smoky Bourbon-Glazed Turkey Legs

(Photo, page 282)

ACTIVE 55 MIN. · TOTAL 2 HOURS, 35 MIN.,
PLUS 12 HOURS BRINING

SERVES 6

- 4 cups apple cider
- 1 cup kosher salt
- 10 (5-inch) fresh thyme sprigs, plus leaves for garnish
- 1¾ cups packed dark brown sugar, divided
- 8 cups ice
- 6 (about 1 to 1¼ lb. each) bone-in, skin-on turkey drumsticks
  Pecan wood chunks
- ¾ cup bourbon
- 6 Tbsp. unsalted butter

1. Bring cider, salt, thyme sprigs, and 1 cup of the brown sugar to a simmer in a large (about 12-quart) stockpot over high. Simmer, stirring occasionally, until salt and brown sugar are dissolved, about 5 minutes. Remove from heat; stir in 4 cups cold water. Add ice and turkey legs. Cover; refrigerate at least 12 hours or up to 24 hours.
2. Remove turkey legs from brine; discard brine. Pat turkey dry with paper towels; let stand at room temperature for about 40 minutes.

EASIEST
DRY-BRINED
TURKEY

WHY DRY BRINE?
It takes a lot of liquid to brine a whole turkey. This method deeply seasons the meat with much less mess and effort.

3. Completely open the bottom vent of a charcoal grill. Light a charcoal chimney starter filled with briquettes. When briquettes are covered with gray ash, pour them onto the bottom grate and push them to 1 side of grill. Scatter pecan wood chunks over hot coals. Cover grill, adjusting vents as needed until grill thermometer shows an internal temperature of 350°F, 15 to 20 minutes. Coat top grate with oil; place on grill. Place turkey legs, meaty-skin side up, on oiled grates over the side without the coals. Grill, covered, about 1 hour.
4. While turkey cooks, bring bourbon, butter, and remaining ¾ cup brown sugar to a simmer in a small saucepan over medium, stirring often. Simmer, stirring often, until sugar is dissolved and mixture is slightly thickened, 5 to 7 minutes. Measure ½ cup glaze into a small heatproof bowl, and set aside until ready to serve. Cover remaining glaze in saucepan, and set aside for brushing.
5. After about 1 hour of the turkey cook time, light another charcoal chimney starter halfway filled with briquettes. When briquettes are covered with gray ash, turkey legs turn dark golden brown, and a meat thermometer inserted into thickest portion registers 165°F, remove turkey from grill. Transfer to a large plate or baking sheet. Carefully lift grate, and pour briquettes over existing coals.

Cover and let grill temperature rise to medium-high (450°F to 500°F). Carefully recoat grate with oil, and return to grill.
6. Brush turkey with some of the bourbon glaze in saucepan. Place legs, skin side down, on oiled grates over the side with the coals. Grill, uncovered, brushing with glaze in saucepan and turning turkey often, until charred in spots and a meat thermometer inserted into thickest portion registers 175°F, about 4 minutes total. Transfer turkey to a cutting board; cover loosely with foil, and let rest 15 minutes. Brush with reserved ½ cup glaze in bowl. Garnish with thyme leaves.

PLENTY FOR EVERYONE
Avoid the inevitable fight over the drumsticks by grilling a batch of these to serve alongside your Thanksgiving turkey.

SMOKY
BOURBON-GLAZED
TURKEY LEGS
(PAGE 280)

DOWNSIZE AND UPGRADE
If you're hosting a smaller group, this recipe is just the ticket. Bonus: The gravy comes together right in the pot with no extra steps.

DUTCH OVEN
TURKEY BREAST
(PAGE 280)

Special-Request Sides

Even the most prepared hosts welcome holiday help. Enter nine please-all dishes

THANKSGIVING is the most glorious feast of the year but can be the most challenging for home cooks. Guests come from near and far—often with an array of dietary restrictions. Oven space is a hot commodity, and time is a limited resource. But don't worry—our Test Kitchen came up with solutions to common write-in dilemmas. You'll be extra grateful this year for these freeze-ahead and no-oven-required recipes, plus our gluten-free spins on classics.

Freezer-Friendly Favorites

It pays to get ahead. Whip these up months in advance, and breathe easier on the big day

Freezer-Friendly Braised Southern Greens

Don't miss out on this Thanksgiving side—it pairs perfectly with cornbread dressing.

ACTIVE 45 MIN. · TOTAL 2 HOURS, 15 MIN. (PLUS 1 HOUR COOLING AND 24 HOURS THAWING IF MAKING AHEAD)

SERVES 10

- 2 Tbsp. olive oil
- 1 large yellow onion, sliced (about 3½ cups)
- 2 Tbsp. minced garlic (from 6 garlic cloves)
- 1 tsp. kosher salt, plus more to taste
- ½ tsp. black pepper
- ¼ tsp. crushed red pepper
- 3 bunches collard greens, stemmed and cut into ½-inch ribbons (about 13 cups)
- 4 cups chicken stock
- 1¾ lb. smoked ham hocks (about 2 pieces)
- 2 fresh bay leaves
- 2 tsp. apple cider vinegar (optional)

1. Heat olive oil in a large Dutch oven over medium. Add onion; cook, stirring often, until lightly browned, about 10 minutes. Stir in garlic, salt, black pepper, and crushed red pepper; cook, stirring constantly, until garlic is fragrant, about 1 minute. Add greens, stirring to coat. Add stock, ham hocks, and bay leaves; bring to a simmer over medium-high. Reduce heat to low; cover and simmer until greens are tender, about 1 hour, 15 minutes. Remove from heat.
2. Discard bay leaves. Transfer ham hocks to a cutting board; let cool 5 minutes. Remove and discard skin. Using a fork, shred meat; discard bones. Return shredded meat to greens; stir to combine. If serving right away, skip to Step 4.
3. Let cool to room temperature, about 1 hour. Transfer greens mixture to an airtight freezer-safe container. Freeze up to 6 months. Transfer container to refrigerator until greens are thawed, about 24 hours. Transfer greens to a large Dutch oven. Cook over medium-high, stirring often, until heated through, about 15 minutes.
4. Stir in apple cider vinegar, if desired. Season with additional salt to taste. Serve.

Best-Ever Freezer-Friendly Yeast Rolls

These buttery rolls have been beloved by readers for years; now you can prepare them weeks beforehand.

ACTIVE 30 MIN. · TOTAL 3 HOURS, 15 MIN. (PLUS 12 HOURS, 30 MIN. FREEZING, THAWING, AND RISING IF MAKING AHEAD)

MAKES 32

- 2 (¼-oz.) envelopes active dry yeast (4½ tsp.)
- 1¼ cups warm water (105°F to 115°F), divided
- 3 large eggs, lightly beaten
- ½ cup vegetable shortening, melted
- ½ cup granulated sugar
- 2 tsp. kosher salt
- 5 to 5¼ cups all-purpose flour, as needed, divided, plus more for work surface
- ¼ cup butter, melted
- 2 tsp. flaky sea salt

1. Stir together yeast and ¼ cup of the warm water in a large bowl; let stand until mixture is foamy, about 5 minutes.
2. Add eggs, shortening, sugar, kosher salt, 2 cups of the flour, and remaining 1 cup warm water to yeast mixture. Beat with a wooden spoon until well combined and smooth, about 2 minutes. Gradually stir in 3 cups of the flour until a soft dough forms, adding up to ¼ cup remaining flour if dough is too sticky.
3. Cover bowl with plastic wrap or a clean dish towel; let rise in a warm place (about 80°F) until doubled in size, about 1 hour.
4. Punch down dough in bowl. Turn dough out onto a floured work surface, and knead until slightly smoother, 3 or 4 times. Divide in half. Working with 1 portion at a time and keeping remaining dough covered, shape each portion evenly into 16 balls (about 2 heaping tablespoons each). If baking right away, skip to Step 6.
5. To freeze, arrange dough balls about 1 inch apart on a baking sheet lined with parchment paper. Cover with plastic wrap. Freeze until solid, about 4 hours. Transfer to a zip-top plastic freezer bag. Seal bag, and freeze up to 3 months.
6. Arrange fresh or frozen dough balls in 2 lightly greased (with cooking spray) 9-inch square metal baking pans. Cover each pan with plastic wrap. (If frozen, refrigerate until dough is thawed, about 8 hours. Remove thawed dough from refrigerator; do not remove plastic wrap.) Let rise in a warm place (about 80°F) until slightly more than doubled in size, about 1 hour. If dough balls were frozen, let rise about 1 hour, 30 minutes.
7. Preheat oven to 375°F. Remove plastic wrap from baking pans. Bake until golden brown, 15 to 18 minutes. Remove from oven, brush evenly with butter, and sprinkle with flaky sea salt. Serve warm.

Freezer-Friendly Shoepeg Corn Casserole

If frozen, let the casserole thaw completely before adding the topping. Pop the dish in the oven just before guests arrive.

ACTIVE 15 MIN. · TOTAL 45 MIN. (PLUS 24 HOURS THAWING IF MAKING AHEAD)

SERVES 8

- 3 Tbsp. unsalted butter, melted, divided
- 1 cup chopped scallions (from 7 scallions)
- ½ cup chopped celery (from 1 celery stalk)
- 2 (11-oz.) cans white shoepeg corn, drained
- 1 (10¾-oz.) can condensed cream of celery soup
- 1 (8-oz.) container sour cream
- 4 oz. extra-sharp Cheddar cheese, shredded (about 1 cup)
- 2 cups cornflakes cereal, crushed
- ¼ tsp. kosher salt
- ¼ tsp. garlic powder

1. Heat 1 tablespoon of the melted butter in a medium skillet over medium. Add scallions and celery; cook, stirring occasionally, until tender, about 7 minutes. Remove from heat.

2. Stir together cooked vegetables, corn, condensed soup, sour cream, and cheese in a large bowl until well combined. Spoon into a 2-quart freezer-safe baking dish. If making right away, skip to Step 4.

3. Tightly wrap baking dish with plastic wrap. Freeze up to 6 months. Transfer frozen casserole to refrigerator until thawed, about 24 hours. Unwrap baking dish; stir mixture until smooth and creamy.

4. Preheat oven to 350°F. Stir together crushed cornflakes, salt, garlic powder, and remaining 2 tablespoons melted butter in a medium bowl until well combined. Sprinkle evenly over mixture in baking dish.

5. Bake in preheated oven until topping is lightly browned, 20 to 23 minutes. Remove from oven; let cool slightly, about 10 minutes. Serve warm.

FREEZER-FRIENDLY BRAISED SOUTHERN GREENS

FREEZER-FRIENDLY SHOEPEG CORN CASSEROLE

BEST-EVER FREEZER-FRIENDLY YEAST ROLLS

GLUTEN-FREE MAC
AND CHEESE

GLUTEN-FREE
CORNBREAD
DRESSING

GLUTEN-FREE
BUTTERMILK BISCUITS

Gluten-Free Go-Tos

These revamped staples work for those who are sensitive to gluten—and are just as tasty as the originals

Gluten-Free Buttermilk Biscuits

Our Test Kitchen knocked this one out of the park—your guests will never know these tender and flaky biscuits are made without a speck of wheat flour.

ACTIVE 20 MIN. - TOTAL 55 MIN.

MAKES 10

- 3½ cups gluten-free all-purpose flour (such as King Arthur), plus more for work surface
- 2 Tbsp. granulated sugar
- 1 Tbsp. kosher salt
- 1 Tbsp. gluten-free baking powder
- ½ tsp. baking soda
- 1 cup cold unsalted butter, cubed
- 1¼ cups cold whole buttermilk
- 1 large egg, beaten
- 1 tsp. flaky sea salt

1. Preheat oven to 425°F. Line a baking sheet with parchment paper; set aside. Stir together flour, sugar, kosher salt, baking powder, and baking soda in a large bowl. Using 2 forks or a pastry blender, cut in cold butter until pieces are pea-size. If there are large chunks of butter, use your fingers to gently flatten. Add buttermilk; stir until a shaggy dough forms and clumps when squeezed together.
2. Turn dough out onto a work surface lightly dusted with flour. Pat into an 8- x 6-inch rectangle, and cut into fourths. Stack quarters; pat down into a rectangle again. Repeat process 3 times until dough comes together (it will be very crumbly the first 2 rounds). Pat or roll into 1-inch thickness. Using a 2¼-inch square cutter dipped in flour, cut into 10 biscuits, rerolling scraps once. Arrange biscuits 1 inch apart on prepared baking sheet. Freeze, uncovered, until cold, about 10 minutes.
3. Remove biscuits from freezer. Brush evenly with egg; sprinkle with flaky salt. Bake in preheated oven until biscuits are golden brown, 15 to 18 minutes. Let cool on baking sheet for 5 minutes. Serve warm.

Gluten-Free Cornbread Dressing

Pick up a gluten-free cornbread mix, and prepare it in a 9-inch skillet according to package directions. Or make it from scratch using our tried-and-true recipe (southernliving.com/glutenfreecornbread).

ACTIVE 40 MIN. - TOTAL 1 HOUR, 40 MIN., PLUS 24 HOURS DRYING

SERVES 12

- 14 cups 1-inch cubes gluten-free cornbread
- ½ cup unsalted butter, melted, divided
- 1 large yellow onion, chopped (about 2½ cups)
- 1½ cups chopped celery (from 4 large celery stalks)
- 1 Tbsp. finely chopped garlic (from 3 garlic cloves)
- ¼ cup chopped fresh flat-leaf parsley, plus more for garnish
- 2 Tbsp. chopped fresh sage
- 1 Tbsp. chopped fresh thyme
- 4 cups gluten-free chicken broth
- 2 tsp. kosher salt
- 1 tsp. black pepper
- 4 large eggs, lightly beaten

1. Spread cornbread cubes in an even layer on a baking sheet. Cover with a clean dish towel, and let stand at room temperature until dry, about 24 hours.
2. Preheat oven to 350°F with rack 6 inches from heat source. Heat ¼ cup of the butter in a large skillet over medium-high. Add onion and celery; cook, stirring often, until vegetables are tender, about 8 minutes. Add garlic; cook, stirring often, until fragrant, about 1 minute. Remove from heat. Stir in parsley, sage, and thyme.
3. Whisk together broth, salt, pepper, and eggs in a large bowl. Add onion mixture and cornbread cubes, and fold gently to combine. Let stand, stirring gently and occasionally, until cornbread has absorbed most of the liquid, about 10 minutes.
4. Spoon mixture into a 3-quart broiler-safe baking dish lightly coated with cooking spray. Pour remaining ¼ cup melted butter evenly over the top of the mixture. Cover with aluminum foil.
5. Bake in preheated oven for 30 minutes. Uncover and bake until dressing is set around the edges, about 15 minutes. Increase oven temperature to broil (do not remove baking dish from oven). Broil until top is golden brown, about 5 minutes. Remove from oven; let cool 10 minutes. Garnish with additional parsley before serving, if desired.

Gluten-Free Mac and Cheese

Creamy fontina cheese and two layers of Colby Jack make everyone's favorite side dish extra delicious.

ACTIVE 30 MIN. - TOTAL 40 MIN.

SERVES 12

- 1 lb. uncooked gluten-free elbow macaroni
- 4 Tbsp. unsalted butter
- ¼ cup gluten-free all-purpose flour (such as King Arthur)
- 2½ cups whole milk
- 2 tsp. gluten-free stone-ground mustard
- 1½ tsp. kosher salt, plus more for salting water
- ¾ tsp. black pepper
- 1 lb. fontina cheese, shredded (about 4 cups)
- 8 oz. Colby Jack cheese, shredded (about 2 cups), divided
- ¼ cup cooked and crumbled gluten-free bacon (from 4 bacon slices)

1. Coat a 13- x 9-inch broiler-safe baking dish with cooking spray; set aside. Cook pasta in boiling salted water according to package directions until al dente, about 8 minutes; drain, and set aside.
2. Meanwhile, melt butter in a large saucepan over medium. Add flour; cook, whisking constantly, until mixture turns light golden brown, about 3 minutes. Gradually whisk in milk until smooth. Bring to a simmer over medium; simmer, whisking often, until mixture thickens enough to coat the back of a spoon, about 3 minutes. Stir in mustard, salt, and pepper.
3. Reduce heat to medium-low; gradually stir in fontina until melted and sauce has thickened. Fold in cooked pasta until fully coated in cheese sauce. Remove from heat.
4. Pour half of the pasta mixture (about 4½ cups) into prepared baking dish. Sprinkle evenly with 1 cup of the Colby Jack. Top with remaining pasta mixture, and sprinkle evenly with remaining Colby Jack.
5. Preheat broiler with oven rack 6 inches from heat source. Place baking dish in oven, and broil until cheese is fully melted and browned in spots, about 7 minutes. Remove from oven; let cool 10 minutes. Sprinkle with crumbled bacon, and serve.

Savvy Stovetop Solutions

Roasting a turkey creates a traffic jam of dishes waiting for the oven. Skip the line with these fast-fix options

Stovetop Broccoli Casserole

After cooking the filling, sprinkle it with shredded Cheddar and cover the skillet— the residual heat will melt the cheese. When you're ready to eat, uncover and add the toasted crackers for a big finish.

ACTIVE 50 MIN. - TOTAL 1 HOUR

SERVES 8

- 1 (2-lb.) pkg. fresh broccoli florets (about 2-inch pieces, around 13 cups total)
- 5 Tbsp. unsalted butter, divided
- 1 cup crushed round buttery crackers (such as Ritz)
- 2 Tbsp. chopped fresh flat-leaf parsley
- 1 cup chopped yellow onion (from 1 medium onion)
- 1 Tbsp. finely chopped garlic (about 3 garlic cloves)
- ¼ cup all-purpose flour
- 1½ cups whole milk
- 2 tsp. Dijon mustard
- 1 tsp. kosher salt, plus more to taste
- 1 tsp. black pepper
- 12 oz. sharp Cheddar cheese, shredded (about 3 cups), divided
- ½ cup mayonnaise

1. Place broccoli and ¼ cup water in a large microwavable bowl. Cover loosely with plastic wrap, and poke holes in wrap to vent. Microwave on HIGH until fork-tender, about 8 minutes. Uncover and set aside.
2. Melt 1 tablespoon of the butter in a medium-size cast-iron skillet over medium. Stir in crushed crackers; cook, stirring occasionally, until crackers are lightly toasted, about 2 minutes. Remove from heat, and stir in parsley. Transfer mixture to a small bowl, and set aside. Wipe skillet clean.
3. Add remaining 4 tablespoons butter to skillet; melt over medium-high. Add onion; cook, stirring occasionally, until softened, about 5 minutes. Add garlic; cook, stirring occasionally, until fragrant, about 1 minute. Sprinkle evenly with flour; cook, stirring constantly, until mixture is light brown, about 1 minute. Gradually whisk in milk, and bring to a simmer over medium-high. Simmer, whisking constantly, until mixture is very thick, about 2 minutes. Reduce heat to medium-low; stir in Dijon mustard, salt, pepper, and 2 cups of the cheese. Cook, stirring constantly, until cheese is melted and smooth, about 2 minutes (mixture will be very thick). Stir in mayonnaise. Fold in steamed broccoli until well combined. Cook, stirring occasionally, until sauce has thickened again, 12 to 15 minutes. Season with additional salt to taste.
4. Sprinkle casserole with remaining 1 cup cheese. Remove from heat, and cover; let stand, covered, until cheese is fully melted, about 10 minutes. Uncover and sprinkle with toasted crackers. Serve warm.

Cranberry-Glazed Green Beans

ACTIVE 40 MIN. - TOTAL 40 MIN.

SERVES 8

- 1 lb. fresh green beans, trimmed
- 2 thick-cut bacon slices, chopped
- 2 small shallots, thinly sliced crosswise (¾ cup)
- ½ cup sweetened dried cranberries
- ¼ cup pure maple syrup
- 2 tsp. kosher salt, plus more for salting water
- ¼ tsp. black pepper

1. Bring a large pot of salted water to a boil over high. Add green beans; cook, undisturbed, until tender-crisp, 3 to 5 minutes. Drain and rinse under cold water. Transfer to a paper towel-lined baking sheet, and pat dry; set aside.
2. Heat a large nonstick skillet over medium. Add bacon; cook, stirring occasionally, until crisp, about 8 minutes. Remove from heat. Transfer bacon to a paper towel-lined plate; reserve drippings in skillet.
3. Add sliced shallots to bacon drippings in skillet. Cook over medium, stirring often, until shallots are translucent, 3 to 5 minutes. Add cranberries and maple syrup; cook, stirring often, until cranberries are fully coated and sauce is well combined, 2 to 3 minutes. Stir in cooked green beans, salt, and pepper; cook, stirring occasionally, until green beans are tender and sauce thickens enough to lightly coat beans, about 6 minutes. Remove from heat; sprinkle with cooked bacon. Serve warm.

Brown Butter Mashed Sweet Potatoes

Enriched with nutty brown butter and a handful of crispy fried herbs, these creamy sweet potatoes make an elegant accompaniment for this festive meal.

ACTIVE 20 MIN. - TOTAL 50 MIN.

SERVES 10

- 4 large sweet potatoes, peeled and cut into 1-inch pieces (about 9 cups)
- 2 garlic cloves, smashed
- 2½ tsp. kosher salt, divided, plus more to taste
- ½ cup unsalted butter
- 15 small fresh sage leaves, rosemary sprigs, or thyme sprigs (or any combination), patted dry
- ½ cup whole milk, divided, plus more as needed
- 2 Tbsp. pure maple syrup
- ¾ tsp. coarsely ground pepper

1. Place 2 quarts cold tap water, sweet potatoes, garlic, and 1 teaspoon of the salt in a large Dutch oven; bring to a boil over medium-high. Reduce heat to medium-low. Cook, undisturbed, until sweet potatoes are fork-tender, 15 to 20 minutes. Drain well, and set aside.
2. Meanwhile, heat butter in a medium skillet over medium, stirring constantly, until it melts and begins to turn golden brown, 4 to 5 minutes. Add herbs; cook, undisturbed, until crisp, 30 seconds to 1 minute. Working quickly, remove skillet from heat. Using a slotted spoon, transfer fried herbs to a paper towel-lined plate. Pour brown butter into a small heatproof bowl; set aside.
3. Transfer half of the sweet potatoes to a food processor, and add ¼ cup of the milk. Process until almost smooth, about 1 minute. Add maple syrup, pepper, and 2 tablespoons of the brown butter. Add remaining sweet potatoes, ¼ cup milk, and 1½ teaspoons salt. Process until whipped and smooth, 1 to 2 minutes, stopping to scrape down sides as needed. Add more milk 2 tablespoons at a time, if needed, until mixture reaches desired consistency. Season with additional salt to taste.
4. Transfer mixture to a serving dish. Drizzle with remaining brown butter, and sprinkle with fried herbs. Serve warm.

CRANBERRY-
GLAZED GREEN
BEANS

STOVETOP
BROCCOLI
CASSEROLE

BROWN BUTTER
MASHED SWEET
POTATOES

Hold the Marshmallows

Our wholesome take on the classic side is just as good with less sugar

Meringue-Topped Sweet Potato Casserole

ACTIVE 20 MIN. - TOTAL 2 HOURS, 10 MIN.

SERVES 8

- 4½ lb. sweet potatoes, scrubbed (5 large sweet potatoes)
- ¼ cup unsalted butter
- ¼ cup packed light brown sugar
- ¼ cup half-and-half
- 1 tsp. ground cinnamon
- ½ tsp. ground ginger
- ½ tsp. vanilla extract
- 3 large eggs, separated
- ¾ tsp. plus ⅛ tsp. kosher salt, divided
- ¼ tsp. cream of tartar
- 6 Tbsp. superfine sugar

1. Preheat oven to 400°F. Prick sweet potatoes all over using a fork. Place on an aluminum foil–lined large rimmed baking sheet. Bake until very tender, 1 hour, 10 minutes to 1 hour, 20 minutes. Let cool slightly, about 10 minutes. Reduce oven temperature to 350°F.
2. Carefully peel sweet potatoes, and place flesh in a large bowl; discard skins. Add butter, brown sugar, half-and-half, cinnamon, ginger, vanilla, egg yolks (reserve whites for meringue), and ¾ teaspoon of the salt; beat with an electric mixer on medium-high speed until smooth, about 1 minute. Remove and clean beaters.
3. Coat an 11- x 7-inch baking dish with cooking spray. Spoon potato mixture into prepared baking dish, and spread into an even layer. Bake at 350°F until edges start to pull away from sides of dish, about 30 minutes.
4. Meanwhile, beat reserved egg whites with cream of tartar and remaining ⅛ teaspoon salt in a large bowl with an electric mixer on high speed until foamy, 20 to 30 seconds. Gradually add superfine sugar, 1 tablespoon at a time, beating on high speed until stiff peaks

form, about 2 minutes. Spoon meringue over potato mixture in baking dish. Using the back of the spoon, gently spread the meringue to cover potatoes, leaving a ¼-inch border around edges. Bake at 350°F until the meringue topping is golden brown, 10 to 15 minutes.

GOOD FOR YOU!
Sweet potatoes are naturally rich in beta-carotene, which your body uses to make vitamin A.

Before Recipe Makeover:

CALORIES: **470** – SUGAR: **41 G** – FAT: **17 G**

After Recipe Makeover:

CALORIES: **308** – SUGAR: **24 G** – FAT: **9 G**

Granola Goals

This warmly spiced make-ahead breakfast is great for overnight guests

SIMPLE SWAP
You can use the same amount of sliced almonds or chopped walnuts or pistachios in place of the pecans.

Honey-Chai Granola

ACTIVE 5 MIN. · TOTAL 1 HOUR, 30 MIN.
SERVES 24

- 3 cups uncooked old-fashioned regular rolled oats
- 1 cup unsweetened shredded coconut
- 1 cup pecan halves, roughly chopped
- ½ cup packed light brown sugar
- 1 tsp. kosher salt
- 1 Tbsp. ground cinnamon
- 2 tsp. ground ginger
- ¾ tsp. ground cardamom
- ¼ tsp. allspice
- ¼ tsp. ground cloves
- ¼ tsp. black pepper
- ½ cup honey
- ½ cup liquid coconut oil
  Orange segments and whole-milk strained (Greek-style) yogurt

1. Preheat oven to 300°F with racks in top third and lower third positions. Line 2 baking sheets with parchment paper or aluminum foil. Stir together oats, coconut, pecans, brown sugar, and salt in a large bowl until combined. Add cinnamon, ginger, cardamom, allspice, cloves, and pepper; stir until combined. Set aside.

2. Stir together honey and coconut oil in a microwavable glass measuring cup. Heat on MEDIUM (50% power) until honey is runny, 30 seconds to 1 minute. Remove from microwave; whisk until combined. Pour over oat mixture in bowl. Stir together thoroughly until combined.

3. Divide mixture evenly between prepared baking sheets; bake in preheated oven, stirring every 15 minutes, until granola is evenly golden brown and toasted, 40 to 45 minutes. Let cool completely on baking sheets, about 45 minutes. Serve with orange segments and yogurt. Store in an airtight container for up to 2 weeks.

COOKING SCHOOL

TIPS AND TRICKS FROM THE SOUTH'S MOST TRUSTED KITCHEN

Gobble Up Leftovers

How to get more mileage out of your Thanksgiving feast

Southern Staple
Tabasco Brand Pepper Sauce

Edmund McIlhenny created Tabasco hot sauce in 1868. A keen gardener, he was given the seeds of *Capsicum frutescens* peppers. After growing his first commercial crop on Avery Island, Louisiana, he made them into a sauce that he sold to local grocers for $1 a bottle. McIlhenny called it Tabasco, the plant's common name. It is thought that the moniker has Indigenous Mexican origins and roughly translates to "place where the soil is humid" or "place of the coral or oyster shell." Over 150 years later, this condiment is the default in much of the country and is sold all over the world.

Turkey Pita Pockets
Toss together ½ cup each sliced **cucumber** and **tomatoes**, ¼ cup sliced **red onion**, 2 Tbsp. chopped **Kalamata olives**, 2 Tbsp. **olive oil**, and 1 Tbsp. **lemon juice** in a bowl. Sauté 3 cups cooked **turkey** with 1 Tbsp. **olive oil** and ¾ tsp. **Greek seasoning** in a skillet until warm. Divide among 6 **pita rounds**; add tomato mixture, **lettuce**, and **tzatziki sauce**. Serves 6

Creamy Turkey Pasta Bake
Sauté 6 cups sliced **collard greens** and 3 cups sliced **mushrooms** with 2 Tbsp. **oil** in a skillet over medium until tender. Stir in 1 lb. cooked **pasta**, 3 cups cooked **turkey**, 2½ cups **cream**, 1¼ cups shredded **Parmesan**, 2 tsp. **kosher salt**, and ¾ tsp. **black pepper**. Transfer to a 13- x 9-inch baking dish; top with 1½ cups shredded **mozzarella**. Bake at 375°F for 15 minutes. Serves 8

Turkey Frittata
Sauté ½ cup sliced **red onion** in 1 Tbsp. **olive oil** in a 10-inch cast-iron skillet over medium until tender. Stir in 2 cups cooked **vegetables** and 1 cup cooked **turkey**. Remove from heat. Whisk 12 **large eggs**, 1 cup shredded **Gruyère**, 1 tsp. **kosher salt**, and ½ tsp. **black pepper** in a bowl; pour into skillet. Bake at 400°F until set, 18 to 20 minutes. Serves 8

Barbecue Turkey Sandwiches
Bring ½ cup **barbecue sauce**, ¼ cup **cranberry sauce**, and 1 Tbsp. **apple cider vinegar** to a simmer in a saucepan over medium. Cook until slightly thickened, about 5 minutes. Stir in 2 cups cooked **turkey**. Divide mixture among bottoms of 4 toasted **hamburger buns**. Add **coleslaw** and **dill pickle slices**, and cover with hamburger bun tops. Serves 4

December

CRANBERRY
POINSETTIA
PUNCH

CRANBERRY
OLD-FASHIONEDS

BOOZY
CRANBERRIES

CRANBERRY
MARGARITAS

Yes, You Cran!

Brighten up your cocktails with cranberries

Cranberry Old-Fashioneds

ACTIVE 5 MIN. - TOTAL 5 MIN.
SERVES 2

Place 2 large **cocktail ice cubes** in
2 chilled rocks glasses. Divide ½ cup
bourbon, 2 Tbsp. **Cranberry Simple
Syrup** (recipe below) and 4 dashes
orange-flavored bitters evenly between
glasses, and stir to combine. Place
Boozy Cranberries (recipe at far right)
and an **orange peel strip** in each glass.
(Alternatively, thread cranberries
onto wooden picks and set on rims of
glasses.) Serve immediately.

Cranberry Margaritas

ACTIVE 10 MIN. - TOTAL 10 MIN.
SERVES 2

Place ¼ cup **Cranberry Simple Syrup**
(recipe at far right) in a small shallow
dish; place **margarita salt** in a separate
shallow dish. Invert 2 glasses into
simple syrup to coat rims. Place each
glass into margarita salt to coat rims. Set
aside. Add ½ cup **blanco tequila**, 2 Tbsp.
orange liqueur (such as Cointreau),
6 Tbsp. **fresh lime juice** (from about
2 limes), and 6 Tbsp. **Cranberry Simple
Syrup** to a cocktail shaker filled with
ice. Shake until well chilled, about
15 seconds. Fill prepared glasses with
ice, and strain margarita into glasses.
Garnish with **lime wheels**, and serve
immediately.

Cranberry Poinsettia Punch

ACTIVE 20 MIN. - TOTAL 20 MIN.,
PLUS 9 HOURS FREEZING
SERVES 12

Prepare the ice mold: Stir together
2 cups **cranberry juice blend** and
1 cup **water** in a liquid measuring cup
until combined. Scatter 1 cup **frozen
cranberries** around bottom of a
decorative Bundt pan. Slice 1 **medium
blood orange** into thin rings; arrange
evenly around cranberries. Pour 1½ cups
of the juice mixture over cranberries
and orange slices. Freeze, uncovered,
until firm, about 1 hour. Meanwhile, store
remaining juice mixture in refrigerator.
Once ice mold is firm, remove from
freezer. Scatter with additional 1 cup
frozen cranberries. Pour remaining
juice mixture over cranberries. Freeze,
uncovered, until completely frozen, at
least 8 hours or up to 1 week. Prepare
the punch: Stir together 2 cups chilled
cranberry juice blend, 1 cup chilled
fresh blood orange juice (from about
6 blood oranges), and 1 cup **orange
liqueur** (such as Grand Marnier) in a
12-cup punch bowl until combined.
Store, covered, in refrigerator up to
2 days. To serve, remove ice mold from
freezer. Fill a large bowl with **hot water**,
and gently lower Bundt pan into hot
water to loosen ice mold, holding for
10 to 15 seconds. Invert onto a baking
sheet, and remove pan. Carefully
transfer ice mold from baking sheet
into mixture in punch bowl. Gently
pour 2 (750-milliliter) bottles chilled
sparkling dry rosé down sides of punch
bowl. Serve immediately garnished with
blood orange slices.

Boozy Cranberries

ACTIVE 15 MIN. - TOTAL 1 HOUR
MAKES ABOUT 1 CUP

Stir together ½ cup packed **light brown
sugar**, ⅓ cup **water**, 3 (3- x 1-inch) **orange
peel strips** plus 2 Tbsp. **fresh juice** (from
1 medium orange), 1 (3-inch) **cinnamon
stick**, 3 **whole cloves**, and ¼ tsp. **kosher
salt** in a medium saucepan. Bring to
a boil over high, stirring constantly.
Boil, stirring constantly, until sugar has
dissolved, about 2 minutes. Reduce heat
to medium-low, and add 1 cup **dried
cranberries.** Simmer over medium
to medium-low, stirring occasionally,
until cranberries start to soften, about
5 minutes. Remove from heat, and stir
in ¼ cup **bourbon**. Let stand, uncovered,
45 minutes. Transfer to a jar or
resealable container. Store, covered, in
refrigerator up to 1 month.

Cranberry Simple Syrup

ACTIVE 20 MIN. - TOTAL 35 MIN.
MAKES 2 CUPS

Combine 1½ cups **water**, ½ cup
granulated sugar, ½ cup **maple syrup**,
2 cups **fresh cranberries**, and ¼ tsp.
kosher salt in a medium saucepan.
Bring to a simmer over high, stirring
occasionally. Reduce heat to medium-
low, and simmer, stirring occasionally,
until cranberries have softened and
burst, about 10 minutes. Cook 3 minutes,
mashing cranberries with a wooden
spoon. Remove from heat, and let
cool slightly, about 10 minutes. Pour
cranberry mixture through a fine mesh
strainer into a medium bowl; discard
solids. Transfer Cranberry Simple Syrup
to a jar or resealable container. Store,
covered, in refrigerator up to 2 weeks.

Juicy Fruit

Sweet-tart satsumas deliver sunny citrus flavor all winter long

Satsuma Upside-Down Cake

ACTIVE 25 MIN. - TOTAL 1 HOUR, 15 MIN.

SERVES 8 TO 10

Baking spray

2 Tbsp. unsalted butter, melted

1 cup granulated sugar, divided

8 medium satsumas, divided

2 cups bleached cake flour

¼ cup packed light brown sugar

2½ tsp. baking powder

1 tsp. kosher salt

¼ tsp. ground cloves

⅔ cup whole buttermilk, at room temperature

2 large eggs, at room temperature, beaten

⅓ cup canola oil

2 tsp. vanilla extract

Whipped cream (optional)

1. Preheat oven to 350°F. Spray a 9- x 2-inch round cake pan with baking spray. Line bottom of pan with parchment paper; coat parchment paper evenly with melted butter and ¼ cup of the granulated sugar.

2. Grate zest from satsumas to yield 1 teaspoon; place zest in a large bowl. Peel 6 satsumas, and cut crosswise into ⅜-inch-thick slices; pat slices dry with paper towels. Arrange slices, cut sides down, in prepared pan, covering bottom of pan in a single, even layer and trimming slices as needed to fit.

3. Add flour, brown sugar, baking powder, salt, cloves, and remaining ¾ cup granulated sugar to large bowl with satsuma zest, whisking until combined and no sugar clumps remain. Juice remaining 2 satsumas to yield ⅓ cup. Whisk in buttermilk, eggs, juice, oil, and vanilla just until combined. Spread batter evenly over satsumas in pan.

4. Bake in preheated oven until a wooden pick inserted in center comes out clean and cake starts to pull away from sides of pan, 38 to 42 minutes. Let cool in pan on a wire rack for 10 minutes. Run a knife around edge of cake to loosen; invert onto a serving plate. Serve warm or at room temperature. Top slices with whipped cream, if desired.

Satsuma Paloma

ACTIVE 10 MIN. - TOTAL 10 MIN.

SERVES 1

Stir together 4 tsp. **granulated sugar**, 1 Tbsp. **kosher salt**, and ½ tsp. **chile powder** on a small plate. Squeeze juice of 1 **satsuma** into a small bowl. Dip rim of a glass in juice and then in sugar mixture. Fill a glass two-thirds full with **ice**. Fill a cocktail shaker two-thirds full with **ice**; add ¼ cup **blanco tequila**, ¼ cup **fresh satsuma juice**, 1 Tbsp. **fresh lime juice**, and 1 Tbsp. **light agave nectar**. Cover and shake vigorously until chilled, 15 to 30 seconds. Strain into prepared glass, and top with 2 Tbsp. **grapefruit-flavored sparkling water**. Garnish drink with a **satsuma slice**.

SATSUMA PALOMA

CITRUS TO SAVOR
Take advantage of these sweet Southern gems before their season draws to a close. Add satsuma segments to grain or vegetable salads for a pop of color (they're lovely with bitter greens like radicchio and endive), or blend them into fruit smoothies. You can also roast satsuma halves alongside ham, pork chops, or chicken and then squeeze them over the meat before serving for a bright finish.

SATSUMA
UPSIDE-DOWN
CAKE

Southern Heart, Filipino Soul

A humble fritter combines chef Cristina Quackenbush's two biggest
food influences in one memory-filled appetizer

CRISTINA QUACKENBUSH isn't a native Southerner, but the first time she set foot in New Orleans, she knew she belonged. "It was 1999," she remembers. "Everyone was all abuzz because Y2K was going to happen and they thought the world was going to end. I fell so in love with this place that I didn't want to leave. Within two weeks, I had moved my entire family down."

More than two decades later, New Orleans is still her home, but it's also a much bigger part of her story than she would have ever imagined. Quackenbush, who was born in the Philippines, has built her own community near the place where Filipino people first settled in America around 260 years ago. She has also fostered a successful cooking career and a reputation as the "Queen of Filipino Soul Food" in the South.

Quackenbush moved to Evansville, Indiana, from the Philippines at the age of 4 when her mom married her American stepfather. The transition was hard, she says. Eager to assimilate, her mom stopped speaking to her in Tagalog and enrolled her in school to help her learn English. The only tether Quackenbush had to her culture was food. Staple Filipino dishes like mechado (stew), adobo, and curry were on the weeknight dinner rotation, but special occasions were when her mother really showed out.

"At the holidays, everyone asked my mom to cook Filipino food," she remembers. "She was the one person who brought something that wasn't American food, and everyone always wanted what she made."

One of Quackenbush's favorite Christmas dishes is shrimp ukoy, a crispy seafood fritter that was often the first appetizer snapped up at large gatherings with her extended stepfamily. It's the perfect mash-up of her two cultures: The fried patty laced with sweet potato and carrot was similar to the Southern-style fritters prepared by her stepfather's relatives, and the vinegar dipping sauce sated Quackenbush's craving for the tangy and sour flavor profiles common in Filipino cuisine.

Now, when Christmas rolls around each year, Quackenbush steps into her mother's shoes. In the kitchen of her Victorian-style shotgun house, she sets to work making the Filipino dishes that her family grew up on and that her grandkids are already requesting by name.

Shrimp Ukoy

ACTIVE 45 MIN. - TOTAL 45 MIN.
SERVES 10 TO 12

FRITTERS
- 2 lb. medium-size peeled and deveined raw shrimp, finely chopped
- 1 cup grated sweet potato (from 1 small peeled sweet potato)
- ½ cup shredded carrot (from 1 large peeled carrot)
- 1 large egg, lightly beaten
- 2 Tbsp. fish sauce
- 3 garlic cloves, finely chopped
- ½ tsp. black pepper
- 1 cup cornstarch
- ½ cup all-purpose flour
- 2 cups vegetable oil
- Kosher salt, to taste

DIPPING SAUCE
- ¾ cup apple cider vinegar
- 1 Tbsp. finely chopped shallot (from 1 small shallot)
- 1 Tbsp. light brown sugar
- 1 Tbsp. soy sauce
- 1 Tbsp. fish sauce
- 1 Tbsp. chopped fresh cilantro
- 1½ tsp. finely chopped garlic (about 2 medium cloves)

1. Prepare the Fritters: Preheat oven to 200°F. Stir together shrimp, sweet potato, carrot, egg, fish sauce, garlic, and pepper in a large bowl. Whisk together cornstarch, flour, and 1¼ cups water in a separate large bowl. Add shrimp mixture to bowl with cornstarch mixture, and stir to combine.
2. Pour oil into a large cast-iron skillet, and heat over medium-high to 360°F. Working in batches, spoon about ¼ cup batter for each Fritter into hot oil, using a spoon to spread batter into 2- to 3-inch-wide circles or ovals. Use a slotted spoon to coax any stray batter pieces to join with circles. Fry until golden brown and crispy on both sides, about 2 to 3 minutes total, flipping halfway through frying. Using a slotted spoon, transfer Fritters to a paper towel-lined plate or baking sheet to drain. Transfer hot Fritters to a wire rack set over a baking sheet, and sprinkle with salt to taste. Keep Fritters warm in preheated oven until ready to serve. Repeat procedure with remaining batter, stirring in bowl between batches as cornstarch will separate and settle.
3. Prepare the Dipping Sauce: Stir together vinegar, 3 tablespoons water, shallot, brown sugar, soy sauce, fish sauce, cilantro, and garlic in a small bowl until brown sugar has dissolved. Pour Dipping Sauce into 1 bowl or several small bowls, and serve with hot Fritters.

The Legend of Great-Aunt Inez's Sand Tarts

Not all icons are born. Some are baked by a 1950s home economics teacher with a penchant for pecans

IT WAS 2016, and it was my first Christmas without my Great-Aunt Inez, my Maw Maw's second-oldest sister, who was the yin to my yang, my Ya-Ya with the most endearing eccentricities, a kindred spirit who encouraged my creative pursuits and curious nature. She was the first person to say to me, after I'd performed a one-woman show at age 5 in her kitchen, "Bébé, someday you're going to New York City!" She believed in me, so I believed in myself.

I was still trying to make my dream as a writer in New York City come true when I got the news that she'd passed away peacefully at 92.

That year, I thought I'd bake her famous sand tarts for the first time and share them with new friends in her honor. I dug up her handwritten recipe card, a photo I'd saved on my phone's camera roll from my last visit home. The cookies came out warm and tan, just like her. I coated them in "Louisiana snow"—powdered sugar—then braced for the chill of the real thing en route to the Upper East Side.

"Did you bring something Cajun?" the host asked. She was a food editor, so I knew she'd appreciate them. It was my shtick, being Cajun, something I could rely on when I felt out of place in the concrete jungle. In a city where I knew no one, at least I knew myself. Or so I thought.

I didn't know I'd be walking into one of the most embarrassing moments of my adult life.

She grabbed a tart, took a bite, made a face, and asked, "Aren't these just Pennsylvania Dutch cookies?"

"Look them up," she said. "I think they're the same." Before I could say anything else, she'd turned to greet the next guest. I ran to the bathroom to Google "Dutch tarts Pittsburgh." There it was. With my back against the door, I scrolled through aliases like "Pecan Snowball Cookies," "Sandies," and "Mexican Wedding Cookies." Mais là! She was right. I wasn't just mortified; I was shaken to my core. No one had questioned my Cajunness before.

Alone on the subway, I wondered: How could Great-Aunt Inez's sand tarts not be Cajun? They were a part of my Boudreaux-LeBlanc family traditions from baptisms to boucheries.

I became obsessed with discovering the origins of this recipe, and oddly, when I finally uncovered the mystery, I liked the real story even better.

"She got it from a cafeteria worker at the school," my cousin Tommy, her son, told me.

When she was a home economics teacher, no one could keep her away from the cafeteria between classes. She loved to veillée, or visit, and learn tricks from the skilled cooks in the kitchen. Of course she added her own touch to the passed-on cookie recipe. Instead of keeping the tarts sphere-shaped, she pinched them into rounded rectangles (and sometimes half-moons), so she could monitor the edges. Golden corners meant they were ready. She also added five times the amount of nuts the recipe called for. She didn't have pricey ingredients or high-tech appliances, but she had plenty of pecan trees.

I learned that the thing Great-Aunt Inez loved most was teaching others about what food could do for the survival of our culture. In this case, it meant turning an American dish into her own, and incorporating it into our South Louisiana customs.

That's when it clicked. Suddenly, I felt closer to my Great-Aunt Inez than I ever had when she was alive. She made Pennsylvania Dutch cookies—or sandies or whatever you want to call them—with the ingredients she had on hand. That's the Cajun way, and that's what I am doing in this new city of mine. I think she'd be proud. —Megan Broussard

Inez's Sand Tarts

The original card reads: "This recipe was handed to me by word of mouth. I have changed it at times. For instance, it called for 1 cup of pecans. I have added 1 and then 3, depending on the harvest of my 3 pecan trees. The oven temperature depends on the stove and times for baking may vary."

ACTIVE 30 MIN. · TOTAL 2 HOURS

MAKES ABOUT 38

- 1 **lb. butter, at room temperature**
- 1 **cup powdered sugar, plus more for rolling**
- 2 **tsp. vanilla extract**
- 5 **cups all-purpose flour, divided**
- 3 **cups chopped pecans**

1. Place butter in a large bowl. Cream butter and powdered sugar together with a spoon.
2. Add vanilla, 3 cups of flour, and pecans. Continue creaming with spoon until combined.
3. Preheat oven to 350°F.
4. Stir in remaining 2 cups flour. This will make a very stiff dough and may be a little messy. Shape into small rectangles, and place on two ungreased baking sheets.
5. Bake in batches for 25 to 30 minutes or to your desired degree of brownness.
6. Let cookies cool thoroughly, and roll in powdered sugar.

Host a Drop-In Gathering

Get everyone in the spirit with easy, elegant starters and fun drinks

Fancy Pigs in Blankets

Finishing touch: Sprinkle these pastry-wrapped bites with everything-bagel seasoning for a flavor boost.

ACTIVE 35 MIN. · TOTAL 50 MIN.

MAKES 40

- 2 frozen puff pastry sheets, thawed (from 1 [17.3-oz.] pkg.)
  All-purpose flour, for work surface
- 1 (1-lb.) pkg. hickory-smoked sausage (such as Conecuh), halved lengthwise and cut into 2-inch pieces (40 pieces)
- 2 large eggs, lightly beaten
- 2 Tbsp. poppy seeds
- ½ cup mayonnaise
- ¼ cup sour cream
- 3 Tbsp. Dijon mustard
- 3 Tbsp. honey
- ¼ tsp. kosher salt
  Snipped fresh chives, for garnish

1. Preheat oven to 400°F. Line 2 baking sheets with parchment paper; set aside.
2. Unfold 1 pastry sheet on a lightly floured work surface; roll into a 15- x 10-inch rectangle. Prick all over with a fork. Cut pastry sheet into 20 (2½-inch) squares. Repeat with remaining pastry sheet.
3. Place 1 sausage piece diagonally in center of 1 pastry square. Fold 1 corner over sausage, tightly tucking corner under sausage. Fold opposite corner over sausage, overlapping pastry and tucking corner under bottom side. Transfer to 1 prepared baking sheet. Repeat with remaining pastry squares and sausage, spacing 1 inch apart on prepared baking sheets. Brush with egg; sprinkle evenly with poppy seeds; chill for 15 minutes.

4. Meanwhile, in a medium bowl stir together mayonnaise, sour cream, mustard, honey, and salt until well combined. Chill sauce until ready to serve.
5. Bake pastries in preheated oven until golden brown, 18 to 20 minutes. Transfer to a platter. Garnish with chives and serve with sauce.

Ambrosia Party Punch

ACTIVE 10 MIN. · TOTAL 10 MIN.

SERVES 12

- 4 cups orange juice
- 3 cups chilled coconut water (such as Vita Coco)
- 1¼ cups chilled pineapple juice
- ¼ cup syrup from maraschino cherries (from 1 [10-oz.] jar), plus cherries for garnish
- 1 small lemon, thinly sliced crosswise
- 1 small orange, thinly sliced crosswise
- 1 (750-milliliter) bottle chilled sparkling rosé or 3 (11½-oz.) cans sparkling lemon beverage (such as San Pellegrino)
  Fresh mint leaves

1. Stir together orange juice, coconut water, pineapple juice, and syrup in a punch bowl or large pitcher. Top with lemon and orange slices.
2. Pour about ¾ cup punch into each cup; top with about ¼ cup sparkling rosé or sparkling-lemon beverage; garnish with cherries and mint leaves.

From trimming the tree to setting the table, nobody celebrates the season better than Southerners.

AMBROSIA
PARTY PUNCH

FANCY
PIGS IN
BLANKETS

TWO-LAYER
PIMIENTO-AND-
CHEESE DIP
WITH SMOKED
ALMONDS

CORNBREAD
CROSTINI

PERFECTLY SPICY
PEPPER-JELLY
MEATBALLS

Cornbread Crostini

ACTIVE 20 MIN. - TOTAL 1 HOUR, 40 MIN.
SERVES 12

- ¼ cup vegetable oil, divided
- 2 cups self-rising yellow cornmeal mix
- ¼ cup cooked and crumbled bacon (3 slices)
- ½ tsp. black pepper
- ¼ tsp. cayenne pepper
- 1 cup whole buttermilk
- 4 oz. smoked Cheddar cheese, shredded (about 1 cup)
- ½ cup canned collard greens, drained
- 2 large eggs, lightly beaten
- ½ cup butter, melted

1. Preheat oven to 425°F. Add 2 tablespoons of the oil to a 10-inch cast-iron skillet; place in oven to preheat.
2. Meanwhile, in a medium bowl, stir together cornmeal mix, bacon, black pepper, cayenne, buttermilk, Cheddar, collard greens, eggs, and remaining 2 tablespoons oil until combined.
3. Carefully remove hot skillet from oven. Immediately add cornmeal mixture to skillet; do not stir. Bake in preheated oven until a wooden pick inserted in center comes out clean, about 20 minutes. Immediately invert cornbread onto a wire rack, and let cool completely, about 30 minutes. Reduce oven temperature to 300°F.
4. Line 2 baking sheets with parchment paper, and set aside. Cut cornbread in half to create 2 half-moons. Cut crosswise into ¼-inch-thick slices; place on prepared baking sheets. Brush both sides of slices with melted butter. Bake, turning halfway through cook time, until crispy, 35 to 40 minutes. Let cool 10 minutes; serve.

Two-Layer Pimiento-and-Cheese Dip with Smoked Almonds

ACTIVE 15 MIN. - TOTAL 15 MIN.
SERVES 12

- 8 oz. sharp white Cheddar cheese, shredded (about 2 cups)
- 4 oz. cream cheese, softened
- ⅞ tsp. kosher salt, divided
- ½ tsp. cayenne pepper
- ¾ cup half-and-half
- 3 (4-oz.) jars sliced pimientos, drained and patted dry
- 1 (1½-oz.) sourdough bread slice, torn and lightly toasted (about 1 cup torn)
- ¼ cup chopped smoked almonds, plus more for garnish
- 1 garlic clove
- 1½ tsp. red wine vinegar
- ¼ cup extra-virgin olive oil
- Torn fresh flat-leaf parsley leaves
- Smoked paprika, for garnish
- For serving: endive leaves, baby heirloom carrots, and Smoky Cornbread Crostini (at left)

1. Add Cheddar, cream cheese, ¾ teaspoon salt, and cayenne to food processor bowl; process until crumbly, 30 seconds, stopping to scrape down sides as needed. Add half-and-half; process until smooth, about 1 minute. Transfer to a medium serving bowl; set aside. Let stand at room temperature while preparing pimiento sauce.
2. Wipe processor bowl clean. Add pimientos, bread, almonds, garlic, vinegar, and remaining ⅛ teaspoon salt to processor bowl; process until finely chopped, about 30 seconds, stopping to scrape down sides as needed. With processor running, gradually pour olive oil through food chute, and process until smooth, about 1 minute.
3. Top Cheddar mixture in bowl with pimiento sauce. Garnish with additional chopped almonds, parsley, and smoked paprika. Serve with endive, carrots, and Smoky Cornbread Crostini.

Perfectly Spicy Pepper-Jelly Meatballs

ACTIVE 25 MIN. - TOTAL 3 HOURS, 40 MIN.
SERVES 10 TO 12

- 2 lb. 85/15 lean ground beef
- 2 large eggs, lightly beaten
- ⅔ cup dry breadcrumbs
- 2 tsp. Worcestershire sauce
- 1 tsp. kosher salt, divided
- ½ tsp. black pepper, divided
- 2 (13-oz.) jars red pepper jelly
- ½ cup bottled chili sauce
- ½ cup bottled barbecue sauce
- 1 tsp. Dijon mustard
- ½ tsp. cayenne pepper
- ¼ cup finely chopped Peppadew peppers (from 5 peppers)
- ¼ cup finely chopped fresh flat-leaf parsley

1. Preheat oven to 400°F. Line 2 large rimmed baking sheets with aluminum foil. Lightly coat an 8-quart slow cooker with cooking spray; set aside.
2. In a large bowl, stir together ground beef, eggs, breadcrumbs, Worcestershire sauce, ½ teaspoon of the salt, and ¼ teaspoon of the black pepper. Mix thoroughly. Shape into 34 meatballs (about 2 tablespoons each). Arrange on prepared baking sheets.
3. Bake in preheated oven until a thermometer inserted in center registers 160°F, about 14 minutes. Remove from oven; transfer meatballs to prepared slow cooker, discarding any liquid from baking sheets.
4. Whisk together pepper jelly, chili sauce, barbecue sauce, mustard, cayenne, remaining ½ teaspoon salt, and remaining ¼ teaspoon black pepper in a medium bowl. Pour mixture over meatballs in slow cooker; toss to coat. Cover and cook on LOW, stirring halfway through cook time, until sauce thickens, 3 to 4 hours. Transfer meatballs to a platter; top with Peppadew peppers, parsley, and sauce.

Feast with Your Family

A special (and doable) meal to wow everyone

ROASTED
BROCCOLINI
WITH PECANS
AND LEMON

SOUTHERN
CRACKLIN' PORK
ROAST WITH
LEMONY HERB
SAUCE

TWICE-BAKED
DUCHESS
POTATOES

Southern Cracklin' Pork Roast with Lemony Herb Sauce

ACTIVE 1 HOUR, 10 MIN. - TOTAL 5 HOURS, PLUS 12 HOURS CHILLING

SERVES 12

1 (8- to 10-lb.) pork belly with skin
2 Tbsp. olive oil
1 medium-size yellow onion, chopped (1½ cups)
8 cups chopped fresh collard greens (from 1 [12-oz.] bunch)
1 Tbsp. fennel seeds
4 Tbsp. plus 1 tsp. kosher salt, divided
1 cup chopped fresh flat-leaf parsley
12 garlic cloves, minced (about ¼ cup)
2 Tbsp. finely chopped fresh rosemary (from 4 [6-inch] sprigs)
4 tsp. finely grated lemon zest (from 2 lemons)
1 Tbsp. black pepper
Lemony Herb Sauce (recipe follows)

1. Place pork belly, skin side down, on a work surface. Using a sharp knife, score meat in a crosshatch pattern, about 1 inch deep by 2 inches wide. Starting with one short side, roll pork belly into a tight spiral; cut a shallow line in skin to mark where it overlaps. Unroll spiral; turn pork belly skin side up. Using shallow line as a guide, slice to remove skin from portion of pork belly that will be inside the roll. (Any skin left inside roll will not get crispy.) Carefully score remaining skin in a crosshatch pattern, about ¼ inch deep by 1 inch wide. Turn pork belly skin side down; set aside.
2. Heat the oil in a large skillet over medium-high. Add onion; cook, stirring often, until translucent, about 3 minutes. Add collard greens, fennel seeds, and 1 teaspoon of the salt; cook, stirring often, until just wilted, about 2 minutes. Remove from heat; let cool, uncovered, 10 minutes.
3. With skin side down, sprinkle pork belly evenly with parsley, garlic, rosemary, lemon zest, pepper, collard greens mixture, and remaining 4 tablespoons salt; pat mixture into pork. Starting with the shorter, skin-removed side, reroll pork belly into a tight spiral (skin-removed side should be on the interior of the spiral). Tie spiral tightly in 1-inch intervals with kitchen twine. Place in a roasting pan fitted with a rack, and chill, uncovered, 12 hours.
4. Preheat oven to 275°F. Bake until a thermometer inserted into thickest

portion of pork registers 160°F, 4 to 6 hours. Remove from oven, and increase oven temperature to 500°F. Bake until skin is crispy and deeply browned, about 25 minutes, basting with drippings during last 10 minutes of cook time. Remove from oven, and let rest 30 minutes. Slice with a serrated knife. Serve with Lemony Herb Sauce.

Lemony Herb Sauce

ACTIVE TIME 5 MIN. - TOTAL TIME 5 MIN.

MAKES ABOUT 1½ CUPS

Stir together 3 cups chopped **fresh flat-leaf parsley**, 1½ tsp. **kosher salt**, ¾ tsp. grated **garlic**, 1 tsp. **lemon zest**, 6 Tbsp. **lemon juice**, and ½ tsp. **black pepper** in a medium bowl. Stir in ¾ cup **extra-virgin olive oil** until combined. Serve immediately, or cover and refrigerate up to 2 days. Let come to room temperature and stir to recombine before serving.

Roasted Broccolini with Pecans and Lemon

ACTIVE 10 MIN. - TOTAL 25 MIN.

SERVES 12

2 large lemons, divided
4 bunches fresh Broccolini (about 2½ lb. total), trimmed
8 garlic cloves, smashed and divided
6 Tbsp. extra-virgin olive oil, divided
2½ tsp. kosher salt, divided
½ tsp. black pepper, divided
1 cup coarsely chopped pecan halves

1. Preheat oven to 450°F. Thinly slice 1 of the lemons. Halve any large stalks of Broccolini. Toss together half of the lemon slices, half of the Broccolini, 4 of the garlic cloves, 3 tablespoons of the olive oil, 1¼ teaspoons of the salt, and ¼ teaspoon of the black pepper on a rimmed baking sheet until combined. Repeat with remaining lemon slices, Broccolini, garlic, olive oil, salt, and pepper on another rimmed baking sheet.
2. Bake in preheated oven until Broccolini begins to brown on 1 side, about 8 minutes. Sprinkle both pans evenly with pecans. Bake, stirring halfway through cook time, until pecans are toasted and Broccolini is tender and browned, 6 to 8 minutes. Transfer to a platter; finely zest remaining lemon over Broccolini mixture.

Twice-Baked Duchess Potatoes

ACTIVE 30 MIN. - TOTAL 1 HOUR, 40 MIN.

MAKES 12

9 large russet potatoes, scrubbed
¾ cup unsalted butter
4 garlic cloves, minced (about 1 Tbsp.)
½ cup whole milk
3½ oz. Parmesan cheese, grated (about 1 cup)
5½ tsp. kosher salt
½ tsp. black pepper, plus more for garnish
6 large egg yolks
2 Tbsp. olive oil
Chopped fresh flat-leaf parsley (optional)
Flaky sea salt (optional)

1. Preheat oven to 425°F. Place potatoes directly on oven rack, and bake until fork-tender, about 1 hour. Remove from oven, and let stand at room temperature until cool enough to handle, about 15 minutes. (Potatoes should still be hot.)
2. Meanwhile, melt butter in a small saucepan over medium. Add garlic, and cook, stirring often, until aromatic, about 2 minutes. Stir in milk, and cook until just warm, about 30 seconds. Remove from heat, and keep warm.
3. Cut potatoes in half lengthwise. Scoop out cooked potato from halves, leaving about ⅛ inch potato flesh on skin; place remaining cooked potato in a large bowl. Reserve 12 potato skins, and set aside. (Discard any remaining potato skins.)
4. Using a whisk or potato masher, whisk or mash cooked potatoes until smooth with no lumps, 1 to 2 minutes. Stir warm milk mixture, Parmesan, salt, and pepper into potato mixture. Using a whisk, vigorously beat egg yolks, 1 at a time, into potato mixture until combined, scraping down sides of bowl as needed.
5. Brush outsides of reserved potato skins with oil, and place on a large rimmed baking sheet. Working in batches, transfer potato mixture to a piping bag fitted with a large open star tip. Pipe potato mixture into prepared potato skins in a decorative pattern, if desired.
6. Bake in preheated oven until piped potato mixture is lightly browned on top, 20 to 25 minutes. Remove from oven; garnish with pepper, parsley, and flaky sea salt, if desired.

Fix a Big, Beautiful Breakfast

Make-ahead recipes and shortcuts for a merry morning

FIVE GOLDEN RINGS
FRUIT SALAD

CRISPY GRITS
BREAKFAST
CASSEROLE

Crispy Grits Breakfast Casserole

ACTIVE 1 HOUR, 10 MIN. · TOTAL 2 HOURS, 40 MIN.,
PLUS 1 HOUR CHILLING

SERVES 10

- 1 lb. hot ground pork sausage
- 1 cup chopped scallions (from 1 bunch), plus more for garnish
- 12 large eggs
- 1 cup whole milk
- ½ tsp. kosher salt
- ¼ tsp. black pepper

Crispy Grits Croutons
(recipe opposite)

- 4 oz. sharp Cheddar cheese, shredded (about 1 cup)

1. Preheat oven to 350°F. Heat a 12-inch cast-iron skillet over medium-high. Add sausage; cook, stirring often, until crumbled and browned, 6 to 8 minutes. Stir in scallions; cook, stirring often, until aromatic, about 1 minute. Remove from heat; transfer to a paper towel-lined plate. Wipe skillet clean.

2. Whisk together eggs, milk, salt, and pepper in a large bowl. Fold in sausage mixture until fully combined. Arrange Crispy Grits Croutons in 2 layers in cast-iron skillet. Pour egg mixture evenly over croutons, and sprinkle evenly with Cheddar. Cover and refrigerate 1 hour or overnight, if desired.

3. Bake in preheated oven until set and golden brown, 35 to 40 minutes. Garnish with scallions, and serve.

Crispy Grits Croutons

ACTIVE 1 HOUR · TOTAL 2 HOURS,
PLUS 1 HOUR CHILLING
MAKES ABOUT 7 CUPS

- 1   Tbsp. plus 1½ tsp. kosher salt, divided
- 2   cups uncooked yellow stone-ground grits
- 4   oz. sharp Cheddar cheese, shredded (about 1 cup)
- ½   cup heavy whipping cream
- 3   Tbsp. unsalted butter
- 2   tsp. black pepper, divided
- 1½ cups plain yellow cornmeal

1. Line a 13- x 9-inch baking pan with plastic wrap, leaving a 2-inch overhang on short sides; set aside. In a large saucepan, bring 7 cups water and 1 tablespoon of the salt to a boil over medium-high. Add grits, stirring constantly. Reduce heat to medium-low; cover and simmer, stirring occasionally, until grits are very thick and tender, about 30 minutes.
2. Remove grits from heat, and let stand 5 minutes. Stir in cheese, cream, butter, and ½ teaspoon of the pepper until smooth, about 1 minute. Spread grits in an even layer in prepared baking pan. Chill, uncovered, until grits are firm, at least 1 hour or up to 3 days.
3. Preheat oven to 425°F. Line 2 large rimmed baking sheets with aluminum foil, and coat lightly with cooking spray; set aside. Invert chilled grits onto a cutting board. Discard plastic wrap; cut grits into 1-inch cubes. Combine cornmeal and remaining 1½ teaspoons salt and 1½ teaspoons pepper in a shallow dish. Dredge grit cubes in cornmeal mixture, shaking off excess. Place on prepared pans; lightly coat with cooking spray.
4. Bake in preheated oven until golden brown, 45 to 50 minutes. Let cool completely. If desired, refrigerate in an airtight container up to 2 days.

Five Golden Rings Fruit Salad

ACTIVE 30 MIN. · TOTAL 30 MIN.
SERVES 10

Heat ½ cup **honey** in a saucepan over medium-low. Cook, stirring occasionally, until honey deepens in color, about 8 minutes. Add 1 cup **apple cider vinegar,** and cook, swirling pan occasionally, until sauce has thickened slightly, 15 to 20 minutes. Remove from heat, and stir in ½ tsp. **ground ginger** and ¼ tsp. **kosher salt.** Set aside. Peel 2 **small grapefruit,** 3 **small navel oranges,** 3 **small Cara Cara oranges,** and 3 **small blood oranges.** Cut 2 **medium-size fresh pineapples** (peeled and cored) and citrus crosswise into ¼-inch-thick slices. Layer fruit on a serving platter; drizzle evenly with honey mixture. Garnish with **fresh mint.**

Take a Shortcut
Three spins on refrigerated cinnamon rolls

Eggnog-Spiced Rolls

ACTIVE 10 MIN. · TOTAL 1 HOUR, 5 MIN.
MAKES 10

Preheat oven to 350°F. Coat 2 (9-inch) round cake pans with cooking spray. Whisk together 2 cups **whipping cream,** 1 tsp. **vanilla,** and ½ teaspoon **nutmeg** in a bowl until combined. Whisk together 1 cup **brown sugar,** ½ cup melted **butter,** and 1½ tsp. **cinnamon** in another bowl until well combined; set aside. Separate 2 (17½-oz.) cans **jumbo cinnamon roll dough** into 10 rolls. Place 5 rolls in each prepared pan. Pour cream mixture around rolls. Spread about 1½ tablespoons brown sugar mixture over each roll. Cover pans with aluminum foil. Bake in preheated oven 35 minutes. Uncover; bake until tops are browned, about 10 minutes more.

Cinnamon-Pecan Twists

ACTIVE 45 MIN. · TOTAL 1 HOUR, 5 MIN.
MAKES 20

Preheat oven to 375°F. Line 2 baking sheets with parchment. Combine ½ cup **brown sugar** and 1 tsp. **cinnamon** in a bowl. Place ½ cup finely chopped **pecans** in another bowl. Separate 1 (17½-oz.) can **jumbo cinnamon roll dough** into 5 rolls; unroll into long strips. Cut each strip into 8 (4½-inch-long) pieces. Brush with ¼ cup melted **butter.** Press buttered side of 20 strips into sugar mixture; press 20 strips into pecans. Twist one of each together; pinch ends to seal. Repeat with remaining strips. Bake on prepared pans 14 minutes. Whisk together 1 cup **powdered sugar,** 4 oz. softened **cream cheese,** 1 tsp. **vanilla,** and ¼ cup **milk** until smooth. Serve with twists.

Orange-Roll Muffins

ACTIVE 40 MIN. · TOTAL 1 HOUR, 5 MIN.
MAKES 10

Preheat oven to 375°F. Coat 10 cups of a 12-cup muffin tray with **baking spray.** Stir together ½ cup plus 2 Tbsp. **orange marmalade** and 2 Tbsp. grated **orange zest** in a small bowl. Separate 2 (17½-oz.) cans **jumbo cinnamon roll dough** into 10 rolls. Unroll into long strips; spread each with 2 teaspoons of marmalade mixture. Add 1 dough strip to each cup, marmalade side in, starting at the rim and spiraling inward. Repeat with remaining strips. Brush tops with ¼ cup melted **butter.** Bake until browned, 15 to 18 minutes. Whisk together 1½ cups **powdered sugar,** 2½ tablespoons marmalade mixture, and 2 tablespoons **orange juice** in a bowl. Drizzle over rolls.

Crowd Control

Hearty, big-batch meals to feed all your hungry houseguests

HALF & HALF
For a different look, divide the sauces down the dish lengthwise so that everyone gets a taste of both red and green enchiladas.

Christmas-Style Enchiladas

ACTIVE 30 MIN. - TOTAL 45 MIN.
SERVES 6

- 3 cups shredded rotisserie chicken (from 1 [2-lb.] whole rotisserie chicken)
- 4 oz. Monterey Jack cheese, shredded (about 1 cup)
- ½ cup crema Mexicana, plus more for drizzling
- 2 Tbsp. finely chopped pickled jalapeño chiles plus 2 Tbsp. liquid from jar (from 1 [12-oz.] jar)
- ¾ tsp. kosher salt
- 2 (8-oz.) pkg. green enchilada sauce, divided
- 2 (8-oz.) pkg. red enchilada sauce, divided
- 12 (6-inch) corn tortillas, warmed
- 1½ oz. Cotija cheese, crumbled (about ⅓ cup)
  Fresh cilantro leaves, thinly sliced radishes, and chopped avocado

1. Preheat oven to 350°F. Gently stir together chicken, Monterey Jack cheese, crema, jalapeños, pickled jalapeño liquid, and salt in a medium bowl until combined; set aside.

2. Spread ¾ cup green enchilada sauce on half of the bottom of a 13- x 9-inch baking dish; spread ¾ cup red enchilada sauce on remaining half so sauces divide the dish in half crosswise and meet in the middle. Place remaining 1¼ cups each green and red enchilada sauces in separate shallow bowls or pie plates.

3. Dip 1 side of 1 tortilla into green sauce, letting excess drain back into bowl; lay tortilla, dipped side up, on a clean work surface. Spoon about ¼ cup chicken mixture down center of tortilla. Roll up tortilla, and place, seam side down, in prepared baking dish over green sauce. Repeat process with 5 more tortillas dipped into green sauce and 6 tortillas dipped into red sauce, placing rolled tortillas in dish over corresponding sauces. Spoon ⅓ cup of each sauce over corresponding rolled tortillas.

4. Bake enchiladas in preheated oven until warmed through, about 15 minutes. Drizzle with additional crema, and top with Cotija cheese, cilantro, radishes, and avocado. Serve remaining enchilada sauces on the side.

GET A JUMP START
These can be made up
to 4 hours ahead. Keep
refrigerated. Brush with egg
right before baking and bake
for 25 to 28 minutes.

Beef Pot Pies

ACTIVE 1 HOUR · TOTAL 1 HOUR, 15 MIN.
SERVES 8

- 1 (17.3-oz.) pkg. frozen puff pastry sheets (2 sheets), thawed
- 2 lb. top sirloin steak (about 1½ inches thick), cut into ½-inch pieces
- ½ tsp. black pepper
- 2½ tsp. kosher salt, divided
- 5 Tbsp. unsalted butter, divided
- ⅓ cup all-purpose flour, plus more for work surface
- 2 Tbsp. tomato paste
- 6 garlic cloves, finely chopped (2 Tbsp.)
- 2½ cups beef broth
- 2 Tbsp. Worcestershire sauce
- 1 Tbsp. creamy prepared horseradish
- 2 (10-oz.) pkg. frozen mixed vegetables (such as green beans, peas, corn, and carrots)
- 2 cups frozen cubed hash brown potatoes (from 1 [32-oz.] pkg.)
- 1 large egg, beaten

1. Preheat oven to 425°F with rack in top third position. Working with 1 puff pastry sheet at a time, roll out each on a lightly floured work surface to a 12- x 10-inch rectangle. Using a 10-ounce ramekin as a guide, cut 4 rounds from each pastry sheet ½ inch wider than ramekin rim all the way around. Reserve remaining dough for another use. Place pastry rounds on a parchment paper–lined baking sheet; cover with plastic wrap, and refrigerate until ready to use.
2. Toss sirloin with pepper and 1 teaspoon of the salt. Melt 2 tablespoons of the butter in a 12-inch cast-iron skillet over high until foam subsides. Working in 2 batches, add sirloin in a single layer, and cook, undisturbed, until bottom sides are lightly browned, about 4 minutes. Transfer to a plate. Do not wipe skillet clean.
3. Melt remaining 3 tablespoons butter in skillet over medium-high. Add flour, tomato paste, and garlic; cook, stirring constantly, until mixture darkens slightly, about 1 minute. Gradually whisk in broth. Bring to a simmer over medium; cook, stirring often, until thickened, about 2 minutes. Remove from heat, and stir in Worcestershire sauce, horseradish, mixed vegetables, potatoes, browned sirloin, and remaining 1½ teaspoons salt; set aside.
4. Divide sirloin mixture evenly among 8 (10-ounce) ramekins, and place on a parchment-lined baking sheet. Brush edges of each dough round with beaten egg, and place, egg side down, on top of each filled ramekin. Using a paring knife, cut 4 small slits into top of each dough round. Brush top of each dough round with remaining beaten egg. Bake in preheated oven until puffed and browned, 15 to 17 minutes.

TRY IT IN A SKILLET
Omit Step 1. Preheat oven to 375°F with rack in top third position. Prepare Steps 2 and 3 as directed, replacing the 12-inch cast-iron skillet with a 10-inch cast-iron skillet. Omit Step 4. Roll 1 **puff pastry sheet** out on a lightly floured work surface to a 12-inch square. Trim about 1½ inches from each corner to form a rough circle. Roll pastry up onto rolling pin. Working quickly, unroll pastry over filling in skillet. Fold excess pastry edges under, and then gently tuck inside skillet (do not press pastry into filling). Using kitchen shears, cut 4 (1-inch-long) slits into top of pastry. Brush top with beaten egg. Place skillet in oven, and bake at 375°F until edges turn light golden, about 15 minutes. Reduce temperature to 350°F; continue baking until pastry is puffed, golden, and crisp, 30 to 35 minutes.

WELCOME HOME
Transfer this soup to your slow cooker so it stays nice and warm for guests no matter what time they roll in.

Ultimate Tomato Soup and Big-Batch Grilled Cheese

ACTIVE 1 HOUR · TOTAL 1 HOUR, 15 MIN.
SERVES 8

3 Tbsp. olive oil

1 medium-size yellow onion, thinly sliced (about 1¾ cups)

3 small carrots, peeled and thinly sliced (about ¾ cup)

2½ tsp. kosher salt, divided

1 Tbsp. finely chopped garlic (from 3 garlic cloves)

1 Tbsp. grated fresh ginger

⅛ to ¼ tsp. cayenne pepper

5 (5-inch) fresh thyme sprigs

2 (28-oz.) cans whole peeled San Marzano plum tomatoes, crushed

2 tsp. light brown sugar

2 cups vegetable stock

½ to ¾ cup heavy whipping cream

1 (20- to 22-inch) baguette, split lengthwise

½ cup red pepper jelly

6 oz. aged white Cheddar cheese, thinly sliced

6 oz. smoked Gouda cheese, thinly sliced

1. Preheat oven to 425°F. Heat oil in a large Dutch oven over medium-high. Add onion, carrots, and ½ teaspoon of the salt; cook, stirring often, until vegetables are golden brown around edges, 10 to 12 minutes. Add garlic, ginger, cayenne pepper, and thyme; cook, stirring often, until fragrant, about 1 minute.
2. Stir tomatoes and sugar into Dutch oven. Bring to a simmer over medium-high. Simmer, stirring often, until slightly thickened, about 10 minutes. Add vegetable stock, and bring to a simmer over medium-high. Simmer, stirring occasionally, until flavors meld, about 10 minutes. Remove from heat. Remove and discard thyme sprigs.
3. Process tomato mixture using an immersion blender until smooth, about 1 minute. (Alternatively, working in 2 batches, ladle tomato mixture into a blender. Secure lid on blender, and remove center piece to allow steam to escape. Place a clean towel over opening; process until smooth, about 30 seconds. Return to Dutch oven.) Stir in ½ cup of the cream and remaining 2 teaspoons salt. For a creamier consistency, add up to ¼ cup additional cream, if desired.
4. Cut split baguette in half crosswise; arrange halves side by side and cut sides up on a parchment paper–lined baking sheet. Hollow out bread from rounded top halves of baguette. Spread pepper jelly evenly over cut sides of baguette. Stuff cheeses evenly into hollowed-out baguette halves. If needed, place some of the cheese on bottom baguette halves.
5. Bake in preheated oven until cheese is melted, 10 to 12 minutes. Carefully place top baguette halves, cheese side down, over bottom baguette halves. Cut each half crosswise into 4 slices for a total of 8 sandwiches. Serve with soup.

Sausage-and-Black-Eyed Pea Soup with Greens

ACTIVE 1 HOUR, 25 MIN. · TOTAL 1 HOUR, 25 MIN.
SERVES 8

- 3 Tbsp. olive oil
- 1½ lb. sweet Italian pork sausage
- 1 medium-size yellow onion, thinly sliced (2 cups)
- 6 garlic cloves, thinly sliced (about 3 Tbsp.)
- 1 tsp. kosher salt
- 1 Tbsp. finely chopped fresh rosemary
- 2 tsp. grated lemon zest (from 1 lemon)
- ½ tsp. crushed red pepper, plus more for garnish
- ¼ cup dry white wine
- 1 large bunch fresh collard greens, stemmed and chopped (8 packed cups)
- 2 (15½-oz.) cans black-eyed peas, drained and rinsed
- 6 cups lower-sodium chicken broth
  Grated Parmesan cheese

1. Heat oil in a large Dutch oven over medium-high. Break sausage into large clumps, and add to Dutch oven. Cook, undisturbed, until bottom side is browned, 3 to 4 minutes. Cook over medium-high, breaking up sausage into smaller pieces using a wooden spoon and stirring constantly, until cooked through, about 3 minutes. Add onion, garlic, and salt; cook, stirring often, until softened, about 6 minutes. Add rosemary, lemon zest, and crushed red pepper, and cook, stirring constantly, until fragrant, about 30 seconds. Add wine, and cook over medium-high, stirring often, until mostly evaporated, about 2 minutes.

2. Stir collard greens, black-eyed peas, and chicken broth into Dutch oven. Bring to a vigorous simmer over high. Reduce heat to medium, and simmer, stirring occasionally, until flavors meld and greens are tender but still have a bite, 40 to 45 minutes. Divide soup evenly among 8 bowls, and garnish with additional crushed red pepper; sprinkle with cheese.

LUCKY YOU

If you don't get to this comforting soup at Christmas, prepare it on New Year's Day to help bring you good fortune and prosperity in 2024.

Pastitsio

ACTIVE 55 MIN. - TOTAL 1 HOUR, 50 MIN.
SERVES 10

- 3 Tbsp. olive oil
- 2 lb. 85/15 lean ground beef
- 1 medium-size yellow onion, finely chopped (1½ cups)
- 6 garlic cloves, finely chopped (2 Tbsp.)
- 2 tsp. dried oregano
- ¾ tsp. ground cinnamon
- 2 Tbsp. tomato paste
- ½ cup dry red wine
- 1 (28-oz.) can crushed tomatoes
- 2¾ tsp. kosher salt, divided
- 12 oz. large pasta shells
- 2½ cups whole-milk ricotta cheese
- 2 large eggs, beaten
- 3 oz. Parmesan cheese, grated (about ¾ cup), divided

1. Preheat oven to 400°F. Bring a large pot of salted water to a boil over high. While water comes to a boil, heat oil in a large Dutch oven over medium-high. Break beef into large clumps, and add to Dutch oven. Cook, undisturbed, until bottom side is browned, 6 to 8 minutes. Stir and cook over medium-high, stirring and breaking up meat into small pieces using a wooden spoon, until cooked through, about 4 minutes. Add onion, garlic, oregano, and cinnamon; cook, stirring often, until onion softens, about 4 minutes. Add tomato paste; cook over medium-high, stirring often, 2 minutes. Add wine; cook, stirring often, until almost completely reduced, 1 to 2 minutes. Stir in crushed tomatoes and 1 teaspoon of the salt. Bring to a simmer over medium-high. Simmer, stirring occasionally, until mixture thickens slightly, about 8 minutes. Remove from heat, and stir in 1 teaspoon of the salt.

2. Cook pasta according to package directions for al dente. Drain pasta, and stir pasta into beef mixture in Dutch oven. Spread mixture into an ungreased 13- x 9-inch baking dish.

3. Stir together ricotta, eggs, ½ cup of the Parmesan, and remaining ¾ teaspoon salt in a medium bowl until blended. Dollop ricotta mixture over pasta mixture, and gently spread to evenly cover; sprinkle with remaining ¼ cup Parmesan. Bake in preheated oven until cheese is browned in spots, 35 to 38 minutes. Remove from oven, and let cool slightly before serving, about 10 minutes.

GREEK TO ME
Traditionally crowned with a homemade béchamel, this weeknight riff on "Greek lasagna" gets the job done with an easier ricotta topping.

Marvelous Muffins

Everything you love about sausage balls but revamped for breakfast

Sausage-Cheddar Muffins

ACTIVE 30 MIN. · TOTAL 55 MIN.
MAKES 12

- 2 Tbsp. olive oil
- 1 lb. breakfast sausage (such as Jimmy Dean)
- 1½ tsp. kosher salt, divided
- ½ cup unsalted butter
- ½ tsp. grated garlic (from 2 garlic cloves)
- 2 large eggs
- 1 cup whole buttermilk
- 1 Tbsp. pure maple syrup
- 2 cups all-purpose flour
- 2 tsp. baking powder
- ½ tsp. baking soda
- 8 oz. sharp Cheddar cheese, shredded (about 2 cups), divided
- Chopped fresh chives

1. Preheat oven to 400°F. Coat a 12-cup muffin tray with cooking spray; set aside. Heat oil in a large nonstick skillet over medium-high. Add sausage and ½ teaspoon of the salt; cook, stirring often to break up meat into small crumbles, until well browned and crispy, 7 to 10 minutes. Remove from heat. Transfer sausage to a paper towel-lined plate; set aside.

2. Microwave butter and garlic in a medium microwavable bowl on HIGH until butter is melted, about 45 seconds. Stir together to incorporate. Let cool to room temperature, about 5 minutes. Whisk in eggs, buttermilk, and maple syrup until smooth. Set aside.

3. Whisk together flour, baking powder, baking soda, and remaining 1 teaspoon salt in a separate medium bowl. Add buttermilk mixture, sausage, and

1¾ cups of the cheese; stir until just combined (do not overmix). Lightly coat a ⅓-cup measuring cup with cooking spray; spoon batter evenly into prepared muffin cups. Sprinkle evenly with remaining ¼ cup cheese.

4. Bake in preheated oven until muffins are puffed and golden brown, 22 to 25 minutes. Remove from oven. Transfer muffin tray to a wire rack, and let cool 10 minutes. Gently run a knife or offset spatula around edges of each muffin, and remove from tray. Garnish with chives, and serve warm. Cooled muffins may be stored in an airtight container in refrigerator up to 3 days; reheat before serving.

A Southern–Fried Hanukkah

Paducah chef Sara Bradley draws from her Jewish heritage and Kentucky roots to cook up a celebratory feast

FREIGHT HOUSE
FRIED CHICKEN

"HANUKKAH, for me growing up, was all about potato latkes, doughnuts, and—believe it or not—fried chicken," says Sara Bradley, chef and proprietor of Freight House in Paducah, Kentucky. All three of her childhood Hanukkah staples made use of oil—a symbolic nod to the origins of the holiday rooted in the miracle of oil used to light the menorah lasting for eight days. Her family made latkes at home but outsourced the doughnuts from Red's Donut Shop, a Paducah institution. Today, she makes sufganiyat, an Israeli donut topped with powdered sugar.

Bradley says she struggled with her Jewish identity when she was growing up, especially at this time of year. She and her siblings longed for a Christmas tree—Bradley's mother, Bev, conceded to a ficus, which they decorated in lights and homemade ornaments and dubbed the Hanukkah bush. Inspired by a *Saturday Night Live* sketch, she and her siblings would joke that "Hanukkah Harry" was coming to visit as their substitute for Santa Claus. "We were children, and we didn't really understand at that time that, while we were different, being Jewish was something really special—less than 1% of the world's population is Jewish," she says.

She credits Camp Ben Frankel with helping her appreciate her identity. Located in southern Illinois, the camp attracted kids from small towns in nearby states. She spent 12 summers there, where she learned to braid and bake challah (among many camp activities) and made lifelong friendships with people who shared her heritage. As an adult, Bradley moved back to the South following time spent in Chicago and New York and reconnected with her ancestry. She now teaches cooking classes in conjunction with her childhood summer camp and her local synagogue, helping pass down recipes.

Every Tuesday, her 4-year-old daughter, Lula Bea Martin, comes to the restaurant after eating her dinner and clears diners' finished plates. Bradley is excited to pass on that restaurant work ethic to her children, and also Jewish traditions, particularly those around food. She says, "As a parent and someone who is reconnecting with being Jewish after a while. I'm holding those things so dear to my heart."

Freight House Fried Chicken

ACTIVE 1 HOUR, 15 MIN. - TOTAL 1 HOUR, 45 MIN., PLUS 4 HOURS MARINATING

SERVES 4 TO 8

- 2 cups whole buttermilk
- ¼ cup hot sauce
- 3½ Tbsp. kosher salt, divided, plus more to taste
- 8 (about 4 lb. total) bone-in, skin-on chicken thighs, trimmed
- 4 cups all-purpose flour
- 1 Tbsp. granulated garlic
- 1 Tbsp. granulated onion
- 1½ tsp. smoked paprika
- ¼ tsp. cayenne pepper
  Canola oil, for frying

1. Whisk together buttermilk, hot sauce, and 1½ tablespoons of the salt in a large zip-top plastic bag; add chicken thighs. Remove excess air from bag; seal bag, and place in a baking dish or on a rimmed baking sheet. Place in refrigerator, and let marinate at least 4 hours or preferably up to 12 hours.
2. Whisk together flour, granulated garlic, granulated onion, paprika, cayenne, and remaining 2 tablespoons salt in a large bowl. Set aside.
3. Fill a large, heavy-bottomed pot with oil to a depth of 2½ inches, making sure there's enough room to add chicken without oil bubbling over. Heat oil over medium-high until a deep-fry thermometer registers 355°F. Place a wire rack over a baking sheet; set aside.
4. Drain chicken from marinade, but do not pat it dry; dredge each thigh in flour mixture to thoroughly coat. Reserve remaining flour mixture. Discard remaining marinade in bag. Transfer chicken thighs to prepared wire rack; let stand 5 minutes.
5. Working in 4 batches, dredge 2 thighs lightly in flour mixture again, and carefully add to hot oil. (Temperature of oil will gradually start to drop.) Adjust heat as needed to reduce oil temperature to 325°F, and cook chicken until an instant-read thermometer inserted into thickest portion of chicken registers 160°F, 8 to 12 minutes. Using tongs, remove chicken from oil, and let drain on a clean wire rack placed over a clean rimmed baking sheet. Season with salt to taste. Return oil to 355°F over medium-high. Repeat process with remaining chicken and flour mixture.

Cheesy Savory Keugel

(Photo, page 318)

ACTIVE 50 MIN. - TOTAL 2 HOURS, 35 MIN.

SERVES 12

- 1 lb. uncooked wide egg noodles
- ½ cup unsalted butter
- 2 cups chopped yellow onions (from 2 medium onions)
- ¼ tsp. ground fennel seed
- 3 Tbsp. kosher salt, divided
- 12 large eggs
- 1½ lb. sour cream (about 3 cups)
- 1½ lb. 4% milk fat cottage cheese (about 2¾ cups)
- 8 oz. goat cheese, crumbled (about 1 cup)
- ¼ cup honey
- 1 Tbsp. granulated onion
- 1 tsp. black pepper

1. Coat a 13- x 9-inch baking pan with cooking spray. Cook noodles according to package directions; drain and set aside.
2. Heat butter in a large skillet over medium-high until melted and bubbly. Add onions, fennel, and 1 tablespoon of the salt; cook, stirring often, until onions are softened and translucent, 5 to 7 minutes. Remove from heat, and let cool slightly, about 20 minutes. Meanwhile, preheat oven to 325°F.
3. Whisk eggs in a large bowl until well combined; set aside. Gently stir together cooled onion mixture, sour cream, cottage cheese, goat cheese, honey, granulated onion, pepper, and remaining 2 tablespoons salt in a separate very large bowl until combined. Stir in eggs until incorporated. Fold in cooked noodles.
4. Pour mixture into prepared pan, and spread in an even layer; cover with aluminum foil. Bake in preheated oven for 45 minutes (edges of keugel will be just starting to set). Remove foil, and bake until light golden and set in the middle, 22 to 30 minutes. Transfer to a wire rack, and let cool at least 15 minutes or up to 3 hours. Serve warm, cold, or at room temperature.

CHEESY
SAVORY KEUGEL
(PAGE 317)

BRUSSELS SPROUTS
WITH POMEGRANATE
MOLASSES
AND WALNUTS

Brussels Sprouts with Pomegranate Molasses and Walnuts

ACTIVE 30 MIN. - TOTAL 30 MIN.
SERVES 4

- 2 Tbsp. vegetable oil
- 1 lb. Brussels sprouts, halved lengthwise (about 4⅓ cups)
- 1 tsp. kosher salt
  Freshly ground black pepper, to taste, plus more for garnish
- 1 Tbsp. finely chopped shallot
- 1 Tbsp. pomegranate molasses
- 1½ tsp. red wine vinegar
- 2 Tbsp. toasted walnut pieces
- 1 Tbsp. chopped fresh flat-leaf parsley
- 1 Tbsp. chopped fresh cilantro

1. Pour oil into a cold 12-inch cast-iron skillet. Working in batches, arrange Brussels sprouts, cut side down, in a single layer in skillet. Place skillet over medium-high heat, and cook, undisturbed, until cut sides of sprouts are very caramelized and sprouts are tender-crisp, 6 to 10 minutes. Transfer to a bowl or platter; stir in salt until well combined, and season with pepper to taste.
2. Whisk together shallot, molasses, and vinegar in a small bowl until well combined. Drizzle mixture over warm Brussels sprouts. Sprinkle with walnuts, parsley, and cilantro. Garnish with additional pepper. Leftovers may be stored in an airtight container in refrigerator up to 7 days.

Sufganiyat

ACTIVE 1 HOUR, 15 MIN. - TOTAL 1 HOUR, 15 MIN.
SERVES 6

SUFGANIYAT
- 1½ cups all-purpose flour
- ½ cup granulated sugar
- 1 tsp. baking powder
  Pinch of kosher salt
- ½ cup whole buttermilk, at room temperature
- 2 large eggs, at room temperature, separated
- 1 Tbsp. unsalted butter, melted
- 1½ tsp. grated orange zest plus 1 Tbsp. fresh juice (from 1 large orange)
- 1 tsp. vanilla extract
  Canola oil, for frying

SUFGANIYAT

GLAZE
- ¼ cup orange marmalade
- 1 Tbsp. bourbon

ADDITIONAL INGREDIENT
Powdered sugar

1. Prepare the Sufganiyat: Whisk together flour, granulated sugar, baking powder, and salt in a large bowl until well combined. Whisk together buttermilk, egg yolks, butter, orange zest and juice, and vanilla in a medium bowl until combined. Fold buttermilk mixture into flour mixture just until nearly combined. (Batter will be thick; do not overmix.)

2. Fill a large, heavy-bottomed pot with oil to a depth of 2½ to 3 inches. Heat over medium-high until a deep-fry thermometer in oil registers 350°F to 360°F. Beat egg whites in a medium bowl with a hand mixer fitted with a whisk attachment on high speed until medium peaks form, 1 to 2 minutes. Gently fold whipped whites into flour batter in 2 additions.

3. Working in batches of 4 or 5 scoops at a time, use a 1-tablespoon spring-loaded scoop to drop batter into hot oil. Fry, using a slotted spoon or spider strainer to stir and flip Sufganiyat constantly, until golden brown and cooked through,

2 to 3 minutes per batch, adjusting heat as needed to maintain oil temperature. Using a slotted spoon or spider strainer, remove Sufganiyat from oil, and let drain on a paper towel-lined plate. Repeat process with remaining batter.

4. Prepare the Glaze: Stir together marmalade and bourbon in a small bowl until combined. Drizzle Sufganiyat with Glaze and garnish with powdered sugar. Serve immediately.

Not-So Vanilla

Ever in the background, this humble pantry staple takes center stage in these showstopping winter desserts

FOLKS TEASE ME when I tell them my favorite ice-cream flavor is vanilla.

Let them laugh—those hecklers don't know what they're taking for granted. Second in scarcity and price only to saffron, vanilla "beans" are the fruit of an orchid that is meticulously cultivated in just a handful of places on the planet. Pollinated, picked, and smoothed by hand, these precious beans are cured up to 90 days before being transformed into the tiny bottles of extract that nearly every Southerner has tucked away in their cupboard.

Often imitated, pure vanilla's nuanced aroma is the sum of hundreds of compounds that mingle, mature, and intensify as the pods age and are exposed to light, heat, and pressure. All these act in concert, yielding a singular ingredient with surprising depth. A sensitive nose and a trained palate can savor the multitude of notes that compose the symphony that is vanilla— floral, fruity, woodsy, winey, smoky, and buttery, to name a few.

Flashier ingredients often upstage this humble flavor, but we see you, vanilla. We've taken four fundamental recipes—cake, custard, meringue, and buttercream—and combined them to create dramatic holiday desserts that allow vanilla to shine. One glimpse (and hopefully a taste) and you'll never call vanilla "boring" again. —Josh Miller

White Christmas Bûche de Noël

ACTIVE 1 HOUR, 15 MIN. - TOTAL 2 HOURS, 15 MIN., PLUS 4 HOURS COOLING AND CHILLING AND 1 HOUR STANDING
SERVES 12 TO 16

    Vanilla Chiffon Cake (recipe, page 324), freshly baked and still hot

2 Tbsp. powdered sugar, plus more for garnish

1½ cups heavy whipping cream

2 Tbsp. vanilla bean paste or 4 tsp. vanilla extract

1 Tbsp. granulated sugar

1 cup Ultimate Vanilla Custard (recipe, page 325)

    Vanilla Syrup (recipe follows)

    Essential Vanilla Buttercream (recipe, page 325)

    Vanilla Bean Meringue Mushrooms (recipe, page 325)

    Fresh rosemary sprigs, for garnish

1. Quickly loosen Vanilla Chiffon Cake edges in baking pan with a butter knife, and dust top with powdered sugar. Place a clean kitchen towel on cake. Place a large wire rack or rimless baking sheet on top of towel; carefully flip to invert cake. Lift off baking pan, and gently peel off parchment from cake. Working from 1 long edge, carefully roll up cake and towel together, jelly roll style, into a log. Place log, seam side down, on a wire rack. Let cool completely, about 1 hour.

2. Beat cream, vanilla bean paste, and granulated sugar in a large bowl with an electric mixer on medium-high speed until medium peaks form, 2 to 3 minutes. Gently fold in Ultimate Vanilla Custard until combined.

3. Carefully unroll cake log. Remove towel, and brush cake evenly with Vanilla Syrup.

4. Spread whipped cream mixture evenly over cake; reroll cake, without towel, into a log. Place, seam side down, on a platter. If desired, diagonally cut 1 (5-inch) piece off 1 end; position alongside cake log as a branch. Frost as desired with Essential Vanilla Buttercream, reserving ¼ cup for decorating. Using fork tines, create a bark-like texture in buttercream. Loosely cover cake with plastic wrap; chill at least 3 hours or up to 24 hours.

5. Remove from refrigerator; let come to room temperature, about 1 hour. Decorate cake and platter, adhering meringue mushrooms with reserved buttercream; garnish with rosemary and powdered sugar.

Vanilla Syrup

ACTIVE 10 MIN. - TOTAL 40 MIN.
MAKES ⅓ CUP

Cook ¼ cup **granulated sugar** and ¼ cup **water** in a small saucepan over medium-high, stirring often, until mixture boils and sugar dissolves. Pour mixture into a small heatproof bowl; whisk in ½ tsp. **vanilla bean paste or extract** until well combined. Chill about 30 minutes. Use immediately, or store in an airtight container in refrigerator up to 1 week.

WHITE CHRISTMAS
BÛCHE DE NOËL

LET IT SNOW PAVLOVA
(PAGE 324)

TRIPLE-VANILLA TRIFLE
(PAGE 324)

Valuable Vanilla

Three flavorful forms

Vanilla Extract

Pure extracts use alcohol to draw out the taste from vanilla beans, without added sugar or artificial colors and flavors. Make it at home by soaking a few beans in vodka or bourbon. You can substitute a tablespoon of extract for one vanilla bean in most recipes.

Vanilla Beans

When purchasing vanilla beans, look for pods that are pliable and shiny—indicators that they're fresh. To access the seeds inside the pod, split the bean lengthwise with a paring knife and then scrape the cut halves with the back of the knife to release the seeds and pulp. Save the spent pods for making your own extract.

Vanilla Bean Paste

While the pods can dry out and lose potency, the paste can be stored in the pantry up to three years and provides the same concentrated flavor and beautiful black specks. Consisting of vanilla bean seeds, extract, and a thickener, it can be swapped for the same amount of vanilla extract in most recipes.

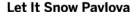

Let It Snow Pavlova

(Photo, page 322)
ACTIVE 40 MIN. - TOTAL 40 MIN.
SERVES 12 TO 16

- 1¼ cups heavy whipping cream
- 3¾ tsp. vanilla bean paste or 2 tsp. vanilla extract
- 3¾ tsp. granulated sugar
- Vanilla Bean Meringues (recipe opposite)
- 2⅓ cups Ultimate Vanilla Custard (recipe opposite)
- Powdered sugar, for garnish

1. Beat cream, vanilla bean paste, and granulated sugar in a large bowl with an electric mixer on medium-high speed until medium-stiff peaks form, 2 to 3 minutes. Set aside.
2. Place the 9-inch Vanilla Bean Meringue on a platter. Spread evenly with about 1 cup Ultimate Vanilla Custard. Top with about 1 cup whipped cream. Repeat layering process with 7-inch, 5-inch, and 3-inch meringues; custard; and whipped cream, reducing custard and whipped cream by about ¼ cup or more per layer as needed. Top with 1-inch meringue cone. Garnish with powdered sugar.

Triple-Vanilla Trifle

(Photo, page 323)
ACTIVE 20 MIN. - TOTAL 2 HOURS, 20 MIN.
SERVES 14 TO 16

- Vanilla Chiffon Cake Trifle Variation (recipe at right)
- 3 cups heavy whipping cream
- 3 Tbsp. vanilla bean paste or 1½ Tbsp. vanilla extract
- 3 Tbsp. granulated sugar
- Ultimate Vanilla Custard (recipe opposite)
- Vanilla Bean Meringue Mushrooms Variation (recipe opposite), roughly crushed (optional)

1. Cut cake into 1½-inch cubes (to yield 10 cups); set aside.
2. Beat cream, vanilla bean paste, and granulated sugar in a large bowl with an electric mixer on medium-high speed until medium peaks form, 3 to 4 minutes. Set aside.
3. Spoon one-third of the Ultimate Vanilla Custard (about 1⅓ cups) into bottom of a 14-cup trifle dish or bowl.

Top with one-third of the cake cubes (about 3⅓ cups). Reserve 3 cups of the whipped cream for topping the trifle; top the cake-cube layer with half of the remaining whipped cream (about 1⅓ cups). Repeat layers twice. Cover and chill at least 2 hours or up to 12 hours.
4. Just before serving, uncover and top with reserved 3 cups whipped cream and crushed meringue mushrooms, if using.

Vanilla Chiffon Cake

ACTIVE 25 MIN. - TOTAL 40 MIN.
MAKES 1 (17½- X 12½-INCH) CAKE

- 5 large eggs, separated
- ¼ tsp. cream of tartar
- 1 cup granulated sugar, divided
- ¼ cup vegetable oil
- 2 tsp. vanilla bean paste or vanilla extract
- 1 tsp. vanilla extract
- 1 cup all-purpose flour
- 1 tsp. baking powder
- ¼ tsp. kosher salt

1. Preheat oven to 400°F. Coat a 17½- x 12½-inch rimmed baking sheet with cooking spray; line with parchment paper, and recoat with cooking spray. Set aside.
2. Beat egg whites and cream of tartar with a stand mixer fitted with a whisk attachment on medium speed until foamy, 1 to 2 minutes. Increase mixer speed to high; gradually add ½ cup of the sugar, beating until stiff, glossy peaks form, 2 to 3 minutes total. Transfer mixture to a medium bowl; set aside. (Do not wipe mixer bowl or whisk attachment clean.)
3. Add egg yolks, oil, vanilla bean paste, vanilla extract, and remaining ½ cup sugar to mixer bowl; beat with whisk attachment on medium-high speed until pale yellow, about 3 minutes. Sift together flour, baking powder, and salt in a medium bowl. Reduce mixer speed to low; gradually add flour mixture, beating just until combined, about 1 minute. Gradually and gently fold in egg white mixture just until combined.
4. Pour batter into prepared baking sheet; using an offset spatula, gently and evenly spread batter to edges. Bake in preheated oven until center of cake springs back when pressed,

about 12 minutes. Remove from oven. If making the White Christmas Bûche de Noël, proceed with Step 1 of that recipe (page 320) immediately, while cake is still hot.

Vanilla Chiffon Cake Trifle Variation

ACTIVE 25 MIN. · TOTAL 40 MIN.
MAKES 1 (13- X 9-INCH) CAKE

In Step 1, preheat oven to 350°F. Coat a 13- x 9-inch metal baking pan with cooking spray; line with parchment paper, leaving a 2-inch overhang on long edges, and recoat with cooking spray. Set aside. Proceed with Steps 2 and 3 as directed. In Step 4, pour batter into prepared pan; gently and evenly spread batter to edges. Bake until center of cake springs back when pressed, 15 to 17 minutes. Remove from oven. Let cool completely on a wire rack, about 1 hour. Use immediately, or store, covered, at room temperature up to 1 day, or freeze up to 1 month.

Ultimate Vanilla Custard

ACTIVE 25 MIN. · TOTAL 25 MIN.,
PLUS 2 HOURS CHILLING
MAKES 4 CUPS

9 large egg yolks
¾ cup granulated sugar
¼ cup cornstarch
½ tsp. kosher salt
1 vanilla bean pod
3 cups whole milk
2 Tbsp. unsalted butter, cubed
2 tsp. vanilla extract

1. Whisk together egg yolks, sugar, cornstarch, and salt in a medium-size heatproof bowl until smooth. Set aside.
2. Halve vanilla bean pod lengthwise. Using the back of a paring knife, scrape vanilla seeds from pod halves into a medium saucepan; add scraped pod halves and milk. Bring to a simmer over medium, stirring occasionally. Remove from heat.
3. Gradually ladle half of hot milk mixture into egg yolk mixture, whisking constantly. Return egg yolk mixture to remaining milk mixture in saucepan. Cook over medium, whisking constantly, until mixture boils and thickens, 8 to 10 minutes. Remove from

heat; stir in butter and vanilla extract until combined. Pour through a fine mesh strainer into a large heatproof bowl. Remove and discard vanilla pod halves. Cover custard with plastic wrap pressed directly onto surface. Chill until cold, about 2 hours. Store, with plastic wrap still pressed against surface, in refrigerator up to 3 days.

Essential Vanilla Buttercream

ACTIVE 15 MIN. · TOTAL 15 MIN.
MAKES ABOUT 4 CUPS

1½ cups unsalted butter, at room temperature
1 Tbsp. plus 1 tsp. vanilla bean paste or 2 tsp. vanilla extract
4½ cups powdered sugar
2 Tbsp. whole milk
¾ tsp. kosher salt

Beat butter and vanilla bean paste in a large bowl with an electric mixer on medium speed until light and fluffy, about 2 minutes. Gradually beat in powdered sugar ½ cup at a time. Add milk and salt; beat until smooth, about 1 minute. Use immediately, or store in an airtight container in refrigerator up to 1 week. (If chilled, let buttercream come to room temperature and whip again with an electric mixer just before using.)

Vanilla Bean Meringues

ACTIVE 30 MIN. · TOTAL 2 HOURS, 30 MIN.,
PLUS 3 HOURS COOLING
MAKES 5 MERINGUES OF SPECIFIED SIZES

9 large egg whites, at room temperature
¼ tsp. cream of tartar
Pinch of kosher salt
2¼ cups granulated sugar
2 Tbsp. vanilla bean paste or 1 Tbsp. vanilla extract

1. Preheat oven to 250°F with racks in top third and lower third positions. Line 2 rimmed baking sheets with parchment paper; set aside.
2. Beat egg whites, cream of tartar, and salt with a stand mixer fitted with a whisk attachment on medium-high speed until foamy, about 1 minute. Increase mixer speed to high, and gradually stream in sugar. Beat until stiff peaks form, 8 to 10 minutes. (Mixture should be glossy, and sugar should be

completely dissolved.) Beat in vanilla bean paste until combined.
3. Using a pencil, trace 1 (9-inch) circle and 1 (5-inch) circle on 1 baking sheet. Trace 1 (7-inch), 1 (3-inch), and 1 (1-inch) circle on remaining baking sheet. Turn both parchment sheets to face pencil side down. Spread or pipe meringue within traced circles in an even layer about 1 inch thick (for the 1-inch circle, pipe or dollop the meringue into a cone or round shape).
4. Bake in preheated oven until meringues are a pale off-white color and firm to the touch, about 2 hours. Turn off oven; let meringues cool, undisturbed, in oven until completely dry and crisp, at least 3 hours or up to 12 hours. Wrap tightly in plastic wrap, and store at room temperature up to 1 day.

Vanilla Bean Meringue Mushrooms Variation

ACTIVE 40 MIN. · TOTAL 2 HOURS, 40 MIN.,
PLUS 3 HOURS COOLING
MAKES 20 MERINGUE MUSHROOMS

Proceed through Step 2 of Vanilla Bean Meringues as directed, reducing ingredient amounts to 3 **large egg whites**, a pinch of **cream of tartar**, a pinch of **kosher salt**, ¾ cup **granulated sugar**, and 2 tsp. **vanilla bean paste (or 1 tsp. vanilla extract)**. Omit Step 3. To form the mushroom caps, dollop meringue mixture to form 2-inch rounds spaced ¾ inch apart on prepared baking sheets. To form the mushroom stems, pipe meringue into ¾-inch-wide cones spaced ½ inch apart. (You will have about 20 rounds and 20 cones total.) Proceed with Step 4 as directed. Once meringues are completely dry and crisp, assemble mushrooms. Using a small sharp knife, pierce a small hole in the bottom of 1 mushroom cap. Using a small spoon, place a dab of **Essential Vanilla Buttercream** (recipe above left) into hole in bottom of mushroom cap. Gently press the pointed end of 1 mushroom stem into hole. Repeat process with remaining caps, stems, and buttercream.

Cookies in Color

Bake a brighter batch using sparkling sprinkles, dyed doughs, and festive frostings

Add your favorite colors to these doughs and frostings to create your own signature recipes

Vanilla Bean Dough

Your go-to extract is fine for this recipe, but splurge for vanilla bean paste to give the cookies a pretty, speckled look.

ACTIVE 15 MIN. - TOTAL 45 MIN.

MAKES ABOUT 2 LB. DOUGH

1½	cups powdered sugar
1	cup unsalted butter, softened
¼	cup granulated sugar
1	large egg, at room temperature
2½	tsp. vanilla bean paste
½	tsp. almond extract
3⅓	cups all-purpose flour
¾	tsp. baking powder
½	tsp. kosher salt

1. Beat powdered sugar, butter, and granulated sugar with a stand mixer fitted with a paddle attachment on low speed just until combined, about 30 seconds. Increase speed to medium-low; beat until light and fluffy, 2 to 3 minutes, stopping to scrape down sides as needed. Beat in egg, vanilla bean paste, and almond extract until combined, 15 to 30 seconds.
2. Whisk together flour, baking powder, and salt in a medium bowl until combined. With mixer on low speed, gradually add flour mixture to butter mixture and beat just until dough comes together, about 2 minutes, stopping to scrape down sides as needed.
3. Divide dough in half; shape each half into a disk, and wrap in plastic wrap. Chill at least 30 minutes or up to 2 days before using.

Chocolate Dough

Don't skip the instant espresso in this recipe; combined with the salt, it coaxes out the subtle notes of the cocoa.

ACTIVE 20 MIN. - TOTAL 20 MIN.

MAKES ABOUT 14 OZ. DOUGH

½	cup unsalted butter, softened
6	Tbsp. granulated sugar
1	large egg yolk, at room temperature
1	Tbsp. vanilla extract
2	tsp. heavy whipping cream
1⅓	cups all-purpose flour
3	Tbsp. Dutch process cocoa
¾	tsp. baking powder
½	tsp. instant espresso granules
¼	tsp. kosher salt

1. Beat butter and sugar with a stand mixer fitted with a paddle attachment on medium speed until light and fluffy, about 2 minutes, stopping to scrape down sides as needed. Add egg yolk, vanilla, and cream; beat on medium speed until combined, about 15 seconds.
2. Whisk together flour, cocoa, baking powder, espresso granules, and salt in a medium bowl until well combined.
3. With mixer on low speed, gradually add flour mixture to butter mixture, beating until combined, 30 seconds to 1 minute, stopping to scrape down sides as needed. Use immediately, or wrap tightly in plastic wrap; refrigerate for up to 24 hours. Let dough stand at room temperature until softened before using, about 30 minutes to 1 hour.

Spiced Spritz Cookie Dough

The trio of warm baking spices melds with the butter in this recipe, yielding cookies with a subtle, cozy flavor.

ACTIVE 15 MIN. - TOTAL 15 MIN.

MAKES ABOUT 1½ LB. DOUGH

1	cup unsalted butter, softened
½	cup granulated sugar
⅓	cup powdered sugar
1½	tsp. vanilla extract
1	large egg, at room temperature
2⅓	cups all-purpose flour
1½	tsp. ground cinnamon
½	tsp. ground ginger
¼	tsp. ground nutmeg
¼	tsp. kosher salt
⅛	tsp. baking powder

1. Beat butter, granulated sugar, powdered sugar, and vanilla with a stand mixer fitted with a paddle attachment on medium speed until light and fluffy, 2 to 3 minutes, stopping to scrape down sides as needed. Add egg; beat on medium speed until well combined, about 30 seconds.
2. Whisk together flour, cinnamon, ginger, nutmeg, salt, and baking powder in a medium bowl until well combined. With mixer on low speed, gradually add flour mixture to butter mixture, beating just until combined, about 1 minute, stopping to scrape down sides as needed. Use immediately.

Vanilla Buttercream

Once it sets, this frosting develops a delicate, sugary crust, which is a lovely contrast to the creamy texture beneath.

ACTIVE 20 MIN. - TOTAL 20 MIN.

MAKES ABOUT 6 CUPS

- 1 cup vegetable shortening
- 1 cup unsalted butter, softened
- 2 (16-oz.) pkg. powdered sugar, sifted
- 5 to 6 Tbsp. whole milk, divided
- 1½ tsp. vanilla extract
- ½ tsp. kosher salt

1. Beat shortening with a stand mixer fitted with a paddle attachment on medium speed until smooth, about 30 seconds. Add butter, and beat until smooth and well combined, about 1 minute, stopping to scrape down sides as needed.
2. With mixer on low speed, gradually add powdered sugar alternating with 5 tablespoons of the milk, beating just until combined. Add vanilla and salt; beat on low speed just until combined, about 15 seconds. Add up to 1 tablespoon remaining milk, 1 teaspoon at a time, beating until smooth and spreadable. Increase speed to medium, and beat until fluffy, about 1 minute. Use immediately, refrigerate in an airtight container for up to 1 week, or freeze up to 1 month. Let frosting return to room temperature, and whisk until smooth before using.

Cookie Glaze

A splash of milk can take this recipe from thick to runny; add it gradually to achieve the perfect consistency for your needs.

ACTIVE 10 MIN. - TOTAL 10 MIN.

MAKES 1 CUP

- 3 cups powdered sugar
- 3 Tbsp. light corn syrup
- 1 tsp. vanilla extract (clear, if possible)
- ¼ tsp. kosher salt
- 3 to 4 Tbsp. whole milk, divided

Stir together powdered sugar, corn syrup, vanilla, salt, and 3 tablespoons of the milk in a medium bowl until combined. Stir in up to remaining 1 tablespoon milk, ½ to 1 teaspoon at a time, until desired consistency is reached (thicker for Chocolate Stockings, p. 329; thinner for Tie-Dye Glazed Ornaments, p. 330).

BUTTER COOKIE WREATHS

MERRY MITTEN COOKIES (PAGE 329)

Butter Cookie Wreaths

In lieu of sprinkles, dust these tiny wreaths with powdered sugar for a snowy look.

ACTIVE 35 MIN. - TOTAL 1 HOUR, 35 MIN.

MAKES ABOUT 3 DOZEN

- Spiced Spritz Cookie Dough (recipe opposite)
- Leaf green food coloring gel
- Red candy sprinkles
- Powdered sugar

1. Preheat oven to 350°F. Stir together Spiced Spritz Cookie Dough and food coloring gel in a bowl until the desired color is reached.

2. Spoon a portion of the dough into a piping bag fitted with a ⅝-inch open star piping tip. Pipe dough into 2¼-inch rings onto ungreased baking sheets, spacing about 1 inch apart. Repeat with remaining dough, refilling piping bag as needed. Top piped dough with sprinkles as desired.

3. Bake in preheated oven, 1 pan at a time, until set, 10 to 12 minutes. Immediately transfer cookies to a wire rack, and let cool completely, about 30 minutes. Dust with powdered sugar before serving. Store in an airtight container at room temperature for up to 5 days.

EVERGREEN
SPRITZ
COOKIES

CHOCOLATE
THUMBPRINTS

SPRINKLE LINZER
COOKIES

CHOCOLATE
STOCKINGS

Evergreen Spritz Cookies

Swap the green sparkling sugar for red, or use a variety to mimic multicolor Christmas lights.

ACTIVE 30 MIN. · TOTAL 1 HOUR, 40 MIN.
MAKES ABOUT 8 DOZEN COOKIES

> Spiced Spritz Cookie Dough (recipe, page 326)
>
> Light and dark green sparkling sugar

1. Preheat oven to 350°F. Place a portion of Spiced Spritz Cookie Dough in a cookie press fitted with desired attachment.
2. Press cookies onto ungreased baking sheets, spacing about 1 inch apart. Repeat with remaining dough, refilling press and changing attachment as needed. Sprinkle tops with sparkling sugars as desired.

3. Bake in preheated oven, 1 pan at a time, until lightly golden and set, 9 to 12 minutes.
4. Immediately transfer cookies to a wire rack, and let cool completely, about 30 minutes. Store in an airtight container at room temperature for up to 5 days.

Sprinkle Linzer Cookies

Try this versatile recipe with other fillings, such as cranberry preserves or orange marmalade.

ACTIVE 1 HOUR · TOTAL 2 HOURS, 5 MIN.
MAKES 40 COOKIES

> Vanilla Bean Dough (recipe, page 326)
>
> Red, green, gold, and silver sparkling sugars

½ cup lemon curd (from 1 [11-oz.] jar)
½ tsp. ground cardamom
 Lemon yellow food coloring gel (optional)
½ cup seedless strawberry jam (from 1 [18-oz.] jar)

1. Preheat oven to 375°F. Line 4 baking sheets with parchment paper. Roll half of Vanilla Bean Dough between 2 sheets of parchment paper to ⅛-inch thickness.
2. Remove top piece of parchment paper from dough. Cut dough using a lightly floured 2-inch fluted round cutter; use 1-inch fluted star, tree, and/ or candy cane cookie cutters to cut out centers of half of dough rounds; do not remove scraps. Transfer cut dough on parchment paper to a baking sheet; chill in freezer until firm, about 5 minutes. Place cut dough shapes ¾ inch apart on

prepared baking sheets. Sprinkle cutout dough circles with sparkling sugars as desired. Reroll, cut, and chill dough scraps as needed. Repeat process with remaining dough half.

3. Bake in preheated oven, 1 baking sheet at a time, until edges are set, 7 to 9 minutes. Let cool on baking sheets for 3 minutes; transfer cookies to a wire rack, and let cool completely, 30 minutes to 1 hour.

4. Whisk together lemon curd and cardamom in a bowl until combined; stir in yellow food coloring gel (if using), adding more until desired color is reached. Whisk strawberry jam in a separate bowl until smooth. Spread lemon curd mixture over half of uncut cookies. Spread strawberry jam over remaining uncut cookies.

5. Place cutout cookies on top of jam- or curd-covered cookies, pressing gently to adhere. Store in an airtight container at room temperature for up to 3 days.

Chocolate Stockings

If you're a fan of sprinkles and want to skip a step, glaze the entire surface of the cookies before dipping them.

ACTIVE 1 HOUR, 10 MIN. - TOTAL 1 HOUR, 50 MIN., PLUS 1 HOUR DRYING

MAKES ABOUT 16 COOKIES

> Chocolate Dough (recipe, page 326)
> ½ cup Cookie Glaze (recipe, page 327)
> ½ cup holiday sprinkles

1. Preheat oven to 350°F. Roll Chocolate Dough between 2 sheets of parchment paper to ¼ inch thickness. Transfer dough on parchment paper to a baking sheet; chill in freezer until firm, about 5 minutes. Cut dough using a 2½- to 3-inch stocking cookie cutter. Place cut dough shapes ¾ inch apart on a large parchment paper–lined baking sheet. (Reroll, freeze, and cut dough scraps as needed.)

2. Bake in preheated oven until tops are dry, about 8 minutes. Let cool completely on baking sheet on a wire rack.

3. Place Cookie Glaze in a piping bag fitted with a ⅛-inch round tip. Place sprinkles on a large rimmed plate. Pipe glaze within sock portion of stocking, leaving cuff portion unglazed. Dip cookie, glazed side down, into sprinkles until glazed portion is completely covered. Turn cookie, glazed side up;

pipe glaze within cuff portion. Let cookies stand, uncovered at room temperature, until glaze is set, 1 to 2 hours. Store in an airtight container at room temperature for up to 5 days.

Merry Mitten Cookies

(Photo, page 327)

If you don't have mitten shapes, you can duplicate this look using any combination of large and small cookie cutters. Trade out the hearts for stars, Christmas trees, or even simple circles.

ACTIVE 45 MIN. - TOTAL 1 HOUR, 5 MIN., PLUS 1 HOUR CHILLING AND COOLING

MAKES ABOUT 30 COOKIES

> Vanilla Bean Dough (recipe, page 326; prepared through Step 2)
> Super red food coloring gel
> Leaf green food coloring gel

1. Preheat oven to 375°F. Line 2 baking sheets with parchment paper.

2. Turn out Vanilla Bean Dough onto a clean work surface, and divide in half. Place 1 half in a mixing bowl; knead in red food coloring gel using a gloved hand until desired color is reached (gloves are not required, but dye will stain your hands). Transfer dough to a clean work surface. Place remaining half of dough in mixing bowl; knead in green food coloring gel using a gloved hand until desired color is reached. Wrap each half in plastic wrap, and refrigerate for at least 30 minutes or up to 2 days.

3. Roll red dough between 2 sheets of parchment paper to ¼-inch thickness. Repeat process with green dough and 2 more sheets of parchment paper.

4. Remove top piece of parchment paper. Cut red dough using a 3½-inch mitten cookie cutter; use a 1-inch heart-shape cookie cutter to cut in top of mitten. (Do not remove heart shape.) Repeat process with green dough, cutting out same number of mittens and hearts as red dough. Transfer dough shapes on parchment paper to baking sheets; freeze until firm, about 5 minutes.

5. Carefully remove heart-shape cutout from each mitten. Transfer mitten-shape cookies to prepared baking sheets, spacing at least ¾ inch apart. Press red hearts into holes left in green mittens and green hearts into holes left in red mittens. Reroll, cut, and chill dough scraps as needed.

6. Bake in preheated oven, 1 baking sheet at a time, until edges are set, 8 to 10 minutes. Let cool on baking sheets on a wire rack 5 minutes; transfer cookies to a wire rack, and let cool completely, about 30 minutes. Store in an airtight container at room temperature for up to 5 days.

Chocolate Thumbprints

For a different look, pipe red, green, or white Vanilla Buttercream (recipe, page 327) into the indentations instead of filling them with glaze.

ACTIVE 50 MIN. - TOTAL 1 HOUR, 30 MIN., PLUS 1 HOUR DRYING

MAKES ABOUT 2 DOZEN COOKIES

> ½ cup holiday sprinkles
> Chocolate Dough (recipe, page 326)
> ½ cup Cookie Glaze (recipe, page 327)
> Red food coloring gel
> Leaf green food coloring gel

1. Preheat oven to 350°F. Place sprinkles in a small bowl. Scoop and roll dough into 1-tablespoon balls; roll in sprinkles until evenly covered, and place about ¾ inch apart on a parchment paper–lined baking sheet. Make an indentation in center of each ball using back of a ½-teaspoon scoop. Smooth any cracks in edges.

2. Bake in preheated oven until tops appear dry, 8 to 10 minutes. Remove from oven, and gently press down centers with ½-teaspoon scoop. Let cool completely on baking sheet on a wire rack, about 30 minutes to 1 hour.

3. Divide Cookie Glaze evenly among 3 small bowls; stir red and green food coloring gels separately into 2 of the bowls, adding more to reach desired shades. Leave third bowl plain.

4. Spoon or pipe glazes into indentations in centers of cooled thumbprints as desired. Let stand until mostly set before serving, 1 to 2 hours. Store in an airtight container at room temperature for up to 5 days.

Tie-Dye Glazed Ornament Cookies

Pro tip: Let refrigerated dough sit at room temperature for about 30 minutes to make rolling much easier.
ACTIVE 2 HOURS · TOTAL 2 HOURS, 30 MIN., PLUS 1 HOUR COOLING AND 4 HOURS STANDING
MAKES ABOUT 40 COOKIES

> **Vanilla Bean Dough (recipe, page 326)**
>
> **Cookie Glaze (recipe, page 327)**
>
> **Teal, Christmas red, or leaf green food coloring gel**
>
> **Gold luster dust (optional)**

1. Preheat oven to 375°F. Line 3 baking sheets with parchment paper. Roll half of Vanilla Bean Dough between 2 sheets of parchment paper to ¼-inch thickness. Remove top piece of parchment paper. Cut dough using lightly floured 2½- to 3½-inch ornament cookie cutters; do not remove scraps. Transfer cut dough on parchment paper to a baking sheet; freeze until firm, about 5 minutes. Place cut dough shapes at least ¾ inch apart on prepared baking sheets. Reroll, cut, and chill dough scraps as needed. Repeat process with remaining dough half.
2. Bake in preheated oven, 1 pan at a time, until edges are set, 8 to 10 minutes. Let cool on pans for 5 minutes; transfer cookies to a wire rack, and let cool completely, about 1 hour.
3. Place ½ cup Cookie Glaze in a medium bowl; set aside. Divide remaining glaze between 2 small bowls. Stir desired food coloring gel into 1 bowl of Cookie Glaze, adding until a deep shade is reached. Stir a smaller amount of the same food coloring gel to second bowl, adding until a lighter shade is reached. Transfer each tinted glaze to a piping bag; cut a ¼-inch hole in the tip.
4. Make a crosshatch pattern in reserved plain Cookie Glaze by drizzling thin lines of deep shade of glaze and topping with thin lines of lighter shade. Dip top of a cooled cookie into pattern in bowl; twist and pull up, letting excess drip off. Place cookie, glaze side up, on a wire rack; wipe edges as needed. Repeat process with remaining cookies, adding tinted glaze in crosshatch pattern into bowl as needed.
5. Let cookies stand until set, about 4 hours. Using a clean paintbrush, decorate tops of cookies with luster dust, if desired. Store in an airtight container at room temperature for up to 5 days.

Frosted Sugar Cookie Snowflakes

When adding food coloring to frosting, a little goes a long way. Start with a small amount; stir, then increase gradually.
ACTIVE 1 HOUR, 30 MIN. · TOTAL 2 HOURS, PLUS 1 HOUR COOLING
MAKES ABOUT 2 DOZEN COOKIES

> **Vanilla Bean Dough (recipe, page 326)**
>
> **Vanilla Buttercream (recipe, page 327)**
>
> **Fuchsia, super red, neon green, and teal food coloring gels**
>
> **White, gold, and turquoise pearl sprinkles**

1. Preheat oven to 375°F. Line 3 baking sheets with parchment paper.
2. Roll half of Vanilla Bean Dough between 2 sheets of parchment paper to ¼-inch thickness. Remove top piece of parchment paper. Cut dough using a lightly floured 4-inch snowflake cookie cutter; do not remove scraps. Transfer dough on parchment paper to a baking sheet, and freeze until firm, about 5 minutes. Place cut dough shapes at least ¾ inch apart on parchment-lined baking sheets. Reroll, cut, and chill dough scraps as needed. Repeat process with remaining dough half.
3. Bake in preheated oven, 1 pan at a time, until edges are set, 8 to 10 minutes. Let cool on pans for 5 minutes; transfer cookies to a wire rack, and let cool completely, about 1 hour.
4. Place ½ cup Vanilla Buttercream in a piping bag fitted with a ⅛-inch round pastry tip, and set aside. Divide remaining Vanilla Buttercream among 4 bowls. Stir together fuchsia and red food coloring gels in 1 bowl of frosting, adding gels until desired magenta color is reached. Stir only red food coloring gel into another bowl of frosting, adding gel until desired color is reached. Stir green and teal food coloring gels separately into remaining 2 bowls of frosting, adding gels until desired colors are reached.
5. Spoon each tinted frosting into a separate piping bag, and fit each with a coupler. Fit 1 piping bag with a ¼-inch French open star piping tip; pipe tinted frosting over a cooled cookie as desired. Use reserved white buttercream to pipe a snowflake design over tinted frosting as desired. Garnish with pearl sprinkles. Repeat with remaining cookies, tinted frosting, and white buttercream, cleaning piping tip and transferring it to other piping bags as needed. Serve immediately, or store in an airtight container at room temperature for up to 5 days.

Chocolate-Peppermint Bars

To achieve this "Christmas sweater" look, use different-size star tips and pipe a combination of straight and squiggly lines.
ACTIVE 45 MIN. · TOTAL 55 MIN., PLUS 1 HOUR, 30 MIN. COOLING
SERVES 9

> **Chocolate Dough (recipe, page 326)**
>
> 2½ cups **Vanilla Buttercream (recipe, page 327)**
>
> ¼ tsp. **peppermint extract**
>
> **Super red food coloring gel**
>
> **Leaf green food coloring gel**
>
> **Electric pink food coloring gel**
>
> **Gold pearl sprinkles (optional)**

1. Preheat oven to 350°F. Grease an 8-inch square baking pan with cooking spray; line with parchment paper, leaving a 2-inch overhang on all sides. Pat Chocolate Dough into an even layer in prepared pan. Bake until edges are set but center is still soft, about 10 minutes. Let cool completely in pan on a wire rack, 1½ to 2 hours.
2. Stir together Vanilla Buttercream and extract in a bowl. Spread 1 cup of the frosting over cookie. Divide remaining frosting among 3 bowls; stir food coloring gel into each to reach desired shades.
3. Spoon each tinted frosting into a piping bag fitted with desired decorative tip. Pipe alternating lines of each color as desired, about ¾ inch apart. Decorate with pearl sprinkles (optional). Using parchment paper as handles, remove from pan. Cut into bars. Store in an airtight container at room temperature for up to 5 days.

CHOCOLATE-PEPPERMINT BARS

FROSTED SUGAR COOKIE SNOWFLAKES

TIE-DYE GLAZED ORNAMENT COOKIES

MARBLE STAR
COOKIES

Marble Star Cookies

The mesmerizing swirls of these stars are surprisingly easy to achieve—just follow the step-by-step photos at right. Use any single food coloring you like, or try a combination.

ACTIVE 45 MIN. - TOTAL 1 HOUR, 30 MIN, PLUS 1 HOUR CHILLING AND COOLING

MAKES ABOUT 30 COOKIES

> Vanilla Bean Dough (recipe, page 326; prepared through Step 2)
> Royal blue food coloring gel
> White sparkling sugar (optional)

1. Preheat oven to 375°F. Line 3 baking sheets with parchment paper.
2. Turn out Vanilla Bean Dough onto a clean work surface, and divide into thirds. Reserve one-third plain dough. Place one-third of dough in a mixing bowl; add small amount of food coloring gel, beating on low speed until desired light blue color is reached, about 30 seconds. Transfer dough to a clean work surface. Place next third of dough in mixing bowl; add food coloring gel, increasing amount as desired, beating until desired deep blue color is reached, about 30 seconds. Keep the remaining third of dough plain.
3. Divide each piece of dough in half to yield 6 portions total. Shape 1 plain dough portion into a 6-inch square on a sheet of parchment paper; shape 1 light blue dough portion into a 6-inch square, and place on top of plain dough square. Shape 1 deep blue dough portion into

a 6-inch square; place on top of light blue square. Repeat layers once with remaining dough. Fold stacked dough in half toward yourself, creating a taco-like shape. Slice dough crosswise into quarters. Turn quarters cut sides up; press dough quarters together, creating a swirled design. Cut dough in half; shape each half into a disk, and wrap in plastic wrap. Chill in refrigerator for at least 30 minutes or up to 2 days.
4. Roll 1 dough disk between 2 sheets of parchment paper to ¼-inch thickness. (If dough has been refrigerated for a long period, let stand at room temperature until slightly softened, 30 minutes to 1 hour.)
5. Remove top piece of parchment paper. Cut dough using a very lightly floured 3- to 3¾-inch star cookie cutter; do not remove scraps. Transfer dough on parchment paper to a baking sheet, and freeze until firm, about 5 minutes. Place cut dough shapes at least 1 inch apart on prepared baking sheets. Reroll, cut, and chill dough scraps as needed. (Stars will become more blue than marbled with each reroll.) Sprinkle tops with sparkling sugar (if desired).
6. Bake in preheated oven, 1 pan at a time, until edges are set, 8 to 10 minutes. Let cool on pans 5 minutes; transfer cookies to wire rack, and let cool completely, 30 minutes to 1 hour. Store in an airtight container at room temperature for up to 5 days.

How To Decorate Marble Star Cookies

1. Stack colored doughs as desired; fold into a "taco" shape.

2. Cut folded dough into four equal pieces; turn cut side down.

3. Press pieces together, gently forming into a disk.

Candy Crush

Three beautiful chocolate bark recipes for sharing (or not...)

CRANBERRY-PISTACHIO BARK

MOCHA BARK

GINGERBREAD BARK

Cranberry-Pistachio Bark

ACTIVE 15 MIN. - TOTAL 1 HOUR, 15 MIN.
SERVES 10

- 2 cups 60%-70% cacao dark chocolate chips (about 12 oz.)
- ¼ cup chopped pistachios
- ½ cup sweetened dried cranberries
- ¼ cup lightly salted toasted coconut chips (such as Dang)
  Flaky sea salt (optional)

1. Line a baking sheet with parchment paper; set aside.
2. Fill a medium saucepan with water to a depth of 1 to 2 inches. Bring to a simmer over medium. Carefully place a slightly smaller heatproof bowl on top of saucepan (the bowl should nestle comfortably in pan without touching water). Place chocolate in bowl; cook, stirring often, until melted, 4 to 5 minutes. Remove bowl from heat. (Alternatively, microwave chocolate in a microwavable bowl on HIGH for 1 minute. Stir, then continue microwaving in 30-second intervals,

stirring after each interval, until fully melted, about 1 minute, 30 seconds.)
3. Pour melted chocolate onto prepared baking sheet. Using an offset spatula, spread chocolate into a roughly ⅛-inch-thick rectangle (about 10 x 13 inches).
4. Sprinkle chocolate evenly with pistachios, cranberries, and coconut; if desired, sprinkle with flaky sea salt.
5. Chill bark, uncovered, in refrigerator until set, about 1 hour. Break into pieces. Store bark in an airtight container in refrigerator up to 1 week.

Mocha Bark

Prepare recipe through Step 2 as directed, using 1½ cups **white chocolate chips** and ½ cup **dark chocolate chips** (melting them in separate bowls) instead of all dark chocolate. Omit Steps 3 and 4. Pour melted white chocolate onto prepared baking sheet, using an offset spatula to spread it into a ⅛-inch-thick rectangle. Stir 2 tsp. **instant espresso granules** into melted dark chocolate. Drizzle dark chocolate mixture evenly

over white chocolate. Using a butter knife or the tip of the offset spatula, swirl dark chocolate into white chocolate. Sprinkle with ¼ cup chopped **chocolate-covered espresso beans** and, if desired, sprinkle with **flaky sea salt.** Proceed with Step 5 as directed.

Gingerbread Bark

Prepare recipe through Step 2 as directed, replacing dark chocolate with 2 cups **white chocolate chips** and stirring ¼ tsp. each **ground ginger** and **ground cinnamon** into the melted white chocolate. Proceed with Step 3 as directed. Omit Step 4. Sprinkle white chocolate evenly with about ¼ cup coarsely crushed **gingersnaps** and ¼ cup **chopped crystallized ginger.** Using a Microplane grater, grate zest from half of 1 **orange** (about 2 tsp.) evenly over top of melted white chocolate. If desired, garnish with **flaky sea salt** and **sprinkles.** Proceed with Step 5 as directed.

The Last Cheese Straw

Some taste memories grow fonder over time

ACCORDING TO MY PARTICULAR PALATE, the "perfect" cheese straws are 30 seconds away from being too toasted, a dash of cayenne short of being too spicy, and just teetering on the edge of being too salty. They are tiny sticks of flavor dynamite, dangerous for their ability to destroy any notions of temperance.

My grandmother May gets the credit for my personal obsession with this snack. Her simple recipe calls for just five ingredients: Cheddar cheese, butter, flour, salt, and cayenne pepper. But when I shared her method with the *Southern Living* Test Kitchen, their batches came out shockingly flat. It was perplexing–until we started thinking like a Southern grandmother. Instead of weighing the flour, we scooped it by the cupful. This small change resulted in the ideal balance of fat to flour, yielding cheese straws with the proper posture.

Family recipes take a perilous journey on their way to us. The wisdom and intuition of our predecessors simply can't fit on an index card. Unlike my generation, which documents nearly every meal on social media, folks back then never took any pictures of their food. In my memory, my grandmother's cheese straws are perfectly golden brown, crispy, and deftly dusted with paprika (that she neglected to include in her recipe). But knowing my grandmother, her batches were likely a little different from year to year, depending on how meticulously (or not) she measured the flour or if she got sidetracked and baked them for five minutes too long (I inherited her distractibility). What matters is that she made them well enough to earn them a permanent spot in our taste memories, solidifying the savory delights as a prerequisite for all our Christmas gatherings.

A full tin of cheese straws turns my family into snack predators. The hollow, metallic thwunk of the lid being opened is like blood in the water, signaling us to circle like sharks and snatch a handful while we can. Our entire stash is usually gone within two days. Mostly, that is. The portions shrink as the supply diminishes...until there's just one left, lonely in his crumb-riddled tin. Eventually, somebody gives in and opens the container for the final time. We're sad, but not devastated, because my grandmother taught my mother how to make them, my mother taught me and my father, my father taught my husband, and one day I'll teach my nephew. My grandmother may no longer be with us, but her cheese straws always will be. And as long as we keep making them, there will never truly be a last one.
–Josh Miller

Spicy Cheese Straws

These are inspired by my grandmother's recipe, but kicked up just a bit. If you don't have Aleppo pepper, substitute regular paprika.

ACTIVE 15 MIN. · TOTAL 1 HOUR, 50 MIN.

SERVES 8

- 1 lb. sharp Cheddar cheese, shredded (about 6 cups loosely packed)
- 1¼ cups butter, softened
- 1½ tsp. cayenne pepper
- 1 tsp. kosher salt
- 1 tsp. smoked paprika
- 3½ cups all-purpose flour
- Aleppo pepper, for sprinkling
- Flaky sea salt, for sprinkling

1. Preheat oven to 400°F with racks in top third and lower third positions. Add shredded cheese to the bowl of a stand mixer fitted with a paddle attachment; let stand until room temperature, at least 30 minutes. Add butter, cayenne, salt, and smoked paprika; beat on medium speed until creamy, about 2 minutes. Reduce mixer speed to low; gradually add flour, beating until a thick dough forms, scraping down sides of bowl as needed, about 3 minutes.

2. Line 2 rimmed baking sheets with parchment paper. Divide dough in half; spoon half of dough into a cookie press fitted with a star disk or into a piping bag fitted with an open star tip (about ½ inch wide). Press or pipe dough onto pans, spacing lines about 1 inch apart. Sprinkle with Aleppo pepper and flaky sea salt.

3. Bake in preheated oven until lightly golden brown, 12 to 14 minutes, rotating pans from top to bottom rack halfway through bake time. Let cool completely on pans, about 20 minutes; break into pieces as desired. Repeat piping procedure with remaining dough; bake and cool as directed. Serve or store in an airtight container at room temperature up to 4 days.

A Redbird Christmas

Celebrated author and Southern icon Fannie Flagg
shares her story of one very special Christmas

THE REDBIRD CAKE
(PAGE 337)

WHEN I WAS A CHILD living in South Alabama, my mother had a sweet friend named Frances Cleverdon, who resided on an oak-lined street in the little town of Magnolia Springs, Alabama. I always loved joining my mother on visits to "Miss Frances" in her beautiful old home on the river. Magnolia Springs was a true nature's paradise, with so many varieties of birds and other wildlife. It was such fun to be there, especially around Christmastime when Miss Frances would dress up as Mrs. Claus and hand out toys and sacks of delicious homegrown pecans. Even after we moved up to Birmingham, my mother would plan a trip or two every year to see Miss Frances.

Later when I was grown up, I was living and working in New York City, a long way from Alabama. There's a particular year I want to tell you about—it was not a good one for me. My mother had passed away only a few months earlier, and I had become increasingly unhappy in my career. I was feeling rather lost. Needless to say, when the holiday season rolled around, I was certainly not in a joyful mood.

Then one afternoon, quite out of the blue, the phone rang. It was Miss Frances calling from Alabama, inviting me to spend Christmas with her. "You need to come home, honey," she said. And so I did. Although I had not seen her for years, I figured it would be better than moping around my lonely apartment. I managed to get a few days off from work and headed down to Magnolia Springs. It was a long and exhausting trip. When I finally arrived, it was well after ten o'clock on Christmas Eve night. She and I caught up for a while, but she could see I was tired. After a cup of hot chocolate, I was taken up to the guest bedroom where my mother and I had stayed so many times before—the one with the pretty view of the backyard, all the way down to the river. But as I closed the curtains that

HISTORICALLY HUMMINGBIRD
On page 206 of the February 1978 issue of *Southern Living*, you'll find our first recipe for Hummingbird Cake, submitted by Mrs. L.H. Wiggins of Greensboro, North Carolina. We've baked up a lot of variations since then, but this is one of our favorites.

night, the winter trees—their bare black branches blowing in the wind—looked as sad and bleak as I felt. I crawled into the big feather bed with a heavy heart, wondering why I had even bothered to make the trip. This was going to be a very sad Christmas, no matter where I was.

Early the next morning, I heard a soft knock on my door. A smiling Miss Frances came in with coffee and set it on my nightstand. She walked over to the window, threw open the curtains, and announced, "Honey, I have a surprise for you. Come see." I forced myself to get up and look out. What a sight. The dark, dreary yard had turned into a living Christmas card. The sky was filled with big, fluffy, swirling snowflakes, and flocks of redbirds were soaring above the ground all the way down to the water.

I hardly had time to catch my breath when all at once, a streak of crimson shot straight up in the air. A huge redbird landed right on the windowsill. He cocked his head, looked me right in the eye, and began jumping up and down as if to say, "Get up; come outside and play." I was suddenly wide awake. "Wow! Did

you see that?" I asked. Miss Frances laughed and said, "Yes, I did. You know, your mother loved redbirds."

"I remember," I replied. "She always said they were her favorites. I wish she were here with us to see them."

Miss Frances smiled and said, "Well, honey, how do you know she's not?"

Looking back, I can truthfully say that when I left Magnolia Springs that holiday, the deep grief I had arrived with had disappeared. Someone or something must have known that trip was exactly what I needed.

I later learned that in many cultures across the world, going back thousands of years, a redbird sighting is believed to have a special meaning.

Early European settlers in America called them "cardinals" and said they were angels or spirits sent from heaven as a sign of hope and comfort. Others view them as a visit from a departed loved one, sent as a reminder that you are not alone.

Of course, we are all free to believe what we want. But for me, I will always think that seeing a redbird in December is nature's way of saying "Merry Christmas," straight from Heaven.

The Redbird Cake

Inspired by our perennially popular Hummingbird Cake, this festive twist is spruced up with maraschino cherries and a comforting blend of warm baking spices. The redbird cookies add a nostalgically sweet finishing touch.

ACTIVE 1 HOUR, 15 MIN. - TOTAL 1 HOUR, 35 MIN., PLUS 2 HOURS, 40 MIN. COOLING AND 30 MIN. CHILLING

SERVES 10

CAKE LAYERS

Baking spray

3 cups all-purpose flour

1¼ tsp. kosher salt

1¼ tsp. ground cinnamon

1 tsp. baking soda

1 tsp. ground ginger

½ tsp. ground allspice

1 (8-oz.) can crushed pineapple in juice

3 large eggs, at room temperature

2 cups granulated sugar

1¼ cups canola oil

⅔ cup mashed ripe bananas (from 2 medium bananas)

½ cup whole buttermilk, at room temperature

3 Tbsp. unsalted butter, melted

2 tsp. vanilla bean paste or extract

1 (16-oz.) jar stemless maraschino cherries, drained, finely chopped, and patted dry (about ¾ cup)

⅔ cup finely chopped toasted pecans

FROSTING

2 (8-oz.) pkg. cream cheese, softened

1 cup unsalted butter, softened

½ tsp. kosher salt

½ tsp. ground ginger

¼ tsp. ground cinnamon

1 (32-oz.) pkg. powdered sugar

1 Tbsp. vanilla bean paste or extract

DECORATIONS

Garnishes: Fresh rosemary sprigs, fresh sage sprigs, fresh bay leaves, and cinnamon sticks

Marzipan Pinecones (recipe follows)

Frosted Redbird Cookies (recipe, page 338)

Powdered sugar, for sprinkling

1. Prepare the Cake Layers: Preheat oven to 350˚F. Coat 3 (8-inch) round cake pans with baking spray; line bottoms using parchment paper. Set aside.
2. Whisk together flour, salt, cinnamon, baking soda, ginger, and allspice in a large bowl until well combined; set aside. Pour pineapple through a fine mesh strainer set over a large bowl; press solids to extract juice. Transfer pineapple to a cutting board, and finely chop. Add pineapple to strained juice in bowl. Whisk in eggs, granulated sugar, oil, bananas, buttermilk, butter, and vanilla until well combined. Add pineapple mixture to flour mixture; whisk until nearly combined. Fold in cherries and pecans.
3. Divide batter evenly among prepared pans (about 2⅔ cups per pan). Gently tap bottoms of pans on the countertop a few times to remove air bubbles.
4. Bake in preheated oven until a wooden pick inserted in centers of Cake Layers comes out clean, 22 to 25 minutes. Let cool in pans on wire racks 10 minutes. Remove from pans, and transfer, parchment side down, to wire racks; let cool completely, 2 hours, 30 minutes to 3 hours.
5. Prepare the Frosting: Beat cream cheese, butter, salt, ginger, and cinnamon with a stand mixer fitted with a paddle attachment on medium-low speed until smooth, 1 to 2 minutes, stopping to scrape down sides as needed. Reduce mixer speed to low, and gradually add powdered sugar, beating until combined after each addition. Add vanilla, and increase mixer speed to medium-high; beat until fluffy, 1 to 2 minutes.

6. Using a serrated knife, trim domed tops of Cake Layers; discard trimmings. Remove and discard parchment paper. Place 1 layer, trimmed side up, on a cake plate; spread top with 1¼ cups Frosting. Top with second layer, trimmed side up, and spread with 1¼ cups Frosting. Top with third layer, trimmed side down. Spread a very thin layer of Frosting over top and sides of cake to form a crumb coat. Chill, uncovered, until Frosting is mostly set, 30 to 40 minutes.
7. Remove cake from refrigerator. Spread remaining Frosting over top and sides of cake. Arrange rosemary, sage, bay leaves, and cinnamon sticks around top and bottom of cake. Add Marzipan Pinecones and Frosted Redbird Cookies to top and sides of cake, and dust with powdered sugar, if desired. Frosted undecorated cake may be stored in an airtight container in refrigerator up to 5 days; let cake return to room temperature before decorating and serving.

Marzipan Pinecones

ACTIVE 10 MIN. - TOTAL 10 MIN.

MAKES 2

Divide 2 Tbsp. marzipan in half; roll 1 Tbsp. of the marzipan between your hands into an egglike shape and place on a small piece of parchment paper. Starting at 1 pointed end of marzipan, insert sliced almonds in overlapping, shingled rows to create a pinecone-like exterior. Repeat with remaining 1 Tbsp. marzipan and almonds. Store in an airtight container up to 3 days.

Frosted Redbird Cookies

Packaged cookie icing (find it in the baking aisle of the grocery store) makes these cheery cardinals a snap to decorate.

ACTIVE 1 HOUR, 30 MIN. - TOTAL 1 HOUR, 45 MIN., PLUS 5 HOURS, 30 MIN. COOLING AND DRYING

MAKES 10 COOKIES

- ½ cup powdered sugar
- 6 Tbsp. unsalted butter, softened
- 2 Tbsp. granulated sugar
- 1 large egg yolk, at room temperature
- ½ tsp. vanilla extract
- 1¼ cups all-purpose flour, plus more for rolling and cutting
- ⅛ tsp. kosher salt
- ⅛ tsp. baking soda
- 1 (7-oz.) pkg. red cookie icing
  Red sanding sugar
- 1 (7-oz.) pkg. black cookie icing
- 1 (7-oz.) pkg. orange cookie icing

1. Preheat oven to 375°F. Beat powdered sugar, butter, and granulated sugar with a stand mixer fitted with a paddle attachment on low speed until just combined. Increase mixer speed to medium-low; beat until mixture is light and fluffy, 2 to 3 minutes, stopping to scrape down sides as needed. Beat in egg yolk and vanilla until combined.
2. Whisk together flour, salt, and baking soda in a small bowl. Reduce mixer speed to low; gradually add flour mixture to powdered sugar mixture, beating until dough just comes together, 1 to 2 minutes, stopping to scrape down sides as needed.
3. Roll dough out on a 13- x 18-inch sheet of parchment paper to ¼-inch thickness; transfer to a baking sheet, and freeze

5 minutes. Using a lightly floured 4½-inch cardinal cookie cutter, cut dough into as many birds as you can. Transfer dough cutouts to a second baking sheet lined with another sheet of parchment paper, spacing cutouts about 1 inch apart. Reroll scraps; repeat freezing and cutting with remaining dough.
4. Bake in preheated oven until edges are light golden, 8 to 10 minutes. Remove from oven, and transfer baking sheet to a wire rack; let cool 5 minutes. Transfer cookies to wire rack, and let stand until completely cool, about 30 minutes.
5. Place 1 cooled cookie on a clean work surface. Pipe a thin border of red icing around cookie edges, leaving an open space for the "beak" and "mask" portions; pipe red icing to fill most of the space within the piped border. Using a wooden pick, spread icing to create an even layer. Generously sprinkle icing with red sanding sugar. Transfer iced cookie to a wire rack. Repeat decorating process with remaining cookies, red icing, and sanding sugar. Let cookies stand until red icing is dry to the touch, about 40 minutes.
6. Gently brush off excess sugar from iced cookies. Working with 1 cookie at a time, pipe a border of black icing along edge of open space closest to red icing to form the "mask," leaving a diamond-shape open area for the "beak." Let stand until black icing is mostly dry to the touch, about 15 minutes.
7. Working with 1 cookie at a time, pipe and fill the remaining "beak" space with orange icing; spread using a wooden pick as needed. Let cookies stand at room temperature until icing has completely dried, at least 4 hours. Store in an airtight container at room temperature up to 3 days.

How To Ice Redbird Cookies

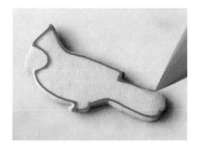

1. Pipe a thin border of red icing around the edges of the cooled cookie, leaving a blank space for the "mask" and "beak."

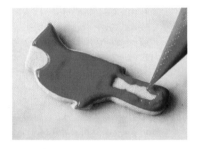

2. Fill in outlined area with red icing, adding a little at time and spreading with a wooden pick for even coverage.

3. Pipe a thin line of black icing to form the "mask." Let dry, then fill in remaining space with orange icing for the "beak."

Double-Dip

Help yourself to seconds with this healthier take on an old-school favorite

Baked Three-Cheese Spinach-Artichoke Dip

ACTIVE 15 MIN. - TOTAL 55 MIN.

SERVES 8

- 1 (8-oz.) pkg. ⅓-less-fat cream cheese, softened
- ½ cup sour cream
- ½ cup mayonnaise
- 1 Tbsp. hot sauce
- 2 tsp. garlic powder
- 2 tsp. onion powder
- 1½ tsp. grated lemon zest (from 1 lemon)
- ½ tsp. kosher salt
- 2 (14-oz.) cans chopped artichoke hearts, drained (about 3 cups)
- 1 (15-oz.) pkg. frozen chopped spinach, thawed and squeezed dry
- 8 oz. Monterey Jack cheese, shredded (about 2 cups), divided
- 3 oz. Parmesan cheese, finely shredded (about 1 cup), divided
   Crudités, for serving
   Whole grain chips, for serving

1. Preheat oven to 375°F. Spray a 2-quart baking dish with cooking spray; set aside. Whisk together cream cheese, sour cream, mayonnaise, hot sauce, garlic and onion powders, lemon zest, and salt in a large bowl until mostly smooth. Fold in artichokes, spinach, 1½ cups of the Monterey Jack, and ⅔ cup of the Parmesan until combined.
2. Spoon mixture into prepared dish, spreading into an even layer. Sprinkle evenly with remaining ½ cup Monterey Jack and ⅓ cup Parmesan.
3. Bake in preheated oven until golden brown and bubbly, 35 to 40 minutes. Serve hot with crudités and tortilla chips.

Before Recipe Makeover:

CALORIES: **748** – SODIUM: **1,440 MG** – FAT: **70 G**

After Recipe Makeover:

CALORIES: **412** – SODIUM: **822 MG** – FAT: **30 G**

GOOD FOR YOU!
Eating better doesn't have to mean giving up the foods you crave. This dip delivers big flavor with about half the cheese in traditional recipes.

Her Magic Touch

Craig Melvin's mom, Betty Jo, is behind his most treasured memories

CRAIG MELVIN GOT HIS LOVE for Christmas from his mother. "When we were growing up, my mom did everything to make the holidays extra special for us, and I've been trying to do the same for my own kids," says the *Today* show anchor; journalist; and Columbia, South Carolina, native. Betty Jo Melvin makes a ritual of decorating her home every year, starting on the day after Thanksgiving "and not a minute after," she adds. Bowls filled with fruits, nuts, and peppermints are set on tabletops, and red and pink poinsettias are displayed throughout every room, a festive touch she learned from her own mother. But the shining stars are the two artificial trees wrapped in strands of clear twinkling lights, one trimmed with an assortment of homemade and vintage baubles, the other adorned with her beloved collection of angel ornaments. "The trees have always been an elaborate production. Mom would leave them up until April if she could," says Craig jokingly. Betty Jo doesn't disagree: "I would keep them up forever. There's something about those trees that brings me a sense of peace."

Betty Jo was born in Cayce, South Carolina. By the time she turned 10, her family had moved across the river to Columbia, and she has called it home ever since. She's the eldest of four children, the first in her family to graduate college, a retired teacher, an avid cook and baker, and the memory maker for her two sons, Craig and Ryan. "When I was a kid, I was lucky to have aunts, uncles, cousins, and my two grandmothers all around us in Columbia," says Craig. "We could bounce from house to house and celebrate with everyone. That's what makes Christmastime so unforgettable for me. It was magical."

And it wouldn't be Christmas—or any Melvin gathering—without Betty Jo's famous macaroni and cheese (recipe at right). "Mom's mac and cheese is the official family side dish. If someone can't attend a get-together, they'll call ahead to request a plate be set aside," says Craig. Like many Southern recipes that are passed down through generations, this classic was shared with Betty Jo by her mother, Florence, who prepared it every Sunday when they were growing up. Over the years, she has put her own signature spin on the decadent side by adding more types of cheeses than the original and admits it's definitely a crowd-pleaser. "I always get in trouble if there's not enough!" says Betty Jo, laughing.

The holidays look a little different these days for Craig, who now resides in Connecticut with his wife, Lindsay Czarniak, and their two children (Delano, 9, and Sybil, 7), but they always try to make it to Columbia to visit family and friends, catch the Lights at Riverbanks Zoo, and create new traditions in his hometown. No matter where they're celebrating on December 25, you can count on seeing Betty Jo's macaroni and cheese on the table.

Betty Jo Melvin's Macaroni and Cheese

ACTIVE 20 MIN. · TOTAL 1 HOUR, 10 MIN.

SERVES 10

6	Tbsp. butter, cubed, plus more for baking dish
12	oz. uncooked elbow macaroni (about 3 cups)
1	(12-oz.) can evaporated milk
1	cup plus 2 Tbsp. whole milk
3	large eggs, lightly beaten
1½	oz. processed cheese (such as Velveeta), cut into ½-inch cubes
1½	tsp. kosher salt
½	tsp. black pepper
11½	oz. preshredded sharp Cheddar cheese (about 3 cups), divided
4½	oz. preshredded mild Cheddar cheese (about 1½ cups), divided

1. Preheat oven to 425°F. Grease a 9- x 13-inch baking dish with butter, and set aside.
2. Prepare macaroni according to package directions for al dente. Drain, and transfer to a large bowl.
3. Stir butter into hot macaroni until melted. Stir in evaporated milk, whole milk, and eggs until well combined. Fold in processed cheese, salt, pepper, 2½ cups of the sharp Cheddar, and 1 cup of the mild Cheddar.
4. Transfer macaroni mixture to prepared baking dish. Sprinkle evenly with remaining ½ cup each sharp Cheddar and mild Cheddar.
5. Bake, uncovered, in preheated oven until golden and bubbly, 45 to 50 minutes. Serve immediately.

"Mom's mac and cheese is the official family side dish."

On a Roll

Senior Test Kitchen Pro Ivy Odom bakes up a new tradition with these savory pinwheels

GROWING UP, we always had Christmas breakfast at my Nana and Papa's house, and it was an elaborate Southern affair. Nana pulled out her Franciscan Ivy china and coordinating green glassware a week before, gave it all a good polish, and set up everything on a festive tablecloth in the dining room. On the morning of our gathering, while her grandchildren were up early opening presents at their own houses, Nana was hard at work in the kitchen. Her menu was extensive: biscuits and yeast rolls, patty and link sausages, bacon and fried cube steak (with gravy), rice and grits—she wanted to make sure everyone had their favorites. Now that these cooking duties have been passed on to my mama and me, we keep most of Nana's menu the same—she'd have a fit if we didn't. But every year, I try to add my own spin on her classics, like a new biscuit recipe, a special gravy, or these Pimiento Cheese Sausage Rolls. Whether you serve them with a pretty fruit salad on your best china or eat them straight from the pan, consider them a hug from my little corner of the South.

Pimiento Cheese Sausage Rolls

ACTIVE 15 MIN. - TOTAL 1 HOUR, PLUS 40 MIN. STANDING

SERVES 12

- 1   lb. fresh pizza dough
- 12 oz. hot ground pork sausage
- 4   oz. sharp Cheddar cheese, shredded (about 1 cup), plus more for sprinkling
- 4   oz. cream cheese, softened
- 1   (7-oz.) jar diced pimientos, drained
- 1   Tbsp. grated sweet onion
- 1   tsp. garlic powder
     All-purpose flour, for work surface

1. Let pizza dough stand, covered, at room temperature until no longer cold to the touch, about 30 minutes. Meanwhile, place sausage, Cheddar, cream cheese, pimientos, onion, and garlic powder in a large bowl. Using your hands or a rubber spatula, mix ingredients together until well combined. Cover and refrigerate until ready to use.

2. Preheat oven to 375°F. Roll out dough on a lightly floured work surface, and gently stretch into a 16- x 12-inch rectangle. Using an offset spatula or your hands, spread sausage mixture evenly over dough rectangle, leaving a ½-inch border on each long edge of dough and spreading mixture out fully to shorter edges of dough. Starting with 1 long edge, roll up dough, jelly roll style, to create a log. Using a serrated knife, cut log crosswise evenly into 12 (about 1¼-inch-wide) slices.

3. Lightly grease a 7- x 11-inch glass or ceramic baking dish with cooking spray. Arrange sausage rolls in prepared baking dish in 4 rows of 3. Sprinkle tops of rolls with desired amount of additional Cheddar; cover dish with aluminum foil.

4. Bake in preheated oven for 20 minutes. Remove foil, and continue baking until tops of rolls are golden brown and a thermometer inserted into the thickest portion of the sausage mixture registers 165°F, 20 to 25 minutes. Remove sausage rolls from oven, and let stand 10 minutes. Serve warm, or store, covered, in refrigerator up to 3 days.

BAKING SCHOOL

TIPS AND TRICKS FROM THE SOUTH'S MOST TRUSTED KITCHEN

Make Your Mark

Stamps are a fun and effortless way to decorate cookies

For a big impression without making and fussing over royal icing, try cookie stamps. They create intricate, three-dimensional embossed designs in any dough—no artistic skills required. Pro tip: Dip the stamps in flour or powdered sugar between uses to guarantee the best results. *nordicware.com*

Did you know that **instant espresso granules** enhance the flavor of chocolate? Simply stir a small amount (it's potent stuff) into icings, batters, and doughs. The powder can also be used to make hot brewed coffee in a flash for cake and brownie batters.

FLAVOR BOOSTERS

Add these items to your pantry and punch up your baking

Good for more than just milkshakes, **malted milk powder** helps cookies brown and adds nutty caramel notes to baked goods. You can fold it into any dough, but it does contain salt, so consider adjusting your recipe accordingly.

Give It a Rest

You rest steaks before serving, but did you know that you should give your cookie dough a break too? Resting allows the flour to hydrate, the dough to firm up, and the flavors to meld and deepen—yielding superior results. Even if you have just 30 minutes to spare, you'll taste the difference that a little bit of time in the fridge can make.

Well Rounded

Even professional bakers make imperfect cookies, but you'd never know it, thanks to this kitchen hack. You'll need a drinking glass (or a biscuit cutter) that is slightly wider than the cookies you're making. Immediately after they come out of the oven, turn the glass or cutter upside down and place it over a cookie. Gently swirl the glass in a circular motion until the edges become smooth and even. Work quickly; the edges won't budge once they've cooled.

COOKING SCHOOL

TIPS AND TRICKS FROM THE SOUTH'S MOST TRUSTED KITCHEN

Southern Staple
Worcestershire Sauce

Worcestershire sauce was created in 1837 in Worcester, England, when two chemists named John Wheeley Lea and William Henry Perrins first concocted the condiment made with malt vinegar, anchovies, and garlic. After allowing the sauce to age for 18 months, they put it on the market and soon began exporting it abroad, bestowed with a name tied to where it was invented. Although the sauce has British origins, Southern cooks consider its savory-salty flavor an irreplaceable part of many recipes. Here are a few ways to put the condiment to good use.

- Fold it into a cheese ball for added savoriness

- Add a splash to your michelada or Bloody Mary

- Stir a few tablespoons into chili or beef stew to amp up the meatiness

Fresh Isn't Always Best

Dried herbs are better for long braises because they won't turn bitter, making them ideal for rubs because they help create a delicious crust. They're also more concentrated than fresh, especially when stored properly away from light, heat, air, and moisture. Generally, you should substitute a third of the amount of dried herbs for fresh in recipes. You'll also want to add them in the earlier stages of the cooking process, unlike fresh, which are typically saved until the end.

Just a Pinch

It can be expensive and wasteful to buy full jars of spices, but Occo Spices sells them in half-teaspoon pods that come in mix-and-match packs, for a space- and money-saving way to sample new flavors or replace old jars.
eatocco.com

Our Favorite Pies & Cakes Recipes

When you need to whip up a dessert for a crowd, it's more than likely your go-to is a special pie or cake. In this collection of our favorites, you'll find the perfect recipe for any season or occasion. For Thanksgiving, consider Elegant Pumpkin-Walnut Layered Pie (page 346). For a summer barbecue, toss together Piña Colada Icebox Pie (page 348) in minutes. Got a birthday dinner? Celebrate with Chocolate Marble Sheet Cake (page 349) or Chocolate-Peppermint Candy Cupcakes (page 350). With any of these best-of recipes, your special occasion will be a slice!

Pies

Single-Crust Pie Pastry
ACTIVE 10 MIN. - TOTAL 2 HOURS, 10 MIN.
MAKES 1 CHILLED DOUGH DISK

- 1½ cups all-purpose flour
- ½ tsp. salt
- 6 Tbsp. cold unsalted butter, cubed
- 2 Tbsp. cold shortening, cubed
- 3 to 4 Tbsp. ice water

1. Pulse flour and salt in a food processor until combined, 3 to 4 times. Add butter and shortening, and pulse until mixture resembles small peas, 4 to 5 times. Sprinkle 3 tablespoons ice water over top of mixture. Pulse 4 times. Add up to 1 more tablespoon of water, 1 teaspoon at a time, pulsing after each addition until dough just begins to clump together.
2. Turn dough out onto a lightly floured work surface; knead until dough comes together, 2 to 3 times. Shape and flatten dough into a disk. Wrap in plastic wrap, and chill 2 hours or up to 2 days.

Double-Crust Pie Pastry
ACTIVE 15 MIN. - TOTAL 2 HOURS, 15 MIN.
MAKES 2 CHILLED DOUGH DISKS

- 3 cups all-purpose flour
- 1 tsp. kosher salt
- ¾ cup cold unsalted butter, cubed
- ¼ cup cold shortening, cubed
- 4 to 6 Tbsp. ice water

1. Pulse flour and salt in a food processor until combined, 3 to 4 times. Add butter and shortening, and pulse until mixture resembles small peas, 4 to 5 times. Sprinkle 4 tablespoons ice water over top of mixture. Pulse 4 times. Add up to 2 more tablespoons of water, 1 tablespoon at a time, pulsing after each addition until dough just begins to clump together.
2. Turn dough out onto a lightly floured work surface; gently knead until dough comes together, 2 to 3 times. Divide dough in half. Shape and flatten each half into a disk. Wrap each disk in plastic wrap. Chill 2 hours or up to 2 days.

Sliced Sweet Potato Pie with Molasses Whipped Cream
ACTIVE 1 HOUR - TOTAL 2 HOURS, 30 MIN., PLUS 4 HOURS COOLING
SERVES 8

CRUST
Double-Crust Pie Pastry (recipe left)

SWEET POTATO FILLING
- 3 lb. sweet potatoes (about 6 medium-size sweet potatoes)
- 1¼ cups granulated sugar
- 2 Tbsp. all-purpose flour
- ¼ tsp. ground allspice
- ½ tsp. ground ginger
- ½ tsp. ground nutmeg
- ¼ tsp. ground cloves
- ¼ cup sorghum syrup, molasses, pure cane syrup, or honey
- ⅓ cup cold unsalted butter, chopped into small pieces

EGG WASH
- 1 large egg
- 1 Tbsp. water
- 2 Tbsp. granulated sugar (optional)

ADDITIONAL INGREDIENT
Molasses Whipped Cream (p. 346)

1. Prepare the Crust: Unwrap chilled pie dough disks from Double-Crust Pie Pastry, and place on a lightly floured surface. Let stand at room temperature until slightly softened, about 5 minutes. Sprinkle each disk with flour. Roll 1 disk into a 12-inch circle. Carefully fit dough circle into a 9-inch deep-dish glass pie plate, leaving a 1½-inch overhang. Refrigerate until ready to use. Roll remaining disk into a 10-inch circle, and refrigerate until ready to use.
2. Prepare the Sweet Potato Filling: Place whole, unpeeled sweet potatoes in a large pot with water to cover by 2 inches. Bring to a rolling boil over high. Reduce heat to medium, maintaining a gentle boil. Cook until sweet potatoes are just tender enough to be sliced, but not so tender that they fall apart, 25 to 35 minutes. (Remove any smaller sweet

Continued on page 346

Continued from page 345

potatoes as they are done, allowing larger ones to cook until they reach the ideal texture.)

3. Stir together sugar, flour, allspice, ginger, nutmeg, and cloves in a small bowl.

4. Drain sweet potatoes, and transfer to a platter to cool. Peel potatoes; trim and discard any fibers. Cut potatoes crosswise into ¼-inch-thick rounds. (You will need about 4 cups to fill piecrust generously.) Gently toss sweet potatoes with sugar-spice mixture.

5. Preheat oven to 350°F. Cover bottom of piecrust in pie plate with a layer of Sweet Potato Filling; continue to layer to fill piecrust. Add additional filling to center, building it up a little higher than outer edges. Sprinkle all remaining sugar-spice mixture in bowl over top of pie; drizzle with sorghum syrup, and dot with butter pieces.

6. Carefully place 10-inch dough circle over filling. Fold edges of bottom crust up and over edges of top crust, and press firmly to seal. Using the tines of a fork, press dough around piecrust edge to make a decorative design. Using a sharp knife, cut 8 slits in top piecrust for steam to escape.

7. Prepare the Egg Wash: Stir together egg and water in a small bowl. Using a pastry brush, brush egg mixture evenly over piecrust. Sprinkle sugar over crust, if desired. Place pie on a baking sheet.

8. Bake in preheated oven until crust is browned, filling is bubbly, and sweet potatoes are tender all the way through, about 1 hour.

9. Transfer pie to a wire rack, and cool to room temperature, about 4 hours. Serve with Molasses Whipped Cream (below).

Molasses Whipped Cream
ACTIVE 5 MIN. - TOTAL 5 MIN.
MAKES ABOUT 2¼ CUPS

- 1 cup heavy whipping cream, cold
- 2 Tbsp. molasses (not blackstrap), pure cane syrup, or sorghum syrup
- ½ tsp. vanilla extract

Using chilled beaters and a large chilled bowl, beat cream with an electric mixer on high speed until thickened, about 2 minutes. Add molasses, and beat until stiff peaks form, about 2 minutes. Add vanilla extract; beat 1 minute. Cover and chill whipped cream until ready to serve.

Elegant Pumpkin-Walnut Layered Pie
ACTIVE 20 MIN. - TOTAL 1 HOUR, 20 MIN., PLUS 1 HOUR COOLING AND 2 HOURS CHILLING
MAKES 8 SERVINGS

- 1 cup chopped walnuts
- 1 (14.1-oz.) pkg. refrigerated piecrusts (2 crusts), divided
- 1 large egg, lightly beaten
- 3 Tbsp. butter, melted
- ¼ tsp. vanilla extract
- 1¼ cups firmly packed light brown sugar, divided
- 1 (8-oz.) pkg. cream cheese, softened
- 2 large eggs
- 1 (15-oz.) can pumpkin
- 2 Tbsp. all-purpose flour
- 1 tsp. ground cinnamon
- ½ tsp. ground ginger
- ½ tsp. ground allspice
- ¼ tsp. ground nutmeg
  Vanilla ice cream, for serving (optional)

1. Preheat oven to 350°F. Bake walnuts in a single layer in a shallow pan until toasted and fragrant, 8 to 10 minutes, stirring occasionally. Remove from oven; increase temperature to 425°F.

2. Unroll 1 piecrust, and cut out pastry leaves using a 2-inch leaf-shape cutter. Brush leaves with beaten egg. Place leaves on an ungreased baking sheet.

3. Bake until golden, 6 to 7 minutes. Let cool on a wire rack.

4. Meanwhile, fit remaining piecrust into a 9-inch pie plate; fold edges under, and crimp. Prick bottom and sides of piecrust with a fork. Bake until lightly browned, 6 to 8 minutes.

5. Combine toasted walnuts, butter, vanilla, and ½ cup of the brown sugar; spread walnut mixture in bottom of prepared piecrust.

6. Beat cream cheese with an electric mixer on medium speed until creamy. Gradually add the remaining ¾ cup brown sugar, beating well. Add eggs and pumpkin, beating well.

7. Combine flour, cinnamon, ginger, allspice, and nutmeg. Add to cream cheese mixture, beating until blended. Pour cream cheese mixture over walnut mixture.

8. Bake at 425°F for 10 minutes. Reduce oven temperature to 350°F, and bake until pie is set, 30 to 35 minutes.

Cool on wire rack 1 hour. Chill for at least 2 hours.

9. Arrange pastry leaves around edge of pie. Served chilled pie with vanilla ice cream, if desired.

Pecan-Chewy Pie
ACTIVE 35 MIN. - TOTAL 1 HOUR, 10 MIN.
MAKES 2 (9-INCH) PIES

CRUST AND STREUSEL
- 1¼ cups all-purpose flour
- 1 cup granulated sugar
- 5 Tbsp. cold butter, divided
- 2 cups very finely chopped pecans
- 1 Tbsp. cold water
- 1 large egg, beaten

CHEWY PECAN FILLING
- 1 cup white chocolate chips
- ½ cup salted butter
- ½ cup dark brown sugar
- 4 large egg yolks, at room temperature
- 1 cup heavy whipping cream, at room temperature
- 1½ cups roughly chopped toasted pecans
- ⅔ cup all-purpose flour
- 1 tsp. kosher salt

ADDITIONAL INGREDIENT
  Ice cream

1. Prepare Crust and Streusel: Preheat oven to 350°F. Stir together flour and granulated sugar in a medium bowl. Using a fork or pastry cutter, cut 4 tablespoons of the butter into flour mixture until it resembles small pebbles. Stir in pecans, water, and egg until mixture is damp. Grease 2 (9-inch) pie pans with remaining 1 tablespoon butter. Divide pecan mixture into thirds; place a third into each pan, pressing to cover bottom and sides. Set aside remaining third. Bake crusts in preheated oven on middle rack of oven until the edges are lightly browned, about 10 minutes. Cool 10 minutes.

2. Prepare the Filling: Melt white chocolate chips and butter in a double boiler over low. (Mixture may separate.) Whisk together brown sugar and egg yolks in a medium bowl until combined. Pour white chocolate mixture into brown sugar mixture, and whisk to combine. Whisk in cream. Stir together pecans, flour, and salt in a small bowl;

fold into white chocolate mixture just until incorporated.

3. Reduce oven temperature to 325°F. Divide filling mixture between 2 crusts. Sprinkle remaining streusel over pies. Bake until golden brown and set, about 35 minutes. Serve warm or at room temperature with ice cream.

Salted Caramel-Chocolate Pecan Pie

ACTIVE 25 MIN. - TOTAL 1 HOUR, 20 MIN.
SERVES 8

CHOCOLATE FILLING
- 1½ cups granulated sugar
- ¾ cup butter, melted
- ⅓ cup all-purpose flour
- ⅓ cup unsweetened cocoa powder
- 1 Tbsp. light corn syrup
- 1 tsp. vanilla extract
- 3 large eggs
- 1 cup toasted chopped pecans
- 1 (9-inch) unbaked deep-dish piecrust shell

SALTED CARAMEL TOPPING
- ¾ cup granulated sugar
- 1 Tbsp. fresh lemon juice
- ⅓ cup heavy whipping cream
- 4 Tbsp. butter
- ¼ tsp. kosher salt
- 2 cups toasted pecan halves
- ½ tsp. sea salt

1. Prepare Filling: Preheat oven to 350°F. Stir together sugar, butter, flour, cocoa, corn syrup, and vanilla in a large bowl. Add eggs, stirring until well blended. Fold in chopped pecans. Pour mixture into crust.
2. Bake in preheated oven 35 minutes. (Filling will be loose but will set as it cools.) Remove from oven to a wire rack.
3. Prepare Topping: Bring sugar, lemon juice, and ¼ cup water to a boil in a medium saucepan over high. Boil, swirling occasionally after sugar begins to change color, 8 minutes or until dark amber. (Watch carefully as the sugar could burn quickly once it begins to change color.) Remove from heat; add cream and butter. Stir constantly until bubbling stops and butter is incorporated (about 1 minute). Stir in kosher salt.
4. Arrange pecan halves on pie. Top with warm caramel. Cool 15 minutes; sprinkle with sea salt.

Cranberry-Apple Pie

Sparkling sugar can be found in specialty supermarkets and stores that carry cake-decorating products.
ACTIVE 15 MIN. - TOTAL 1 HOUR, PLUS 1 HOUR COOLING
SERVES 8

- 1 (14.1-oz.) pkg. refrigerated piecrusts (2 crusts), divided
- 1 large egg, lightly beaten Cranberry-Apple Pie Filling (recipe follows)
- 4 Tbsp. sparkling sugar,* divided

1. Preheat oven to 400°F. Fit 1 piecrust into a 9-inch pie plate according to package directions. Brush edges of piecrust with egg. Spoon Cranberry-Apple Pie Filling into piecrust, mounding filling in center of pie.
2. Unroll remaining piecrust on a lightly floured surface. Brush piecrust lightly with egg; sprinkle with 2 tablespoons sparkling sugar. Using the width of a ruler as a guide, cut the piecrust into 9 (1-inch-wide) strips. Arrange strips in a lattice design over filling; fold excess bottom piecrust under and along edges of top piecrust. Gently press ends of strips, sealing to bottom piecrust. Brush lattice with egg; sprinkle with remaining 2 tablespoons sparkling sugar. Place pie on a baking sheet.
3. Bake in preheated oven on lower oven rack 45 minutes, shielding with aluminum foil after 30 minutes to prevent excessive browning. Remove from oven, and let cool on a wire rack 1 hour.
***Note:** Regular or turbinado sugar may be substituted.

Cranberry-Apple Pie Filling

ACTIVE 30 MIN. - TOTAL 1 HOUR, 15 MIN.
MAKES ENOUGH FOR 1 (9-INCH) PIE

- 12 large cooking apples, peeled (about 6 lb.)
- 1½ cups granulated sugar
- ⅓ cup all-purpose flour
- ½ cup butter
- 1 cup sweetened dried cranberries

Cut apples into wedges; toss with sugar and flour. Melt butter in a large skillet over medium; add apple mixture to skillet, and sauté 10 to 15 minutes or until apples are tender. Stir in sweetened dried cranberries; remove from heat, and let cool completely, about 45 minutes.

Tiramisú Toffee Trifle Pie

ACTIVE 25 MIN. - TOTAL 25 MIN., PLUS 8 HOURS CHILLING
SERVES 8 TO 10

- 1½ Tbsp. instant coffee granules
- ¾ cup warm water
- 1 (10.75-oz.) frozen pound cake, thawed
- 1 (8.8-oz.) pkg. mascarpone or cream cheese, softened
- ½ cup powdered sugar
- ½ cup chocolate syrup
- 1 (12-oz.) container frozen whipped topping, thawed, divided
- 2 (1.4-oz.) English toffee candy bars, coarsely chopped*

1. Stir together coffee and water until coffee is dissolved. Let cool.
2. Meanwhile, cut cake into 14 slices. Cut each slice in half crosswise. Place cake slices in bottom and overlapping up sides of a 9-inch deep-dish pie plate. Drizzle coffee mixture over cake slices.
3. Beat mascarpone cheese, sugar, and chocolate syrup with an electric mixer on medium speed until smooth. Add 2½ cups whipped topping, and beat until light and fluffy.
4. Spread cheese mixture over cake. Dollop remaining whipped topping in center of pie. Sprinkle with chopped candy bars. Cover and chill 8 hours.
***Note:** 10 miniature English toffee candy bars (from 1 [12-oz.] pkg.), coarsely chopped, may be substituted.

Fudgy Peanut Butter Cup Pie

ACTIVE 15 MIN. - TOTAL 30 MIN., PLUS 2 HOURS FREEZING
MAKES 8 SERVINGS

- 1 (1.75-qt.) container vanilla ice cream with peanut butter cups swirled with fudge
- ½ cup creamy or chunky peanut butter
- 1 (6-oz.) prepared chocolate crumb piecrust
- 6 (0.55-oz.) peanut butter cup candies, halved
- ½ cup chocolate-peanut butter shell coating

1. Allow ice cream to stand at room temperature until softened, 20 to 30 minutes.

Continued on page 348

Continued from page 347

2. Meanwhile, spread peanut butter over the crust and freeze 10 minutes.

3. Spread softened ice cream evenly over peanut butter in crust. Arrange peanut butter cup candy halves, cut sides down, around edges of crust. Drizzle chocolate–peanut butter shell coating over ice cream. Freeze at least 2 hours.

4. To serve, cut frozen pie with a warm knife.

Piña Colada Icebox Pie

ACTIVE 25 MIN. · TOTAL 2 HOURS, 20 MIN., PLUS 4 HOURS CHILLING

SERVES 8

- 2 cups pecan shortbread cookie crumbs (about 16 cookies)
- 1 cup sweetened flaked coconut
- ¼ cup butter, melted
- ⅓ cup granulated sugar
- 2 Tbsp. cornstarch
- 1 (8-oz.) can crushed pineapple in juice
- 1 (8-oz.) pkg. cream cheese, softened
- 1½ cups cream of coconut, divided
- 2 large eggs
- 1 cup heavy whipping cream
  Lightly toasted shaved coconut, pineapple wedges, fresh pineapple mint sprigs, for garnish (optional)

1. Preheat oven to 350°F. Lightly coat a 9-inch pie plate with cooking spray. Stir together cookie crumbs, coconut, and butter; firmly press on bottom and up sides of pie plate. Bake until lightly browned, 10 to 12 minutes. Transfer to a wire rack; cool completely, about 30 minutes.

2. Stir together sugar and cornstarch in a small heavy saucepan; stir in pineapple. While stirring constantly, bring to a boil over medium–high; cook, stirring constantly, until thickened, about 1 minute. Remove from heat; cool completely, about 20 minutes.

3. Beat cream cheese at medium speed with a heavy-duty electric stand mixer fitted with the whisk attachment until smooth. Gradually add 1 cup cream of coconut, beating at low speed just until blended. (Chill remaining ½ cup cream of coconut until ready to use.) Add eggs, 1 at a time, beating just until blended after each addition.

4. Spread cooled pineapple mixture over bottom of piecrust; spoon cream cheese mixture over pineapple mixture.

5. Bake in preheated oven until set, 40 to 45 minutes. Cool completely on a wire rack, about 1 hour. Cover and chill 4 hours.

6. Beat whipping cream on high speed until foamy. Gradually add remaining ½ cup cream of coconut, beating until soft peaks form; spread over pie. Garnish with coconut, pineapple, and/or mint leaves, if desired.

Salted Caramel-Apple Hand Pies

ACTIVE 20 MIN. · TOTAL 35 MIN., PLUS 30 MIN. COOLING

MAKES 16

- 2 Granny Smith apples, peeled and cut into small cubes (2 cups)
- ¼ cup granulated sugar
- 2 tsp. all-purpose flour, plus more for work surface
- 2 tsp. fresh lemon juice (from 1 lemon)
- ½ tsp. ground cinnamon
- ¼ tsp. kosher salt
- 2 (14.1-oz.) pkg. refrigerated piecrusts (4 crusts total)
- 8 soft caramel candies, roughly chopped
  Pinch of flaky sea salt
- 1 large egg
  Sanding sugar (optional)

1. Preheat oven to 375°F. Line a baking sheet with parchment paper. Stir together apples, granulated sugar, flour, lemon juice, cinnamon, and kosher salt in a bowl until combined.

2. Unroll 1 of the piecrusts on a lightly floured surface, and cut out 8 circles using a 3-inch cookie cutter. (Discard dough scraps, or reserve for another use.) Repeat process with remaining 3 piecrusts.

3. Arrange 16 of the dough rounds on prepared baking sheet. Spoon 1 heaping tablespoon of the apple filling mixture onto center of each of the 16 rounds, leaving a ¼-inch border around filling. (Reserve remaining filling for another use.) Sprinkle chopped caramel candies evenly onto filling mounds, and sprinkle with sea salt.

4. Whisk together egg and 1 tablespoon water in a small bowl, and brush some

of the mixture over edges of the 16 filled dough rounds. Top filled dough rounds with remaining 16 dough rounds. Crimp together top and bottom dough-round edges using a fork, sealing each pie. Brush pie tops with remaining egg mixture. Cut small slits (about ½ inch long) into each pie top. Sprinkle pies with sanding sugar, if desired.

5. Bake in preheated oven until pies are golden brown, 15 to 20 minutes. Let cool completely on baking sheet, about 30 minutes.

Cakes

Chocolate Pound Cake

ACTIVE 10 MIN. · TOTAL 1 HOUR 10 MIN., PLUS 10 MIN. COOLING

MAKES 1 (10-INCH) CAKE

- ½ cup shortening
- 1 cup margarine, softened
- 3 cups granulated sugar
- 5 large eggs
- 3 cups all-purpose flour
- ½ tsp. baking powder
- ½ tsp. kosher salt
- ½ cup unsweetened cocoa powder
- 1¼ cups milk
- 1 tsp. vanilla extract
  Creamy Chocolate Glaze (recipe follows)
  Chopped pecans, for topping

1. Preheat oven to 350°F. Beat shortening and margarine with an electric mixer on high speed until well combined; gradually add sugar, beating until light and fluffy. Add eggs, one at a time, beating well after each addition.

2. Combine flour, baking powder, salt, and cocoa powder in a bowl; mix well. Add to shortening mixture alternating with milk, beginning and ending with flour mixture. Stir in vanilla. Pour batter into a greased and floured 10-inch tube pan.

3. Bake in preheated oven until a wooden pick inserted in center comes out clean, about 1 hour 15 minutes. Cool in pan 10 to 15 minutes; invert onto a serving plate. Spoon Creamy Chocolate Glaze over top of warm cake, allowing it to drizzle down sides. Sprinkle with chopped pecans.

Creamy Chocolate Glaze

ACTIVE 10 MIN. - TOTAL 10 MIN.

MAKES ABOUT 2 CUPS

2¼ cups sifted powdered sugar

3 Tbsp. unsweetened cocoa powder

¼ cup margarine, softened

3 to 4 Tbsp. milk

Combine sugar and cocoa, mixing well. Add margarine and milk; beat until smooth.

Chocolate Velvet Cupcakes

ACTIVE 20 MIN. - TOTAL 2 HOURS, 40 MIN.

MAKES 3 DOZEN

1½ cups semisweet chocolate chips

½ cup butter, softened

1 (16-oz.) pkg. light brown sugar

3 large eggs

2 cups all-purpose flour

1 tsp. baking soda

½ tsp. kosher salt

1 (8-oz.) container sour cream

1 cup hot water

2 tsp. vanilla extract

Browned Butter-Cinnamon-Cream Cheese Frosting (recipe follows)

1. Preheat oven to 350°F. Microwave chips in a microwaveable bowl on HIGH 1 to 1½ minutes or until melted and smooth, stirring at 30-second intervals.

2. Beat butter and sugar in a bowl with an electric mixer on medium speed until well blended, about 5 minutes. Add eggs, 1 at a time, beating just until blended after each addition. Add melted chocolate, and beat until mixture is blended.

3. Sift together flour, baking soda, and salt. Gradually add to chocolate mixture alternately with sour cream, beginning and ending with flour mixture. Beat on low speed just until blended after each addition. Gradually add hot water in a slow, steady stream, beating on low speed just until blended. Stir in vanilla.

4. Place 36 paper baking cups in 3 (12-cup) muffin pans; spoon batter into cups, filling three-fourths full.

5. Bake in preheated oven until a wooden pick inserted in centers comes out clean, 18 to 20 minutes. Remove from pans to wire racks, and let cool completely, about 45 minutes.

6. Pipe frosting onto cupcakes.

Browned Butter-Cinnamon-Cream Cheese Frosting

ACTIVE 15 MIN. - TOTAL 1 HOUR, 15 MIN.

MAKES 5 CUPS

Cook ½ cup **butter** in a small heavy saucepan over medium, stirring constantly, until butter begins to turn golden brown, 6 to 8 minutes. Immediately remove from heat. Pour butter into a bowl. Cover and chill 1 hour or until butter is cool and begins to solidify. Beat butter and 2 (8-oz.) pkg. softened **cream cheese** with an electric mixer on medium speed until creamy; gradually add 2 (16-oz.) pkg. **powdered sugar**, and beat until light and fluffy. Stir in 1 tsp. **ground cinnamon** and 2 tsp. **vanilla extract**.

Fudge Cake

ACTIVE 15 MIN. - TOTAL 1 HOUR 30 MIN., PLUS 30 MIN. COOLING

SERVES 16

1 cup unsalted butter

4 (1-oz.) squares semisweet baking chocolate, finely chopped

1¾ cups granulated sugar

4 large eggs

1 cup all-purpose flour, sifted

Dash of kosher salt

1 cup chopped toasted pecans

1 tsp. vanilla extract

Cooking spray

Powdered sugar

1. Preheat oven to 300°F. Place butter and chocolate in a large microwaveable bowl. Microwave on HIGH until completely melted, about 1 minute, stirring every 20 seconds. Add granulated sugar, and stir until well combined. Cool 10 minutes. Add eggs, 1 at a time, and stir until blended after each addition. Fold in flour and salt. Stir in pecans and vanilla.

2. Coat a 9-inch square baking pan with cooking spray. Line bottom and sides of pan with parchment paper, allowing 4 to 5 inches to extend over sides. Coat parchment paper with cooking spray. Pour cake mixture into prepared pan.

3. Bake in preheated oven until a wooden pick inserted in center comes out clean, 45 to 50 minutes. Cool in pan on a wire rack 30 minutes. Lift cake from pan, using parchment paper sides as handles, and cool completely, about 30 minutes. Cut into squares, and dust with powdered sugar before serving.

German Chocolate Snack Cake

ACTIVE 15 MIN. - TOTAL 1 HR., 15 MIN., PLUS 1 HOUR COOLING

MAKES 18 SQUARES

½ cup chopped pecans

1 (18.25-oz.) pkg. German chocolate cake mix

4 large eggs, divided

½ cup butter, melted

1 (16-oz.) pkg. powdered sugar

1 (8-oz.) pkg. cream cheese, softened

1. Preheat oven to 350°F. Arrange chopped pecans in a single layer in a shallow pan. Bake 5 to 7 minutes or until toasted and fragrant. Reduce oven temperature to 300°F.

2. Stir together cake mix, 1 egg, butter, and toasted pecans in a medium bowl; press mixture into bottom of a lightly greased 13- x 9-inch pan.

3. Beat sugar, cream cheese, and remaining 3 eggs with an electric mixer on medium speed until smooth. Pour powdered sugar mixture over batter in pan, spreading to edges.

4. Bake until a wooden pick inserted in the center comes out clean, about 1 hour. Cool completely on a wire rack, about 1 hour. Cut cake into 2½- to 3-inch squares.

Chocolate Marble Sheet Cake

ACTIVE 20 MIN. - TOTAL 45 MIN., PLUS 1 HOUR COOLING

MAKES 12 SERVINGS

1 cup butter, softened

1¾ cups granulated sugar, divided

2 large eggs

2 tsp. vanilla extract

2½ cups all-purpose flour

1 Tbsp. baking powder

½ tsp. kosher salt

1 cup half-and-half

¼ cup unsweetened cocoa powder

3 Tbsp. hot water

Mocha Frosting (recipe follows)

1. Preheat oven to 325°F. Beat butter and 1½ cups sugar with a heavy-duty electric stand mixer on medium speed until creamy, 4 to 5 minutes. Add eggs, 1 at a time, beating just until blended after each addition. Beat in vanilla.

2. Sift together flour, baking powder, and salt. Add to butter mixture alternately with half-and-half, beginning and ending

Continued on page 350

Continued from page 349

with flour mixture. Beat on low speed just until blended after each addition, stopping to scrape bowl as needed.

3. Spoon 1¼ cups of the batter into a bowl. Stir in cocoa, water, and remaining ¼ cup sugar until well blended.

4. Spread remaining vanilla batter into a greased and floured 15- x 10-inch jelly-roll pan. Spoon chocolate batter onto vanilla batter in pan; gently swirl with a knife or small spatula.

5. Bake in preheated oven until a wooden pick inserted in center comes out clean, 25 to 30 minutes. Let cool completely in pan on a wire rack, about 1 hour. Spread top of cake with Mocha Frosting.

Mocha Frosting

ACTIVE 10 MIN. - TOTAL 10 MIN.

MAKES: 2½ CUPS

- 3 cups powdered sugar
- ⅔ cup unsweetened cocoa powder
- 3 Tbsp. hot brewed coffee
- 2 tsp. vanilla extract
- ½ cup butter, softened
- 3 to 4 Tbsp. half-and-half

1. Whisk together sugar and cocoa in a medium bowl. Combine coffee and vanilla.

2. Beat butter with a heavy-duty electric stand mixer on medium speed until creamy; gradually add sugar mixture alternately with coffee mixture, beating on low speed until blended. Beat in half-and-half, 1 tablespoon at a time, until smooth and mixture has reached desired consistency.

Chocolate-Peppermint Candy Cupcakes

ACTIVE 25 MIN. - TOTAL 1 HOUR, 5 MIN., PLUS 45 MIN. COOLING AND 30 MIN. CHILLING

MAKES 3 DOZEN

- 1½ cups semisweet chocolate morsels
- ½ cup butter, softened
- 1 (16-oz.) pkg. light brown sugar
- 3 large eggs
- 2 cups all-purpose flour
- 1 tsp. baking soda
- ½ tsp. kosher salt
- 1 (8-oz.) container sour cream
- 1 cup hot water
- 2 tsp. vanilla extract

- 1 (12-oz.) pkg. white chocolate morsels
- ½ cup crushed peppermint candy canes
  Vanilla Buttercream Frosting (recipe follows)

1. Microwave semisweet chocolate in a microwaveable bowl on HIGH 1½ minutes or until melted and smooth, stirring at 30-second intervals. Beat butter and brown sugar with an electric mixer on medium speed until well blended, about 5 minutes. Add eggs, 1 at a time, beating just until blended after each addition. Add melted chocolate, beating just until blended.

2. Sift together flour, baking soda, and salt. Gradually add to chocolate mixture alternating with sour cream, beginning and ending with flour mixture. Beat on low speed just until blended after each addition. Gradually add hot water in a slow, steady stream, beating on low speed just until blended. Stir in vanilla.

3. Preheat oven to 350°F. Place 36 paper baking cups in 3 (12-cup) muffin pans; spoon batter evenly into baking cups, filling two-thirds full.

4. Bake in preheated oven until a wooden pick inserted in centers comes out clean, about 18 minutes. Remove from pans to wire racks, and let cool completely, about 45 minutes.

5. Microwave white chocolate in a microwaveable bowl on HIGH 1½ minutes or until melted and smooth, stirring at 30-second intervals. Spread melted white chocolate in a ¼-inch-thick layer on an aluminum foil–lined baking sheet. Sprinkle with crushed candy. Chill until firm, about 30 minutes. Remove from baking sheet, and chop.

6. Spread cupcakes with Vanilla Buttercream Frosting; sprinkle with chopped candy mixture.

Vanilla Buttercream Frosting

ACTIVE 10 MIN. - TOTAL 10 MIN.

MAKES 4½ CUPS

- 1 cup butter, softened
- ¼ tsp. salt
- 1 (32-oz.) pkg. powdered sugar
- 6 to 7 Tbsp. milk
- 1 Tbsp. vanilla extract

Beat butter and salt at medium speed with an electric mixer 1 to 2 minutes or until creamy; gradually add powdered

sugar alternating with 6 tablespoons milk, beating at low speed until blended and smooth after each addition. Stir in vanilla. If desired, beat in remaining 1 tablespoon milk, 1 teaspoon at a time, until Frosting reaches desired consistency.

Coconut-Pecan Cupcakes

ACTIVE 20 MIN. - TOTAL 2 HOURS, 15 MIN.

MAKES 3 DOZEN

- ½ cup butter, softened
- ½ cup shortening
- 2 cups granulated sugar
- 5 large eggs, separated
- 1 Tbsp. vanilla extract
- 2 cups all-purpose flour
- 1 tsp. baking soda
- 1 cup buttermilk
- 1 cup sweetened flaked coconut
- 1 cup finely chopped pecans, toasted
  Caramel Frosting (p. 350)
  Chopped roasted salted pecans, for garnish (optional)

1. Preheat oven to 350°F. Beat butter and shortening in a bowl with an electric mixer on medium speed until fluffy. Gradually add sugar, beating well. Add egg yolks, 1 at a time, beating until blended after each addition. Add vanilla; beat until blended.

2. Combine flour and baking soda; add to butter mixture alternately with buttermilk, beginning and ending with flour mixture. Beat at low speed just until blended after each addition. Stir in coconut and finely chopped pecans.

3. Beat egg whites on high speed until stiff peaks form, and fold into batter. Place 36 paper baking cups in 3 (12-cup) muffin pans; spoon batter into cups, filling half full.

4. Bake in preheated oven until a wooden pick inserted in centers comes out clean, 18 to 20 minutes. Remove from pans to wire racks, and let cool completely, about 45 minutes.

5. Pipe Caramel Frosting onto cupcakes. Garnish with chopped salted pecans.

Caramel Frosting

ACTIVE 15 MIN. - TOTAL 45 MIN.

MAKES 4½ CUPS

Microwave 1 (14-oz.) pkg. **caramels** and ½ cup **heavy whipping cream** in a microwavable bowl on HIGH 1 to

2 minutes or until smooth, stirring at 30-second intervals. Let caramel mixture cool until lukewarm (about 30 minutes). Beat 1 cup softened **butter** in a bowl with an electric mixer on medium speed until creamy. Gradually add 5 cups **powdered sugar** alternating with caramel mixture, beating on low speed until blended and smooth after each addition. Stir in 2 tsp. **vanilla extract**.

Dark Chocolate Bundt Cake

ACTIVE 30 MIN. - TOTAL 1 HOUR, 50 MIN., PLUS 1 HOUR 15 MIN. COOLING

MAKES 12 SERVINGS

- 1 (8-oz.) pkg. semisweet chocolate baking squares, coarsely chopped
- 1 (16-oz.) can chocolate syrup
- 1 cup butter, softened
- 2 cups granulated sugar
- 4 large eggs
- 2½ cups all-purpose flour, plus more for the pan
- ½ tsp. baking soda
- ¼ tsp. kosher salt
- 1 cup buttermilk
- 1 tsp. vanilla extract
  Powdered sugar, for garnish (optional)

1. Preheat oven to 325°F. Melt chocolate in a microwaveable bowl on HIGH 1½ minutes or until melted and smooth, stirring at 30-second intervals. Stir in chocolate syrup until smooth.
2. Beat butter with an electric mixer on medium speed until creamy. Gradually add sugar, beating on medium speed until light and fluffy. Add eggs, 1 at a time, beating just until blended after each addition.
3. Sift together flour, baking soda, and salt. Add to butter mixture alternately with buttermilk, beginning and ending with flour mixture. Beat on low speed just until blended after each addition. Stir in vanilla and melted chocolate just until blended. Pour batter into a greased and floured 14-cup Bundt pan.
4. Bake in preheated oven until a long wooden pick inserted in center comes out clean, about 1 hour and 20 minutes. Let cool in pan on a wire rack 15 minutes. Remove from pan to wire rack, and cool completely, about 1 hour. Garnish with powdered sugar, if desired.

Brown Sugar-Bourbon Bundt

ACTIVE 20 MIN. - TOTAL 2 HOURS, 35 MIN., PLUS 1 HOUR COOLING

MAKES 12 SERVINGS

- 1 cup butter, softened
- ½ cup shortening
- 1 (16-oz.) pkg. light brown sugar
- 5 large eggs
- 1 (5-oz.) can evaporated milk
- ½ cup bourbon
- 3 cups all-purpose flour, plus more for dusting pans
- ½ tsp. baking powder
- ½ tsp. kosher salt
- 1 Tbsp. vanilla bean paste
  Shortening, for greasing pan
- 2 Tbsp. powdered sugar
  Candied oranges, magnolia leaves (optional)

1. Preheat oven to 325°F. Beat butter and shortening with a heavy-duty electric stand mixer on medium speed until creamy. Gradually add brown sugar, beating on medium speed until light and creamy. Add eggs, 1 at a time, beating just until blended after each addition.
2. Stir together evaporated milk and bourbon in a bowl. Stir together flour, baking powder, and salt in another bowl. Add flour mixture to butter mixture alternately with milk mixture, beginning and ending with flour mixture. Beat on low speed just until blended after each addition. Stir in vanilla bean paste. Pour batter into a greased and floured 10-inch (12-cup) Bundt pan.
3. Bake in preheated oven until a long wooden pick inserted in center comes out clean, 1 hour 5 minutes to 1 hour 10 minutes. Cool in pan on a wire rack 10 to 15 minutes; remove from pan to wire rack. Cool completely, about 1 hour. Dust top lightly with powdered sugar. Garnish with candied oranges and magnolia leaves, if desired.

Classic Cola Cake

ACTIVE 10 MIN. - TOTAL 40 MIN., PLUS 1 HOUR COOLING

MAKES 12 SERVINGS

- ¾ cup chopped pecans
- 1 cup cola soft drink
- ½ cup buttermilk
- 1 cup butter, softened
- 1¾ cups granulated sugar

- 2 large eggs, lightly beaten
- 2 tsp. vanilla extract
- 2 cups all-purpose flour
- ¼ cup unsweetened cocoa powder
- ¼ tsp. baking soda
- 1½ cups miniature marshmallows
  Classic Cola Frosting (recipe follows)

1. Preheat oven to 350°F. Arrange pecans in a single layer in a shallow pan. Bake until toasted and fragrant, about 5 minutes.
2. Combine cola and buttermilk in a small bowl; set aside.
3. Beat butter with an electric mixer on low speed until creamy. Gradually add sugar, beating until blended. Add eggs and vanilla; beat on low speed just until blended.
4. Combine flour, cocoa, and baking soda in a bowl. Add to butter mixture alternately with cola mixture, beginning and ending with flour mixture. Beat at low speed just until blended after each addition. Stir in marshmallows. Pour batter into a greased and floured 13- x 9-inch pan.
5. Bake in preheated oven until a wooden pick inserted in the center comes out clean, 30 to 35 minutes. Remove from oven; cool 10 minutes.
6. Pour Classic Cola Frosting over warm cake; sprinkle with toasted pecans.

Classic Cola Frosting

ACTIVE 10 MIN. - TOTAL 15 MIN.

MAKES 2¼ CUPS

- ½ cup butter
- ⅓ cup cola soft drink
- 3 Tbsp. unsweetened cocoa powder
- 1 (16-oz.) pkg. powdered sugar
- 1 Tbsp. vanilla extract

1. Combine butter, cola, and cocoa powder in a large saucepan. Bring to a boil over medium, stirring until butter is melted. Remove from heat; whisk in sugar and vanilla. Use immediately.

Cranberry-Almond Streusel Cake

ACTIVE 45 MIN. - TOTAL 2 HOURS, 20 MIN.

SERVES 12 TO 16

Shortening, for greasing pan

2 tsp. baking powder

½ tsp. baking soda

½ tsp. kosher salt

2½ cups cake flour, plus more for dusting pans

¾ cup unsalted butter, softened

1 cup granulated sugar

¾ cup packed light brown sugar

3 large eggs

1¼ cups sour cream

2 tsp. orange zest (from 1 orange)

1½ tsp. vanilla extract

½ tsp. almond extract

3 cups fresh or frozen cranberries

Almond Streusel (recipe follows)

½ cup chopped almonds, toasted

½ cup jarred sea salt caramel sauce

1. Preheat oven to 350°F. Grease and flour a 10½-inch Bundt pan or 10-inch tube pan. Whisk baking powder, baking soda, salt, and 2¼ cups plus 2 tablespoons of the flour in a medium bowl.

2. Combine butter, granulated sugar, and brown sugar in the bowl of a heavy-duty stand mixer fitted with paddle attachment; beat on medium speed until light and fluffy, about 5 minutes. Add eggs, 1 at a time, beating well after each addition. Stir in sour cream, zest, and extracts. Gradually add flour mixture, beating on low speed just until blended after each addition.

3. Toss together cranberries and remaining 2 tablespoons cake flour in a small bowl until coated. Fold cranberries into batter. Pour half of batter into prepared pan; smooth batter, and top with Almond Streusel. Pour remaining batter over streusel, and smooth batter.

4. Bake in preheated oven until golden brown and a wooden pick inserted in center comes out clean, 50 minutes to 1 hour. Cool cake in pan on a wire rack 10 minutes. Remove cake from pan to wire rack, and let cool at least 30 minutes before serving. Combine almonds and 2 tablespoons of the caramel sauce; arrange on top of cake. Drizzle with remaining caramel sauce.

Almond Streusel

ACTIVE 10 MIN. - TOTAL 10 MIN.

MAKES 1½ CUPS

¼ cup packed light brown sugar

¼ cup cake flour

½ tsp. ground cinnamon

¼ tsp. kosher salt

1 cup chopped almonds

2 Tbsp. unsalted butter, melted

Stir together brown sugar, flour, cinnamon, and salt in a small bowl. Stir in almonds and butter until crumbly.

Fresh Apple Cake

ACTIVE 25 MIN. - TOTAL 2 HOURS

SERVES 12 TO 15

1½ cups chopped pecans

½ cup butter, melted

2 cups granulated sugar

2 large eggs

1 tsp. vanilla extract

2 cups all-purpose flour

2 tsp. ground cinnamon

1 tsp. baking soda

1 tsp. kosher salt

2½ lb. Granny Smith apples (about 4 large), peeled and cut into ¼-inch-thick wedges

Shortening, for greasing pan

Browned-Butter Frosting (recipe follows)

1. Preheat oven to 350°F. Bake pecans in a single layer in a shallow pan until lightly toasted and fragrant, stirring halfway through, 5 to 7 minutes.

2. Stir together butter, sugar, eggs, and vanilla in a large bowl until blended.

3. In a medium bowl, combine flour, cinnamon, baking soda, and salt; add to butter mixture, stirring until blended. Stir in apples and 1 cup pecans. (Batter will be very thick, similar to a cookie dough.) Spread batter into a lightly greased 13- x 9-inch pan.

4. Bake in preheated oven until a wooden pick inserted in center comes out clean, about 45 minutes. Cool completely in pan on a wire rack, about 45 minutes. Spread Browned-Butter Frosting over cake; sprinkle with remaining ½ cup pecans.

Browned-Butter Frosting

ACTIVE 20 MIN. - TOTAL 1 HOUR, 20 MIN.

MAKES ABOUT 3½ CUPS

1 cup butter

1 (16-oz.) pkg. powdered sugar

¼ cup milk

1 tsp. vanilla extract

1. Cook butter in a small saucepan over medium, stirring constantly, 6 to 8 minutes or until butter begins to turn golden brown. Remove pan from heat immediately, and pour butter into a small bowl. Cover and chill 1 hour or until butter is cool and begins to solidify.

2. Beat butter with an electric mixer on medium speed until fluffy; gradually add powdered sugar alternating with milk, beginning and ending with powdered sugar. Beat mixture on low speed until well blended after each addition. Stir in vanilla.

Pumpkin-Spice Magic Cake

ACTIVE 25 MIN. - TOTAL 2 HOURS, 40 MIN., PLUS 45 MIN. COOLING

SERVES 12

CAKE

Cooking spray

½ cup butter, softened

½ cup granulated sugar

½ cup packed light brown sugar

1 large egg, at room temperature

2¼ cups all-purpose flour

1 tsp. pumpkin pie spice

¾ tsp. baking powder

¾ tsp. baking soda

¼ tsp. salt

½ cup canned pumpkin

⅓ cup whole buttermilk

1 tsp. vanilla extract

½ cup jarred cajeta (Mexican caramel sauce) or caramel sauce, divided

FLAN

1 (14-oz.) can sweetened condensed milk

1 (12-oz.) can evaporated milk

4 oz. cream cheese, softened

3 large eggs

1 Tbsp. vanilla extract

ADDITIONAL INGREDIENTS

⅓ cup chopped toasted pecans

Cajeta (Mexican caramel sauce) or caramel sauce, for serving

1. Prepare the Cake: Fill a large roasting pan with hot water to a depth of 2 inches; place on rack in lower third of oven. Preheat oven to 350°F. Generously coat a 14-cup light-color Bundt pan with cooking spray.

2. Beat butter, granulated sugar, and brown sugar in bowl of a heavy-duty stand mixer on medium speed until light and fluffy, about 3 minutes. Add egg; beat just until blended. Sift together flour, pumpkin pie spice, baking powder, baking soda, and salt in a bowl. Whisk together pumpkin, buttermilk, and vanilla in a separate bowl. Add flour mixture to butter mixture alternating with pumpkin mixture, beginning and ending with flour mixture, beating on low speed after each addition. (Batter will be thick.)

3. Evenly pour ¼ cup of the cajeta into prepared Bundt pan. Gently spoon batter over cajeta; smooth top of batter. Set aside.

4. Prepare the Flan: Place condensed milk, evaporated milk, cream cheese, eggs, and vanilla in a blender. Process on high speed until completely combined, about 30 seconds, stopping to scrape down sides as needed. Pour mixture over batter in Bundt pan. Cover loosely with aluminum foil.

5. Carefully remove roasting pan with hot water from preheated oven. (Water should be steaming when removed from oven.) Gently place Bundt pan in prepared roasting pan, and return to oven. Bake in preheated oven until a wooden pick inserted in center comes out clean, 1 hour 30 minutes to 1 hour 45 minutes, rotating Bundt pan halfway through bake time.

6. Remove Bundt pan from roasting pan; transfer to a wire rack to cool until slightly warm, about 45 minutes. Gently invert onto a rimmed serving plate. Spoon remaining ¼ cup cajeta over top; sprinkle with pecans. Serve additional cajeta on the side.

Caramel Apple Coffee Cake
ACTIVE 35 MIN. - TOTAL 4 HOURS, 50 MIN.
SERVES 8 TO 10

- 2 Tbsp. butter
- 3 cups peeled and sliced Granny Smith apples (about 3 large)
  Pecan Streusel Topping (recipe follows)
  Caramel Sauce (recipe follows)

- ½ cup butter, softened
- 1 cup granulated sugar
- 2 large eggs
- 2 cups all-purpose flour, plus more for dusting pan
- 2 tsp. baking powder
- ½ tsp. salt
- ⅔ cup milk
- 2 tsp. vanilla extract
  Shortening, for greasing pan

1. Preheat oven to 350°F. Melt 2 tablespoons butter in a large skillet over medium-high; add apples, and sauté 5 minutes or until softened. Remove from heat; cool completely, about 30 minutes.

2. Meanwhile, prepare Streusel Topping and Caramel Sauce. Reserve ½ cup Caramel Sauce for another use.

3. Beat softened butter with an electric mixer on medium speed until creamy; gradually add sugar, beating well. Add eggs, 1 at a time, beating until blended after each addition.

4. Combine flour, baking powder, and salt in a bowl; add to butter mixture alternately with milk, beginning and ending with flour mixture. Beat on low speed until blended after each addition. Stir in vanilla. Pour batter into a greased and floured shiny 9-inch springform pan; top with apples. Drizzle with ½ cup Caramel Sauce; sprinkle with Streusel Topping.

5. Bake in preheated oven 45 minutes. Cover loosely with aluminum foil to prevent excessive browning; bake until center is set, 25 to 30 minutes. (A wooden pick will not come out clean.) Cool in pan on a wire rack 30 minutes; remove sides of pan. Cool completely on wire rack, about 1½ hours. Drizzle with ½ cup Caramel Sauce.

Pecan Streusel Topping
ACTIVE 15 MIN. - TOTAL 45 MIN.
MAKES ABOUT 2½ CUPS

Stir together 1½ cups **all-purpose flour**, 1 cup chopped **pecans**, ½ cup melted **butter**, ½ cup firmly packed **light brown sugar**, ¼ cup **granulated sugar**, 1½ tsp. **ground cinnamon**, and ¼ tsp. **kosher salt** until blended. Let stand 30 minutes or until firm enough to crumble into small pieces.

Caramel Sauce
ACTIVE 20 MIN. - TOTAL 35 MIN.
MAKES ABOUT 1½ CUPS

Bring 1 cup firmly packed **light brown sugar**, ½ cup **butter**, ¼ cup **whipping cream**, and ¼ cup **honey** to a boil in a medium saucepan over medium-high, stirring constantly; boil, stirring constantly, 2 minutes. Remove from heat, and cool 15 minutes before serving. Store in an airtight container in refrigerator up to 1 week. To reheat, microwave on HIGH until just warm, 10 to 15 seconds; stir until smooth.

Blackberry-Peach Coffee Cake
ACTIVE 20 MIN. - TOTAL 1 HR., 30 MIN., PLUS 1 HOUR, 30 MIN. COOLING
MAKES 8 SERVINGS

  Streusel Topping (recipe follows)
- ½ cup butter, softened
- 2 large eggs
- 2 cups all-purpose flour
- 2 tsp. baking powder
- ½ tsp. kosher salt
- ⅔ cup milk
- 2 tsp. vanilla extract
- 2 cups sliced and peeled fresh firm, ripe peaches (about 2 large peaches, 7 oz. each)
- 1 cup fresh blackberries
  Powdered sugar
  Fresh blackberries, sliced peaches, for garnish (optional)

1. Preheat oven to 350°F. Prepare Streusel Topping.

2. Beat butter with an electric mixer on medium speed until creamy; gradually add granulated sugar, beating well. Add eggs, 1 at a time, beating until blended after each addition.

3. Combine flour, baking powder, and salt in a bowl; add to butter mixture alternately with milk, beginning and ending with flour mixture. Beat on low speed until blended after each addition. Stir in vanilla. Pour batter into a greased and floured 9-inch springform pan; top with peaches and blackberries. Pinch off 1-inch pieces of Streusel Topping, and drop over fruit.

4. Bake in preheated oven until center of cake is set (a wooden pick inserted into center will not come out clean), about 1 hour 10 minutes. Let cool completely

Continued on page 354

Continued from page 353

on a wire rack, about 1 hour 30 minutes. Dust with powdered sugar. Garnish with additional fresh blackberries and peaches, if desired.

Streusel Topping

ACTIVE 10 MIN. · TOTAL 10 MIN.
MAKES 1½ CUPS

½	cup butter, softened
½	cup granulated sugar
½	cup firmly packed light brown sugar
⅔	cup all-purpose flour
1	tsp. ground cinnamon
½	tsp. ground nutmeg

1. Beat butter with an electric mixer at medium speed until creamy; gradually add granulated sugar and brown sugar, beating well. Add flour, cinnamon, and nutmeg; beat just until blended.

Pecan Pound Cake

ACTIVE 25 MIN. · TOTAL 2 HOURS, 25 MIN., PLUS 1 HOUR COOLING
SERVES 10 TO 12

2	cups butter, softened
1¼	cups granulated sugar
1¼	cups firmly packed light brown sugar
6	large eggs
1	Tbsp. vanilla extract
1½	tsp. baking powder
¼	tsp. kosher salt
4	cups all-purpose flour, divided, plus more for dusting pan
1	cup milk
4	cups chopped toasted pecans
	Shortening, for greasing pan
	Citrus Glaze (recipe follows)

1. Preheat oven to 325°F. Beat butter with a heavy-duty electric stand mixer on medium speed until creamy. Gradually add granulated sugar and brown sugar, beating until light and fluffy, 3 to 5 minutes. Add eggs, 1 at a time, beating just until blended after each addition. Stir in vanilla.
2. Stir together baking powder, salt, and 3¾ cups flour in a medium bowl. Add flour mixture to butter mixture alternating with milk, beginning and

ending with flour mixture. Beat on low speed just until blended after each addition. Stir together pecans and remaining ¼ cup flour in a small bowl; add to batter, and stir just until combined. Pour batter into a greased and floured 10-inch tube pan.
3. Bake in preheated oven until a long wooden pick inserted in center comes out clean, 1 hour 15 minutes to 1 hour 30 minutes, shielding with aluminum foil after 55 minutes to prevent excessive browning. Cool in pan on a wire rack 15 minutes; remove cake from pan to wire rack. Cool 20 minutes.
4. Spoon Citrus Glaze over cake. Cool completely, about 1 hour.

Citrus Glaze

ACTIVE 10 MIN. · TOTAL 10 MIN.
MAKES ABOUT ¾ CUP

Whisk together 2½ cups **powdered sugar**; 2 Tbsp. **butter**, melted; 1 tsp. **orange zest**; 1 tsp. **lemon zest**; 2 Tbsp. fresh **orange juice**; and 1 Tbsp. fresh **lemon juice** until smooth. Whisk in up to 1 Tbsp. more **lemon juice**, 1 tsp. at a time, until desired consistency is reached.

Key Lime Cheesecake with Strawberry Sauce

ACTIVE 20 MIN. · TOTAL 1 HOUR, 45 MIN., PLUS 1 HOUR, 30 MIN. COOLING AND 8 HOURS CHILLING
MAKES 10 TO 12 SERVINGS

2	cups graham cracker crumbs
1½	cups granulated sugar, divided
½	cup butter, melted
3	(8-oz.) pkg. cream cheese, softened
3	large eggs
1	(8-oz.) container sour cream
1½	tsp. lime zest
½	cup Key lime juice
	Fresh strawberries, for garnish (optional)
	Strawberry Sauce (recipe follows)

1. Preheat oven to 350°F. Stir together graham cracker crumbs, ¼ cup sugar, and the butter in a medium bowl Press onto bottom and 1 inch up sides of a greased 9-inch springform pan. Bake in preheated oven for 8 minutes; let cool. Reduce oven temperature to 325°F.

2. Beat cream cheese with an electric mixer on medium speed until fluffy; gradually add the remaining 1¼ cups sugar, beating until blended. Add eggs, 1 at a time, beating well after each addition. Stir in sour cream, zest, and juice. Pour batter into crust.
3. Bake at 325°F for 1 hour 5 minutes; turn oven off. Let stand in oven, with door partially open, 15 minutes. Remove from oven, and immediately run a knife around edge of pan, releasing sides.
4. Let cool completely in pan on a wire rack, about 1 hour 30 minutes. Cover and chill 8 hours. Garnish with fresh strawberries, if desired, and serve with Strawberry Sauce.

Strawberry Sauce

ACTIVE 5 MIN. · TOTAL 5 MIN.
MAKES 1 CUP

1¼	cups fresh strawberries
¼	cup granulated sugar
1½	tsp. lime zest

1. Combine strawberries, sugar, and lime zest in a food processor. Process until smooth, stopping to scrape down sides.

Baking at High Altitudes

Liquids boil at lower temperatures (below 212°F) and moisture evaporates more quickly at high altitudes. Both of these factors significantly impact the quality of baked goods. Also, leavening gases (air, carbon dioxide, water vapor) expand faster. If you live at 3,000 feet or below, first try a recipe as is. Sometimes few, if any, changes are needed. But the higher you go, the more you'll have to adjust your ingredients and cooking times.

A Few Overall Tips

- Use shiny new baking pans. This seems to help mixtures rise, especially cake batters.
- Use butter, flour, and parchment paper to prep your baking pans for nonstick cooking. At high altitudes, baked goods tend to stick more to pans.
- Be exact in your measurements (once you've figured out what they should be). This is always important in baking, but especially so when you're up so high. Tiny variations in ingredients make a bigger difference at high altitudes than at sea level.
- Boost flavor. Seasonings and extracts tend to be more muted at higher altitudes, so increase them slightly.
- Have patience. You may have to bake your favorite sea-level recipe a few times, making slight adjustments each time, until it's worked out to suit your particular altitude.

Ingredient/Temperature Adjustments

CHANGE	AT 3,000 FEET	AT 5,000 FEET	AT 7,000 FEET
Baking powder or baking soda	Reduce each tsp. called for by up to 1/8 tsp.	Reduce each tsp. called for by 1/8 to 1/4 tsp.	Reduce each tsp. called for by 1/4 to 1/2 tsp.
Sugar	Reduce each cup called for by up to 1 Tbsp.	Reduce each cup called for by up to 2 Tbsp.	Reduce each cup called for by 2 to 3 Tbsp.
Liquid	Increase each cup called for by up to 2 Tbsp.	Increase each cup called for by 2 to 4 Tbsp.	Increase each cup called for by to 3 to 4 Tbsp.
Oven temperature	Increase 3°F to 5°F	Increase 15°F	Increase 21°F to 25°F

Metric Equivalents

The recipes that appear in this cookbook use the standard United States method for measuring liquid and dry or solid ingredients (teaspoons, tablespoons, and cups). The information on this chart is provided to help cooks outside the U.S. successfully use these recipes. All equivalents are approximate.

METRIC EQUIVALENTS FOR DIFFERENT TYPES OF INGREDIENTS

A standard cup measure of a dry or solid ingredient will vary in weight depending on the type of ingredient. A standard cup of liquid is the same volume for any type of liquid. Use the following chart when converting standard cup measures to grams (weight) or milliliters (volume).

Standard Cup	Fine Powder (ex. flour)	Grain (ex. rice)	Granular (ex. sugar)	Liquid Solids (ex. butter)	Liquid (ex. milk)
1	140 g	150 g	190 g	200 g	240 ml
¾	105 g	113 g	143 g	150 g	180 ml
⅔	93 g	100 g	125 g	133 g	160 ml
½	70 g	75 g	95 g	100 g	120 ml
⅓	47 g	50 g	63 g	67 g	80 ml
¼	35 g	38 g	48 g	50 g	60 ml
⅛	18 g	19 g	24 g	25 g	30 ml

USEFUL EQUIVALENTS FOR LIQUID INGREDIENTS BY VOLUME

¼ tsp.					=	1 ml	
½ tsp.					=	2 ml	
1 tsp.					=	5 ml	
3 tsp.	=	1 Tbsp.			=	½ fl oz.	=	15 ml
		2 Tbsp.	=	⅛ cup	=	1 fl oz.	=	30 ml
		4 Tbsp.	=	¼ cup	=	2 fl oz.	=	60 ml
		5⅓ Tbsp.	=	⅓ cup	=	3 fl oz.	=	80 ml
		8 Tbsp.	=	½ cup	=	4 fl oz.	=	120 ml
		10⅔ Tbsp.	=	⅔ cup	=	5 fl oz.	=	160 ml
		12 Tbsp.	=	¾ cup	=	6 fl oz.	=	180 ml
		16 Tbsp.	=	1 cup	=	8 fl oz.	=	240 ml
		1 pt.	=	2 cups	=	16 fl oz.	=	480 ml
		1 qt.	=	4 cups	=	32 fl oz.	=	960 ml
						33 fl oz.	=	1000 ml	=	1 l

USEFUL EQUIVALENTS FOR DRY INGREDIENTS BY WEIGHT

(To convert ounces to grams, multiply the number of ounces by 30.)

1 oz.	=	¹⁄₁₆ lb.	=	30 g
4 oz.	=	¼ lb.	=	120 g
8 oz.	=	½ lb.	=	240 g
12 oz.	=	¾ lb.	=	360 g
16 oz.	=	1 lb.	=	480 g

USEFUL EQUIVALENTS FOR LENGTH

(To convert inches to centimeters, multiply the number of inches by 2.5.)

1 in.				=	2.5 cm
6 in.	=	½ ft.		=	15 cm
12 in.	=	1 ft.		=	30 cm
36 in.	=	3 ft.	=	1 yd.	=	90 cm

USEFUL EQUIVALENTS FOR COOKING/OVEN TEMPERATURES

	Fahrenheit	Celsius	Gas Mark
Freeze Water	32°F	0°C	
Room Temperature	68°F	20°C	
Boil Water	212°F	100°C	
Bake	325°F	160°C	3
	350°F	180°C	4
	375°F	190°C	5
	400°F	200°C	6
	425°F	220°C	7
	450°F	230°C	8
Broil			Grill

Recipe Title Index

This index alphabetically lists every recipe by exact title

General Recipe Index

This index lists every recipe by food category and/or major ingredient.

DOTDASH MEREDITH CONSUMER MARKETING
Director, Direct Marketing-Books: Daniel Fagan
Marketing Operations Manager: Max Daily
Marketing Manager: Kylie Dazzo
Senior Marketing Coordinator: Elizabeth Moore
Content Manager: Julie Doll
Senior Production Manager: Liza Ward

WATERBURY PUBLICATIONS, INC.
Editorial Director: Lisa Kingsley
Creative Director: Ken Carlson
Associate Design Director: Doug Samuelson
Contributing Copy Editor: Andrea Cooley
Contributing Proofreader: Carrie Truesdell
Contributing Indexer: Mary Williams

Recipe Developers and Testers: Dotdash Meredith Food Studios

ISBN: 978-0-8487-8453-9
ISSN: 0272-2003

First Edition 2023
Printed in the United States of America
10 9 8 7 6 5 4 3 2 1
Call 1-800-826-4707 for more information.

Pictured on front cover:
The Redbird Cake, page 337